THE NEXT WAVE

THE NEXT WAVE

Financing Women's Growth-Oriented Firms

SUSAN COLEMAN and **ALICIA M. ROBB**

STANFORD ECONOMICS AND FINANCE
An Imprint of Stanford University Press • Stanford, California

Stanford University Press
Stanford, California

Special discounts for bulk quantities of titles in the Stanford Economics and Finance imprint are available to corporations, professional associations, and other organizations. For details and discount information, contact the special sales department of Stanford University Press. Tel: (650) 725-0820, Fax: (650) 725-3457

Printed in the United States of America on acid-free, archival-quality paper

Library of Congress Cataloging-in-Publication Data

Names: Coleman, Susan, 1951– author. | Robb, Alicia M., author.
Title: The next wave : financing women's growth-oriented firms / Susan
    Coleman and Alicia M. Robb.
Description: Stanford, California : Stanford Economics and Finance, an
    imprint of Stanford University Press, 2016. | Includes bibliographical
    references and index.
Identifiers: LCCN 2016014110 (print) | LCCN 2016014373 (ebook) |
    ISBN 9780804790413 (cloth : alk. paper) | ISBN 9781503600003 (pbk. : alk. paper) |
    ISBN 9781503600980 (electronic)
Subjects: LCSH: Women-owned business enterprises—United States—Finance. |
    Women-owned business enterprises—United States—Management. | Success in
    business—United States.
Classification: LCC HG4061 .C638 2016 (print) | LCC HG4061 (ebook) |
    DDC 658.15/224082—dc23
LC record available at http://lccn.loc.gov/2016014110

Typeset by Bruce Lundquist in 10/14 Minion

To my husband, Bill, with grateful thanks for your love, encouragement, and support—Susan Coleman

To my good friend, Paula Kantor, who dedicated her life to women's empowerment. She was killed by the Taliban in Afghanistan on May 13, 2015—Alicia Robb

CONTENTS

Preface and Acknowledgments   ix

1   Introduction: Why Growth?   1

2   A Status Report on Growth-Oriented Women Entrepreneurs   17

3   What We Know About the Challenges for
Growth-Oriented Women   34

4   A Star Is Born! Financing Strategies for Nascent Entrepreneurs   56

5   First Things First: Financing Strategies for Early Stage Firms   79

6   The White Knuckle Flight:
Survival Stage Strategies for Growth-Oriented Firms, Part I   97

7   Brave New World:
Survival Stage Strategies for Growth-Oriented Firms, Part II   119

8   Crowdfunding: The New Kid on the Block   141

9   Liftoff! Financing Strategies for Scaling Up and Managing
Rapid Growth   158

10   Going for Gold: Harvesting Value   179

11   No Rest: Life After Harvesting Value   203

12   Let the Circle Be Unbroken: Women Investors   220

Appendix: Resources   243

Notes   261

Interviews   263

References   265

Index   281

PREFACE AND ACKNOWLEDGMENTS

One of our greatest frustrations in writing our first book, *A Rising Tide: Financing Strategies for Women-Owned Firms,* was the limited amount of time and space that we could devote to growth-oriented firms. In light of that, we are delighted that Stanford University Press has given us the opportunity to expand upon our earlier work and devote an entire book to the topic of financing strategies for growth-oriented women entrepreneurs. In this book, *The Next Wave: Financing Women's Growth-Oriented Firms,* we follow the journey of high-growth entrepreneurs from their firms' earliest stages through to maturity, harvest, and even beyond.

The most recent U.S. Census data reveal that there are nearly ten million women-owned firms in the United States (*2012 Survey of Business Owners*). Although the majority of these firms are small, a growing cohort of women is launching firms with significant growth potential. Their motives for doing so are as diverse as the firms themselves. Some of these growth-oriented entrepreneurs are motivated by a desire to pursue an opportunity or an unmet need in the marketplace. Others are frustrated by the constraints imposed by a "glass ceiling" that prevents them from reaching the most senior ranks of corporations. Still others are drawn by the financial and economic rewards that can come from leading a firm that achieves scale. Whatever their motivations, data reveal that an increasing number of women are choosing entrepreneurship as a career path, and of those, a growing number of them share aspirations for growth.

In *The Next Wave* we focus on the financial strategies employed by growth-oriented women entrepreneurs. As we will show, these are more varied and complex than the strategies used by lifestyle entrepreneurs. Firms that grow typically require larger amounts of financial capital, and both prior research and anecdotal data reveal that women often encounter a variety of barriers in their attempts to secure financing at all stages of their firms' development.

Some of these barriers are structural in nature, while others are social and cultural. In light of that, our goal has been to recognize the barriers but also to highlight the financial strategies that have worked and can work for growth-oriented women entrepreneurs.

In addition to delivering a contemporary account of financing strategies from the growth-oriented entrepreneur's perspective, *The Next Wave* also addresses investor perspectives on financing. To date, most books on growth-oriented entrepreneurship have focused on the entrepreneur's challenges and strategies, but have ignored the investor side of the equation. This approach tells only half of the story. Since growth-oriented firms often require substantial amounts of both external debt and equity, the investor perspective is critical. We address this gap by detailing the development of a new generation of women investors—women who have risen through the corporate or professional ranks or have launched their own successful firms and have thus acquired significant funds to reinvest in the entrepreneurial firms of others. These women are in a unique position to serve as investors for a new generation of entrepreneurs. We envision this as a type of "virtuous circle" whereby women entrepreneurs make the transition from being recipients of human, social, and financial capital to being providers of those key resource inputs to the next generation of growth-oriented women entrepreneurs.

The Next Wave combines research findings from our own scholarly work using the Kauffman Firm Survey with that of other highly regarded researchers in the United States and abroad. In addition, we provide interviews with real-world growth-oriented women entrepreneurs in a broad range of industries to illustrate how our entrepreneurs actually apply the principles and practices of finance. Our interviews with these amazing entrepreneurs are what give *The Next Wave* its "spark," because we had the opportunity to share in the passion, successes, frustrations, and failures of women who aspire to growth.

In addition, consistent with our desire to strengthen the link between women as entrepreneurs and women as investors, we provide insights from angel investors and venture capitalists, who are an important part of the next wave of growth-oriented women's entrepreneurship.

Writing *The Next Wave* has been a labor of love for both of us, and we have many people to thank for the successful completion of this book. We would first like to thank the wonderful women entrepreneurs and investors who have taken the time to share their experience, insights, and wisdom with us. *The Next Wave* could not have been written without them. We would also like to thank the Ewing Marion Kauffman Foundation for providing access to the Kauffman Firm Survey, which provides data on a cohort of over four thousand U.S. firms launched in 2004 and tracked over an eight-year period. We have used these invaluable data as the basis for much of our analytical work. We wish to note, however, that although we have used the KFS data to produce research findings for this book, the opinions and recommendations expressed are our own and not necessarily those of the Kauffman Foundation.

We would like to thank the Kauffman Foundation yet again for the generous financial support that has allowed us to write *The Next Wave* and to attend key conferences where we developed and tested our ideas. We would also like to thank the University of Hartford's Barney School of Business for a summer research grant to support the development of early drafts of *The Next Wave*. The Barney School also provided graduate assistant support that allowed us to gather prior research and data. In particular, graduate assistants Ece Karhan, Mert Karhan, and Isha Sen have played an invaluable role in the book's development. We would like to thank the University of Hartford's Women's Education and Leadership Fund for a grant that helped support the development of case studies on our women entrepreneurs.

We have been doubly blessed in our publisher, Stanford University Press, which also published our first book, *A Rising Tide: Financing Strategies for Women-Owned Firms*. We are deeply appreciative for SUP's recognition of the need for a second book to delve more deeply into the phenomenon of growth-oriented women's entrepreneurship. Many thanks to our wonderful editor, Margo Beth Fleming, who has provided guidance and constant encouragement. Similarly, we are grateful for the work of our editorial assistant, James Holt, who so ably shepherded *The Next Wave* through the production process. We would like to take this opportunity to recognize and thank our two reviewers, Babson College's Victoria Sassine and Julie Weeks, president and CEO of Womenable. Their thorough reviews and detailed comments were instrumental in helping us expand and improve upon earlier versions of this book.

Last but not least, we would like to thank our families and friends for their support, love, and patience through this process. In particular, Susan thanks her husband, Bill Coleman, for his enduring love, encouragement, and support, as well as her sister, Maureen Distasio, her brother, David Flint, and David's partner, Becky Wilson, for being the best sisters and brother anyone could ever ask for. She would also like to thank her nephews, Mick and Lou Distasio, her grandson, Ben Coleman, and her University of Hartford students for their unfailing belief that she can do anything she puts her mind to. Alicia would like to thank all the amazing women in her life who continually support and inspire her, including her mother, Jackie, her aunts, Barbara and Brenda, her niece, Maria, her cousins, Samantha and Sabrina, her friends Jeanne Lavin, Erin Pinto, and Krista Katsantonis, as well as as the many women who agreed to share their stories, their expertise, and their advice that we highlight in this book. Alicia would also like to thank her colleagues and friends at the Kauffman Foundation, especially E. J. Reedy, Dane Stangler, Mette Kramer, Michelle St. Claire, Barbara Pruitt, Arnobio Morelix, Amisha Miller, Alex Krause, and Kauffman's CEO, Wendy Guillies. She thanks her partner, Mark Patrick, for his love and support. Finally, in the last year of this project, Alicia lost a good friend, Paula Kantor, to whom she dedicated this book, who was killed in Kabul by the Taliban. Paula was a passionate advocate for women and dedicated her life to empowering women around the world. We hope that we can continue to do our small part in continuing Paula's work. She will not be forgotten.

THE NEXT WAVE

1

INTRODUCTION

Why Growth?

"My own butt was the inspiration for all of this," said Sara Blakely, founder of Spanx, an entrepreneurial firm in the shapewear industry with an estimated market value of $1 billion (Wolfe, 2013). Sara is both a surprised and a surprising role model for growth-oriented women entrepreneurs. As the daughter of an attorney, she attended Florida State University with the goal of becoming a lawyer like her father. Low scores on the LSAT derailed her plan, however, and she ended up selling fax machines. Long hours on the road gave her time to fantasize about creating a product that she could sell and others would be willing to buy. Consistent with her vision, she founded Spanx at the age of twenty-seven. Originally, Spanx produced a lower body shaper for women that filled the gap between the girdles of yesteryear and the much more sheer women's underwear of today. The product's appeal is that it allows women to feel more confident by smoothing out bulges and bumps, while remaining relatively comfortable. Endorsements from Oprah Winfrey helped launch Spanx in 2000, and the following year, Sara started selling her products on QVC, the home shopping channel. Spanx were and continue to be sold in department stores where Sara has marketed the product using "before" and "after" photos of her derriere. After the success of her initial product line, Sara branched out into additional offerings including denim leggings, swimwear, workout clothing, and men's Spanx. In 2013, Sara was the first woman to join Bill Gates and Warren Buffett's Giving Pledge by agreeing to donate over half of her wealth to charity. Today, Sara remains the sole owner of Spanx, which had sales of almost $700 million in 2013.

We could not resist Sara Blakely's story as a way to launch our own entre-preneurial venture, a book that focuses on the financing strategies of growth-oriented, women-owned firms. Sara is part of a new and growing vanguard of women who are taking the plunge and growing their firms to achieve sig-nificant size and scope. For these women, the sky's the limit, and they are pav-ing the way for those who follow. Although today only a small percentage of women own firms with revenues in excess of $1 million, entrepreneurs like Sara Blakely are breaking new ground, developing market-driven products and ser-vices, and designing strategies to achieve success on their own terms. This book is a celebration of their accomplishments, as well as an examination of the fi-nancial strategies that have helped them succeed.

Before we delve into the details, however, let's start with some preliminary questions: Why growth? Why women entrepreneurs? Why now? Traditionally, women-owned firms in the United States have been small. Even today, the vast majority of women-owned firms have no employees aside from the entrepre-neur herself (*2012 Survey of Business Owners*). Similarly, women-owned firms have been "small" in terms of revenues. Thus, women-owned enterprises have typically been low-growth or no-growth "lifestyle" firms, often home-based and concentrated in service and retail sectors. A primary motivation for women entrepreneurs like these has been the desire to supplement family income in ways that allow them to be at home with children while they are young. We fea-tured one such entrepreneur, Debbie Gadowsky, the founder of Cookies Direct, in our first book, *A Rising Tide: Financing Strategies for Women-Owned Firms* (Coleman and Robb, 2012). Debbie initially launched her firm at home with the goal of helping to finance college educations for her two children. She has done that and more, and now ships cookie baskets all over the world, achieving revenues of $500,000 per year while still operating out of her home.

More recently, however, a new cohort of women entrepreneurs has emerged. Unlike Debbie, who launched with the specific goal of establishing a relatively small and manageable home-based firm, these women start their firms with the intent to achieve significant size and scale. In this sense, they are a "new breed" that has emerged from the economic, social, and cultural characteristics of our time. Sara Blakely typifies entrepreneurs of this type in that she is young, well educated, creative, and visionary. She is also motivated not only by the innova-tive nature of her products but also by the economic rewards that they provide to her as an entrepreneur. Further, she values recognition as well as the op-portunity to make an impact at a national or even international level. As a way to begin answering our questions Why growth? Why women? and Why now? let's examine the factors that have "made" Sara Blakely as well as other growth-oriented women entrepreneurs like her.

Economic Impacts of Growth-Oriented Entrepreneurship

Every year, thousands of firms are launched, and simultaneously thousands of standing firms die or cease to exist through a variety of means. This pattern illustrates economist and political scientist Joseph Schumpeter's theme of "creative destruction," which is at the heart of the entrepreneurial process (Schumpeter, 1934). In the United States, the vast majority of firms are young and small. Some of these firms will grow into large enterprises, but most of those that manage to survive the first few years will remain small. The U.S. Small Business Administration defines a "small business" as a firm having five hundred or fewer employees, and 99 percent of all firms in this country fall into that category. In fact, most of these firms are "very small," with ten or fewer employees and annual revenues of $100,000 or less (Lowrey, 2011). Nevertheless, the firms that we continually hear about in the business press are the big ones.

Why are we so focused on this small percentage of very large firms? Our preoccupation with growth-oriented firms can be explained by two major considerations: their ability to contribute to economic growth and their potential for creating a significant number of new jobs (Haltiwanger, Miranda, and Jarmin, 2013; Audretsch, 2007; Wennekers and Thurik, 1999). Prior research reveals that young, growth-oriented entrepreneurial ventures disproportionately create jobs in the United States (Haltiwanger, Hyatt, McEntarfer, and Soufa, 2012; Haltiwanger, Jarmin, and Miranda, 2010). While firms under ten years of age only account for about 25 percent of overall employment, they account for about 40 percent of job creation (Figure 1.1).

The job creation potential of new growth-oriented firms is particularly important now. Although the United States has emerged from a global financial crisis and the worst recession in eighty years, the job market continues to pose challenges. The current national unemployment rate is 5.5 percent (U.S. Bureau of Labor Statistics, 2015a). However, this national percentage masks the stark nature of the job market for some segments of the population. As examples, the unemployment rate for young people, those in the twenty-to-twenty-four-year age range, is 10.6 percent, and for those in the eighteen-to-nineteen-year

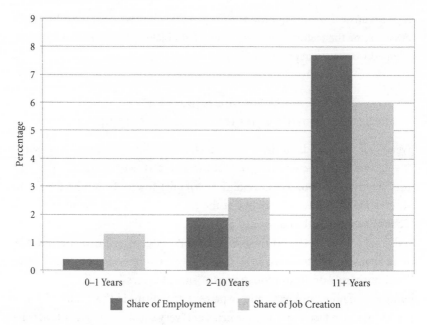

FIGURE 1.1. Share of Employment and Job Creation by Firm Age
Source: Kauffman Foundation BDS Statistics Briefing (Haltiwanger and others, 2012)

age range it's 16.8 percent (U.S. Bureau of Labor Statistics, 2015b). For black and Hispanic young adults, the rate is even higher. This age range is the point at which young adults typically launch their careers, get married, buy cars and houses, and start families. Their inability to find jobs postpones that entire process and reduces the likelihood of positive outcomes.

These factors help us in answering the questions Why growth? and Why now? However, our third question, Why women?, remains. Several scholars have pointed out that women entrepreneurs represent an economic resource that has yet to be fully tapped. Although women represent roughly 50 percent of the population, they represent only about one-third of entrepreneurs (Minnitti, 2010; *2012 Survey of Business Owners*). The "gender gap" in growth-oriented entrepreneurship is even wider. A recent report from the Kauffman Foundation points out,

> With nearly half of the workforce and more than half of our college students
> now being women, their lag in building high-growth firms has become a major
> economic deficit. The nation has fewer jobs—and less strength in emerging
> industries—than it could if women's entrepreneurship were on a par with

men's. Women capable of starting growth companies may well be our greatest under-utilized economic resource. (Mitchell, 2011, p. 2)

In spite of this persistent gap between men and women in the level of growth-oriented entrepreneurship, a number of factors are contributing to positive change. Some of these factors represent changing trends in education, society, and culture, while others represent motivational drivers that are prompting more women to take the plunge. Taken together, these various factors have contributed to a changing entrepreneurial landscape and a blurring of many boundaries that have traditionally separated the types of firms that women launch from those launched by men. Let's take a few moments to review some of these changes.

Educational, Social, and Cultural Factors

Today's women entrepreneurs are better educated, better trained, and better prepared than ever before. From the standpoint of education, the number of women graduating from college actually exceeds the number of men. Although men are still more likely to have graduate degrees, women are gaining rapidly. Thanks to initiatives at the local, state, and federal levels, women are also diversifying their fields of study to encompass previously male-dominated disciplines such as science, technology, engineering, and math (STEM) (Landivar, 2013). These academic disciplines are important because they often serve as a gateway for entry into fields such as health care, information technology, and manufacturing, all of which are fertile ground for innovation and entrepreneurship. Continued progress in this area will help to break down the "industry segregation" that has constrained women to service and retail fields, which are highly competitive, less growth-oriented, and less profitable (Hudson, 2006; Wang, 2013).

In addition to these educational gains and the new opportunities they unlock for women entrepreneurs, a major social and cultural change has been the number of women who work outside of the home. Working women are not necessarily a new phenomenon, but a growing number of these women are now holding positions of influence and power in both large and small corporations (*2012 Catalyst Census*). These positions help women develop skills in a broad range of areas, including the ability to manage others, the ability to make important and often difficult decisions, and the ability to see the "big picture." Taken together, these educational and workplace changes have helped to equip a growing number of women with the human capital required to launch growth-oriented firms.

In spite of these changes, however, women still face challenges in corporate environments. Although women are now well represented in middle management positions, few have reached the executive suite or board of directors level (Ding, Murray, and Stuart, 2013; Nelson and Levesque, 2007). Studies conducted by Catalyst, an organization devoted to expanding opportunities for women, found that women held only 4.2 percent of the CEO positions in Fortune 500 firms in 2012. Similarly, women held only 16.6 percent of the board seats for these firms (Missing Pieces, 2013). In a study on the development of "high potentials" capable of serving on boards for both public and private companies, the authors noted that

> men are more likely than women to have career experiences managing people, being responsible for profit functions, and attaining executive status in their current jobs. (Carter and others, 2013, p. 6)

A number of the women entrepreneurs we have spoken with allude to the "glass ceiling," which prevented them from advancing to the most senior ranks of their former firms—creating an impetus to start their own. From a public policy perspective, one of our challenges going forward is to ensure that women have advancement opportunities in their firms and organizations. As in the case of educational and experiential gains, these types of leadership opportunities will help to equip them with the skills needed to launch growth-oriented firms.

Financial Rewards as a Motivator: Oprah Winfrey

In addition to basic advancement, an important motivator for growth-oriented entrepreneurs, both male and female, is the potential for significant financial and economic gains. Consider the case of Oprah Winfrey, who is not only a highly successful growth-oriented entrepreneur, but also one of the wealthiest individuals in the United States.

Oprah Winfrey was born to a teenage single mother in rural Mississippi. Raised in an inner city neighborhood in Milwaukee, Winfrey was sexually abused by family members and friends of her mother as a child. She became pregnant at the age of fourteen, and gave birth to a son who later died. Oprah subsequently moved to Nashville, Tennessee, to live with her father. While there, she enrolled in Tennessee State University and began working in local radio and TV in 1971. After graduating from college, Winfrey embarked on her broadcasting career in earnest, hosting her first television chat show in 1976. This led to the launch of the now famous Oprah Winfrey Show as a nationally syndicated program in 1986. Winfrey launched her own production company, Harpo (Oprah spelled backward) to house the show, which became increasingly popular and increasingly profitable. Her show focused on issues and topics that resonate with women, highlighting both the joys and challenges of everyday life. Simultaneously, she addressed difficult topics such as sexual abuse, sexual preference, substance abuse, and marital fidelity. When the trend toward "trashy talk shows" emerged in the 1990s, Winfrey bucked it and signaled her respect for her audience by avoiding tawdry topics. In contrast, she focused increasingly on topics relating to self-improvement, strategies for overcoming adversity, and spirituality.

Winfrey went on to launch additional entrepreneurial initiatives, including Oprah's Book Club, O: the Oprah Magazine, Oxygen Media, and the Oprah Winfrey Network. As a role model and thought leader, Oprah has inspired many women to take control of their destinies by getting out of bad relationships, taking charge of their emotional and physical well-being, and improving their lives. For almost three decades, she has served as an enduring example of courage, dignity, common sense, and spunk. In 2013, Oprah Winfrey had a net worth of $2.9 billion and held the distinction of being America's only African-American billionaire. In addition to the many accolades and awards that she has received in her field, including numerous Emmys and a Lifetime Achievement Award by the National Academy of Television Arts and Sciences, Winfrey has been recognized as a member of the Forbes 400, a listing of the four hundred wealthiest individuals in the United States (http://www.forbes.com). In 2013, Forbes also recognized Winfrey as number 13 on its list of the world's most powerful women.[1] While women like Oprah show the earning potential of a high-growth women entrepreneur, traditionally, women's earnings have lagged those of men. This persists even today.

Recent data from the U.S. Bureau of Labor Statistics indicate that full-time women workers' earnings are only about 81 percent of that of their male counterparts. The pay gap is even greater for African-American and Latina women, with African-American women earning 64 cents and Latina women earning 56 cents for every dollar earned by a Caucasian man (U.S. Bureau of Labor

Statistics, 2013). A number of reasons have been put forth for this discrepancy, including the fact that women are more likely to have career interruptions associated with the birth of children or their subsequent care in the home. Further, as noted above, many women have gravitated to fields that simply do not pay as well as others, such as teaching, nursing, and clerical work versus manufacturing, computer science, and engineering. These boundaries are shifting, however, as more women assume the role of primary wage earner for their families. A record 40 percent of all households with children under the age of eighteen include mothers who are either the sole or primary source of income for the family, according to a new Pew Research Center analysis of data from the U.S. Census Bureau. The share was just 11 percent in 1960[2] (Wang, Parker, and Taylor, 2013). Similarly, women are now well represented in a number of previously male-dominated fields such as medicine, accounting, and law. These factors have raised women's aspirations and expectations for higher earnings and opportunities for career advancement.

Being Recognized as a Leader

Another motivator for growth-oriented women entrepreneurs is the opportunity for recognition as a leader in their field at either a national or even an international level. Beyond the firm, leadership roles allow women to shape the direction of their industries and provide input on key issues such as legislation, regulations, and public policy, all of which will have an impact on them. Like well-known male entrepreneurs such as Bill Gates or Steve Jobs, women entrepreneurs want to be recognized as "movers and shakers." They want to be taken seriously, and they believe they have earned that right. This is a motivator that surfaced in our first book, *A Rising Tide*, as several of the women entrepreneurs that we interviewed spoke of their desire to reach their full potential and to be respected, valued, and looked up to for their accomplishments. They wanted to validate their own capabilities and talent through their entrepreneurial ventures, but they wanted external validation as well.

These themes are especially prominent in women entrepreneurs who aspire to growth. Kiran Mazumdar-Shaw established her biotech firm, Biogen, in Bangalore, India, in 1978, operating out of her garage and starting with the equivalent of approximately $200 in funding (Anderson, 2012). In 2004, Biogen went public with a market value of over $1 billion and now operates on a global scale. One of Mazumdar-Shaw's goals has been to make health care more affordable and more accessible, particularly for the poor. In a 2012 interview with CNN she stated,

> India is a country where 80% of healthcare is out of pocket; where 80% of healthcare infrastructure is in the private sector; where most people don't have access to quality healthcare (Anderson, 2012).

In the face of these grim statistics, Mazumdar-Shaw resolved to be an agent of change by using technology to bring down the cost of developing new drugs. She has earned global acclaim and was recognized as a Technology Pioneer by the World Economic Forum. She has also received national awards presented by the president of India for her pioneering work in the field of biotechnology. (http://www.biocon.com)

Making an Impact

Each of the growth-oriented women entrepreneurs we have referenced—Sara Blakely, Oprah Winfrey, and Kiran Mazumdar-Shaw—has sought ways to have an impact beyond the boundaries of her company. Each of our entrepreneurs has used her wealth and influence to address issues and causes on a larger scale. As noted, Sara Blakely has made a commitment to donate half of her wealth to charity. Her efforts to date have been focused on initiatives that help women and girls. One such project was the Empowerment Plan, a Detroit-based program that works to create jobs for homeless women (Spanx Mogul Sara Blakely Becomes First Female Billionaire to Join Gates-Buffett Giving Pledge, 2013). Her pledge letter states,

> Since I was a little girl I have always known I would help women. In my wildest dreams I never thought I would have started with their butts. As it turns out, that was a great place to start! At Spanx we say it's our goal to make the world a better place, one butt at a time. With this pledge my goal is to make the world a better place . . . one woman at a time. (http://www.givingpledge.org)

Oprah Winfrey has provided generous financial support to a broad range of individuals and causes. One of the initiatives that has been most important to her is the Leadership Academy for Girls located in South Africa, which Winfrey established in 2002 and has been funding ever since (The Education of Oprah Winfrey, 2012). Beyond that, her visibility as a celebrity has enabled her to take positions of social and political issues. As an example, in the 2008 presidential campaign Winfrey was an outspoken supporter of then little-known candidate Barack Obama. Her support is credited with persuading roughly one million voters to support Obama in a race that led to the election of America's first black president. (McClatchy, 2007)

In addition to her desire to lower the costs associated with developing new drugs, Kiran Mazumdar-Shaw wanted to start a firm that would help to arrest the "brain drain" of bright young scientists from India to other nations. Today her firm employs almost five thousand scientists, including a significant number of women who were previously sidelined and bypassed for the most desirable jobs in science and technology fields (Anderson, 2012). These examples highlight our belief that growth-oriented women often have societal goals and aspirations driving their choices. The fact that they have been so successful in launching and growing their firms provides them with a platform for addressing other issues and causes for which they have a passion.

Growth-Oriented Women Entrepreneurs as Role Models

Women entrepreneurs who have successfully grown their firms can also have an impact by serving as role models and mentors for other women contemplating entrepreneurship or attempting to launch their businesses. This is particularly important given the continuing gap between the numbers of women- and men-owned firms. This gap is even more pronounced for growth-oriented firms. Women such as Sara Blakely, Oprah Winfrey, and Kiran Mazumdar-Shaw serve as an inspiration for the thousands of women who dream of following in their footsteps. Each of these remarkable women has also taken it upon herself to help other women and girls reach their educational, career, or entrepreneurial goals. In *A Rising Tide* one of our key strategies for women entrepreneurs was to "pay it forward" (Coleman and Robb, 2012, p. 244). We advised aspiring women entrepreneurs to get mentors, and we urged successful women entrepreneurs to be mentors. These measures are all a part of the "rising tide" of women's entrepreneurship that we addressed in that book. In order for women entrepreneurs to succeed, they have to help and support each other. In other words, women's entrepreneurship is not a zero sum game in which some women can succeed only if others fail. In contrast, entrepreneurship is a "big boat," and there is plenty of room for more talented, energetic, and determined women like those we have described in this chapter. In *The Next Wave*, we will highlight the importance and impact of successful women entrepreneurs on the launch and development of other growth-oriented women-owned ventures.

Growth-Oriented Women Entrepreneurs as Investors

One of the newest and most exciting ways in which successful women can have an impact is by investing in other emerging entrepreneurs. Many of these investors are professional women such as attorneys, doctors, and accountants, but a growing number are women entrepreneurs who have launched their own successful growth-oriented firms. In recognition of this trend, organizations such as Springboard Enterprises, Astia, Pipeline Angels, and Golden Seeds provide both training and opportunities for women to invest. For example, Golden Seeds has established a "Knowledge Institute" to train and empower both women entrepreneurs and investors (http://www.goldenseeds.com). Over thirty training modules are available on topics such as the risks and rewards of angel investing, structuring a deal, financial due diligence, and board membership. For successful women entrepreneurs, investing in and supporting other women entrepreneurs is one of the many ways they can give back. More examples and resources are provided in later chapters. This motivation to give back and support other women is particularly important, because, as we will demonstrate in this book, one of the major challenges for growth-oriented women entrepreneurs is the challenge of securing adequate financial capital to launch and grow their ventures. In light of that, we need those successful women entrepreneurs, the Sara Blakelys and the Oprah Winfreys of the world, to "pay it forward" by investing in the entrepreneurial dreams of others.

Financing Strategies for Growth-Oriented Women Entrepreneurs

As we have observed in this chapter, the profile of women entrepreneurs is changing, and changing in positive ways thanks to educational, workplace, social, and cultural shifts. Each of these has had the effect of opening the door to growth-oriented entrepreneurship a bit wider for women. As we have also shown, a growing number of factors are not only creating opportunities but also providing the motivation for women to pursue growth. One barrier that still remains, however, is the barrier of securing adequate financial capital to launch and grow a firm. Current research suggests that women entrepreneurs have largely leveled the playing field in terms of access to debt capital, although they continue to borrow smaller amounts than men (Coleman and Robb, 2009; Haynes and Haynes, 1999). A significant gap between women and men remains, however, when it comes to securing sources of equity capital in the form of angel investments, venture capital, or private equity (Brush, Carter, Gatewood, and Hart, 2004; Harrison and Mason, 2007; Robb, 2013). This is not necessarily a problem for smaller firms, which tend to rely on internal sources of capital and external debt in the form of bank loans. Nevertheless, accessing sufficient amounts of external equity capital is a major impediment for women entrepreneurs who launch growth-oriented firms. As we ride the "next wave" together, we will explore the financial challenges faced by growth-oriented women as well as the financial strategies that successful women have employed to overcome those challenges.

In addition to delivering a contemporary account of financing strategies from the entrepreneur's perspective, we will address investor perspectives on financing. To date, most books on growth-oriented entrepreneurship have focused on the entrepreneur's challenges and strategies but have ignored the investor side of the equation. Since growth-oriented firms typically require large amounts of external equity, the investor perspective is critical. We will address this gap by detailing the development of a new generation of women investors. Accordingly, we will discuss strategies for mobilizing, educating, and training this cohort of potential female investors, while also teaching women entrepreneurs how to effectively engage with these counterparts. In this sense, we see *The Next Wave* as a "must read" for the thousands of women who are contemplating growth-oriented entrepreneurship, as well as those women who have gained sufficient wealth to take a more active role in growth-oriented investing.

Organization of This Book

The format of *The Next Wave* is organized around the life cycle of a growth-oriented firm and the financial issues and challenges that emerge at each stage of the life cycle. In this introductory chapter, we have discussed motivations for growth and have profiled three highly successful growth-oriented women entrepreneurs. In Chapters 2 and 3, we provide a status report on growth-oriented women's entrepreneurship, as we lay out some of the challenges that women face in trying to scale their companies. Chapters 4 and 5 focus on the financial challenges and strategies associated with nascent and early stage growth-oriented firms. Since the survival stage is a "make or break" point in the development of growth-oriented firms, we devote Chapters 6 and 7 to an exploration of the challenges that accompany that stage, as well as the financial strategies used by successful growth-oriented entrepreneurs to overcome them. We look at the emerging phenomenon of crowdfunding in Chapter 8, and how this strategy can be used not only for financing but also for product and price testing, market validation, and more. Chapter 9 focuses on how growth-oriented women entrepreneurs can achieve significant scale and scope. This, in turn, may lead to "harvesting value" in the form of an initial public offering, a process that we describe in Chapter 10. Most books on entrepreneurial finance would end with this particular "happy ending." In our case, we see the harvest event not only as a happy ending, but as a happy beginning for the next stage for growth-oriented women entrepreneurs, the stage that involves their transition from entrepreneur to investor. We describe this transition, as well as its importance, in Chapters 11 and 12.

As we make this journey together, we will rely on both qualitative and quantitative data documenting the motivations, experience, and challenges faced by growth-oriented women as well as their financial strategies for growth. To this end, each chapter will incorporate the stories of "real world" growth-oriented entrepreneurs. In this introductory chapter, we have drawn upon secondary sources to highlight the experience of three very successful high-profile women entrepreneurs, Sara Blakely, Oprah Winfrey, and Kiran Mazumdar-Shaw. Going forward, however, we will share case studies based on interviews done with growth-oriented entrepreneurs at various stages of their firms' life cycles. These case studies feature women who have employed a broad range of financial strategies in their pursuit of entrepreneurial growth. Similarly, the case studies provide examples of growth-oriented entrepreneurship across a broad range of industries.

We will also draw upon prior research in the areas of entrepreneurial finance and women's entrepreneurship to identify the financial issues and challenges associated with firm growth. Finally, we will incorporate our own research using data from the Kauffman Firm Survey, a longitudinal dataset that collected data on more than four thousand U.S. firms launched in 2004, which were tracked over an eight-year period. The KFS is an invaluable resource in that it provides detailed information on owner characteristics and firm performance, as well as financial structure and strategies.

At the end of each chapter, we integrate findings from our entrepreneur interviews with those drawn from current and prior research to "close the loop" by summarizing the chapter's key takeaways. Similarly, each chapter ends with a section titled "What Does This Mean for You?", which is designed to help you, our readers, apply each chapter's takeaways to your own entrepreneurial ventures and journeys.

As we begin this new voyage together, we embrace this opportunity to intertwine findings from the latest research and practice as they relate to the financing strategies of women entrepreneurs who have high-growth aspirations. As we have noted, the entrepreneurial landscape is changing rapidly, and changing in ways that will benefit women entrepreneurs. They are the "next wave," and they are already having a profound effect on business, society, and our economy. These are truly exciting times for us and for them!

Closing the Loop

In this chapter, we have addressed the fundamental question of what motivates women entrepreneurs to grow their firms. In doing so, we have drawn upon the examples of three highly successful growth-oriented entrepreneurs, Sara Blakely, Oprah Winfrey, and Kiran Mazumdar-Shaw. In Sara's case, she was motivated by an opportunity in the marketplace to develop a line of comfortable shapewear products that would increase women's confidence in themselves while also allowing her to enjoy the financial rewards associated with launching a growth-oriented firm. Oprah Winfrey has also enjoyed these same financial rewards and is listed as one of the four hundred wealthiest individuals in the United States. At the same time, however, entrepreneurship has served as a pathway for Oprah to become a role model for millions of women and girls as well as a thought leader on a broad range of issues. Biogen founder Kiran Mazumdar-Shaw has used growth-oriented entrepreneurship as a means for making health care more accessible and affordable on a global scale. As we have seen, each of these remarkable entrepreneurs has been driven by a combination of factors that include the pursuit of an opportunity, financial gain, being recognized as a leader in her field, and making an impact that will improve the lives of countless others.

We have pointed out that, traditionally, women have launched very small firms for a variety of reasons. Although many of these firms are very successful, they do not create the same type of economic impact that larger firms are able to create, leading the Kauffman Foundation's Lesa Mitchell to refer to women who are capable of launching growth-oriented firms as "our greatest under-utilized economic resource." More recently, however, a new generation of women entrepreneurs is embracing both the challenges and the rewards associated with growth.

For these women, educational and workplace gains combined with changing cultural and societal factors have opened a door that was previously closed to many. In effect, these changes have made it much more possible for women who want to grow their firms to do so. In spite of this progress, the path of growth-oriented entrepreneurship is not an easy one. For women, in particular, there continue to be obstacles, some of which are structural and others attitudinal. One such barrier that has been especially intransigent is women's ability to secure sufficient amounts of financial capital to launch and grow their firms. Prior research consistently shows that women start their firms with smaller amounts of financial capital than men and that they go on to raise smaller amounts of capital post-launch. These findings have serious implications not only for the growth of women-owned firms, but for their very survival. Our goal in *The Next Wave* is to take on this challenge by identifying and sharing the financial strategies that have helped women entrepreneurs grow their firms. We will do so through a combination of case studies featuring growth-oriented women entrepreneurs as well as through research using data from the Kauffman Firm Survey.

In addition to focusing on the growth potential of women entrepreneurs, *The Next Wave* will focus on the potential of women as investors. The same factors that are opening doors for growth-oriented entrepreneurs have also created opportunities for women to accumulate significant amounts of wealth in the form of career-generated earnings or the proceeds from their own entrepreneurial ventures. Just as women have been underrepresented in growth-oriented entrepreneurship, they have similarly been underrepresented as investors in entrepreneurial firms. In this book, we will explore ways for unlocking the unrealized potential of women capable of investing in growth-oriented firms, including those launched by other women. This perspective will allow us to address both the entrepreneur and the investor sides of the equation, creating a virtuous circle whereby successful women are able to help and support growth-oriented women entrepreneurs who will eventually be in a position to do the same for others.

What Does This Mean for You?

Although we often associate growth with high-tech firms such as Apple Computer, Google, and Facebook, the examples from this chapter illustrate that every industry has potential for high-growth firms. This is important, because women entrepreneurs are currently more heavily represented in the service, retail, and health care industries than they are in technology-related fields. This is changing, but the point is that women entrepreneurs have growth opportunities, no matter what industry their companies are in.

In *The Next Wave*, our goal is to provide those women entrepreneurs who are pursuing growth with an array of financial strategies that can help them achieve it. With that in mind, we leave you with the following thoughts as we conclude this first chapter:

1. Think about your own appetite for growth. What factors would motivate you to grow your firm? These can include things like the desire to take advantage of an opportunity in the marketplace, the desire to achieve greater financial gains, the desire to assume a leadership role in your industry or community, or the desire to have a positive impact on the lives of others.

2. Correspondingly, what factors are holding you back from growing your firm? Do you lack confidence in your own abilities and skills to manage a larger firm? Are you concerned about possible risks associated with growth? Are you having a hard time securing needed resources, including resources in the form of financial capital? Do you anticipate greater challenges in managing the work-family balance if you grow your firm?

3. Does your firm have growth potential? What opportunities in the form of new products, services, markets, or delivery systems might you pursue to achieve growth?

4. Are you already motivated to grow your firm, but you simply don't know how to go about it? Do you have role models, mentors, advisors, and a network of support to help you move forward?

If any of these questions strike a familiar chord, you have come to the right place. Using the stories of entrepreneurial women just like you, we will navigate the growth process from a firm's earliest stages through to harvesting value and beyond with a focus on the financial strategies that work at each stage. Welcome aboard! It's time to launch!

2

A STATUS REPORT ON
GROWTH-ORIENTED
WOMEN ENTREPRENEURS

Before launching into a discussion of growth-oriented women entrepreneurs, we think it's important to provide an overview of women-owned firms in general. Table 2.1 provides data from the *Survey of Business Owners* as released by the U.S. Census Bureau in 1997, 2002, 2007, and 2012. The data reveal that there were nearly ten million women-owned firms generating $1.6 trillion in revenues in 2012. That represents an increase of 83 percent from 1997 to 2012, compared with an increase of 33 percent for all firms. During the same time frame, the revenues generated by women-owned firms grew by 97 percent, compared with a growth rate of 81 percent for all firms. The shares of firm revenues, payroll, and employment remain small, but grew over the period, which is promising.

In 2012 there were just over a million women-owned firms with more than one employee. This represents nearly 20 percent of all employer firms, a marked increase since 1997. Further, those firms grew their employee ranks more quickly. The data show that women-owned firms increased their number of employees by 27 percent from 1997 to 2012, whereas firms overall increased employment by 11.5 percent. Thus, the percentage of jobs generated by women-owned firms has increased from 6.8 percent of total employment in 1997 to 7.8 percent in 2012. While these comparative statistics suggest that women-owned firms tend to be smaller on average as measured by both revenues and employment, the 2012 numbers help illustrate the potential of women's entrepreneurship.

TABLE 2.1. Women-Owned Businesses (1997–2012)

Women	1997	2002	2007	2012
Firms (Number)	5,417,034	6,489,483	7,793,425	9,932,434
Receipts (Millions of dollars)	$818,669	$940,775	$1,192,781	$1,616,319
Employer Firms (Number)	846,780	916,768	911,285	1,052,876
Receipts (Millions of dollars)	$717,764	$804,097	$1,010,470	$1,383,150
Employees (Number)	7,076,081	7,146,229	7,587,020	8,982,588
Annual payroll (Millions of dollars)	$149,116	$173,709	$218,136	$290,473
All				
Firms (Number)	20,821,934	22,974,685	27,110,362	27,626,362
Receipts (Millions of dollars)	$18,553,243	$22,627,167	$30,181,461	$33,537,004
Employer Firms (Number)	5,295,151	5,524,813	5,752,975	5,424,393
Receipts (Millions of dollars)	$17,907,940	$21,859,758	$29,208,766	$32,478,441
Employees (Number)	103,359,815	110,786,416	118,668,699	115,249,459
Annual payroll (Millions of dollars)	$2,936,493	$3,813,488	$4,886,977	$5,236,468
Women as a Percentage of All				
Firms	26.0%	28.2%	28.7%	36.0%
Receipts	4.4%	4.2%	4.0%	4.8%
Employer Firms	16.0%	16.6%	15.8%	19.4%
Receipts of Employer Firms	4.0%	3.7%	3.5%	4.3%
Employees	6.8%	6.5%	6.4%	7.8%
Annual Payroll	5.1%	4.6%	4.5%	5.5%

Growth Rates	1997–2012		2002–2012	
	Women	All	Women	All
Firms	83.4%	32.7%	53.1%	20.2%
Employer Firms	24.3%	2.4%	14.8%	−1.8%
Receipts	97.4%	80.8%	71.8%	48.2%
Employment	26.9%	11.5%	25.7%	4.0%

Source: U.S. Census Bureau, 1997, 2002, 2007, and 2012 Survey of Business Owners

As academic entrepreneurs, we tend to be "glass half full" rather than "glass half empty" types, and we see these statistics as an opportunity. In light of the gains that women have made in education and the workplace, their level of growth-oriented entrepreneurship should actually be much higher. In this chapter we will explore some of the trends that can help paint a more favorable picture not only for the current status of growth-oriented entrepreneurship for women, but for their future prospects as well. We will begin by providing a global perspective and then focus more specifically on growth-oriented entre-preneurship in the United States.

A Global Perspective

The Global Entrepreneurship Monitor

The Global Entrepreneurship Monitor (GEM) was launched in 1999 to survey and measure the extent of entrepreneurship worldwide. The depth and breadth of the GEM project allows us to examine how the process of entrepreneurship unfolds for different populations, for example in developed versus developing economies, or for women versus men. The GEM's *2012 Women's Report* provides valuable insights into the activities of both nascent women entrepreneurs and women running established businesses (Kelley, Brush, Greene, and Litovsky, 2012).

In terms of numbers, the *2012 Women's Report* estimates that over two hundred million women were either planning to start or already operating businesses in the countries included in the 2012 survey. Approximately half of women-owned firms provide or are expected to provide employment for at least one person. Equally important, an estimated twelve million women expressed the intention to grow their firms over the course of the next five years. In the United States, survey findings indicate that women are starting firms at twice the rate of other developed economies. Nevertheless, and consistent with survey results overall, U.S. women were less likely to engage in entrepreneurship than men. One particularly important finding is that women entrepreneurs in the United States had higher rates of innovation (defined as "the extent to which entrepreneurs offer products or services that are new to some or all customers") than men (36 percent versus 33 percent), as well as higher rates of innovation than all of the other geographic regions sampled.

Aspirations for growth can be measured in a variety of ways, including the entrepreneur's intentions of adding employees or expanding into new geographic territories. The GEM report revealed that, across the regions surveyed, more male than female entrepreneurs anticipated adding employees. Nevertheless, 16 percent of women participants in the United States responded that they expected to add six or more employees over the course of the next five years. U.S. entrepreneurs in general were less inclined to grow by expanding internationally than those in other regions. This was especially true for women, who were less than half as likely as men to internationalize their markets (7 percent versus 16 percent). Given the size, diversity, and innovative nature of

U.S. markets, this suggests an untapped opportunity for women entrepreneurs in particular. The GEM survey summarizes the state of women's entrepreneurship in the United States as follows:

> Entrepreneurship among women in the U.S. appears to be characterized by contrasts: healthy rates but lower than men, having personal resources for this activity but not leveraging the resources of others, and innovating and entering knowledge-intensive industries but not venturing outside the country. (Kelley and others, 2012, p. 41)

Women Entrepreneurs in the OECD

In a report on women's entrepreneurship in the countries included in the Organization for Economic Cooperation and Development (OECD), economist Mario Piacentini (2013) concluded that "important gender gaps in entrepreneurship exist" (p. 4). He found that male entrepreneurs were three times more likely to own businesses with employees than were women, and that women's earnings from self-employment were as much as 60 percent lower than for men. Consistent with the GEM survey, Piacentini noted that women rarely own large businesses, and in doing so highlighted the unrealized economic potential of women-owned firms. Piacentini stressed the potential for employment gains if the rates of entrepreneurial activity for women were more consistent with those of men.

In his analysis of the causes of gender differences in entrepreneurship, Piacentini highlights two factors. The first is market failures that lead to lower endowments for women entrepreneurs in the key areas of human, social, and financial capital. The second is attitudinal differences and stereotypes that discourage women from launching or growing their own firms. From a resource-based perspective, women are more likely to experience career interruptions due to child-bearing and the care of children. Piacentini notes that women entrepreneurs have "double assignments," in that they must manage their firms and their households simultaneously. Thus, consistent with our discussion in Chapter 1, women are less likely to have human capital in the form of prior experience in managerial roles, and are less likely to have previous experience in launching an entrepreneurial firm. Prior research also notes that women have different types of social capital in the form of networks and contacts (Aldrich, 1989; Aldrich, Reese, and Dubini, 1989). In particular, their professional networks tend to be smaller and consist primarily of other women.

Piacentini also points to differences in financial capital as a key factor in gender differences in firm size and growth. He cites data revealing that women rely more heavily on internal rather than external sources of capital, and that they raise less capital overall. Since women earn less than men, they have lower amounts of personal financial capital to invest in their firms. Previous studies also point to women's limited access to external growth capital in the form of angel investments and venture capital. Women entrepreneurs, in other words, launch their firms with smaller amounts of financial capital and have less access to the types of external financial capital that would allow them to grow their firms.

In terms of attitudes, entrepreneurship is typically associated with men rather than women. Entrepreneurs featured in the press, for example, are almost always males who launched large, growth-oriented firms in technology-related fields. In contrast, women, who are more likely to launch service, retail, or health care firms, have fewer role models. Not surprisingly, Piacentini found that women had a significantly lower preference for self-employment in the countries studied, including the United States. Women were less likely than men to view entrepreneurship as a viable career option. Figure 2.1 shows that half of the men surveyed in the United States felt that the pursuit of self-employment was possible compared to roughly 40 percent of women. This same pattern held true for virtually all of the countries surveyed and helps to explain women's lower level of engagement in entrepreneurship from a global perspective. Finally, women had less confidence in their skills and abilities to succeed as entrepreneurs. Their concerns about the risks associated with launching and growing a firm combined with a fear of failure may serve to discourage them from choosing the path of growth-oriented entrepreneurship.

Women-Owned Firms and Growth: A U.S. Perspective

Studies on High-Impact Firms

Shifting from a global perspective to a national one, two recent studies published by the U.S. Small Business Administration introduced the term "high-impact firms." High-impact firms are important, because they increase both revenues and employment rapidly. In the first of the SBA studies, researcher Zoltan Acs and his colleagues (Acs, Parsons, and Tracy, 2008) defined high-impact firms as firms whose sales have doubled over a four-year period and have increased employment by a growth quantifier of two or more. These re-

FIGURE 2.1. Becoming Self-Employed

Source: Piacentini, 2013

searchers found that high-impact firms represent a tiny percentage (between 2 and 3 percent) of all firms. Further, they discovered that high-impact firms emerged in all industries and in all firm sizes. The economic impact of these firms is significant: high-impact firms generated 58 percent of new jobs created between the years of 1994 and 2006. These jobs were fairly evenly split between firms with fewer than five hundred employees and those with more than five hundred employees. Highlighting the role of entrepreneurship, Acs and his colleagues also found that high-impact firms tended to be younger than low-impact firms.

The second study, authored by Spencer L. Tracy Jr. (Tracy, 2011), noted that, on average, high-impact firms grow by over 100 percent, compared to an average growth rate of 6 percent or less. Tracy estimated that there are 350,000 such companies in the United States, representing approximately 6 percent of all employer firms. He contends that the importance of high-impact firms lies in their job creation potential and their ability to sustain the economy through both ups and downs. This study makes the case that, were it not for high-impact firms, the United States would have lost 16.3 million jobs between 1994 and 2008.

Both of these studies found that high-impact firms are found in all geographic regions, and are evenly distributed across all industry sectors. This is particularly noteworthy, because it would seem to disprove the stereotype that growth-oriented firms are concentrated in technology-related fields in which women tend to be underrepresented. Equally important, Tracy's study found that women's level of representation in high-impact entrepreneurship was comparable to their level of representation in entrepreneurship overall. Within this sample of firms, women-owned firms represented 12.4 percent of high-impact firms and 13.2 percent of all other companies (Table 2.2). Thus, although women represent a smaller percentage of high-impact firm owners, they are creating high-impact firms at the roughly the same rate as men.

TABLE 2.2. High-Impact Company Ownership, by Segment and Gender, 2004–2008

| Employment | High Impact Companies | | | | All Other Companies | | | |
| | Women-Owned | | Men-Owned | | Women-Owned | | Men-Owned | |
Category	Number	Percent	Number	Percent	Number	Percent	Number	Percent
1–19	36,069	12.4	255,965	87.6	1,210,832	13.2	7,975,531	86.8
20–499	6,962	9.4	67,216	90.6	47,493	7.8	563,826	92.2
500+	78	3.8	1,972	96.2	418	2.3	17,476	97.7

Source: Tracy, 2011

Findings from the Kauffman Firm Survey

The Kauffman Firm Survey (KFS), which we introduced in Chapter 1, provides yet another source of data on U.S. firms and confirms that very few firms owned by either women or men grow to be large. Table 2.3 provides a comparison of the top twenty-five firms that were owned by women and the top twenty-five owned by men as measured by end-of-period employment in 2011.

Table 2.3 reveals that these firms had average employment of 7 (women-owned) and 22 (men-owned) in their first year of observation. By the year 2011, average employment had grown to 28.6 employees for women-owned firms and 152.4 employees for men-owned firms. The median number of employees, however, was much lower, especially for women. In fact, only one firm owned by a woman employed more than 100 employees, compared with thirteen of the firms owned by men. Thus, although both women- and men-owned firms experience growth in employment, the women-owned top twenty-five started with fewer employees and grew more slowly.

The reality is, however, that most firms are small and do not aspire to growth. The KFS asked respondents what they thought their growth would be over the 2008–2011 period. At the end of the survey period, we were able to measure the actual performance of the firms that survived, thus revealing some interesting differences by gender (Table 2.4). Nearly one-quarter of male-owned firms expected to increase their employment by 30 percent or more, compared with just 16 percent of women. About 38 percent of women-owned firms expected to grow very little, if at all, or even to decrease their employment, compared with about 35 percent of men. When we look at actual growth rates, however, we see that just under a quarter of firms decreased their employment from 2008 to 2011, while 58 percent of women-owned firms and 53 percent of male-owned firms grew by 30 percent or more. This finding suggests that women-owned firms have more potential for growth than their founders realize.

TABLE 2.3. Top 25 Firms by Gender

Variable	Obs	Female Mean	Obs	Male Mean	Percentage Change 2004–2011 Female	Male
Employees (2004)	25	7.1	25	22.0	Female	Male
Employment (2011)	25	28.6	25	152.4	303	591
Revenues (2004)	14	$1,468,764	18	$2,572,944		
Revenues (2011)	21	$3,638,239	24	$22,156,133	148	761

Source: Kauffman Firm Survey microdata, 2012

TABLE 2.4. Growth Expectations and Actual Growth (2008–2011)

	2008-2011 Growth expectations		2008-2011 Actual growth	
	Male	Female	Male	Female
Decrease	15.8%	13.5%	23.3%	22.4%
No change or increase by less than 5%	19.4%	24.4%	22.1%	18.5%
Increase between 5 and 29%	40.7%	46.2%	1.8%	0.9%
Increase by 30% or more	24.1%	16.0%	52.9%	58.2%
	100%	100%	100%	100%

Source: Kauffman Firm Survey microdata, 2012

Data from the Inc. 5000

The Inc. 5000 list, which ranks companies by overall revenue growth over a three-year period, is another source of data on high-growth entrepreneurs in the United States. We were able to analyze data from the first quarter of 2014 to create a sample of 404 founders (57 women, 347 men) who made this list. Thus, while women entrepreneurs remained a minority within this group, they represented almost 15 percent of the total sample, indicating that, consistent with data from our other sources, there is a sizeable cohort of growth-oriented women entrepreneurs in the United States. Although the Inc. 5000 is not a rigorously defined sample that can be generalized to the population of high-growth firms as a whole, data from this sample reveal some noteworthy gender differences, as shown in Table 2.5.

Respondents were asked about the sources of financing used for their current business. Personal savings were the most common source for both men

TABLE 2.5. Inc. 5000 Survey: Sources of Financing for Current Business

	Female	Male
Personal savings	69.6%	72.0%
Family	19.6%	22.5%
Close friends	1.8%	9.2%
Business acquaintances	5.4%	13.5%
Personal or business credit card	26.8%	38.3%
Personal or business loan from a bank	55.4%	51.3%
Government grants (e.g., SBIR or STTR)	5.4%	4.0%
Equity capital from angels or venture capitalists	3.6%	14.4%
Other (Please specify)	10.7%	7.2%
I have not used any financing	10.7%	12.1%
Average Rank on Inc. 5000 List	2,093	1,873
N	57	347

Source: Inc. 5000 Quarterly Survey, 2014; authors' analysis

and women, followed by bank loans. The patterns diverged for other sources of financing, however. While more than 14 percent of men had secured equity capital from angel investors or venture capitalists, only 3.6 percent of women had done so. Men were also much more likely than women to raise capital from close friends (9.2 percent versus 1.8 percent) and business acquaintances (13.5 percent versus 5.4 percent). The average ranking on the Inc. 5000 list was just over 2,000 for women and just under 1,900 for men.

Our review of data from both global and U.S. sources confirms that women entrepreneurs are less likely to engage in growth-oriented entrepreneurship than are men. Nevertheless, these same sources show that there is an emerging cohort of women who are launching firms with the potential for growth. What prompts these intrepid women entrepreneurs to "take the plunge" into growth-oriented entrepreneurship? What challenges do they encounter, and what rewards do they hope to achieve? Most important, as they strive to launch and grow their firms, what are the strategies that work? Our mini-case on Mary Page Platerink, the founder of First Aid Shot Therapy, helps us answer some of these questions.

Mary Page Platerink and First Aid Shot Therapy

Mary Page Platerink is the founder and CEO of First Aid Shot Therapy (www .firstaidshottherapy.com), a firm that provides single-dose liquid shots of over-the-counter drugs that have been approved by the Food and Drug Administration (FDA). These liquid shots are easy to swallow and provide fast-acting relief for pain and upset stomach symptoms. Further, these products are an ideal solution for today's fast-paced society, in which one never knows when a sudden headache or case of indigestion will crop up.

Prior to launching her firm, Mary Page worked for Coca-Cola for a number of years. Coca-Cola's multibillion-dollar acquisition of Vitamin Water prompted her to start thinking about what would be required to build an innovative company capable of creating value throughout the supply chain. Coming from consumer products rather than high tech, she began studying consumer products companies that created value, often through creative packaging and product delivery. Her goal was to create a firm that a larger company (like Coca-Cola) would buy.

Initially Mary Page thought about the consumer products industry, since her background was in that area. She also considered health care, in which her husband worked. The spark for Mary Page's idea actually came one day when she was walking down a shopping aisle for over-the-counter drugs. It occurred to her that companies providing over-the-counter drugs don't always think about the consumer experience. In other words, they do not think in terms of "ready to use" products that can be consumed quickly and on the run. She believed that if she could improve that user experience by delivering fast, effective relief that bordered on instant gratification, she'd have a winning product.

Mary Page discovered that developing a drug product is very different from developing food or drink products. She also discovered that it's not cheap. She knew she would need to find financial capital, so she began talking to potential investors almost immediately. Initially she contacted people she knew who were also knowledgeable about the health care industry. Her first investors, who fell into both categories, were individuals who had also invested in a medical device company. A former boss from Coca-Cola and others from the consumer products industry came on board as investors as well. In spite of these successes, raising financial capital was a challenge. It took Mary Page eighteen months to raise her initial angel round. She found that there weren't a lot of funders in the space she wanted to occupy, so she "didn't fit anyone's investor prospectus." The fact that her firm had no clear exit path for investors presented an additional challenge, making it difficult to connect with the right investors who would provide her firm with a reasonable valuation.

In spite of the challenges, Mary Page learned a lot from her experience. One particularly valuable lesson was how important it is to make sure you get the right investors on board. Often Mary Page's investors were people she sought out for knowledge or advice, rather than money. As these individuals learned more, they became intrigued with her idea and wanted to put money into the business. Thus, these investors added value to the business above and beyond the funding they provided.

Sometimes you get an indication that certain people are not the ones to trust with the company. Listen to your gut and your own instincts. You become really close to the culture of your investors, so it is critical to find a match. Spend time getting to know your investors and make sure they understand your business.

Mary Page's first round was made up entirely of angel investors. She turned down some institutional money at that time, because she wanted to maintain control and have a board composed of people she knew and was comfortable with. In the second round, however, she began actively courting institutional investors, and it took an additional eighteen months to get them over the hump. In light of the time required to raise new capital, Mary Page observed that it's important to prepare for the next round before you close the previous one. She was also quick to note that raising financial capital got easier over time, and that she actually enjoys it now. Ultimately, Mary Page raised money from about fifteen angels and three large institutional health care investors. More than a third of her investors were women who have been a great source of advice and support.

My business is so much better now because I've worked with amazing people who challenged me to think through and improve the business, which made my company better. In the beginning I was pretty naive.

Currently, First Aid Shot Therapy has two products available for sale (and two more on the way), a solid supply chain, and more retailer demand than it can handle. Mary Page attributes her success to perseverance, and says she gets up every day determined to do what needs to be done to achieve her goals. Since launching its first product in December 2013, the firm has grown to ten full-time employees and thirty full-time consultants, all of whom own shares in the company. On the basis of the firm's performance to date, Mary Page is already talking with several companies that are potential acquirers.

Over the course of our discussion, Mary Page provided us with a checklist for raising financial capital that includes the following points:

1. Make a business plan, create milestones, and develop a strategy to reach them.

2. Know when to raise money and how you will turn that investment into value.

3. Have a baseline and measure milestones.

4. Choose investors on the basis of their ability to make you and your company better.

5. Focus on creating the right business.

6. Find individuals you want to work with, and identify people that have expertise in that field.

7. Surround yourself with great people who can help you put together a financial plan and coach you.

8. Practice the pitch. You do get better by pitching and talking to investors.

Real-life experience pitching can be transformational, and you can get things beyond money. One guy persuaded me to change the name of the brand—he didn't invest, but he gave great advice and he was right. It's not a bad process. And there is nothing like the adrenaline that comes from doing it.

Our mini-case on Mary Page Platerink reinforces several of the themes developed in Chapter 1. In particular, our interview with Mary Page reveals two primary motivations. First, she saw an opportunity in the marketplace that would allow her to combine her expertise in consumer products with an unmet need in the area of health care. Second, like many growth-oriented entrepreneurs, Mary Page was motivated by the potential for financial gain. Consistent with that, she established the goal of creating a firm that would be successful enough to attract the interest of a potential buyer.

Mary Page's experience also highlights two fundamental truths about raising growth capital. First, you always need more money than you think you will, and second, it will take you longer to get it than you might like. Mary Page attributed her success in raising financial capital to persistence and getting the right kind of investors, people who could provide advice as well as money, people who understood her business, and people whom she could trust. Her fundraising strategy was one of creating concentric circles of potential investors. She started with people she knew and gradually expanded beyond that to include both angel investors and large institutional investors. This progression is both noteworthy and important, because entrepreneurs sometimes tend to overlook the social capital resources they already have in the form of family, friends, acquaintances, and co-workers.

Mary Page also used the strategy of minimizing her fixed expenses by using a high proportion of consultants rather than permanent employees. This financial strategy allowed her to obtain expertise when she needed it without burdening the firm with ongoing costs. A final lesson to be learned from Mary Page's story is that you never know where your next good idea will come from, so you need to keep an open mind. We can see this in her experience with an investor who didn't actually invest, but nevertheless recommended a name change and provided other valuable advice. If Mary Page had just walked away from that individual because he didn't give her any money, she would not have benefited from the value that he was willing and able to provide.

The Diana Project

Mary Page's story flies in the face of stereotypes suggesting that women are not interested in launching growth-oriented firms. The Diana Project, which focuses specifically on growth-oriented women-owned firms, was launched in 1997 in response to many of the prevailing "myths" about women's entrepreneurship, including the assumption that women use different sources of financing because they do not need or want equity capital to grow their firms. In particular, Candida Brush and her Diana Project colleagues (Brush, Carter, and others, 2001; Gatewood and others, 2009) took issue with the contention that women do not want high-growth businesses. They backed up their position with a study of women entrepreneurs who participated in the Springboard forums. Springboard Enterprises (https://sb.co) is an organization that helps growth-oriented women entrepreneurs prepare for and connect with equity investors. This study and subsequent work associated with the Diana Project helped to document the experiences of women who are, in fact, eager to accept the challenges and risks associated with growth-oriented entrepreneurship.

Using data provided by Springboard on 1,700 women who applied to participate in one of the forums held in 2000, the Diana Project researchers found that 80 percent of applicants wanted to grow their ventures as rapidly as possible and were prepared to raise external equity to achieve that goal. Over half of these applicants estimated the size of their target markets to be more than $15 billion and international in scope. On average, the applicants were seeking $2.5 million in external funding to support their growth aspirations, an amount comparable to ventures launched by men. In contrast, the eighty-four firms that were actually selected to present at one of the Springboard forums that year were seeking an average of $10 million.

The Diana Project and the research that has grown out of it represent a turning point in our understanding of growth-oriented entrepreneurship. Prior to Diana, conventional wisdom indicated that large and growing firms are the domain of men rather than women. The Diana Project opened our eyes to the fact that women are also launching large and growing firms, often in industry sectors that were previously dominated by men. Consistent with these findings, the Diana Project further revealed that growth-oriented women entrepreneurs recognize and accept the need to raise significant amounts of external capital to achieve their goals. In this sense, our book builds upon the findings of the Diana Project and the work that has followed in an effort to share the potential and excitement of growth-oriented entrepreneurship as well as the financial strategies of women like Mary Page Platerink who have succeeded in growing their firms.

- ## Springboard Enterprises

Mary Page Platerink described herself as "pretty naive" during her firm's early stages, and this is certainly the case for many novice entrepreneurs, particularly women who are less likely to have prior entrepreneurial experience. How does a "newbie" get up to speed on raising financial capital in the close-knit and somewhat baffling world of angel investing and venture capital? Increasingly, growth-oriented women entrepreneurs are turning to organizations such as Springboard Enterprises to gain the knowledge, skills, and contacts they need to raise external equity. Founded in 1999, Springboard "sources, coaches, showcases and supports women-led growth companies seeking equity capital for product development and expansions" (https://sb.co).

As of July 2014, 556 women-led companies had participated in Springboard programs, and 84 percent of these have successfully raised financial capital. Equally impressive given the high failure rate of entrepreneurial ventures, 81 percent of the Springboard companies are still in business as independent or merged entities. Eleven firms have gone public, including firms such as Zipcar (ride-sharing), Viacord (cord blood stem cell banking), iRobot (robots), and Xenogen (biotechnology), while an additional 147 have made strategic exits through a merger or acquisition. Springboard firms have raised a total of $6.5 billion to fund their growth, and collectively these firms have created thousands of new jobs. Springboard firms encompass a broad range of industries, although biotechnology/health care and software/IT firms represent over 50 percent of the total. Firms are drawn from all geographic regions in the United States, and Springboard recently expanded its focus to serve women entrepreneurs in other countries as well.

Closing the Loop

In this chapter we have pointed out that growth-oriented entrepreneurship for women remains a study of contrasts. The studies we cite discuss the fact that in the United States and globally as well, women are less likely than men to pursue entrepreneurship as a career option. Further, when women do start firms, these tend to be much smaller in terms of revenues and number of employees. More recently, however, there have been signs that the tide is turning for growth-oriented women's entrepreneurship. In the United States, census data reveal that women are actually launching firms at a faster rate than men, reaching a total of 8.9 million firms in 2012. Similarly, the Global Entrepreneurship Monitor reveals that there were over two hundred million women-owned firms in the countries included in its survey, and twelve million of these women expressed a desire to grow their firms. In a study of high-growth U.S. firms, Tracy (2011) found that although women represented a slightly lower percentage of high-impact owners, they were actually creating high-impact firms at the same rate as men. Consistent with this trend, the Inc. 5000 data reveal that women founders now represent a respectable 15 percent of its designees. Finally, the Diana Project team (Brush, Carter, and others, 2001) makes a vigorous case for the presence of an emerging cohort of growth-oriented women entrepreneurs who are willing to embrace the challenges and risks that come with achieving significant size and scope. The Diana Project is unique in that it focuses specifically on women entrepreneurs who aspire to growth, and in doing so, it has served as an inspiration for this book, which will examine the financial strategies of women who meet those criteria. Thus, in a sense, the Diana Project has served as our initial "launch," and we are eager to explore the progress, changes, and innovations that have occurred as well as their effect on financial strategy since its initial publication. As we will show, many of these changes and innovations have benefited growth-oriented women entrepreneurs by leveling the playing field and providing greater access to the resources and tools they need to succeed. Our mini-case on Mary Page Platerink and her firm, First Aid Shot Therapy, illustrates this trend and provides us with a real-world example of an entrepreneur who is challenging the "myths" about what women entrepreneurs can achieve.

What Does This Mean for You?

This chapter provides several take-aways for women entrepreneurs who are growing or thinking about growing their firms:

1. First, you are not alone. In fact, you are a part of an emerging cohort of women entrepreneurs who aspire to growth. Although the studies we have cited in this chapter illustrate that women-owned firms are relatively small on average, they also attest to the fact that a subset of women is launching firms that attain significant size and scope. This is particularly true in the United States, where women are creating "high impact" firms at the same

rate as men, and where women-owned firms now represent almost 15 percent of the Inc. 5000 firms.

2. Second, in spite of these gains, women still face challenges in their attempts to secure growth capital in the form of angel investments and venture capital. This doesn't mean that it can't be done, but it does mean that women face additional hurdles necessitating different types of strategies.

3. Our featured entrepreneur, Mary Page Platerink, shared some of these strategies that worked for her. These include:

    A. Develop a business plan, create milestones to measure progress, and develop strategies for achieving them.

    B. Choose the "right investors" who share your vision and can add value to the firm in multiple ways, that is, by providing advice and support as well as financial capital.

    C. Practice your fundraising skills, because, like many other skills, they will get better over time.

    D. Recognize that investors may not operate on the same schedule that you do. In other words, raising financial capital takes a lot of time and effort, and it typically takes longer than you think it should.

    E. In light of that, be persistent. You will probably encounter a lot of "no's" in your entrepreneurial journey, but stick with it and keep coming back.

    F. Don't burn any bridges. Just because someone will not invest in your firm, it does not mean that he or she cannot add value in some other way.

4. If you anticipate that your firm will need external equity in the form of angel or venture capital, consider working with an organization like Springboard Enterprises. These organizations can provide valuable advice, training, and contacts with providers of financial capital. Participating in a program of this type can give you the "boost" you need to take your firm to the next level. Beyond that, by participating in the Springboard programs and events, you become part of a vibrant network of growth-oriented women entrepreneurs who can serve as an ongoing source of support and inspiration!

3

WHAT WE KNOW
ABOUT THE CHALLENGES
FOR GROWTH-ORIENTED WOMEN

The sharp discrepancy in firm size between women- and men-owned firms described in Chapter 2 provides us with an opportunity to identify and discuss some of the constraints, beliefs, attitudes, and systemic barriers that may be holding women back from growing their firms. To begin this discussion, we turn to one of the theories underpinning a fairly considerable amount of research in the field of entrepreneurship, the Resource-Based View.

A Resource-Based Perspective

The Research-Based View (RBV) asserts that the firm is a collection of tangible and intangible resources. The task of the entrepreneur is to assemble, develop, and transform the resources required to generate unique capabilities that will create a competitive advantage (Amit and Schoemaker, 1993; Wernerfelt, 1984). According to the RBV, those firms that can assemble and deploy their resources most effectively will achieve superior performance (Brush, Greene, and Hart, 2001; Sirmon and Hitt, 2003). What kind of "resources" are we talking about? Typically, resources are grouped into three major categories: human capital (education and experience), social capital (key networks and contacts), and financial capital (access to sources of debt, equity, or both). More recently, political capital, or the ability to influence legislation, regulations, and policies, has been added to the mix. How do women stack up relative to men in these four resource categories?

Dimensions of Human Capital: Education and Experience
Educational Gains

In the category of human capital, women entrepreneurs, on average, tend to be highly educated. The Kauffman Firm Survey data indicate that 48 percent of women entrepreneurs are college graduates. This is in keeping with recent trends in educational attainment, which reveal that, overall, women are making significant educational gains. Data provided by the National Center for Education Statistics show that in 2010–2011 women were awarded 57.2 percent of undergraduate college degrees, 60.1 percent of master's degrees, and 51.4 percent of doctorates (National Center for Education Statistics, 2013).

In spite of these educational gains, however, women and men tend to focus on different fields of study. In particular, men are more likely to have degrees in the STEM fields, or science, technology, engineering, and math. Data gathered by the National Science Foundation show that in 2010, 36.6 percent of all undergraduate degrees awarded to men were in the fields of science and engineering, compared to 27.7 percent for women (National Science Foundation, 2013). These fields are important because they are a source of entrepreneurial initiatives in key industries such as computer science, technology, and bioscience. Within the STEM disciplines as well, many of the sub-fields, including mathematics, computer science, and engineering, continue to be dominated by men, and studies reveal that women who venture into them often face environments that are unwelcoming and even hostile (Marlow and McAdam, 2013; Ranga and Etzkowitz, 2010). Nevertheless, Table 3.1 illustrates that women are making important inroads in STEM fields at all levels of educational attainment. As an example, the percentage of doctoral degrees going to women in all STEM fields increased from 13.5 percent in 1970 to 46.8 percent in 2010.

What has led to the change over time in the types of degree programs pursued by women? Many of these gains have come about thanks to educational initiatives focused on attracting girls and young women into the STEM fields at the local, state, and national levels. The National Science Foundation (http://www.nsf.gov), in particular, has been instrumental in encouraging and supporting programs designed to attract and engage female students in the fields of science and engineering. Other initiatives have targeted girls at an even earlier age in an attempt to combat gender stereotypes and raise little girls' awareness for the full range of their educational and career opportunities. As more women enter these fields, the power structure will change in ways that will enfranchise and empower the girls and women who follow.

TABLE 3.1. Percentage of Degrees Going to Women by Field, United States, 2010

| Academic Year Ending | All Fields | Science and Engineering Fields | | | | | Non-S&E Fields |
		Biological and Agricultural Sciences	Earth, Atmospheric, and Ocean Sciences	Mathematics and Computer Sciences	Physical Sciences	Engineering	
		Bachelor's Degrees					
1970	43.2	24.1	10.2	36.1	14.5	0.8	51.5
1980	49.2	39.1	23.8	36.4	24.0	10.1	54.9
1990	53.3	48.2	27.9	35.8	32.2	15.4	58.1
2000	57.3	55.8	40.0	32.7	41.1	20.5	60.5
2010	57.2	57.8	39.3	25.6	41.3	18.4	60.4
		Master's Degrees					
1970	39.8	25.8	11.1	25.5	15.1	1.1	47.2
1980	49.5	32.5	18.7	27.6	18.7	7.0	55.3
1990	52.6	45.8	23.7	31.1	27.6	13.6	58.4
2000	58.1	52.3	38.1	35.6	34.6	20.8	62.0
2010	60.3	56.2	47.0	30.6	37.5	22.3	64.0
		Doctoral Degrees					
1970	13.5	12.9	3.1	6.3	5.8	0.4	20.3
1980	30.3	24.3	9.9	12.1	12.8	3.6	41.1
1990	36.3	33.7	19.2	16.8	18.7	8.5	51.0
2000	43.8	42.7	28.2	21.0	24.5	15.7	56.7
2010	46.8	51.7	42.5	25.2	30.3	23.1	60.0

Source: National Science Foundation, 2011

• Debbie Sterling and GoldieBlox

Debbie Sterling didn't even know what engineering was until a high school math teacher encouraged her to consider it as a college major. She listened to that advice when she enrolled in Stanford University and graduated four years later with a degree in mechanical engineering and product design. During her college years, Debbie was struck by how few women were majoring in engineering. In a 2013 interview with Katie Couric, Debbie shared the following:

> I was one of only a handful of women in my engineering program at Stanford. It wasn't easy. I often felt like my ideas were ignored, like I didn't belong. It was a boys club, that program, and my perspective wasn't part of the equation. (Debra Sterling's Mission to Inspire the Next Generation of Female Engineers, 2013)

This prompted Debbie to come up with the idea of designing a toy that would introduce girls to engineering at an early age, and GoldieBlox was born!

GoldieBlox (http://www.goldieblox.com) is a construction toy that encourages young girls to combine their typically strong verbal skills with building. If you have wandered through a toy store lately, you have probably noticed the fairly strong gender segregation of girls' toys versus boys' toys. The "girl" aisles are overwhelmingly pink and filled with dolls, babies, carriages, toy stoves, dishes, makeup kits, and the like. In contrast, the "boy" aisles are filled with action toys (cars, trucks, airplanes), building toys (legos, erector sets, transformers, Bob the Builder), and, what we affectionately refer to as toys that kill other toys (GI Joe, the Hulk, Star Wars). Debbie's goal was to "disrupt the pink aisle."

GoldieBlox, the toy, is a child inventor and engineer (Lindenmayer, 2012). She and her canine sidekick, Nacho, go on adventures that require them to save the day by inventing new things. The GoldieBlox toy set involves hands-on inventing activities as well as a tool set. Many in the toy industry warned Debbie that a building toy for girls would just not sell.

Initially Debbie funded the launch of GoldieBlox with her own savings. In 2012, however, she launched a Kickstarter campaign with the goal of raising $150,000 to produce a minimum order quantity of five thousand units. By October of that year, the campaign had attracted over five thousand investors and raised $285,000 (http://www.kickstarter.com).

> When I launched GoldieBlox on Kickstarter, I had 30 days to raise $150,000, in the hopes of getting GoldieBlox into production. 30 days to prove those toy industry veterans wrong. 30 days to prove that I wasn't the only one who wanted more for our girls.
> I hit my goal in 5 days. (Debra Sterling's Mission to Inspire the Next Generation of Female Engineers, 2013)

Currently, the GoldieBlox flagship toy, "GoldieBlox and the Spinning Machine" is available in every Toys"R"Us store in the United States. Going forward, Debbie's goal is to create an entire series of GoldieBlox building stories in which Goldie learns about and employs a wide variety of engineering concepts, including gears, pulleys, circuits, and coding.

The Role of Prior Experience

Along with education, previous experience is the other major type of human capital, and serves as a major building block for entrepreneurial firms. Experience can come in the form of prior work experience in general, experience working in a particular industry, managerial experience, or previous experience

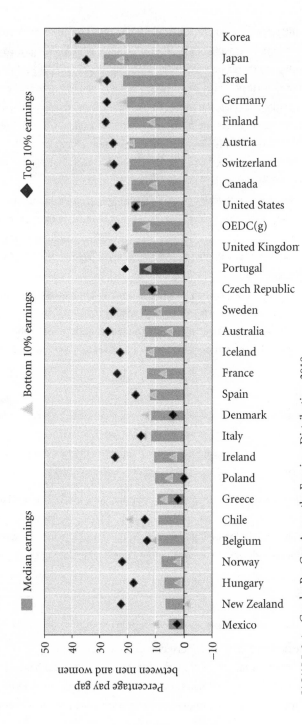

FIGURE 3.1. Gender Pay Gap Across the Earnings Distribution, 2010

Source: OECD, 2012

in launching an entrepreneurial firm. As in the case of education, women have made impressive gains in the workplace, and the number of women working outside the home has increased dramatically since the Second World War. The Bureau of Labor Statistics reported that 53.2 percent of women aged sixteen and older were employed in 2011, compared to 40.8 percent in 1970 (*Women in the Labor Force*, 2013). The percentage of women employed during the prime working years of twenty-five to fifty-four was even higher, 74.7 percent.

Women have also made workplace gains by advancing into managerial roles and are well represented in the middle management ranks of most major corporations. In spite of these gains, however, women are still underrepresented at the most senior management levels. Similarly, women continue to be underrepresented on boards of directors. Thus, although women have acquired a tremendous amount of workplace, industry, and middle management experience, they have gained less experience in making the types of decisions that involve senior-level strategic planning and priority setting. To illustrate this point, Catalyst (http://www.catalyst.org), an organization devoted to expanding opportunities for women in business, reported that in 2012 women held 14.3 percent of chief executive officer positions and 16.6 percent of board of director seats for the Fortune 500 companies.

As with senior-level managerial experience, prior entrepreneurial experience helps to prepare women for leading new ventures. Since women are less likely to be entrepreneurs than men, they are also less likely to have the types of leadership and decision-making skills that come with launching and growing a new firm. This experiential gap has important implications for financial strategy, because providers of growth capital tend to gravitate toward founders who have successfully launched previous firms.

Women's experiences in the workplace affect their entrepreneurial readiness in other ways as well. Women are significantly more likely to work part time and to have career interruptions associated with the birth of children and care of family members (OECD, 2012). These employment patterns make it more difficult and often less attractive for women to pursue senior-level positions, which may require long hours, work-related travel, and limited flexibility. In turn, women who are passed over for senior-level positions, as well as those who exclude themselves from consideration for reasons associated with family, have lower levels of earnings and wealth. Figure 3.1 provides a snapshot of the pay gap between women and men in a number of countries including the United States. It reveals that, for those women who do succeed in advancing to more senior levels, the pay gap actually widens. This discrepancy between women and men is also important from the standpoint of financial strategy, because the personal financial resources of the entrepreneur are a major source of financing for new ventures during the earliest stages of their development. Thus, if women have fewer opportunities to accumulate wealth, they will be less likely to start their own firms, and, if they do, they will start them with smaller amounts of financial capital.

Social Capital: It's Who You Know

Like human capital, social capital is a key resource for growth-oriented entrepreneurs. Social capital refers to the people you know and the groups or organizations that you are a part of. The importance of social capital lies in the fact that it serves as a means for helping entrepreneurs generate the resources they need to launch and grow their firms. This is particularly true for growth-oriented entrepreneurs who require substantial resources in the form of people, facilities, and funding. In this sense, social capital is an essential building block for success for growth-oriented entrepreneurs. Recent research suggests that, although women entrepreneurs have made impressive human capital gains in the areas of education and workplace advancement, they still lag men in terms of developing the types of social capital needed to launch and grow firms that will achieve significant size. Stated simply, women entrepreneurs are less likely to know the "right people" or be a part of networks that would give them access to those individuals. This distinction has implications for their ability to raise financial capital, particularly external equity capital.

The Diana Project, which focuses on women's potential for growth-oriented entrepreneurship, was introduced in Chapter 2. Within the context of social capital, researchers associated with the project found that women entrepreneurs are largely excluded from venture capital networks, which tend to be closely knit and male-dominated (Brush, Carter, and others, 2001; Gatewood and others, 2009). This is a significant disadvantage, because although VC firms invest in a relatively small percentage of ventures, they are an important source of funding for high-growth firms. The Diana Project team also found that VC firms employ fewer women in decision-making roles that could lead to greater investment in women-owned firms (Brush and others, 2004).

Since the original Diana Project study in 2001, several researchers have addressed the issue of "homophily" in the funding patterns of both entrepreneurs and providers of funding. In a study of angel investors, John Becker-Blease and co-author Jeff Sohl (2007) found that entrepreneurs were more likely to seek financing from angel investors of the same sex. Similarly, a study authored by Richard Harrison and Colin Mason (2007) found that women angel investors were at least marginally more likely to invest in women entrepreneurs. These findings highlight the challenges faced by women entrepreneurs given that there are currently so fewer women angel investors. The gender discrepancy in the availability of angel capital helps to explain why women are more heavily reliant on internal rather than external sources of capital (Coleman and Robb, 2009). Further, women start their firms with smaller amounts of capital than men across industries and firm types. These patterns illustrate why organizations like Springboard that provide networks of women entrepreneurs and investors are so important. They help to expand the entrepreneurial ecosystem in ways that will benefit women, particularly those women who aspire to growth.

Dialing for Dollars: Raising Financial Capital

As we learned in Chapter 2, the vast majority of women-owned firms are very small. In fact, 84 percent of women-owned firms have no employees aside from the entrepreneur herself, and 88 percent have revenues of $100,000 per year or less (*2012 Survey of Business Owners*). Women are also more likely to operate home-based businesses, in part because working from the home provides the opportunity to balance work and family. By their nature, the majority of these home-based firms tend to be small and have limited requirements for financing, staff, or equipment. In light of this, women entrepreneurs, particularly those who launch small or home-based firms, rely heavily on internal rather than external sources of financing. Internal sources include the entrepreneur's personal savings, credit cards, home equity lines, and bank loans secured by personal assets. Correspondingly, entrepreneurs who launch these "lifestyle" types of firms are not typically candidates for external sources of capital in the form of business loans, angel investments, or venture capital.

In contrast, the financing profile and requirements for growth-oriented firms is very different. This profile is illustrated by the "financial growth cycle" first described by Berger and Udell in 1998. The premise behind the financial growth cycle is that growth-oriented firms go through different stages. Initially, in the Development Stage, the entrepreneur formulates her idea and begins to gather the resources she needs to launch. The next stage, or Startup Stage, involves the entrepreneur's launch of her firm and the initial sale of her products or services. The Survival Stage is a critical point, because at this stage the firm is generating revenues, but the revenues are not sufficient to cover expenses. Thus, the risk of failure is particularly great if the entrepreneur is not able to secure additional sources of financing to carry her through. The Rapid-Growth Stage is the stage we typically associate with growth-oriented firms. As the name implies, this is a period of rapid and often "explosive" growth during which time sales and revenues increase dramatically. Not surprisingly, this burst of success and growth attracts other competitors. As they enter the market, growth rates slow, and the firm enters its Maturity Stage.

According to Berger and Udell, the entrepreneur faces different financial challenges at each of these stages. Similarly, different financial strategies and sources are available and appropriate at each stage. As an example, entrepreneurs are heavily reliant on personal sources of financing and bootstrapping during the Development and Startup stages. Conversely, firms that go through periods of rapid or explosive growth require significant amounts of funding from external sources.

One criticism of the financial growth cycle is that not all firms go through all stages of the cycle, which is certainly true. The vast majority of firms start small and remain small. These are often referred to as "lifestyle" firms, which do not experience rapid growth. In spite of this criticism, however, the financial growth cycle does a fairly good job of describing the experience of the types of growth-oriented firms that are the focus of this book.

Prior research suggests that women entrepreneurs are both determined and creative when it comes to generating internal sources of capital and bootstrapping (Coleman and Robb, 2012). Their real challenge lies in attempting to raise substantial amounts of external financial capital, particularly in the form of external equity. Work done by the authors has shown that women are significantly less likely than men to use external equity as a source of financing (Coleman and Robb, 2009). Thus, if women entrepreneurs are either unwilling or unable to secure equity capital, it will be much more difficult for them to grow their firms. Research has also shown that women raise smaller amounts of financial capital for their firms than men, regardless of the source (Amatucci and Sohl, 2004; Coleman and Robb, 2009). Failure to raise sufficient amounts of capital can result in lost opportunities, lower growth rates, and even failure of the firm.

Political Capital: The New Kid on the Block

Traditionally, discussions about the types of resources that contribute to firm success and growth have centered on the three areas of human, social, and financial capital. More recently, however, researchers have also started to focus on political capital as a dimension that is particularly relevant for women. In the United States, women are less likely to be elected officials or members of Congress. Although women are well represented in the House of Representatives, their numbers there do not reflect their numbers in the electorate. The gap in representation between women and men is even more significant in the Senate. Similarly, although women have held senior administrative positions such as secretary of state (Hillary Clinton and Condaleeza Rice) they have never held the position of president or vice-president. The gap in political representation is even more pronounced in less developed or less democratic economies where women often don't have the right to be educated, to own property, or to vote.

Political capital is relevant for growth-oriented women entrepreneurs because, like the other types of capital we have discussed, it can provide them with access to key inputs, individuals, and markets. It also provides them with an opportunity to shape the legislation, regulations, and public policies that will affect them. As an example, the U.S. government itself is a major "customer" for many firms, both large and small. A contract to provide goods and services to a major U.S. agency such as the Department of Defense is not only a significant source of revenues but also a boost for the stature of the firm. For many years these contracts were granted almost exclusively to firms owned by men. More recently, however, regulations affecting government procurement practices have required federal agencies to ensure that women- and minority-owned firms also have access to contracting opportunities. The challenge for growth-oriented women entrepreneurs is learning how to take advantage of these opportunities for doing business with governments at the local, state, and national levels.

Increasingly, growth-oriented women entrepreneurs are turning to women-focused networks as a means for gaining access to human, social, financial, and political capital. These networks allow women to find the "strength in numbers" needed to overcome barriers posed by stereotypes about women and male-dominated power structures in education, finance, and government. We have provided a number of examples of these networks in the Appendix under the heading "Entrepreneurship Groups." In addition, there are an increasing number of organizations such as Springboard Enterprises, Astia, Golden Seeds, and 37 Angels that focus specifically on providing the types of training, mentoring, and networks that will help growth-oriented women-owned firms raise financial capital.

Attitudinal Perspectives
on the Challenges to Growth
Motivational Factors: Reluctance to Grow

Prior research suggests that fewer women than men are motivated to grow their firms (Cliff, 1998; Morris, Miyasaki, Watters, and Coombes, 2006). These studies show that women are more concerned about factors such as greater time commitment, difficulty balancing work and family, and higher levels of stress that can come with launching and operating a larger firm. Figure 3.2, based on data collected by the OECD, illustrates that women engage in lower levels of paid

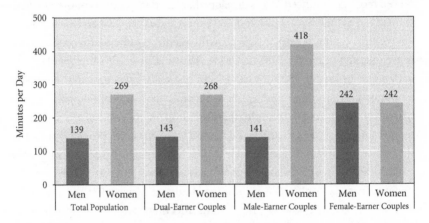

FIGURE 3.2. Minutes Devoted to Unpaid Work, by Gender
Source: OECD, 2012

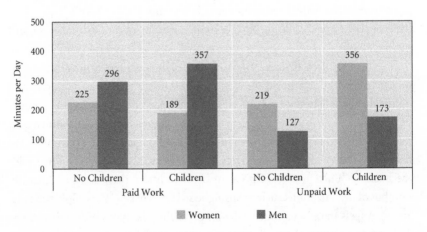

FIGURE 3.3. Gender Gaps in Unpaid and Paid Work, with and Without Children
Source: OECD, 2012

(employment) versus unpaid (home and family) work. This is true for dual-career households in general, as well as for dual-career couples with children.

Figure 3.3 illustrates that the gap between paid and unpaid work for women and men widens after the birth of children. Although men have assumed a more active role in domestic and childcare activities in recent years, women still shoulder the bulk of these responsibilities. In a recent article, Brush, de Bruin, and Welter (2009) addressed the "unequal division of labor and access to household resources that differentially impacts access to the standard 3Ms of markets, money, and management." In the same article these authors asserted that the effect of motherhood "impinge(s) on women's ownership of assets, their access to resources, and the realization of their capabilities" (p. 11).

Greater amounts of time spent on care of the home and children affects women in three important ways. First, their desire for flexibility in scheduling may reduce women's motivation to take on the challenges associated with growth. Second, time spent on home-related or "unpaid" work reduces the number of hours that can be devoted to an entrepreneurial venture. Finally, household roles can affect women indirectly through lower levels of earnings and accumulated wealth if women opt for part-time rather than full-time employment or select jobs that allow them to fulfill household responsibilities (Maani and Cruickshank, 2010). Since the personal financial resources of the entrepreneur are a major source of financing for early stage ventures, this housework-induced wage differential between women and men poses a threat to the intent and ability of women to launch and grow their firms.

- ## Goldman Sachs 10,000 Small Businesses

As noted earlier, the entrepreneur's motivation to grow her firm is an important determinant of firm growth. For those entrepreneurs who do want to grow, several important programs have been designed to help them achieve that goal. One such program is the Goldman Sachs 10,000 Small Businesses program (http://www.gold mansachs.com), launched in 2009 with the goal of helping small business owners grow their firms. A recent report developed by Babson College indicates that roughly 1,300 small business owners have graduated from the program, which is offered at eighteen different locations throughout the United States (*Stimulating Small Business Growth*, 2014). Participants are provided with practical business education, a range of support services, and access to financial capital.

The program's curriculum involves approximately one hundred hours of instruction provided over a three- to four-month period in the form of day-long modules and evening clinics. These modules focus on topics with titles such as Growth Opportunities, Money & Metrics, Being Bankable, and Action for Growth. As a part of the program, participants work with a program advisor to identify growth opportunities for their own businesses and to develop a growth plan. They are also organized into "growth groups" that facilitate peer-to-peer learning and support.

To date, almost half (47.8 percent) of the 10,000 Small Businesses participants have been women. Participant firms are drawn from all types of industries. To qualify, applicants must have been in operation for at least two years. Further, the firm must employ at least four individuals and have revenues of at least $150,000. The selection process also considers the firm's potential to grow as well as the entrepreneur's motivation to do so.

From a financing standpoint, many of the participant firms have been turned down for traditional bank loans. A key element of the program involves increasing participants' awareness for different sources of capital that may be available to them as well as technical assistance on how to become bankable. Thanks to these efforts, program graduates have increased their average funding level from $287,189 before the program to $1.03 million six months after graduation (*Stimulating Small Business Growth*, 2014).

Program results also reveal that 63.7 percent of graduates increased their revenues within six months of graduation, compared to 37 percent of U.S. small businesses overall. Similarly, 44.8 percent of the program graduates added new jobs, compared to 18 percent of all small businesses (*Stimulating Small Business Growth*, 2014).

Attitudes Toward Risk

One explanation that has been put forth for gender discrepancies in firm size and growth has been differences in attitudes toward risk. Prior research suggests that women are more risk averse, which may have an effect on their willingness to grow their firms. A number of these articles focus on the investment decisions and choices of women investors. These studies have revealed, fairly consistently, that women are more conservative in their investment strategies than men and select less risky investment alternatives (Bajtelsmit and VanDerhei, 1997; Hinz, McCarthy, and Turner, 1997; Jianakopolos and Bernasek, 1998; Bajtelsmit, Bernasek, and Jianakoplos, 1999; Sunden and Surette, 1998). Similarly, using data from the 1998 Survey of Consumer Finances, one of your authors (Coleman, 2003) found that women reported a higher level of risk aversion than men, with almost 50 percent of women stating that they were not willing to take any financial risks.

Other studies on gender differences in risk aversion, however, have highlighted the role of context, noting that women may be more risk averse than men in some situations but not necessarily in others. As an example, Schooley and Worden (1996) found that gender was not a significant factor in attitudes toward risk if life cycle stage and employment were held constant. In another study focusing on investment behavior, Sunden and Surette (1998) found that, in addition to gender, marital status affected the ways in which individuals allocated assets in defined contribution plans. Consistent with this theme, Constantinidis, Cornet, and Asandei (2006) studied women entrepreneurs in Belgium to find that their perspectives on growth varied depending upon their level of family responsibilities. Those women entrepreneurs who had families and children had higher levels of risk aversion and were reluctant to invest larger amounts of capital in their firms.

Other studies on attitudes toward risk have focused more specifically on women's decision making within corporate and entrepreneurial contexts. In a study of Spanish graduate students, Canizares and Garcia (2010) found that, when surveyed on their intention to launch an entrepreneurial firm, women exhibited a greater fear of failure than men. Alternatively, male students were more likely to express a desire for new challenges as well as a willingness to take at least moderate risks. Cliff (1998) studied a sample of Canadian firms to find that women were more concerned than men with the risks associated with rapid growth. A second study of Canadian firms conducted by Orser and Hogarth-Scott (2002) echoed these results. Their findings revealed that women entrepreneurs viewed the personal demands associated with growth, such as less time with family and higher levels of stress, more negatively than men. Studies of Australian entrepreneurs have also revealed evidence of higher levels of risk aversion on the part of women entrepreneurs coupled with a desire for more moderate levels of growth (Watson and Newby, 2005; Watson, 2006). Similarly, Kepler and Shane (2007) conducted a study of U.S. firms to find that women entrepreneurs showed a greater preference for launching low risk or low return companies that provide an alternative to paid employment rather than an opportunity for growth.

Self-Efficacy: I Think I Can, I Think I Can . . .

Related to the issue of risk aversion, a number of studies have found that women have lower levels of self-efficacy than men. Within an entrepreneurial context, entrepreneurial self-efficacy (ESE) has been defined as the individual's belief that she has the necessary skills and abilities to launch a firm (Chen,

Greene, and Crick, 1998; Drnovsek, Wincent, and Cardon, 2010). If women entrepreneurs have less confidence in their abilities, they may be less willing to take the types of risks that accompany launching or growing a firm. In a study of teens and MBA students, Wilson, Kickul, and Marlino (2007) found that differences in ESE emerge at an early age. Results from both samples revealed that both girls and women had lower levels of ESE and were less likely to consider entrepreneurship as a career path. Another study involving MBA students (Zhao, Seibert, and Hills, 2005), did not find gender differences in ESE, but did find gender differences in entrepreneurial intentions. These researchers found that women students perceived the task of launching a firm to be more difficult and less rewarding than did men. Using Global Entrepreneurship Monitor (GEM) data from seventeen countries, Koellinger, Minniti, and Schade (2008) found that women were significantly less likely to believe that they had the skills necessary to launch a firm. Further, women had a significantly higher fear of failure. In a study of U.S. entrepreneurs, Kirkwood (2009) found that women had less confidence in their entrepreneurial abilities than men, and were even reluctant to call themselves entrepreneurs.

In terms of the types of competencies required to succeed as an entrepreneur, several studies suggest that women lack confidence in their financial skills and abilities in particular (Hisrich and Brush, 1984; Brush, 1992). One such study focused specifically on the topic of "financial self-efficacy" to find that only 60 percent of the women entrepreneurs interviewed were confident or very confident in the area of financial management (Amatucci and Crawley, 2011). In a similar vein, previous studies on borrowing behavior have shown that women are more likely to be "discouraged" borrowers in the sense that they do not apply for loans because they assume they will be turned down (Coleman, 2000; Freel, Carter, Tagg, and Mason, 2012; Orser, Riding, and Manley, 2006).

The cover story of a recent issue of *The Atlantic* was titled, "The Confidence Gap." Katty Kay, an anchor with the BBC World News, and Claire Shipman, a reporter with ABC News, argued that the persistent disparity between male and female self-assurance keeps women from achieving at the highest levels, including in entrepreneurship (Kay and Shipman, 2014a). They contend that the natural result of low confidence is inaction. Thus, when we don't act, or when we hesitate because we are unsure, we hold ourselves back. Kay and Shipman suggest that, in order to become more confident, we need to stop thinking so much and just act. In fact, they feel so strongly about this message that they wrote an entire book on the topic titled *The Confidence Code: The Science and*

Art of Self-Assurance—What Women Should Know (Kay and Shipman, 2014b). It is a fascinating read, and urges us to move outside of our comfort zones and avoid the trap of "analysis paralysis" that can lure us into prolonged deliberation rather than action. This advice is consistent with what we have observed from our interviews with women entrepreneurs for this book. Although they think things through carefully, they have a definite bias toward action.

What's Different About Growth-Oriented Women Entrepreneurs?

Taken together, the studies we have cited thus far suggest that women entrepreneurs, in general, are more reluctant to take risks, have a greater fear of failure, and have less confidence in their abilities to successfully launch and grow an entrepreneurial venture. In turn, we might anticipate that these factors would affect the types of firms that women start as well as their goals and expectations for these firms. As a counterpoint to these studies, however, Brush, Carter, and others (2001) launched the Diana Project, which attacked many of the "myths" associated with women's entrepreneurship. In particular, these researchers took issue with the contention that women do not want high-growth businesses. They backed up their position with a study of women entrepreneurs who participated in the Springboard forums. As we noted in Chapter 2, Springboard Enterprises (https://sb.co) is an organization that helps growth-oriented women entrepreneurs prepare for and connect with equity investors. This study and subsequent work associated with the Diana Project helped to document the experiences of women who are in fact eager to accept the challenges and risks associated with growth-oriented entrepreneurship.

Similarly, entrepreneur interviews that we conducted in the process of writing our first book, *A Rising Tide* (Coleman and Robb, 2012), revealed that there was a cohort of women who were prepared to embrace the opportunities and challenges of growth. In terms of human capital, these women were highly educated and had accumulated a significant amount of experience in their respective fields. In many instances, these human capital attributes paved the way for social capital in the form of key contacts and access to networks. In other instances, we found women entrepreneurs who systematically developed their social capital in order to gain access to needed resources.

Another take-away from *A Rising Tide* was the incredible level of creativity and determination shown by women entrepreneurs who launched growth-oriented firms. None of the entrepreneurs we interviewed started out with all of the financial capital they needed to launch and grow. In this sense, our growth-oriented entrepreneurs were very different from the lifestyle entrepreneurs that we interviewed. Nevertheless, women who aspired to growth managed to put together an extraordinary array of financing strategies to get through the critical early stages of their firm's life cycle and fund its subsequent growth.

From a motivational and attitudinal perspective, "really scrappy"[1] is a good description for the growth-oriented entrepreneurs we interviewed for *A Rising Tide.* Among other factors, they were motivated by the financial and economic rewards that come with launching and operating a growth-oriented firm. In other instances, they were motivated by the desire to seize an opportunity in the marketplace and run with it. Some of our entrepreneurs saw growth-oriented entrepreneurship as a way to achieve a leadership role not only in their firms but in their industry and in the business community overall. This, in turn, would put them in a position to influence regulations, legislation, and public policy. These women were not afraid or reluctant to dance on a very large stage.

Alexandra Wilkis Wilson and the Gilt Groupe

Alexandra Wilkis Wilson describes her experience in founding the Gilt Groupe (http://www.Gilt.com) as a "roller coaster ride . . . You experience the highest highs and the lowest lows when you launch a rapid-growth firm like Gilt." Alexandra met co-founder Alexis Maybank as an undergraduate at Harvard University. The two became fast friends and continued to remain close as they moved through Harvard's prestigious MBA program. Both were dedicated shoppers, and after graduation sought careers in the rapidly changing retail industry. Alexandra gained international experience in the field of luxury goods with Bulgari and Louis Vuitton, while Alexis plunged into the world of e-commerce at AOL and eBay. The two launched Gilt in November of 2007 with the goal of marrying their love of retailing with their combined expertise in fashion and e-commerce. In launching the firm, they joined forces with another pair of friends, Mike Bryzek and Phong Nguyen, who had expertise in the areas of engineering and computer science and brought in serial entrepreneur Kevin Ryan, who became the fifth member of the team. Kevin became Gilt's first CEO and provided the bulk of Gilt's seed funding. In discussing their strategy for launching Gilt, Alexandra observed,

> We needed a team to establish this particular business, because we needed
> skills in two very different areas, fashion and technology. We also needed

someone like Kevin who had experience in launching a growth-oriented firm
and raising significant amounts of external capital. (Ellsworth Lecture, 2013)

Gilt's innovation was the introduction of Internet "flash sales" for luxury
clothing and goods. Flash sales are sales of specific items that are made available
daily for a limited period of time. In the same way that Marshall's and Loeh-
man's bring designer goods into retail outlets, Gilt sought to bring high-end
designer sample sizes to the Internet at discount prices. As Alexandra describes
it, the objective is to have visitors to the Gilt website "rush through the virtual
doors" in order to secure the sale items (Ellsworth Lecture, 2013). In this sense,
Gilt has two types of customers: Gilt shoppers, who purchase goods, and luxury
retailers such as Marc Jacobs, Valentino, and Jimmy Choo, who sell them.

Gilt membership is by invitation only, so shoppers have the sense that they
belong to an exclusive group. Initially Gilt targeted young women in their
twenties and thirties who want access to designer styles at affordable prices.
The "flash sale" nature of the shopping experience creates a sense of urgency.
Each day at noon, Gilt sends an email to its members alerting them to the day's
sales. Shoppers then have thirty-six hours to make their purchases. A shopper
can put up to five items into her "cart," but the hold time for those items is limited to ten minutes, so she has to decide quickly. Customer satisfaction is one of
Gilt's keys to success. The items buyers purchase are new, with their tags still on
them. Alexandra notes that although the industry average return rate for goods
is 35 percent, Gilt's return rate is much lower.

Gilt's other type of customer, luxury retailers, benefit from their association
with Gilt because it provides them with a way to turn excess inventories into
cash. Service to retailers is also a priority, because Gilt needs them to provide
goods for sale (Ellsworth Lecture, 2013). Within the world of fashion retailing,
Gilt has been a major agent for change in that it has forced luxury brands to
embrace the Internet and e-commerce (Laneri, 2010).

Alexandra and her co-founders aspired to growth from the very outset of
their firm; they wanted to launch a firm that had the potential to "go viral."
In discussing her motivations for growing the firm, Alexandra noted that the
retail industry is very crowded and highly competitive. In light of that, the
founders saw the benefit of scaling the firm rapidly, because they believed that
being the biggest player would provide them with a competitive advantage.
Alexandra highlighted the role and importance of social capital in achieving
scale. During the earliest days of the firm, Gilt's initial customers were gleaned
from the personal networks of the founding team, each of whom contacted

friends, relatives, classmates, business associates, and the like to generate a preliminary cohort of thirteen thousand customers (Ellsworth Lecture, 2013). That initial customer base enabled Gilt to test and modify its revenue model while also demonstrating the potential of the flash sale approach.

Social capital also played an important role in securing the financial resources required to achieve scale and scope. As noted above, CEO Kevin Ryan was a successful entrepreneur with contacts and credibility in the venture capital industry. These contacts combined with his experience in launching and financing a growth-oriented firm enabled Gilt to secure a Series A round of funding for $5 million from Matrix Partners. Gilt subsequently went on to raise additional VC and private equity rounds. Alexandra notes that individuals from these various funding sources also became "great board members" capable of providing strategic direction for the young firm as well as financing.

Today, Gilt generates in excess of $600 million in sales annually to eight million customers located in 180 different countries (Ellsworth Lecture, 2013). Gilt has expanded beyond its initial focus on high-end women's clothing to add other high-end lines, including men's clothing, clothing for babies and children, home goods, and both city and international experiences. Over four thousand brands provide goods for sale on the Gilt website. Headquartered in New York City, Gilt has grown to 1,100 employees in ten locations.

Alexandra encourages other women entrepreneurs to take the risks associated with growing their firms and to be prepared for both the successes and failures that are an inevitable part of the growth process (Ellsworth Lecture, 2013). She also stresses the need for flexibility, noting that she and her co-founders have had to continually refine and build upon their business model. Finally, she emphasizes the importance of the team approach used to launch Gilt. The five members of the founding team had complementary skills and experience, but they were joined by a common sense of purpose and a high level of trust in each other.

Closing the Loop

In this chapter we have employed the Resource-Based View as a framework for examining some of the challenges and systemic barriers faced by women entrepreneurs who aspire to growth. The entrepreneur's task is to assemble, acquire, and deploy these resources to create a competitive advantage. Human capital, which refers to prior education and experience, is a category in which women entrepreneurs have faced challenges. From an educational standpoint, women have been less likely to pursue studies in the areas of science, technology, engineering, and math (STEM). That tide is gradually turning, however, thus providing women with the educational backgrounds and environments required to pursue high-tech, growth-oriented entrepreneurship. Going forward, we need to continue to develop, promote, and fund programs that will encourage girls and women to engage with the STEM disciplines at both the K–12 and college levels.

Also in the category of human capital, women have lagged men in terms of prior work experiences that would prepare them for launching and leading an entrepreneurial firm. Although women have made tremendous gains in the workplace, they are still much more likely to be clustered in the middle and lower ranks of corporations rather than in the most senior leadership positions. Similarly, women are much less likely to have prior entrepreneurial experience than men. These experiential gaps also create financial gaps between women and men, since women have lower earnings and fewer opportunities to accumulate significant amounts of wealth. The earnings discrepancies are often exacerbated by career interruptions associated with the birth and care of children. In light of these experiential and associated financial gaps, we need to ensure that women have equal access to employment and leadership opportunities at all levels, including the most senior levels.

Social capital and political capital both refer to the types of networks that entrepreneurs are a part of. These networks can serve as gateways to needed resources, contacts, and expertise. In the case of political capital, they can provide women entrepreneurs with opportunities to shape and influence the direction of their industries as well as legislation and regulations affecting them. Networks can also be instrumental in providing access to the types of financial capital required to fund high growth. Prior research reveals that women entrepreneurs tend to have different networks from men, and that they are less likely to be an integral part of those networks providing growth capital in particular. Organizations such as Springboard Enterprises have aggressively addressed this challenge by working with growth-oriented women entrepreneurs to prepare them and connect them with providers of equity capital, including angel networks and venture capital firms. Simultaneously, we need to increase the number of women in decision-making and investing roles in these types of organizations, which remain heavily male-dominated.

Our mini-case on the Gilt Groupe highlights the importance of both human and social capital. Alexandra Wilkis Wilson was highly educated and actually met her co-founder while pursuing undergraduate and graduate degrees at Harvard University. Prior to launching Gilt, Alexandra also accumulated valuable experience by working for two major luxury goods retailers, Bulgari and Louis Vuitton. Social capital in the form of key contacts and networks led to the addition of two co-founders who had expertise in the area of technology as well as their own networks, which yielded a fifth co-founder with prior entrepreneurial experience and contacts in the venture capital industry. Having this person on board was a key factor in opening the door to VC funding when Gilt was going through its rapid-growth stage.

Financial capital is also an essential resource for growth-oriented entrepreneurs. As we have noted in this chapter, women often approach entrepreneurship with lower earnings and accumulated wealth than men, thereby putting their new firms at risk. As we will show in subsequent chapters, women entrepreneurs are less reliant on external sources of capital and raise smaller amounts of it than their male counterparts. Both of these factors can hamper the ability of a new firm to secure needed resources, develop innovative products and services, and grow. This is particularly true for high-growth firms that typically require significant amounts of external capital in the form of angel or venture capital. Thus, the financial challenges and strategies of growth-oriented women entrepreneurs serve as the focal point for this book.

As we have also shown in this chapter, attitudinal factors such as growth expectations, attitudes toward risk, confidence, and self-efficacy can all affect the propensity of women to pursue rapid growth. These attitudinal factors and the stereotypes associated with them have contributed to the myth that women are not motivated or equipped to engage in growth-oriented entrepreneurship. However, there is a growing cohort of "myth-busting" women who are embracing the challenges of growth-oriented entrepreneurship with gusto. Debbie Sterling, the founder of GoldieBlox, majored in engineering in college and went on to design a toy that serves as a role model for young girls. Goldie is an engineer, an inventor, and a hero in challenging situations; last but not least, she's cool with her own pet companion and convertible. Similarly, Alexandra Wilkis Wilson, co-founder of the Gilt Groupe, eagerly climbed aboard the "roller coaster ride" of high-growth entrepreneurship, using her networking skills to build a founding team, connect with customers, and raise growth capital. In these two entrepreneurs, as in others we will feature further on, we see the motivation, drive, vision, and just plain gutsiness that have made them and their firms so successful.

What Does This Mean for You?

This chapter highlights the importance of developing both the resources and the attitudes required for growth-oriented entrepreneurship.

1. Take a personal inventory of your resources in the areas of human, social, financial, and political capital. Which of these represent areas of strength, and which will require additional work? For each type of capital, develop an action plan that will take you from where you are to where you would like to be.

2. Evaluate your current contacts and networks. Which of these can serve as "gateways" to resources in the form of human, social, financial, or political capital? Invest the time required to develop and maintain these relationships.

3. Identify additional individuals, groups, or organizations that can help you secure the resources to launch and grow your firm. Develop a plan for gaining access to these groups and building a relationship.

4. Do an honest assessment of your motivations and attitudes toward growth-oriented entrepreneurship. Are you eager to accept both the challenges and the opportunities that come with rapid growth? If not, are there ways to address the factors that are holding you back?

5. Make a list of your accomplishments, both personal and professional. What does this list tell you about your determination, drive, and capabilities?

6. Find a way to spend some time with a successful growth-oriented woman entrepreneur, perhaps over coffee or lunch, and talk about her experience during the early stages of her firm. How did she secure the resources she needed to launch and grow? What challenges did she encounter, and how did she overcome them? What were her motivations and attitudes toward growth? How did she "feel" about the process of entrepreneurship? Was she confident in her abilities from the start, or did she build confidence over time?

4

A STAR IS BORN!

Financing Strategies
for Nascent Entrepreneurs

At one time or another, all firms are nascent firms. The term *nascent* simply means a firm that is just getting started. Thus, when we refer to nascent firms, we typically are referring to firms in their first year of existence. From an economic perspective, nascent firms are important because they are recognized as a potential source of innovation, jobs, and growth. In light of these contributions, researchers and policy makers have sought to identify the factors that encourage entrepreneurship in general, and growth-oriented entrepreneurship in particular (Davidsson and Henrekson, 2002).

Consistent with that, it stands to reason that entrepreneurs launching growth-oriented firms would employ financial strategies different from those used by entrepreneurs launching lifestyle firms. We have already seen evidence of this in our case studies on Mary Page Platerink (First Aid Shot Therapy) and Alexandra Wilkis Wilson (The Gilt Groupe), both of whom anticipated the need to raise significant amounts of financial capital from external investors. These entrepreneurs knew from the earliest stages that they wanted to grow their firms, and they adopted strategies that would allow them to achieve that goal. In this chapter, we will focus on these nascent entrepreneurs and the early stage financial strategies that help them launch their firms and start them on a path toward growth.

Who Are the Nascent Entrepreneurs?

The Panel Study of Entrepreneurial Dynamics (PSED) was undertaken specifically to learn more about the characteristics of nascent firms in the United

States (Reynolds, Carter, Gartner, and Greene, 2004). For this reason, studies using this important dataset will serve as the focal point for our discussion of financing issues. In designing the PSED, more than sixty-four thousand individuals were contacted and screened over an eighteen-month period beginning in July of 1998 to determine the number of people who were engaged in the process of starting new firms. Findings revealed that a total of 6.1 percent of the total sample were involved in starting either a standalone business or a new business within an existing business. Further interviews and questionnaires revealed that one-third of these nascent entrepreneurs were women while two-thirds were men. Thus, although women represent half of the population in the United States, men are twice as likely to start their own firms. In terms of the motivations of these early stage entrepreneurs, research using the PSED has shown that women rated financial success and innovation as being less important than did men (Carter, Gartner, Shaver, and Gatewood, 2003). Since these attainments are typically associated with growth-oriented entrepreneurship, the fact that women place less emphasis on them may help to explain why they are less likely to launch firms with the goal of achieving growth.

The entrepreneur's aspirations and goals play an important role not only in the launch of new firms but also in their subsequent survival and growth. As we have seen from our earlier case studies, the entrepreneur's goals also have an impact on the types and amount of resources that she needs to develop and acquire. Brush, Edelman, and Manolova (2008) found that growth-oriented firms spent a greater amount of time securing and developing organizational resources, including financial capital. Thus, their "first sales" came at a later point than those for firms that were less growth-oriented.

> Ventures with higher aspirations had greater scale of organizational resources, appear to focus more time and effort to build and develop the organizational infrastructure within which growth can take place. When developing this infrastructure, our study suggests that growth-oriented ventures do not rush to sell products but rather build the organization so that it can flourish over time. Alternatively, lower-aspiring firms tended to have a faster first sale." (p. 176)

In addition to providing us with information on the characteristics of very early stage firms and entrepreneurs, the PSED also provides insights into strategies that contribute to survival and sustainability. Research using the PSED data found that just one-third of nascent entrepreneurs actually made the transition to operating firms after one year (Parker and Belghitar, 2006). Firms were more likely to do so if they had established credit with suppliers, and if they had begun to receive some money from operations. These findings demonstrate the importance of financial capital, even during the earliest stages of the firm, particularly in the form of trade credit and earnings from the business. One study that focused specifically on the survival of nascent firms revealed that greater financial resources significantly decrease the likelihood of discontinuance (Liao, Welsch, and Moutray, 2004).

> Our results illustrate the importance of financial capital, particularly personal funding in a firm's survival at the nascent stage, when the liability of newness and smallness is great. Ample financial capital enables entrepreneurs to mainly focus on building a business, rather than being constantly under the pressure of balancing cash flows. Consequently, well-funded start-ups should have a significantly lower probability of discontinuance. (p. 12)

In a provocative article on financing business startups, Cassar (2004) explored the challenges of getting "well-funded." New firms suffer from a high level of "asymmetric" or incomplete information. Early stage firms have a limited track record, they typically are not yet profitable, and some do not even generate revenues during their first year. Further, nascent firms are often based on new products, services, or technologies that have not been tested by the marketplace. This combination of factors makes it very difficult for suppliers of capital to evaluate the firm's prospects or the riskiness of its anticipated cash flows. These challenges are exacerbated for growth-oriented firms, because they typically require larger amounts of external capital to fund their growth. Cassar's results revealed that firm size was an important factor in determining the amount of capital raised. His findings also revealed that asset structure played a role; firms with tangible assets were able to raise larger amounts of financial capital. These assets can be used as collateral on loans, and they also reduce the informational asymmetry associated with new firms. Cassar's findings suggest that growth-oriented firms in asset-intensive industries such as manufacturing, construction, and transportation will have an easier time raising capital. Conversely, however, firms in services, technology, or bioscience may face greater challenges.

New Firm Survival

The first year or two is a critical time for any new firm, because it is not yet fully established and there is a high risk of failure. This is the period during which

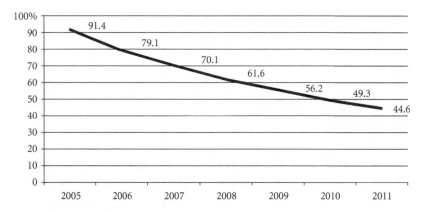

FIGURE 4.1. Firm Survival, 2005–2011
Source: Kauffman Firm Survey Microdata, 2012

the entrepreneur transforms her business idea into action, creates the infrastructure and organization to support the company, begins to develop and sell products and services, and hires employees.

Many new firms fail because they do not have the necessary systems and controls in place. What do we mean by that? We are referring to financial management and reporting systems, and systems for managing cash, receivables, and inventories. All three of these are areas in which new firms often get into trouble. Firms do not necessarily go out of business because they don't have any customers. They go out of business because they don't have any cash. This grim reality highlights the importance of being able to generate sufficient capital from either internal or external sources. This is not necessarily a new-firm phenomenon—nearly 10 percent of all employer firms close down each year, and this percentage has remained remarkably consistent over time.

Not surprisingly, the survival rate for new and young firms is even lower. As the KFS data show, for those firms that started in 2004, more than half closed down by 2011, the last year of the survey (Figure 4.1). These grim statistics illustrate the fact that launching a new firm is indeed a risky business.

New-Firm Growth Rates

Even for those firms that do survive and grow, the vast majority do not experience significant growth. In contrast, most new firms start small, and remain small. Table 4.1, also based on KFS data, reveals that only 52.6 percent of

TABLE 4.1. Employment by Kauffman Firm Survey Firms

	All Firms 2004	Surviving Firms 2011
Firms with Employees	40.9%	52.6%
Average Employment	1.9	4.6
Average Employment (employers only)	4.6	8.7

Source: Kauffman Firm Survey microdata, 2012

surviving firms launched in 2004 had any employees in 2011, eight years later. For those firms that did have employees, the mean number of employees was less than ten. Thus, on average, even those firms that grew didn't grow to be very large. Table 4.1 highlights how unusual are firms like the Gilt Groupe, which has created over a thousand new jobs, and why they are the focus of so much attention.

Financing Strategies for Nascent Firms

Financial resources are often a key to the survival and growth of new firms (Cooper, Gimeno-Gascon, and Woo, 1994). As noted earlier, however, one of the challenges for new firms is the problem of asymmetric information (Ang, 1992; Cassar, 2004). Asymmetric information refers to the fact that, in privately held firms, insiders have more information than outsiders. Thus, it is difficult for outsiders, including external providers of financial capital, to evaluate the prospects of the firm. Consistent with this theme, prior research suggests that the problem of asymmetric information often causes new firms to rely more heavily on internal rather than external sources of financing. Those firms that are able to attract external financing are typically larger, are more growth-oriented, or have tangible assets that can be used as collateral for loans (Cassar, 2004).

We can examine data from the KFS to evaluate the effect of asymmetric information as well as differences in financing between growth-oriented firms and non-growth firms. Table 4.2 shows the financing sources, by gender, for new firms in their first year of operation (2004) and compares the capital structure of firms that grew over the period to those that closed down or stayed small. For this analysis, high-growth-potential firms are those that have at least five employees by the end of the period. While this may seem relatively small, remember that out of around twenty-five million tax returns filed each year,

TABLE 4.2. Startup Capital by Gender, 2004

	All	Women-Owned	Men-Owned	High-Growth Women-Owned	High-Growth Men-Owned
Owner Equity	$32,614.75	$23,914.83	$36,396.68	$44,435.97	$75,537.68
Insider Equity	$2,099.85	$1,896.99	$2,012.66	$774.21	$5,038.02
Outsider Equity	$16,293.75	$1,201.50	$23,473.88	$3,902.39	$56,012.25
Owner Debt	$4,581.50	$3,683.50	$5,023.05	$4,858.43	$15,920.54
Insider Debt	$6,737.29	$6,000.78	$7,217.39	$12,705.44	$18,009.76
Outsider Debt	$49,384.36	$37,601.27	$55,549.22	$69,748.84	$112,355.67
Total Financial Capital	$111,711.50	$74,298.88	$129,672.88	$136,425.28	$282,873.93
Owner Equity	29.20%	32.19%	28.07%	32.57%	26.70%
Insider Equity	1.88%	2.55%	1.55%	0.57%	1.78%
Outsider Equity	14.59%	1.62%	18.10%	2.86%	19.80%
Owner Debt	4.10%	4.96%	3.87%	3.56%	5.63%
Insider Debt	6.03%	8.08%	5.57%	9.31%	6.37%
Outsider Debt	44.21%	50.61%	42.84%	51.13%	39.72%
Total Financial Capital	100.00%	100.00%	100.00%	100.00%	100.00%
Outsider Debt Ratio	20.0%	19.0%	21.0%	22.6%	29.2%

Source: Kauffman Firm Survey microdata, 2006

only about six million businesses have any employees other than the owners themselves. A very small percentage of firms have more than five employees. As such, this was used to proxy for high-growth potential.

Table 4.2 reveals that women, on average, started their firms with roughly half as much financial capital as men. In terms of source, women were more reliant on owner and insider equity. Women-owned firms were also more reliant on all forms of debt, including owner debt, insider debt, and outsider debt. Conversely, they were dramatically less reliant on external equity. Although high-growth firms were launched with twice as much financial capital as firms on average, growth-oriented women entrepreneurs still started with less than half as much financial capital as their male counterparts. As with women-owned firms in general, growth-oriented women-owned firms were more reliant on internal sources of capital and debt than men, while external equity continued to represent only a small proportion of total financing. These distinctions help to explain some of the size differentials for women- and men-owned firms. As we saw in our case studies on First Aid Shot Therapy and Gilt Groupe, external equity typically provided by angel investors and venture capitalists is a major source of financing for high-growth firms. If women are less able to secure this type of financial capital, they will not have the same opportunities for growth that men do.

Table 4.3 documents some of the characteristics associated with high-growth entrepreneurship. From the perspective of human capital, growth-oriented entrepreneurs, both women and men, were more likely to have college or graduate degrees than were entrepreneurs on average. Similarly, growth-oriented firms were more likely to be founded by entrepreneurial teams rather than by single individuals. Team ownership has the advantage of providing a broader mix of experience, skills, and talents. It is also very likely that a founding team can provide more personal financial capital as well as a larger network of potential providers of financial capital. This finding is also consistent with what we observed in our Gilt case. Founders Alexandra Wilkis Wilson and Alexis Maybank teamed up with three other co-founders, one of whom had prior entrepreneurial experience and contacts in the venture capital industry. This paved the way for Gilt to raise substantial amounts of external equity. In this sense, both our KFS findings and our case studies highlight the benefits of building a community to help launch and grow the firm rather than attempting to "go it alone."

TABLE 4.3. Characteristics of High-Growth Firms by Gender, 2011

	All	Women-Owned	Men-Owned	High-Growth Women-Owned	High-Growth Men-Owned
Owner Age	44.9	44.8	44.9	43.1	43.9
Team Ownership	11.5%	8.1%	13.2%	25.9%	30.8%
High School or Less	13.6%	10.6%	15.4%	5.3%	7.9%
Some College	36.7%	42.8%	34.9%	30.6%	25.8%
College Grad	30.0%	28.0%	31.6%	43.2%	40.9%
Graduate Degree	17.5%	18.1%	17.7%	20.9%	25.4%
Total Revenues	$140,121	$85,369	$166,232	$362,468	$376,062
Employment	1.6	1.1	1.9	3.2	4.7
Total Assets	$133,701	$82,158	$159,102	$238,190	$339,675
PPE Ratio	37.5%	36.9%	37.8%	30.2%	30.9%
High Tech	5.5%	2.5%	6.9%	3.6%	8.7%
Any Intellectual Property	19.5%	18.2%	19.9%	16.6%	28.1%
Product Offered	51.8%	54.8%	50.4%	36.8%	59.9%
Home Based	50.1%	51.0%	49.8%	33.2%	18.2%

Source: Kauffman Firm Survey microdata, 2012

Table 4.3 also reveals some important distinctions between the growth-oriented women and men entrepreneurs and their firms. It is noteworthy that these high-growth women-owned firms had average revenues that were roughly comparable to those of men. However, women had fewer employees and assets, however, suggesting that they may actually do a better job of generating revenues from the human, social, and financial assets that they do have. Another noteworthy difference highlighted in Table 4.3 is that high-growth women-owned firms were considerably less likely to be in high-tech fields or to have some type of intellectual property. Alternatively, women-owned firms were much more likely to be in the business of delivering services rather than products. Finally, one-third of the growth-oriented women-owned firms operated out of their homes, compared with fewer than one-fifth of growth-oriented men. This may be a reflection of the different types of firms that women launch, or it may be another sign that women pursue "capital efficient" financial strategies more aggressively than men.

When we break out the "top twenty-five" firms for women and for men as measured by employment, we again see some important distinctions (Table 4.4). Women-owned firms had an average of 7.1 employees during their initial year of operation compared to 22 employees for male-owned firms. The employment gap between women and men was even larger, however, after eight years of operation. Firm revenues exhibit a similar pattern. The top twenty-five women-owned firms generated average revenues of $1.5 million in their first year versus $1.6 million for men. This gap increased to $3.6 million versus $22.2 million by the eighth year, however. These statistics could be viewed as support for the contention that women entrepreneurs prefer slower and more modest rates of growth than men (Cliff, 1998; Morris, Miyasaki, Watters, and Coombes, 2006). Alternatively, however, if we consider both Tables 4.2 and 4.4, they may suggest that women are not necessarily less motivated to grow their firms, but rather less well resourced, particularly in the area of financial capital (Brush, Carter, and others, 2001; Brush, Carter, and others, 2004).

TABLE 4.4. Top 25 Firms by Gender

Variable	Female		Male		Percentage change 2004–2011	
	Obs	Mean	Obs	Mean	Female	Male
Employees (2004)	25	7.1	25	22.0	Female	Male
Employment (2011)	25	28.6	25	152.4	303%	591%
Revenues (2004)	14	$1,468,764	18	$2,572,944		
Revenues (2011)	21	$3,638,239	24	$22,156,133	148%	761%

Source: Kauffman Firm Survey microdata, 2012

Fortunately, the growth-oriented women entrepreneurs that we have chosen to focus on in this book do not dwell on these statistics, nor do they view them as impediments to their own aspirations and goals. They are too busy developing innovative ideas, launching the firms that will bring those ideas to life and securing the resources they need to succeed. Our next entrepreneur, Doreen Block, founder of Poshly, is a case in point.

Doreen Block and Poshly

When we speak with representatives of the new generation of young entrepreneurs, it is energizing to experience their "sky's the limit" attitude. Poshly founder Doreen Block grew up in the midst of Silicon Valley's high-tech culture, in which she was surrounded by innovation and entrepreneurs. That environment had a tremendous impact on her interest in starting her own firm. Doreen majored in business at UC Berkeley and interned at Yahoo for three summers during college, further immersing herself in the world of technology-based entrepreneurship. Armed with education, experience, and motivation, she founded Poshly (http://poshly.com) in the summer of 2012 with the goal of helping beauty product firms do a better job of matching women's coloring and characteristics with individual beauty products. Doreen saw a huge opportunity to bring data analytics into the $380+ billion beauty products industry, in which more than thirty million women in the United States shop for beauty products online. She observed that few technology-oriented firms were serving this space, suggesting an opportunity for new entrants. Her "Ah-hah!" moment came when she saw an ad targeted at redheads and realized that data collection around hair color, eye color, and other characteristics would be valuable to brands that need that kind of information for selling their products. Sensing that there was enormous potential to make a connection between brands and consumers through technology, Doreen decided to take the plunge, and Poshly was born.

We started with the hypothesis that proprietary data can be useful—not IP addresses or click activity—but rather data gathered from directly asking people questions. What color are your eyes? Are you going to prom?, etc. We knew that the data would be valuable. The question became how were we going to monetize all the information we were obtaining? The biggest challenge early on was getting a clear focus that we could communicate and articulate to investors, including how we could scale.

Poshly builds personalization technologies that connect beauty brands with beauty consumers in innovative, data-driven ways. Poshly's first tool was a website devoted to beauty give-aways that culls data from users with fun, easy quizzes. On Poshly, members discover beauty products that are best suited to their personal characteristics and needs. At the same time, beauty brands gain a better understanding for the preferences and personas of their customers in real time. Poshly's innovative approach for combining the power of data analytics and technology has already attracted considerable attention within the beauty products industry. The firm's beauty give-away site has been featured in *InStyle* magazine's "Best of the Web," and was awarded L'Oreal's NEXT Generation Award.

In terms of financial strategy, Block bootstrapped like many early stage entrepreneurs until January of 2014, when she began raising capital from external investors. Prior to that time, money from her own savings and early stage revenues from the business also provided roughly $100,000. Although Poshly's revenues were still relatively modest, Doreen was able to raise nearly a million dollars from seed fund investors. Her initial investors consisted of technology executives from the West Coast (all male). The New York chapter of Golden Seeds and Astia Angels from both coasts were also early stage investors.

In her interview with us, Doreen indicated that she did not have any problem raising the seed round and, in fact, raised a lot more than she needed. Nevertheless, it was not a smooth process by any means.

We had a term sheet, but then it morphed. We got a priced round from an angel group. The other firms in their portfolio were dealing with follow-on funding, so they wanted other investors in our raise. We thought it was a done deal, but then we needed to keep pitching and raise more funding. When we went out and continued raising, the feedback was that it might not make sense to do a priced round.[1] We ended up doing a convertible note instead. Some of the people in the initial angel syndicate did end up investing in that convertible note, but not the syndicate itself.

It was a learning experience for Block, who observed,

I really learned that funding can be a rather creative process and needs to work for you and your investor. It is not a one size fits all. I was initially looking for investors to tell me what to do, but now I'm much more strong in saying what I want to see happen. I found it empowering. The seed round really helped me change my perspective on who can steer the conversation.

Doreen shared with us that that both Golden Seeds and Astia have been instrumental in Poshly's growth.

Mentors have helped us figure out how to package and monetize the data, as well as how to articulate the business model to investors. They have helped me ask the right questions and craft the road map for going forward. Mentors also became our investors. Brainpower and connections were just as important as the financial investments. Astia was a great process because it gave me a platform. I pitched in December, and it was incredible to be in a room of fifty to sixty diverse investors. We closed within a few weeks with some of those individuals. Astia Angels also invested along with other investors who are currently tracking us for a series A.

On the basis of her experience with raising financial capital to date, Doreen offered the following advice:

1. Have a very granular financial plan, and be specific about your assumptions.
2. Have different scenarios for revenue and growth so there is a plan B (and a plan C).
3. Make sure you have a clear picture of what you need to accomplish and develop a "to do" list for each milestone.
4. Be open to different business models and ways to monetize the value your firm provides.
5. Network and find mentors!

Poshly's next milestone involves building an application program interface (API) in order to scale the technology. This step will allow Doreen to approach publishers and other potential partners like *Teen Vogue*, a magazine and website patterned after *Vogue* magazine that provides teens with information on fashion, beauty, celebrities, and entertainment. The API platform will be powered by Poshly, but the look and feel will be *Teen Vogue*. Doreen's seed round will allow her to pay her current staff, grow her team, and build the API. Currently, Poshly employs three full-time employees and two full-time contractors. Doreen is in the process of hiring two more engineers full time.

At the time of our interview, Doreen expected to raise a Series A round of funding in 2014. Poshly's seed round has provided a bridge to the Series A round that will allow the firm to develop its technology faster. Block shared that they are already oversubscribed on investment contingents. The sky is the limit.

Business Plan Versus Lean Startup: Which Is Right for You?

The Benefits of a Comprehensive Business Plan

Traditionally, one of the key tasks of the early stage entrepreneur has been the development of a written plan that (1) identifies the opportunity her firm will address, (2) details the resources required as well as how she will secure them, and (3) explains her revenue model and how she will put these resources to work. Development of a business plan, though time consuming, has been viewed as an essential task that serves both internal and external purposes. From an internal perspective, the business plan is a type of "sanity check" for the entrepreneur. It ensures that she has thought through all the pieces of the business, that those pieces fit together into a cohesive whole, and that they will allow her to achieve the goals that are important to her. Most of us are not experts in all of the functional areas of a business. We may be great at product development or marketing, but we are miserable when it comes to finance or manufacturing. Obviously an entrepreneur does not have to be an expert in all of these areas, but she has to know enough about each to make good decisions during the firm's earliest stages. At that point, there's no money to hire a CFO or a VP of manufacturing. It's just you! In other words, nascent entrepreneurship can be a lonely affair. In light of that, it was not surprising to us that many of the growth-oriented women entrepreneurs that we interviewed for this book actually used a team approach for launching their firms. Whichever path the entrepreneur chooses for launching her firm, the process of creating a business plan guarantees that she has considered all of the key areas and issues, either individually or in collaboration with her founding team members.

A second advantage of a business plan is that it serves as a gateway for helping the entrepreneur gain access to external investors. In this sense, it is necessary but not sufficient in and of itself as a means to secure funding. Providers of capital, both debt and equity, want to make sure that you have thought your idea through and have a viable revenue model, consistent with Doreen Block's recommendation that entrepreneurs develop "a very granular financial plan." They also want to see your progress to date in terms of products, services, clinical trials, regulatory approvals, number of customers, and revenues. As one might anticipate, they are particularly interested in the qualifications of the entrepreneur, both personal and professional. They want to ensure that you have a well-balanced management team with expertise in the different functional areas. As noted earlier, external providers of capital are particularly drawn to "serial entrepreneurs," or those who have previously launched successful businesses. Angel investor networks and venture capital firms receive hundreds of business plans over the course of a year. Key considerations like those we have detailed can make the difference between a second look and a trip to the circular file. In light of that, nascent entrepreneurs should take the task of developing their business plan very seriously.

Although there are a number of benefits associated with developing a comprehensive business plan, a growing number of entrepreneurship scholars and practitioners caution that the entrepreneur should not spend too much time trying to solidify the specifics of her business model before it has been tested and refined. These individuals contend that attempts to "calcify" the business model too early can actually increase the chances of business failure. As an alternative, they encourage early stage entrepreneurs to use a new approach called the Lean Startup Model.

The Lean Startup Model:
A Novel Alternative to the Traditional Business Plan

One of the challenges associated with launching an entrepreneurial venture is that so many of them fail, roughly 50 percent by their sixth year (Figure 4.1). During this span of time, the entrepreneur often consumes a significant amount of time and resources only to learn that her business model is not sustainable. The Lean Startup Model was developed to address the relatively high "infant mortality rate" for new ventures, not necessarily by preventing failure, but rather by encouraging non-viable firms to fail faster and early thus allowing the entrepreneur to move on to a more promising idea.

Entrepreneur Steve Blank laid the groundwork for the lean startup movement with a book titled *The Four Steps to the Epiphany* (2005), in which he stressed that new ventures are not simply smaller versions of established ventures. In light of that, entrepreneurial ventures require a different process for identifying and developing viable business ideas. According to Blank, the lean startup "favors experimentation over elaborate planning, customer feedback over intuition, and iterative design over traditional 'big design up front' development" (Blank, 2013, p. 4).

Blank contends that the entrepreneur's primary task is to find the right business model, not to execute a pre-determined business model which may or may not work. He points out that the entrepreneurial process involves many unknowns. According to Blank, the traditional business planning approach assumes "that it's possible to figure out most of the unknowns of a business in advance, before you raise money and actually execute the idea" (2013, p. 5).

In other words, the traditional business plan approach encourages entrepreneurs to articulate their business idea, amass resources, and start building their product, largely in isolation. Thus, it is only after a considerable amount of time and effort that they realize the business model doesn't actually work. In contrast, the lean approach helps new ventures "launch products that customers actually want, far more quickly and cheaply than traditional methods" (Blank, 2013, p. 7).

Figure 4.2 identifies some of the major differences between the Lean Startup Model approach and the more traditional business planning approach. It highlights the importance of early stage customer involvement, rapid prototyping, incremental improvements, and the incorporation of failure into the entrepreneur's learning process.

The term "lean startup" itself was initially coined by entrepreneur Eric Ries in his book *The Lean Startup*, published in 2011. Unlike bootstrapping, which seeks to minimize expenses and the need to raise external sources of capital, lean management focuses on minimizing waste in the form of either resources or time. The entrepreneur achieves this goal by testing elements of the business model early and often to either validate or reject them. In this fashion, business model development is a process of continuous improvement.

In a subsequent article, Ries and two co-authors (Eisenmann, Ries, and Dillard, 2013) describe the Lean Startup Model as a "hypothesis driven approach," designed to "help reduce the biggest risk facing entrepreneurs: offering a product that no one wants" (p. 1).

They go on to define the business model as "an integrated array of distinctive choices specifying a new venture's unique customer value proposition and how it will configure activities to deliver that value and earn sustainable profits" (p. 2).

The task of the entrepreneur is to develop and test a set of falsifiable hypotheses for each element of the business model. This allows the entrepreneur to build and analyze her business model in an iterative and ongoing fashion. As a part of this process, the entrepreneur develops a series of minimum viable products, or MVPs. An MVP is defined as the smallest set of features or activities needed to go through a build-measure-learn cycle (Ries, 2011), thereby allowing her to test an individual business model hypothesis.

Strategy

Business Model	Business plan
Hypothesis-driven	Implementation-driven

New-Product Process

Customer Development	Product management
Get out of the office and test hypothesis	Prepare offering for market following a linear, step-by-step plan

Engineering

Agile Development	Agile or Waterfall Development
Build the product iteratively and incrementally	Build the product iteratively, or fully specify the product before building it

Organization

Customer and Agile Development Teams	Department by Function
Hire for learning, nimbleness, and speed	Hire for experience and ability to execute

Financial Reporting

Metrics That Matter	Accounting
Customer acquisition cost, lifetime	Income statement, balance sheet, cash
Customer value, churn, viralness	flow statement

Failure

Expected	Exception
Fix by iterating on idea and pivoting away from ones that don't work	Fix by firing executives

Speed

Rapid	Measured
Operates on good-enough data	Operates on complete data

FIGURE 4.2. Lean Startup Model Versus Traditional Business Plan
Source: Blank, 2013

If the MVP test results validate the business model hypothesis, then the entrepreneur perseveres on her current path (Persevere). If the MVP test rejects a critical business model hypothesis, the entrepreneur needs to discontinue the business (Perish). Alternatively, however, if the MVP test is negative or even positive, but other market feedback suggests that a greater opportunity lies elsewhere, the entrepreneur may choose to pivot in a way that preserves some business model elements but rejects others (Pivot). (Eisenmann, Ries, and Dillard, 2013, p. 10). By using this approach, the entrepreneur is able to continuously test and refine the elements of her business model as her venture evolves.

This hypothesis-driven approach is summarized in a tool called the Business Model Canvas (Figure 4.3), which lays out the nine building blocks for a new venture (Osterwalder and Pigneur, 2010). Each "block" in turn includes a series of hypotheses that the entrepreneur must test as described above. Although still relatively new, the Business Model Canvas and the Lean Startup Model are being taught in a growing number of venues, including major universities and "Startup Weekends" throughout the United States. Steve Blank has provided an additional resource in the form of an online course titled *How to Build a Startup: The Lean LaunchPad* that anyone can take for free (http:// www.udacity.com).

Revenue Model Versus Business Model: Same or Different?

One often sees the terms *revenue model* and *business model* used interchangeably. In fact, however, they are quite different. The revenue model is a component of the firm's business model and explains how the venture will generate revenues in excess to expenses, thereby creating profits. In contrast, the business model represents a more comprehensive set of activities that includes not only revenue generation but also key resources, operational processes, and strategic considerations (Johnson, Christensen, and Kagermann, 2008; Morris, Schindehutte, and Allen, 2005). These address the firm's capabilities and challenges as well as the ways in which the firm will create value for its customers. One of the advantages of the Business Model Canvas as described in this chapter is that it provides a way for us to visualize the various components of the business model. Similarly, an earlier article published in the *Harvard Business Review* describes the roles of four key elements for "an effective business model" (Johnson, Christensen, and Kagermann, 2008, p. 62). These are the Customer Value Proposition, the Profit Formula, Key Resources, and Key Processes. These tools help us remember that the firm's business model encompasses more than just revenues minus expenses.

The lean startup movement is growing rapidly and now has its own website (http://www.leanstartup.com), which provides information on resources for

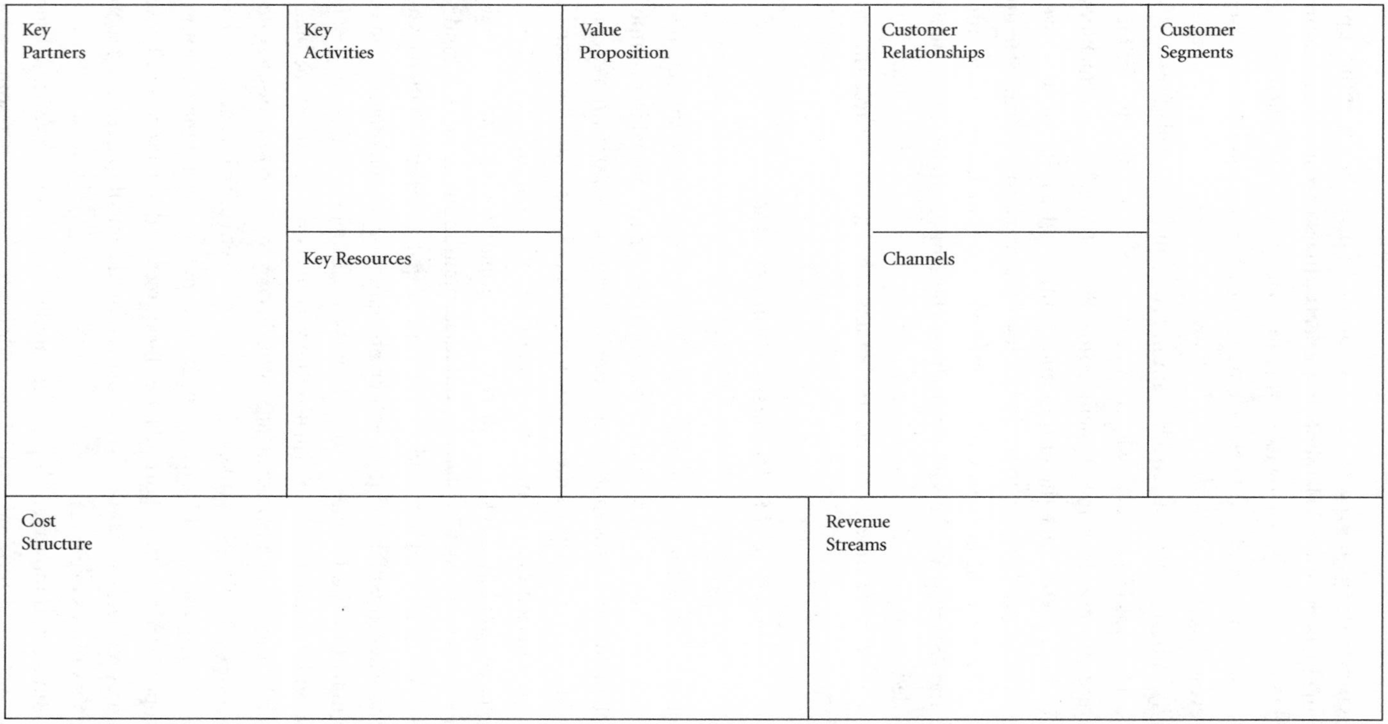

FIGURE 4.3. Business Model Canvas
Source: Osterwalder and Pigneur, 2010, p. 44

learning and adopting this approach. These include an annual national conference as well as regional "MeetUps" throughout the world. Last but not least, the website provides case studies of firms including Dropbox, Wealthfront, Grockit, and Aardvark that have used the Lean Startup Model. At this point, the lean startup approach is still too new for researchers to be able to validate its impact on new-firm survival and growth. Thus, most of the results to date are company-specific and anecdotal in nature. Nevertheless, it is an approach worth looking at, because it provides yet another set of strategies to help growth-oriented entrepreneurs navigate the perilous early stages of a new firm's development.

Which Should You Use?

The question of business plan versus lean startup is often posed as an either/or proposition. We would argue, however, that both are useful at different stages of the firm's development. As described, the Lean Startup Model allows the nascent or early stage entrepreneur to test key elements of her business model before investing significant amounts of time and money. This approach is designed to incorporate small failures into the business planning process as an alternative to large, and potentially fatal, failures down the road. The lean approach also helps ensure that the entrepreneur's time and resources will be invested wisely. In this sense, the Lean Startup Model is particularly appropriate for early stage entrepreneurs.

In contrast, the traditional business plan approach may be better suited to later-stage entrepreneurs who plan to raise significant amounts of external capital. The business plan assumes that the entrepreneur knows what her business model is and that she needs to acquire resources in the form of human, social, financial, and political capital to execute it. A formal business plan is particularly appropriate for entrepreneurs seeking external equity capital from angel networks, venture capital firms, or private equity firms. These are sophisticated investors who want to make sure that the entrepreneur has thought through all of the dimensions of her business, including its risk factors, thoroughly. Further, as we will see in later chapters, negotiations with angels and VCs over issues such as valuation and control can become intense. In situations such as these, the entrepreneur's best defense is to know her business and its financials inside and out. In light of that, the business plan is not only a type of road map for the firm once the business model has been defined, but also a key tool for attracting and negotiating with external investors.

Closing the Loop

During the nascent stage, the entrepreneur is a very busy person, because at that point, nothing is fully formed or in place. This is probably also one of the most difficult stages, because the entrepreneur has to do some serious soul-searching to determine if entrepreneurship is the path she really wants to pursue. As we noted in Chapter 3, this involves an honest assessment of her motivations, goals, and priorities and the development of her "resource inventory." Any new firm will require resources in the forms of financial, human, and social capital. During the nascent stage, the entrepreneur figures out what she already has and what she needs to develop or obtain from other sources.

Although entrepreneurs often select industries in which they have accumulated either education or experience, the nascent stage provides further opportunities for the entrepreneur to gain a deeper understanding of her firm's industry dynamics and structure. Is this a new and growing industry, or is it an industry that has matured and is stagnating? If it is a high-growth industry, it will be much easier for the entrepreneur to grow her firm by riding the wave of industry expansion. In contrast, if she launches a firm in a mature, non-growth, or even declining industry, she will have to take market share from established firms. This can obviously be done through innovative products, services, technologies, or delivery systems, but it is often a challenge to break into the established order. In our Poshly mini-case, Doreen Block realized that she could apply the tools of data analytics to the beauty industry, thereby using technology to link specific consumers with specific brands. Any woman who has spent far too much time at a department store cosmetics counter agonizing about which foundation, eye shadow, blush, and lipstick match not only her coloring but each other can appreciate the benefits of a website that can provide guidance on which beauty products are best for her.

Consistent with this theme, it is important for the nascent entrepreneur to understand the competitive landscape that she is entering. Are there major competitors already in the form of powerful established firms? If so, she may choose to compete with them indirectly by targeting a specific niche or introducing a new delivery system rather than going head to head. Alternatively, if the competitive environment is highly fragmented, there are opportunities for the entrepreneur to grab market share from other firms through the quality of her products and services as well as through effective execution. In the case of entirely new industries, the competitive environment is a blank page, and the entrepreneur can choose to position her firm in ways that will maximize its advantages, strengths, and opportunities for growth.

During the nascent stage, the entrepreneur needs to gain an understanding of what the critical success factors are for her industry. Is it product or service quality, innovation, low cost, customer service, the delivery system, or a combination of these factors? Going back to our Gilt Groupe example from Chapter 3, Gilt was able to combine high-quality designer women's clothing with attractive pricing, an unbeatable combination, particularly for young professional women. Its unique delivery system, the flash sale, was also a home run in that it created a sense of urgency and excitement among buyers. True to the maxim that imitation is the sincerest form of flattery, many other retailers have adopted the flash sale approach in the past few years.

In addition to identifying critical success factors, a key task for the nascent entrepreneur is the development of a revenue model that will ensure the firm's survival and growth. The revenue model is a component of the entrepreneur's overall business model. In essence, the revenue model is a description of how the firm will generate revenues in excess of costs. Although many new firms are unprofitable at startup, this is obviously not an option for the long term. From the standpoint of financing, the sooner a firm can achieve profitability, the more attractive it is to external funding sources, because that eliminates at least one form of uncertainty. This helps us understand why bioscience firms face so many challenges in their attempts to secure capital. These firms typically have development cycles of a decade or more. During that time, money is going out to fund research and development, clinical trials, salaries, and laboratories, but little or no money is coming in. This prolonged period of revenue uncertainty makes it very difficult for these firms to raise investor capital. As an alternative, many rely on government sources of funding in the form of grants and contracts to get them through a fairly lengthy survival stage.

Like the bioscience industry, technology-based firms such as Poshly often face a challenge in attempting to define and sustain a revenue model. Due to the rapid pace of technological innovation and change, today's technology darling may be tomorrow's technology has-been. Entrepreneurs entering industries characterized by rapid technological change must be prepared to innovate continuously as a way to stay ahead, or at least even, with their markets, and continuous innovation requires a constant financial commitment.

In other instances, technology-based firms face difficulties when they try to monetize their innovative ideas. Initially they offer the product or service at no cost or at a subsidized cost to get people to try it, and everyone loves it at that price. The firm's challenge is getting to the point where they can charge enough for their product or service to generate a profit. There are two ways to achieve this goal; either raise the price or reduce the cost. Either or both will work, but one way or another the firm has to get there or it will not survive. Similarly, investors will lose interest if the firm cannot find a way to monetize the value it creates for its customers. Our interview with Doreen Block at Poshly confirmed the importance of developing a viable revenue model as a means for attracting investors. A major challenge during the early stages of her firm was figuring out how to translate the data they gathered on women using the Poshly website into revenues.

In this chapter, we have also taken the opportunity to present and discuss the Lean Startup Model, which has garnered a considerable amount of attention in recent years. Although the Lean Startup Model is sometimes confused with bootstrapping, the two are actually very different. As we have described, the Lean Startup Model was designed to address the vulnerability of early stage firms by minimizing waste and reducing the likelihood of failure. It does this by identifying and testing hypotheses relating to key elements of the entrepreneur's business model. The more traditional business plan approach assumes that the entrepreneur already knows what her business model is and just needs to fill in the blanks for the various functional areas and anticipated results. In contrast, the Lean Startup Model is based on the premise that the entrepreneur's key task is to identify an appropriate business model, because if the business model doesn't work, the business will not survive. Major tenets of the Lean Startup Model include early involvement of customers, rapid and incremental product development, ongoing hypothesis testing, and acceptance of failure as a part of the entrepreneurial process. Although the Lean Startup Model does not necessarily eliminate the need for a business plan, it does provide an alternative approach for early stage firms.

What Does This Mean for You?

In this chapter we focused on those activities that will help the entrepreneur launch her firm and get off to a good start. During the nascent stage, many of those activities will be directed toward solidifying your business idea and developing your skills and resources.

1. Identify resources that you can use to address your areas of weakness. Take part in local startup events in your communities. Several groups have ac-

tivities and chapters in cities around the country. Up Global hosts frequent Startup Weekends, Startup Grind offers monthly fireside chats with successful entrepreneurs, and the Kauffman Foundation hosts weekly events with entrepreneurs through their 1 Million Cups program. Get to know others in your community.

2. Start building your network. Once your firm has launched and begins to grow, you will need investors, managers, employees, suppliers, customers, and individuals with specialized expertise in a variety of areas. During this stage, you may also want to consider the desirability of launching with one or several co-founders who can bring additional skills, resources, and contacts to the table. There are also an increasing number of groups such as Springboard Enterprises and Astia that provide training and support to growth-oriented women entrepreneurs. Others, like our own Rising Tide Program, are emerging even as this book goes into print. Groups such as Emerging Women (www.emergingwomen.com) and the Vinetta Project (www.vinettaproject.com) are communities and networks of women who will be quite valuable in your journey.

3. Find mentors. Ideally these will be entrepreneurs who have successfully launched and grown their firms. These are the people who can share insights that you will never find in any book, even this one. They can also provide support, encouragement, and knowledge borne of experience when you do hit those bumps in the road during the firm's early years.

4. Identify and test your revenue model. How will your firm generate revenues in excess of expenses? Although many new ventures lose money during their early months or years, in the longer term a viable revenue model is essential for the sustainability of your firm. From the standpoint of financial strategy as well, the revenue model is a critical piece of your business, because investors will also scrutinize it carefully.

5. Get comfortable with the numbers. Our featured entrepreneur in this chapter, Doreen Block, talked about the importance of being able to develop detailed financial statements. Although others may help you with this, you need to understand the process and the statements themselves, since they will be scrutinized and questioned by potential investors.

6. Develop alternative scenarios for your firm. Things do not always go as we would like, and during your first year you are almost certain to hit some bumps in the road. As Doreen advised, have a plan B, and a plan C.

7. Explore ways in which the lean startup approach can help you develop and refine your firm's business model. Attend some meetings of the "MeetUp" group in your area to learn how other entrepreneurs are using the Lean Startup Model and what their experiences have been. Although the Lean Startup Model will not necessarily eliminate the need to do a business plan eventually, it does provide a cost- and time-effective means for developing and validating your firm's business model in the early stages.

5

FIRST THINGS FIRST

Financing Strategies for Early Stage Firms

Early stage firms are firms that have moved beyond the nascent stage into execution. Early stage firms have already been launched, so they have products or services as well as customers. However, the firm is generating minimal, if any, revenues, so it is not yet a candidate for most sources of external financing. Major sources of financing include the entrepreneur's own money and savings, personal loans and credit cards, loans or gifts from family and friends, and bootstrapping (minimizing expenses).

This stage is particularly challenging for growth-oriented women entrepreneurs, because data show that they have lower levels of personal earnings and wealth than men. Thus, they have less capital to bring into the firm. This chapter will document the financial strategies that growth-oriented women entrepreneurs have used at this early stage in order to get their firm off to a good start. The three major strategies that we will focus on in this chapter include using your own personal financial resources, soliciting financial support from family and friends, and bootstrapping.

Personal Financial Resources

The entrepreneur's personal financial resources include her savings, earnings from paid employment, and credit obtained in her own name rather than in the firm's name. These are the tried and true financial sources for all entrepreneurial firms, regardless of the founder's gender. Entrepreneurs who can put substantial amounts of personal capital into their startup firms are better positioned to establish a solid foundation for survival and subsequent growth. From the standpoint of wealth accumulation as well, the longer the entrepreneur can delay taking external equity capital by putting in her own capital, the greater her share of ownership and control.

Prior research reveals that although women entrepreneurs rely heavily on personal sources of financing, in dollar amounts they contribute far less to their firms than men (Coleman and Robb, forthcoming). This is because personal savings typically come from accumulated earnings. Statistics reveal that women earn less than men, so they accumulate less in the form of savings and personal wealth (Bobbitt-Zeher, 2007; Goldin, 2014; Manning and Swaffield, 2008). Why is this the case? One reason for women's lower earnings and accumulated wealth is that they are less well represented at the most senior ranks of organizations, where they would receive higher levels of compensation. A second reason is that women are much more likely to have career interruptions, typically associated with the birth and care of children. These interruptions often cause women to be either delayed on or entirely excluded from fast-track career paths. Thus, they reach the top of the economic food chain much more slowly, if they get there at all.

Table 4.2 (Startup Capital by Gender) from our previous chapter revealed that women launch their firms with smaller amounts of owner-provided debt and equity than men. Further, the funding gap between women and men is even larger for growth-oriented firms. What can growth-oriented women entrepreneurs do to compensate for their generally lower level of personal financial resources?

Our entrepreneur interviews revealed that a number of women use a team approach to founding their firms. From the standpoint of financial capital, starting with a team provides several advantages (Eisenhardt, 2013; Ganotakis, 2012; Maschke and Knyphausen-Aufseb, 2012). First, multiple team members can each contribute personal financial capital, thereby increasing the total amount. Second, founding teams are often assembled to provide complementary skills and, in turn, complementary social capital. Thus, different team members have access to different types of contacts and networks, making the whole greater than the sum of its parts. This is particularly relevant for growth-oriented firms that will need significant amounts of external capital. Individual team members may also have a track record of success in founding previous successful businesses. If this is the case, these same team members may already have access to external funding sources such as angel investor networks or venture capital. Consistent with this observation, Julia Hartz, co-founder and president of Eventbrite and keynote speaker at the Female Founders Forum in Dublin (April 2014), urged women entrepreneurs to "Find a co-founder—more than one. You need someone with complementary skills. . . . You will get from point A to point B twice as fast" (Burke, 2014).

Another helpful strategy is the accumulation of a financial "nest-egg" to help carry the firm through the early years of its existence. Although women have lower earnings and accumulated wealth than men, they are, on average, in their forties when they start their firms (Coleman and Robb, 2014). This provides them with the opportunity and time to accumulate financial capital as well as human and social capital. In other instances, entrepreneurs (both women and men) "moonlight" by continuing to work for an employer, either part time or full time. This strategy allows the entrepreneur to pay for her living and other expenses until she reaches the point where her firm generates sufficient revenues to do so. Similarly, married entrepreneurs (both women and men) often receive financial support from a working spouse.

Yet another strategy for early stage entrepreneurs is what we refer to as an "attitude adjustment" about lifestyle and needs versus wants. Given that the early stage entrepreneur will be directing a lot of her financial resources into the firm, she may have to adapt, at least temporarily, to a more modest lifestyle than one she may have enjoyed when she was collecting a regular paycheck. Surprisingly, none of the entrepreneurs we interviewed for this book complained about this adjustment, although many of them experienced it. Their excitement about their entrepreneurial venture and its prospects overcame the inconvenience of driving an older car, shopping less, and eating out less often. It was just part of the package, and they accepted it as a price they had to pay for pursuing an idea they were passionate about.

These strategies and others that we will discuss in this chapter illustrate the theories of effectuation and financial bricolage. Sarasvathy's theory of effectuation (Sarasvathy, 2001; 2004) contends that individuals operate under conditions of environmental uncertainty. In the face of this uncertainty, they respond by selecting a course of action from a range of possible alternatives. This is certainly true of early stage entrepreneurs, who are continually learning and adapting their strategies to manage the risks associated with launching a new firm.

The theory of bricolage is closely related to the Resource-Based View in that it also describes how entrepreneurs acquire the resources that they need to succeed. Bricolage as a term was first introduced by anthropologist Claude Levi-Strauss (Levi-Strauss, 1967) to explain the process of recombining available resources to achieve new ways of solving problems or exploiting opportunities. More recently, bricolage has been identified as a strategy that may be particularly appropriate for resource-constrained organizations like those we are describing in this chapter (Baker, 2007).

According to Baker and Nelson (2005), bricolage has three primary characteristics. First, it incorporates a bias toward action in addressing the problem or opportunity at hand. Second, bricolage frequently involves finding value in inputs that other businesses view as worthless. Finally, bricolage involves the combination of resources to achieve a new purpose. In a recent article, Dafna Kariv and one of your authors, Susan Coleman, proposed a theory of "financial bricolage" for early stage firms (Kariv and Coleman, 2015). They found that small infusions of financial capital during the firm's first two years had a significant impact on firm performance during those years as well as in subsequent years. This was true for necessity-based or smaller firms as well as opportunity-based firms, which tend to be more growth-oriented. These findings highlight the fact that small amounts of capital at critical points in time can make the difference between survival and failure for early stage firms.

Family and Friends

Early stage investors, including family and friends (F&F), are often termed "inside investors" because they have a personal link to the entrepreneur. This personal relationship and belief in the entrepreneur may be as important as, or even more important than, the strength of her firm's revenue model. Family and friend capital can come in a variety of forms, including loans, equity investments in exchange for a portion of ownership, outright gifts, or donations in the form of free labor, space, facilities, or the like. F&F investors also provide intangibles such as emotional support, encouragement, and a sympathetic ear when the firm hits a rough patch.

Although F&F capital is often both flexible and patient, it is important for the entrepreneur to deal professionally and communicate clearly with these types of inside investors, since misunderstandings and miscommunications can lead to both personal and business difficulties. Given its importance and prevalence, it is surprising that there is not more research on F&F financing. One notable exception, however, is an article by Basu and Parker (2001) focusing on a sample of Asian entrepreneurs in the United Kingdom. These researchers found that over half of their sample firms relied on F&F loans at startup, thus making it the second most important source of financing behind personal savings. Basu and Parker's findings also suggest that heavy reliance on F&F loans was not due to credit rationing on the part of banks. Alternatively, respondents chose to use F&F financing, possibly because the terms were more flexible. Nevertheless, these researchers caution that F&F lenders are not necessarily all motivated by altruistic considerations. Some actually want and expect to receive a return as well as the option to call in a favor at some later date. The co-existence of these somewhat conflicting motivations highlights the importance of dealing with F&F infusions of capital in a professional fashion. In the course of researching our previous book, *A Rising Tide*, we found that some of the women entrepreneurs we interviewed used an attorney to draw up a legal document formalizing the terms and conditions for their F&F loans. This approach ensured that both sides understood those terms and conditions up front. Similarly, the agreement spelled out what would happen if, for some reason, the entrepreneur could not pay back the loan. Clarifying these conditions and expectations does not necessarily forestall adverse events such as the failure of the firm, but they do mitigate the fallout from those events to some extent.

A more recent study by Coleman and Robb (2014), using data from the Kauffman Firm Survey (Table 5.1), found a somewhat lower reliance on F&F (or insider) financing than did the Basu and Parker study. This study revealed that 7.9 percent of total financial capital came in the form of insider financing during the startup year. Women founders were more reliant on insider financing than men, however (10.7 percent vs. 7.2 percent). This same study

TABLE 5.1. Insider Financing at Startup, 2004

	All	Women-Owned	Men-Owned	High Growth Women-Owned	High Growth Men-Owned
Insider Equity	$2,100	$1,897	$2,013	$774	$5,038
Insider Debt	$6,737	$6,001	$7,217	$12,705	$18,010
Total Financial Capital	$111,712	$74,299	$129,673	$136,425	$282,874
Insider Equity	1.9%	2.6%	1.6%	0.6%	1.8%
Insider Debt	6.0%	8.1%	5.6%	9.3%	6.4%

Source: Kauffman Firm Survey microdata, 2006

focused on a subsample of firms defined as having high growth potential (HGP). These firms were somewhat less reliant on insider financing in percentage terms, although HGP women were still more reliant than HGP men (9.9 percent vs. 8.2 percent).

Bootstrapping

As we noted in Chapter 4, bootstrapping and lean management as practiced using the Lean Startup Model are often confused, but, in fact, they are quite different. As we discussed, the Lean Startup Model represents an overall firm strategy to help early stage firms minimize waste in the form of time and resources by testing and refining elements of the firm's business model, thereby increasing its chance for survival. In contrast, bootstrapping is a very specific set of strategies designed to either minimize expenses or accelerate cash flows as a means for minimizing the firm's need to raise external financial capital.

In one of the earlier articles highlighting the importance of bootstrapping for new and informationally opaque firms, Harrison, Mason, and Girling (2004) described bootstrapping as "imaginative and parsimonious strategies for marshalling and gaining control of resources" (p. 308). They went on to note that there are two major "flavors" of bootstrapping. The first consists of strategies for raising capital without using formal providers of debt or equity such as banks or venture capitalists. The second pertains to strategies for acquiring resources without actually having to pay for them.

In a later article, Ebben and Johnson (2006) described bootstrapping as "finding creative ways to avoid the need for external financing through reducing overall costs of operation, improving cash flow, or using financial sources internal to the company" (pp. 851–852).

Both of these definitions help us understand why bootstrapping is such an appropriate strategy for early stage entrepreneurs who typically do not have access to formal sources of capital at that point in the firm's development. Bootstrapping also recognizes that early stage entrepreneurs are working with limited financial resources and cannot afford to pay for key inputs such as space, equipment, and labor. Alternatively, bootstrapping encourages them to acquire these resources through "imaginative" means.

What are some common bootstrapping strategies? Ebben and Johnson (2006) noted that different bootstrapping methods come into play at different stages of the firm's development. Some strategies are designed to minimize expenses, for example, "buy used instead of new equipment." Others are geared toward speeding up cash flow in ("offer customers discounts on up-front payments") or slowing down cash flow out ("deliberately delay payments to supplier"). Some bootstrapping methods draw upon the entrepreneur's personal resources ("obtain capital from founder's salary at another business"), while others draw upon resources that may be available in the community ("share business space with another firm").

Although we often tend to think of bootstrapping as a default financial strategy used by entrepreneurs who are unable to secure external capital, it is actually a very empowering financial strategy that can be employed at any point in time. In an article titled "Funding Gap, What Funding Gap?" Lam (2010) observes that bootstrapping allows entrepreneurs to actively manage their demand for and supply of entrepreneurial finance to narrow their funding gap. This perspective is important, because it puts the entrepreneur squarely in the driver's seat where she belongs. Lam's article highlights the fact that, although entrepreneurs must continually monitor and react to their environment, they are also in a position to shape it through their financial strategies and choices. Thus, measures such as foregoing a salary, using volunteer labor, or starting the firm from one's home are all strategies that can increase a firm's chances for survival and success during those critical early days and months.

In addition to its role in empowering early stage entrepreneurs, research suggests that bootstrapping skills and attitudes can also be adapted to the needs of firms during the later rapid-growth stage. Harrison, Mason, and Girling (2004) studied U.K. firms in the software industry to find that larger firms used different bootstrapping strategies from those used by small firms. In particular, the authors noted that larger firms were more reliant on strategies that relied on customer and supplier relationships as a means for generating resources. Similarly, Brush, Carter, Gatewood, and others (2006) studied a sample of women entrepreneurs to find that different bootstrapping techniques were used at different stages of development, consistent with Ebben and Johnson (2006). Their findings revealed, however, that firms in the rapid-growth stage of development were just as likely to use bootstrap financing as early stage firms. In fact, firms that had already acquired some type of external equity were significantly more reliant on bootstrapping, emphasizing the enduring nature of this financing strategy.

As with most sources of entrepreneurial finance, bootstrapping does not occur in a vacuum, and several studies emphasize the link between acquiring capital and the entrepreneur's ability to develop and utilize her social networks (Bruderl and Preisendorfer, 1998; Brush, Carter, Greene, and others, 2002). Within the context of bootstrap finance, Jones and Jayawarna (2010) studied over two hundred early stage ventures to find that social networks played a key role in the acquisition of bootstrapped resources. Further, their results revealed that both "weak ties" in the form of relationships with suppliers and customers and "strong ties" in the form of family and friend relationships were significant, depending on the type of bootstrapping activity. For example, the ability to delay payments may come about through positive relationships with suppliers (weak ties), whereas the ability to obtain free labor is more likely to be provided by family and friends (strong ties). In both cases, Jones and Jayawarna found that social networks had a positive effect on bootstrapping activities, which, in turn, had a positive effect on firm performance as measured by sales growth.

Credit Cards

Some studies categorize the use of credit cards as a particular type of boot-strapping strategy (Ebben and Johnson, 2006; Harrison, Mason, and Girling, 2004; Winborg and Landstrom, 2000). We have chosen to separate them out, however, because of their pervasive use as a means for early stage financing. In a study using data from the Kauffman Firm Survey, Scott (2009) found that 58 percent of firms used credit card debt as a source of financing during the firm's first year. Smaller firms tended to rely more heavily on this source, but 20 percent of larger firms launched with at least three employees also used credit card debt. As a source of early stage financing, credit cards offer the entrepreneur several advantages. First, they are readily available, and just about anyone can get one. Second, credit card debt is unsecured, making it particularly attractive to entrepreneurs who do not have assets that can be used as collateral. In a sense, a credit card serves as a line of credit that can be drawn upon as needed and used for a variety of purposes. Thus, the flexibility of credit card debt is a third important advantage.

The obvious disadvantage of credit card debt is that it is a very costly form of borrowing. Even in today's historically low interest rate environment, interest rates on unpaid balances are in the range of 15 to 21 percent. If we add in fees and late charges, the cost continues to climb. In light of the high cost, we might ask ourselves why a savvy entrepreneur would want to use credit cards as a source of financing at all. Typically, the answer is that she does not have a lot of other alternatives for borrowing. If her firm is new and unprofitable, she cannot get a bank loan for the business. Similarly, if she does not have personal assets such as a house that can be pledged as collateral, she cannot get a personal bank loan that could be used to fund her business. In light of that, availability often trumps cost when it comes to the entrepreneur's decision to use credit card debt. One caution in the use of credit card debt, however, is that it decreases the firm's likelihood of survival (Scott, 2009). High levels of debt obtained through one or multiple credit cards impose a financial burden that new firms with limited revenues may not be able to sustain. This is one of many risks that early stage entrepreneurs need to weigh and balance against the potential advantages of this particular financing source.

In this chapter we have examined four important sources of early stage financing: the entrepreneur's personal funds, support from family and friends, bootstrapping, and credit cards. Let's take a look at another early stage firm, Denizens Brewing Company, to see which of these various sources entrepreneur Emily Bruno used to launch her firm.

Emily Bruno and Denizens Brewing Company

Emily Bruno and her two co-founders, one male and one female, began planning for their firm, Denizens Brewing Company (http://www.denizensbrewingco.com), in January of 2013. Emily always knew that she wanted to have her own firm at some point, and she wanted to select a field that would provide opportunities for growth as well as financial and economic rewards for her as an entrepreneur. One of her co-founders, Emily's brother-in-law, is a brewer and has won awards for his talents in this area. That got Emily thinking about the possibility of launching a craft brewery in the Washington, D.C. area. She had always appreciated craft beers and was drawn to the social nature of the business as well as the ability to manufacture and sell a high-quality product. Although sales growth in the beer industry is relatively stagnant in the United States, the craft beer segment is still growing by double digits every year (http://www.brewersassociation.org; White, 2014). There are a few large national players such as Boston Beer, the maker of Sam Adams ales, but overall the craft beer segment is highly fragmented and comprises many small, local breweries (*The Boston Beer Company, Inc.*, 2000).

Emily's research revealed that the D.C. area is somewhat underserved by craft breweries when compared to other regions. She talked with her brother-in-law and her wife (the third founder), and Denizens Brewery became a reality with the goal of opening for business in June of 2014. Denizens' initial location was planned for downtown Silver Spring within steps of a busy Metro stop. The brewery serves European style lagers, American-style ales, and barrel-aged beers to craft beer enthusiasts as well as those just learning to appreciate the range and quality of craft beers. The venue consists of the brewery itself as well as a bar and beer garden, both of which will eventually serve food in addition to craft beers and other beverages.

In addition to wanting to launch a growth-oriented firm, Emily knew she wanted to work with a founding team rather than going it alone. She conducted further research on the success factors associated with growth-oriented firms, and found that those that were launched by teams generated higher revenues. She noted, "I don't see how one person could possibly do all the things that need to be done, particularly in a firm where achieving scale is an objective."

She further explained that the three founders for Denizens Brewing have complementary areas of expertise. Her brother-in-law is an accomplished brewer, as noted above, her partner is an attorney, and Emily has previous experience with project management as well as an in-depth understanding of entrepreneurial firms based on her time as the research and policy director of the National Women's Business Council. In addition to being able to split up the work that needs to get done, Emily noted that team members are a source of encouragement and emotional support for each other.

Being an entrepreneur can be a really lonely business. It is also a big responsibility. In our case, we raised $250,000 from family and friends. You can't just walk away from that if the business fails. Other people who are not entrepreneurs don't understand that.

During the pre-launch stage of its development, Denizens Brewing used a relatively flat organizational structure, so the three founders discussed major issues and shared decision making. Emily noted that this approach sometimes takes longer in terms of reaching an agreement than would be the case if one person were the CEO, but it works for them at the present time.

Founding as a team has also made it easier to raise early stage financing, because each of the founders provided social capital in the form of friends and family. These, in turn, provided financial support totaling $250,000. This "F&F round" positioned Denizens to go after additional financing in the form of a bank loan. Emily approached ten different banks and ultimately found only one that would consider lending her firm money as a part of a state-guaranteed loan program.

I couldn't believe how hard it was to get a bank loan. The three of us had a tremendous amount of accumulated professional experience, we had already raised $250,000 in six weeks, and I put up my house as collateral as well as the firm's manufacturing equipment. In addition, we had to put up personal guarantees. Even with all that, it took seven months to get the loan.

Asked about the borrowing experience itself, Emily commented,

I was dealing with all guys and I found I had to grovel somewhat, because I felt like I was being punished when I was assertive. They kept telling me that we were too young, but two of us are in their thirties and the third is in his late twenties. When do they think people start businesses? The business press is always touting these young guys in their teens or early twenties who start high-tech or social media firms as role models. And then we get told we're too young? There was also a tremendous amount of documentation required. They even wanted to know who was going to pick out the china. Do you really think they would have asked a male entrepreneur that question? In dealing with banks as lenders, we found that they are extremely risk averse and don't really have any metrics for evaluating new firms. They make decisions within a small box, and if you fall outside that box, they would rather not deal with you.

In addition to providing documentation and a detailed business plan, Emily lined up political support for her firm based on its potential to provide jobs and a positive economic impact. Ultimately, Denizens Brewing was approved for a state-guaranteed loan in the amount of $500,000. This was followed up with a $75,000 working capital loan provided through a local small business revolving loan program.

One of the aspects of entrepreneurship that Emily wanted to discuss was attitudes toward risk. Conventional wisdom has it that women are more risk averse than men, yet in Emily's case, she left a good job, put up her home as collateral, and pledged personal guarantees in order to launch her firm. These are not exactly the marks of a highly risk averse person. She also noted that risk is not necessarily a bad thing and, in fact, can serve as a powerful motivator for entrepreneurs.

We went through a really tough time last winter wondering if things were actually going to come together. One of the things that kept us going during those dark days was the knowl-

edge that we had taken other people's money. They believed in us and were counting on us, so throwing in the towel was not an option.

As we concluded our interview, Emily offered several pieces of advice to early stage entrepreneurs. Some pertain to financing while others are more general in nature:

1. When you start a new firm, there will be a lot of things you don't know. Don't let that overwhelm you, because you will figure things out as you move through the process. Take it one step at a time.

2. Bring people in for help when you need additional expertise. In our case, we sought out advice from mentors in the craft brewing industry as well as from our investors.

3. In terms of going after financial capital, be persistent, and never be the roadblock. If they ask for documentation, give it to them right away. That way, if there is a delay, it's on them, not on you. Never let them use your response, or lack of it, as an excuse to delay or deny funding.

Denizens Brewing Company began serving customers in July of 2014. Their offerings include five flagship beers on tap and four rotating seasonal brews with names such as "the shirtless horseman Russian imperial stout" and "big bad bohemian pale lager." Denizens has also partnered with the BBQ Bus to provide barbecue and "comfort food classics" onsite. In addition to describing their products and hours of operation, Denizens' website provides "inspirational" beer quotes. Our personal favorite, attributed to Kaiser Wilhelm, is "Give me a woman who loves beer and I will conquer the world." In spite of all their hard work, Emily and her co-founders are obviously enjoying themselves and anticipate revenues in excess of $1 million during their first full year of operations.

The National Women's Business Council

Emily Bruno learned a lot about what works and what doesn't in women's entrepreneurship during her time as director of research and policy for the National Women's Business Council (NWBC) (http://www.nwbc.gov). The NWBC was originally established as a part of the Women's Business Ownership Act of 1988. Prior to that time, women in many states were still required to have a male relative co-sign for a business loan. The NWBC was created as a nonpartisan federal advisory council to provide advice and guidance to the president, Congress, and the U.S. Small Business Administration on economic issues that are important to women business owners. To achieve this goal, the council conducts research on key issues, communicates its research findings widely, and provides a platform for change. The council's fifteen members include prominent women business owners as well as the leaders of major women's business organizations. The chair of the council is appointed by the president. Currently, the NWBC's research and activities are focused on four major "pillars": (1) access to capital, (2) access to markets, (3) job creation and growth, and (4) data collection. In the council's 2014 Annual Report, NWBC chair Carla A. Harris wrote,

> Women entrepreneurs have significantly increased their economic impact in the past few decades. Today, women business owners are the fastest growing segment of the economy. The Council remains committed to using research as a springboard for continued action and change as the landscape for women and entrepreneurship shifts. Our hope is to build bridges between influencers, institutions, and entrepreneurs, leveraging the power of research and collaboration, so that we can impact the business climate for women. The numbers confirm that the full economic participation of women and their success in business is critical to the continued economic recovery and job growth in this country—and we are honored to be part of the movement to impact and better the business climate for women. (*Building Bridges: 2014 Annual Report*, 2014, p. 3)

The Benefits and Challenges of Founding Teams

Like Emily Bruno, many growth-oriented entrepreneurs use a team approach to establish their firms (Schjoedt and Kraus, 2009; Vyakarnam, Jacobs, and Handelberg, 1999). As already noted, one of the primary benefits of founding with a team rather than as an individual is that the team is able to provide different types of human and social capital that can help the venture cope with environmental uncertainties and setbacks associated with new firm formation (Chowdhury, 2005). Prior research also suggests that team-based ventures perform better, thus improving their chances of attracting external funding (Baum and Silverman, 2004; Beckman, Burton, and O'Reilly, 2007).

In terms of founding team composition, some previous studies, particularly those focusing on board of director composition, suggest that demographic as well as experiential diversity leads to better decision making and superior performance (Campbell and Minguez-Vera, 2008; Kakarika, 2013; Post and Byron, 2015; Rodriguez-Dominguez, Garcia-Sanchez, and Gellego-Alvarez, 2012). These studies argue that gender diverse boards and entrepreneurial teams better reflect the diversity of potential customers and the economy overall. Further, diversity can enhance creativity and innovation as well as problem-solving ability, because a mixed gender group is more likely to generate and consider more potential solutions.

In spite of its benefits, researchers note that founding as an entrepreneurial team is not without risks (Schjoedt and Kraus, 2009). One such risk is the challenge of finding team members who actually have complementary rather than similar skills. We tend to know and be drawn to individuals who move in circles similar to our own rather than those who have different talents, interests, and social networks. In light of that, entrepreneurs may need to stretch beyond their comfort zones in assembling their teams. A second major risk is the potential for conflict among founding team members. This can pose threats to the venture's daily operations, its ability to raise financial capital, and even its prospects for survival.

The lesson from all this is that growth-oriented entrepreneurs should weigh the benefits of creating a founding team rather than going it alone. Simultaneously, however, they should choose their team members carefully to ensure that they can provide needed skills, experience, contacts, and resources. Finally, they should determine whether or not they can actually work elbow to elbow with potential team members through the inevitable ups and downs that accompany new venture formation and growth.

Closing the Loop

Early stage firms are particularly vulnerable. Although the entrepreneur has typically developed and even tested her revenue model, revenue generation is a relatively minor source of financing at this point. Similarly, external sources of financing are usually not an option, because the firm, its products, and its services are as yet still too new and untested. Thus, early stage firms are often highly resource-constrained and dependent on personal and internal sources of financing. Consistent with this, the entrepreneur's personal savings and wealth are a major early stage source. This poses a challenge for growth-oriented women entrepreneurs, because they tend to have lower earnings and less accumulated wealth than men. Similarly, family and childcare responsibilities can make it both difficult and costly for young women to pursue a path of growth. In response to these challenges, our interviews reveal that women often launch their growth-oriented firms as part of an entrepreneurial team. This team approach allows them to access a broader pool of savings and financial contacts, and it also allows for a distribution of labor that better accommodates work-life balance. Thus, the entrepreneur is less likely to be overwhelmed by the sense that she has to do everything herself. This chapter's entrepreneur, Emily Bruno, used the team approach for launching her craft brewery, Denizens Brewing Company, as a means for gaining access to talent and resources while also splitting up the various tasks that need to be accomplished.

Family and friends who believe in the entrepreneur and her vision are also important early stage investors. They supply capital in the form of loans, equity investments, outright gifts, and free labor or other types of support. F&F investors, in contrast to more formal providers of capital, are also more likely to be patient and forgiving investors, because they typically care more about the entrepreneur than about generating a financial return. Nevertheless, many an entrepreneur has learned the hard way that it can be dangerous to mix family and friends with money. If the firm is not successful, close relationships can end or suffer for years. One strategy for mitigating this risk is to spell out and document the terms of the loan, equity investment, or gift to clarify expectations and avoid potential misunderstandings down the road. An attorney with small business expertise can be used for this purpose. In spite of this risk, however, F&F investors often play a key role in providing early stage emotional support and encouragement. For novice entrepreneurs in particular, this "emotional capital" can be just as important as the financial capital provided. Emily Bruno, our Denizens Brewing entrepreneur, raised her initial financing round of $250,000 from family and friends and shared her difficulties in tapping into more formal types of financial capital in the form of bank loans. Nevertheless, the firm's ability to raise this early stage F&F capital positioned it to raise subsequent funds from other sources.

Although our third source of internal capital, bootstrapping, is often associated with smaller, lifestyle firms, it is actually a strategy that is applicable to growth-oriented firms as well, particularly during the early stages of development when resource constraints can be most pressing. Bootstrapping serves as a means whereby the entrepreneur can acquire needed resources in the form of talent, space, equipment, and capital at minimal expense. It is also a way for the early stage entrepreneur to stretch every dollar that she invests or raises to its limit. This is an essential strategy, because the more productivity she can generate from the capital and resources she invests, the greater the firm's chances for survival. In this sense, bootstrapping helps to position the firm for subsequent rounds of financing from external providers.

Taken from another perspective, bootstrapping is also a strategy that allows the entrepreneur to retain as much ownership and control as possible for a longer period of time. Thus, when she eventually does approach venture capitalists, she is able to do so with a larger and more established firm, thereby reducing the extent to which her equity position will suffer dilution from external rounds of funding. Some researchers caution, however, that growth-oriented entrepreneurs should be careful not to "over-bootstrap," because that can stifle the firm's ability to develop new products and services as well as its growth (Patel, Fiet, and Sohl, 2011). As with many aspects of entrepreneurial finance, bootstrapping represents a delicate balance between minimizing costs and maintaining ownership while also raising sufficient amounts of capital to fund the firm's growth.

Although Emily Bruno did not specifically comment on the use of credit cards to fund her business, a number of the women entrepreneurs we interviewed for our first book, A Rising Tide, indicated that credit cards were a common source of early stage financing. This should not surprise us given the difficulty of securing bank loans for firms that do not have a track record and are not yet profitable. In contrast, credit cards are readily available from multiple sources. As such, they represent an important part of the financing mix required to get the firm to a point where it can obtain other sources of capital.

What Does This Mean for You?

Early stage firms are firms that are "up and running," but still very new and typically not yet profitable. In light of that, it is extremely difficult for their founders to attract or secure external sources of financing in the form of angel investments, venture capital, or bank loans. In contrast, early stage firms are heavily reliant on the entrepreneur's personal financial resources and the support she can generate from those close to her. Our mini-case on Emily Bruno and Denizens Brewing highlights some of the financial strategies that can help entrepreneurs cope with the financial constraints they will encounter at this stage of their development.

1. Consider the possible advantages of founding your firm with a team rather than going it alone. Team members can provide a diverse array of skills, contacts, and networks. They can also provide larger amounts of personal financial capital than one person can by herself. By attending events in your startup community, like those mentioned in Chapter 4, you can find like-minded folks interested in the entrepreneurial process. A new website called Founder Dating (founderdating.com) is another resource for finding co-founders for your team.

2. If you plan to launch a growth-oriented firm, build up a personal financial "nest egg" to help you through the first couple of years. As we have shown, the entrepreneur's personal financial resources are a major source of financing, and this is particularly true for women. The more you can save and sock away prior to your firm's launch, the better.

3. Consider a family and friends round as a source of early stage financing. In Emily's case, Denizens was able to raise $250,000 by doing this. Begin a dialogue with family members and friends who may be willing and financially able to invest. If you do accept F&F funding, work with an attorney or an accountant to ensure that all parties understand the terms, conditions, and risks.

4. Find creative ways to acquire resources and manage your expenses. In this chapter we talked a lot about bootstrapping or strategies designed to minimize expenses. These strategies are critically important for early stage firms and play a key role in helping firms survive and grow. As researchers, we have personally become very fond of bootstrapping strategies, because they show how creative and resourceful highly motivated entrepreneurs can be. We'll talk about another source of financing, crowdfunding, which is also becoming an increasingly popular source of early stage financing, in Chapter 8.

5. Get your credit house in order. Emily Bruno's story illustrates the difficulties that new firms face in their attempts to secure bank loans for the business. In light of that, many early stage entrepreneurs rely on bank loans in their own name or on credit cards. Given their reliance on personal sources of debt during the firm's early stages, it is important for women to maintain good credit as a means for ensuring that they can access loans at a reasonable cost when they need them. This is also true in the case of credit cards.

Although credit card debt is expensive in general, individuals with better credit can obtain cards with better rates and lower fees.

6. Emily Bruno talked about the importance of "persistence" in seeking out early stage funding sources. Although Denizens Brewing was not able to obtain loans from nine different banks, they were able to secure a $500,000 loan from the tenth by using a state guaranteed loan program. Similarly, they obtained a $75,000 working capital loan through a local small business program. In other words, Emily's persistence in looking beyond the more obvious bank-lending products for other alternatives paid off in the end.

7. Never be the roadblock. Emily described the agonizingly slow process of getting approved for her state-guaranteed loan, a process that took seven months and reams of documentation. Nevertheless, she stuck to her guns and provided everything that was requested, because she was not going to give the lenders any excuse to turn her down. We see this pattern in our own states. Entrepreneurs leave money on the table because they do not want to go through the aggravation of filling out all the forms and answering all the questions. Our question to them, and to you, is "How much do you need the money"? If the answer is "a lot," it could be worthwhile to stick with the process in spite of the time and effort required. In general, early stage entrepreneurs grossly underestimate the time that they will have to invest in raising financial capital. This is particularly true for growth-oriented entrepreneurs who have to raise so much of it. Emily's message to us is "Invest the time; it's part of the process."

6

THE WHITE KNUCKLE FLIGHT

Survival Stage Strategies

for Growth-Oriented Firms,

Part I

In this chapter we will begin our discussion of the survival stage, which represents another critical time for growth-oriented entrepreneurs. This is the stage at which the business has started to generate revenues and acquire customers. Nevertheless, expenses far outstrip revenues, so the company is still unprofitable and the rate at which the company is burning through cash exceeds its ability to generate cash. At this point, there is a real risk that the company will fail because it simply runs out of the money needed to keep itself alive. For growth-oriented firms, angel investors are a key source of financing during the survival stage. This is the case because entrepreneurs have largely exhausted their internal sources of financing at this point. As we will show, the pursuit of angel capital represents a special challenge for growth-oriented women entrepreneurs who traditionally have received only a tiny percentage of angel and VC financing. In spite of these challenges, however, this chapter will describe strategies for finding, securing, and working with angel investors, as well as the advantages and disadvantages of doing so.

This chapter will also address the investor perspective by discussing the characteristics that angel investors look for in growth-oriented firms and growth-oriented entrepreneurs. In addition, we will describe changes that have occurred in the angel investor markets over the course of the last decade. These include the increasing sophistication of angel investors, the development of angel investor networks, and the changing preferences of angel investors in the wake of the financial crisis.

The Role of Angel Investors

Angel investors are high-net-worth individuals who invest in new firms. Often these individuals are professionals such as lawyers, doctors, or accountants who are looking for an attractive return on their investment. This motivation has become particularly compelling in our current low-interest-rate environment. In other instances, they are individuals who have gained experience and success in a particular industry and want to support other entrepreneurs in their field. Whereas venture capital firms are organized as financial intermediaries to invest other people's money, angel investors invest their own money, typically in smaller amounts ranging from $10,000 to $250,000. Like VCs, many angel investors also take an active role in the firm, particularly those who have prior managerial or industry experience. As an example, an angel investor might spend one or two days per week "on site" advising the entrepreneur and helping to guide the direction of the firm. Another similarity between angel investors and VCs is that both are "patient" investors in the sense that they are willing to commit financial capital for extended periods of time.

Although angel investors make smaller individual investments than venture capital firms, in aggregate they invest similar amounts in dollar terms. Angels invest in a greater number of companies, however, and in a relatively broad range of industries, making them an essential source of financing for many entrepreneurial firms (Figure 6.1). According to the University of New Hampshire's Center for Venture Research, the angel investor market continued the upward trend

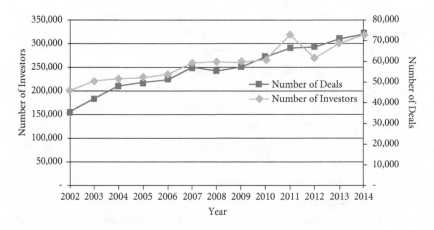

FIGURE 6.1. Angel Deals and Investors Over Time
Source: UNH Center for Venture Research, various years.

started in 2010 in investment dollars and in the number of investments (Sohl, 2014). In 2014, total investments reached $24.1 billion, a decrease of 2.8 percent over 2013. A total of 73,400 entrepreneurial ventures received angel funding in 2014, an increase of 3.8 percent over 2013 investments. The number of active investors in 2014 was 316,600 individuals, an increase of 6.0 percent from 2013. The decrease in total dollars in combination with the increase in the number of investments resulted in a deal size for 2014 that was lower than in 2013 (a decrease in deal size of 6.4 percent from 2013). The $24.1 billion in total investments is still close to the market high of $26.0 billion that occurred in 2007.

From the standpoint of the entrepreneur, angel investors are important because they are often willing to invest at an earlier stage of the firm's development than venture capitalists or banks. This willingness makes angel capital, like personal sources of finance, family and friends, and bootstrapping, a major source of financing in the "R&D" or nascent stage as well as in the startup and early growth stages. Statistics compiled by Professor Jeffrey Sohl at the University of New Hampshire found that in 2013, 21 percent of angel investments were made in the seed stage, while 41 percent occurred in the early stage (Sohl, 2014).

A fairly recent development in the angel investing "space" has been the creation of a growing number of angel investing networks. These networks provide a number of advantages. The first of these is that a network of investors is in a better position to secure, process, and communicate key information about target companies. This helps address the problem of informational asymmetry, which is inherent in new, privately held firms. A second major advantage is that, by pooling the financial resources of multiple investors, an angel network is able to attract and invest in larger deals. Thus, the network approach gets angel investors onto the radar screen of entrepreneurs who are launching firms in growth-oriented industries with attractive options for harvesting value. This brings us to the third advantage, which is that a network has the potential to generate a better deal flow. As we have seen in previous chapters, a big part of the entrepreneurial finance story is who you know and what they can do for you. Angel investing is no different in this respect. If you are a part of an angel network, you will probably see bigger and potentially better deals than you would as an individual investor.

Thanks to the development of angel groups and networks, the distinctions between angel and venture capital investing have become less pronounced. As noted above, by participating in networks, angel investors gain access to a better deal flow and are collectively able to invest larger amounts. Similarly, they are able to participate in multiple rounds of funding for firms that achieve their benchmarks over a period of time. Although the research does not yet reflect this, one might also anticipate that angel networks, like venture capitalists, are more attuned to performance metrics and harvest options than are individual angel investors.

Women and Angel Investing

The experience of women in angel investing has been mixed from the standpoint of women entrepreneurs seeking financial capital as well as from that of women as angel investors. Prior research conducted by entrepreneurship scholars John Becker-Blease and Jeffrey Sohl (2007) reveals that women receive only a small percentage of total angel capital, largely because they don't ask for it. This may be at least partially due to the fact that women tend to launch smaller firms on average, making them less likely to pursue external sources of growth capital. As an increasing number of women entrepreneurs are pursuing strategies to scale their firms, however, we would similarly anticipate that a greater number would want to tap into the market for angel investor capital. In the same study, Becker-Blease and Sohl found that those women who went after angel financing were just as likely to receive it as men, suggesting a problem of demand rather than one of supply. As a final point, Becker-Blease and Sohl found that women entrepreneurs were somewhat more likely to seek and receive funding from women angels. Conversely, men entrepreneurs were more likely to seek funding from male investors. Given the relatively small number of women angel investors, this finding has an indirect if not a direct effect on the supply of angel capital available to growth-oriented women entrepreneurs.

In a related study of British angel investors, researchers Richard Harrison and Colin Mason (2007) found few differences between female and male angel investors. They did find, however, that male investors had stronger networks than female investors, an important distinction, since networks are a major source of deal flow. Consistent with Becker-Blease and Sohl, they also found that women investors were slightly more likely to invest in women-owned firms, although the difference was not significant. One of the major findings from the Harrison and Mason study, however, was the relative invisibility of women angel investors due to their small numbers. Thus, the gender imbalance of angel investors may serve as a type of structural disadvantage for women seeking capital from that source.

One of the good bits of news on the angel investing front is that women's participation as both seekers and providers of funding is increasing. According to the University of New Hampshire's Center for Venture Research (Sohl, 2005), women-owned ventures represented 4.7 percent of entrepreneurs seeking angel capital and approximately 5 percent of angel investors in 2004. In 2014 however, women accounted for 36 percent of the entrepreneurs that were seeking angel capital, compared with 23 percent in 2013. In addition, women constituted 26.1 of the angel investor market, which is a 34.5 percent increase over 2013, when women only represented 19.4 percent of the market (Sohl, 2014). The yield rate was 15 percent for women, compared with 21.6 percent for men, and women-led ventures made up about 28 percent of the deals in 2014. These statistics reveal that there is still a fairly considerable gender imbalance, but the percentages are moving in the right direction.

What has prompted this change in the level of women's participation in the angel market? One important factor has been the emergence of groups such as 37 Angels, Springboard Enterprises, Astia Angels, MergeLane, and Golden Seeds that focus on working with growth-oriented women entrepreneurs and women investors. These organizations help women entrepreneurs prepare for presenting their companies to angel investors and venture capitalists and help train women investors. They also provide links between entrepreneurs and investors, thereby highlighting essential sources of social capital. In this sense, they help women entrepreneurs get a foot in the door. The first section of the Appendix provides a list of resources, including a sample of organizations like these that provide growth-oriented women entrepreneurs with coaching, mentoring, and connections to potential angel investors. A number of these organizations also provide deal flow for potential investors as well as training and preparation for women who want to become angel investors.

Angel investor groups targeting women entrepreneurs serve an important unmet need at the present time, given the smaller percentage of women who receive angel capital or serve in the role of angel investors. These groups are helping to train and develop a critical mass of growth-oriented women entrepreneurs and women investors who will help level the playing field. As noted earlier, several studies have commented on a certain degree of "homophily" within the market for angel capital (Becker-Blease and Sohl, 2007; Harrison and Mason, 2007), in that male entrepreneurs are more likely to seek funding from male investors, while the reverse is true for women entrepreneurs. This creates an obvious problem for women entrepreneurs in an environment in which there are relatively few women angels. In a subsequent study, Becker-Blease and Sohl (2011) found that having a few token women angel investors did not do the trick either and actually resulted in a lower level of funding approvals. This led them to conclude that when women investors have minority status within an angel investing group, they have less confidence and are less willing to invest. Alternatively, however, Becker-Blease and Sohl found that when the percentage of women investors in an angel group exceeded 10 percent, their levels of investment were comparable to those of men. From the standpoint of women entrepreneurs, these findings attest to how important it is for angel investor groups to diversify their mix of investors as well as the firms they consider for investment.

Entrepreneur Perspectives: Peggy Cross and Ecotensils

Peggy Cross refers to herself as a quirk of nature.

I have always known I wanted to develop a product. When I was a junior in college, I knew I'd be in packaging, that I would live for some time in New York and some time in San Francisco, and that after working in packaging I'd start my own packaging firm.

Peggy did, in fact, work in marketing for packaging firms in New York and San Francisco, when the idea of ecopackaging started to gain visibility. She shared with us how, in 2006, spoon lids came out of a perfect storm of (1) her love for packaging and marketing, (2) her search for a product that she could take to market, and (3) being a mom with younger kids and understanding the convenience of packing nutritious lunches all the time. Peggy pointed out that many nutritious products such as applesauce and yogurt need a utensil. Her environmental focus combined with the desire to make a contribution in terms of environmental impact led Peggy to the idea of the ecotensil. Sustainable and cost effective, it was a product that solved several problems. It became clear to Peggy that there was sufficient demand after talking to big yogurt companies, but there were also challenges:

1. How do you get the utensil onto the cup?

2. How do you educate the consumer?

3. How do you gauge consumer acceptance?

While Peggy's initial company idea in 2006 was for spoonlids, she launched Ecotensils in 2010 with an initial product called the Eco-taster, a paper tasting spoon, as a go-to market strategy.

It worked like a charm. We knew we had to grow the tasting spoon market so we utilized in-store demos. Consumers would get experience with a paper utensil, which would prove our market acceptance, which would get us buy-in from companies. Now we've proved our acceptance and education, which was a long process. The tasting spoon was really a means to an end. Now these groups can do their one-package utensils, spoonlids, which was the original product idea as well as the ecotensil product with higher profit margins.

Getting people to try the product was one of the biggest challenges because paper utensils are a new product, and it became clear that customers needed to try them out before they would buy. Peggy attended many trade shows to build credibility. There were upstream challenges as well, because the individuals she spoke with then had to sell it up the chain of command in their respective companies. Through this process, Peggy recognized that finding ways to move the product through the chain of approval was the hump her firm needed to get over. In response, she invested considerable time and energy helping the people she spoke with achieve that goal.

In terms of startup financing, Peggy invested roughly $50,000 of her own funds for the first three years before her firm began selling products, for things like patents, attorneys' fees, and prototyping. By the time she sought out angel investing in 2012, she was well into production and had raised another $150,000 from friends and family. Her original goal for the angel round was $650,000, but she ended up with $860,000.

When asked to describe the experience of raising angel capital, Peggy replied,

Torture. It took nine months to raise the capital; the first eight months there was nothing and then in the last month all this capital came flooding in. It was torture because I was out raising money, which was hard and I wasn't focused on growing the business. It took so long and I was naive going into the process. I started with Keiretsu,[1] and it was a steep learning process and took five months. But out of that we got one investor that was a key player for us. So in return for more equity he became my advocate and mentor for raising more capital. We came up with a plan, he helped me refine my pitch and my slide deck, and he helped me get more polished. We went to eight different angel groups, and it was a time-consuming process. It pushed back our revenue projections, because we were small then. During that time, I was focused on fundraising, and I was not able to grow our business. At the end I liked it because I was getting good, but in the beginning it was torture. To get up and talk in front of a big group of grey hair and suits . . . I wasn't used to that. And then to have a full room of people talking about things that were new to me was quite a hurdle to get over. I'm someone who is not at all from that background; I'm from marketing. I never really did numbers. I'm organized, but not a numbers person.

When asked if she felt she'd have raised the funds faster if she had known more about the process up front, Peggy responded,

I never went through an incubator; maybe that would have helped. I just thought, oh I don't have time to figure out the incubator thing . . . I'm already selling product, going on my own. . . . But in terms of capital raised, introductions they could have made, maybe I'd be further down the road if I had gone through the incubator program. . . . I haven't tapped into resources like networks; it's time-consuming and I often just default to my time is better spent trying to do stuff myself. Networking has never been a strong suit of mine. Early on, it would have been great to have a partner (but not 50-50) who liked to do that stuff. . . .

Incubators Versus Accelerators: What's the Difference?

In our interview with Peggy Cross, she referred to the benefits she might have derived if she had participated in an incubator. In fact, Peggy did participate in Astia, a business accelerator focusing on growth-oriented women-owned firms.[2] What is the difference between the two? The terms *incubator* and *accelerator* are often used interchangeably, and this definitional confusion has made it difficult to identify the discrete activities of each as well as their respective impacts on new and growing firms. A growing body of research helps us clarify the two terms, however, and determine their similarities and differences (Hackett and Dilts, 2004).

For starters, both are dedicated to helping early stage firms get off the ground and circumvent some of the problems associated with the "liability of newness." Both also provide advice and a range of other support services. That's pretty much where the similarities end.

Incubators have been in existence for some time, and they typically provide physical space for startup companies. The majority of incubators are nonprofit entities, and they are often associated with universities, state or municipal governments, or research facilities. Early stage firms are housed within the incubator for a period of time usually ranging from one to five years. In addition to having a physical space in which to operate, these firms have access to support services in the form of training; industry contacts; and access to professional service providers such as attorneys, accountants, consultants, marketing specialists, angel investors, venture capitalists, and volunteers. Often, incubators have economic development goals in the form of facilitating technology transfer, diversifying the region's mix of industries, and job creation. One of the criticisms that has been leveled at incubators, however, is that in their desire to fill the incubator space, they sometimes accept or retain firms that will not ultimately be viable.

A thought-provoking article by Syracuse University professors Alejandro Amezcua and Alexander McKelvie (2011) found that incubators are particularly beneficial to women entrepreneurs. They conducted a study of over eighteen thousand incubated firms to find that women-owned incubated firms outperformed not only women-owned non-incubated firms but men-owned non-incubated and incubated firms as well in measures of survival rate, sales growth, and employment growth. Simultaneously, however, these authors found that the post-incubation performance of women-owned firms decreased significantly, leading them to conclude that the environment outside of the incubator continues to present significant obstacles that prevent women from growing their firms. Alternatively, the authors hypothesize that in order to satisfy their own goal of maintaining a "full house," incubators may encourage and allow women to persist with ventures that have a high risk of failure in the external market.

In contrast to incubators, accelerators are a relatively recent phenomenon. The first accelerator was Y Combinator, established in Northern California in 2005. The accelerator model consists of a short-term and highly intensive program typically lasting for sixty to ninety days designed to help entrepreneurs bring their product to market and connect with potential funding sources. Entrepreneurs are provided with a rigorous program of training, mentoring, and technical assistance to help them grow their firms rapidly (Dempwolf, Auer, and D'Ippolito, 2014). Participants move through the accelerator program as a part of a cohort, thereby establishing lasting relationships with members of their group. The process is highly selective, with a focus on those firms most likely to succeed and grow in specific industries such as software design or mobile application development (Dempwolf, Auer, and D'Ippolito, 2014).

Whereas the majority of incubators are publicly or university-owned and operated, most accelerators are privately owned. While many accelerators do not provide space outside the duration of the program, they do provide seed funding for which they take a portion of each firm's equity. The culminating event of each cohort-based group is a pitch or demo day in which the entrepreneurs "pitch" their firm to groups of angel investors and venture capitalists. In this sense, accelerators are designed to help close the funding gap for early stage firms and the information gap for potential investors (Dempwolf, Auer, and D'Ippolito, 2014). Because accelerators are so new, it has been difficult to evaluate their actual effectiveness and results. Researchers Susan Cohen and Yael Hochberg (2014) report that an average of 41 percent of accelerator graduates receive subsequent financing within one year of financing. As of 2011, however, only 4 percent of graduates had successfully exited through an IPO or sale of their firm. In quoting these statistics, the authors note that accelerators may not have been around long enough to fairly evaluate their impact on successful exits.

The Global Accelerator Network (GAN) (www.gan.co) is a membership of organizations using the seed-stage, mentorship-driven accelerator model and includes fifty of the most respected accelerators from six continents around the world. Their goal is simple: support the top accelerators that grow top companies. Their members, mentors, investors, founders, and strategic partners have achieved some impressive early numbers. They note that founders in GAN accelerators average over half a million dollars in funding. In total, firms have raised nearly a billion dollars as of April 2015, and the accelerated companies have generated employment for thousands of people.

In terms of women's participation in incubator or accelerator programs, prior research suggests that women are even less well represented than they are in entrepreneurship overall. In their study, which includes data on 18,400 firms, Amezcua and McKelvie (2011) found that only 1,150 firms, or roughly 6 percent, were owned by women. This gender imbalance has prompted some researchers to suggest that, rather than providing a protected and neutral environment, incubators perpetuate the masculine norm for what a successful entrepreneur looks like (McAdam and Marlow, 2010; Marlow and McAdam, 2012; 2013). Thus, women participants simply swap a hostile external environment for an equally hostile internal one. Although we were not able to find a gender breakdown for accelerator participants, given their technology focus it is very likely that women are in the minority in that environment as well (Garber, 2013).

Does this mean that women entrepreneurs should avoid incubators and accelerators? Absolutely not! If you have launched a firm with the potential for significant and rapid growth, you should explore all of the potential resources that are available to you. Some accelerators, such as Springboard Enterprises and MergeLane, focus specifically on women-owned firms to ensure that participants gain access to funding sources and have the opportunity to build a network that includes women supporting other women. Other leading accelerators, such as Y Combinator, 500 Startups, and Techstars, serve both women- and men-owned firms. For these options, ask what the gender mix has been for past cohort participants. Also ask about success metrics for past women participants. How many have received follow-on financing? How many have had successful exits? If women are relatively well represented in an accelerator that accepts both genders, you are likely to encounter an environment that is more gender neutral and hospitable. Conversely, if only a small percentage of participants are women, this may suggest that the program is geared more toward the more traditional male stereotype of the entrepreneur. Depending on your personality and the thickness of your skin, you may or may not be comfortable in that type of setting.

The Springboard Enterprises Accelerator

As noted earlier, one of the major business accelerators to focus specifically on women-owned firms was Springboard Enterprises. Springboard Enterprises, which we introduced in Chapter 2, was founded in 1999 and describes itself as "a highly-vetted expert network of innovators, investors, and influencers who are dedicated to building high-growth technology-oriented companies led by women" (https:/sb.co). It achieves this goal by sourcing, advising, and showcasing firms that meet these criteria through a variety of programs and activities. One of these is the Springboard Accelerator. Each year two accelerator cohort programs are conducted, one in life sciences and the second in digital media and technology. Approximately twenty-five to thirty companies participate in each cohort. A key component of the accelerator program is an intensive boot camp that focuses on both the content and the delivery of the company's presentation for investors. Cohort companies are also assigned a personal advisory team that advises the entrepreneur on business strategy and provides contacts and connections relevant for her firm. Following the completion of their accelerator experience, the participants are provided with opportunities to present to groups of investors, industry experts, and other individuals capable of providing valuable connections. Springboard describes the types of women entrepreneurs it is looking for as

- Entrepreneurs who are receptive to coaching and feedback.

- Entrepreneurs whose identified needs align with relationships and expertise we have in our network.

- Entrepreneurs at or about to be at an inflection point of growth.

- Entrepreneurs in whom we can make a long term investment of human capital, and who in turn will invest back in Springboard. (https://sb.co)

Since 2000, 545 women entrepreneurs have participated in the Springboard Accelerators, raising $6.5 billion in financing. This, in turn, has allowed these firms to grow, generating billions of dollars in revenues each year and creating thousands of new jobs. In terms of its success rate, 83 percent of Springboard companies are still in business. Eleven of these firms, including familiar names such as Minute Clinic, Zipcar, and iRobot, have gone public (https://sb.co).

A relatively new entrant into the accelerator space is MergeLane, a new accelerator based in Boulder, Colorado, that discovers, accelerates, and invests in exceptional women and the companies they run. Their first cohort of eight firms started in February of 2015. Their unique model has a reduced residency requirement that enables entrepreneurs with family commitments to participate. While MergeLane requires entrepreneurs to participate in person during the first two weeks and the last week of the twelve-week program in Boulder, it complements that requirement with virtual mentoring and mentor connections in the companies' place of residence to ensure connection throughout the program. The curriculum targets the most critical early stage business issues as well as topics specifically affecting women leaders. MergeLane also provides connections to high-value, gender- and industry-diverse mentors and investors throughout the entire program. It puts a strong focus on accelerating businesses and leaders and building great companies as compared to focusing on a one-off demo-day pitch (http://mergelane.com).

Perspectives of an Angel Investor:
Jo Anne Miller and Golden Seeds

Like Springboard Enterprises, Golden Seeds is an organization that focuses on developing and funding growth-oriented women-owned ventures as well as women who have the potential to invest in them. Jo Anne Miller is a managing director for the Golden Seeds Angel Network. She is also a partner in Milk Street Ventures and a co-founder of SLO (San Luis Obispo) Seed Ventures. In terms of human and social capital, Jo Anne has more than thirty years of tele-communications and computer industry experience in general management, software and hardware systems development, and software engineering and product management for wireless and data communications products. After ten years of entrepreneurial venture-backed startups in cellular and wire line infrastructure equipment manufacturing, she moved into early stage investing in 2003. In addition to her professional qualifications, Jo Anne has an MBA from the University of Chicago, an MS in computer science from the University of Colorado, and a BS in mathematics from the University of Michigan.

When we asked Jo Anne about common mistakes made by entrepreneurs raising angel capital, she responded that one common mistake was not imagining a large enough market or thinking big enough. She stated that women need to "think bigger and take bigger risks." She also said women, even women launching technology-based firms, often "don't feel that they can be a CEO or CTO . . . they think they need to find a male lead on that even if they have a tech background." Consistent with this observation, Jo Anne has noted that women entrepreneurs often go into consumer products, because those types of firms are easier to scale and are in their comfort zones, even if they have a background in technology.

When asked why women entrepreneurs raise too little capital, Jo Anne observed that

women may not be asking for too little per se, but in thinking overall, they might be too conservative in how they are going to spend money and how much total capital they are going to need to get from point A to point B.

With respect to how women pitch their firms, Jo Anne indicated that she definitely sees women coming across with lower confidence levels and deferring to men too often in cases in which there are founding teams. As for pitching to female investors, there are both advantages and disadvantages. One advantage is that women may have a greater comfort level pitching to an investor of the same gender. Alternatively, however, this can create a false sense of security if there is a perception that the investor will be more lenient because she is a woman.

Jo Anne's key recommendations for growth-oriented women entrepreneurs who plan to seek angel or VC funding:

1. Build a strong team and make sure you are pitching something that has a big enough or potentially big enough market.

2. Be thinking about how you want to exit before you pitch.

3. Practice your pitch. Be believable.

4. Take risks! Be passionate, persistent, and willing to put it out there in order to be a really big success, not just big enough.

5. It's hard. You will hear a lot of NOs, you need to have perseverance.

Jo Anne Miller's perspectives as an experienced angel investor are valuable because they highlight some of the points that have been raised in prior research. First, women entrepreneurs don't "think big enough," and because of that they don't raise enough capital to grow their firms to their full potential. Jo Anne's comments suggest that women entrepreneurs need to develop a long-term vision for their firm and its potential rather than focusing exclusively on more immediate needs. This will help them to pursue funding consistent with the big picture. Second, women tend to lack confidence in their ability to navigate the fundraising process. This acts as a signal and can resemble dumping a bucket of blood into a shark tank. Women entrepreneurs need to be able to project confidence, and the best way to achieve that is to know their business and industry from the inside out. This gives them an inherent advantage over investors. Accelerators such as the Springboard Accelerator and MergeLane can help growth-oriented women entrepreneurs prepare and practice their "pitch," so when they get in front of a group of investors, they are ready. Finally, women entrepreneurs may assume that women investors will "give them a break." Studies suggest that women investors are more willing to consider investing in women-owned firms, but they use essentially the same investment criteria for women as for men. In other words, there are no "breaks." Thus, women entrepreneurs need to anticipate the same level of due diligence and questioning from women investors as from men.

Entrepreneur Perspectives: Chinwe Onyeagoro and FundWell[3]

When Chinwe Onyeagoro set out to launch FundWell, a loan-matching service for small businesses, she already had seven years of entrepreneurial success behind her, having previously co-founded and run O-H Community Partners, a consulting firm devoted to helping organizations raise substantial amounts of capital. During that time, she helped clients raise $120 million in grants, loans, tax incentives, and government subsidies (http://www.thefundwell.com). Recognizing the same unmet need in the small business sector, Chinwe decided to turn her financial and fundraising expertise to that sector.

FundWell was launched in 2011 with the mission of "helping small businesses get more and better access to low-cost capital" (http://www.thefundwell .com). To achieve this goal, FundWell focuses on expanding small firms' access to capital through its national network of lenders and by providing financial education. In this sense, Onyeagoro learned from the mistakes of many well-intentioned programs that provide funding for small firms but do not provide the types of education and training that help the entrepreneur make good choices for her firm.

FundWell's clients include small firms throughout the United States that generate at least $100,000 in revenues and have no prior bankruptcies. Through its loan-matching and financial wellness platform (http://www.thefundwell .com), FundWell matches business borrowers with up to three lenders for free. In addition, they provide loan education and assistance to help borrowers select the loan that is best for their firm. Loans can be for as little as $500 or as much as $2 million, and carry varying interest rates. Loans can also come in different forms, including bank loans, SBA loans, equipment loans, factoring, peer-to-peer loans, cash advances, and the like. In addition to loan matching, FundWell provides a Financial Wellness Program designed to educate small business owners and help them prepare for securing capital to fund future growth opportunities. This program includes a customized financial action plan as well as tips and advice to help firm owners improve their financial health over time.

From a financing perspective, Onyeagoro had an inherent advantage in that she had already launched one successful entrepreneurial venture and in doing so developed an extensive national network of contacts. Initially, FundWell was developed as part of her consulting firm's product line. Onyeagoro estimates that approximately $250,000 in profits from O-H Community Partners was devoted to developing this new line of business. Recognizing its longer-term potential, however, Chinwe and her associates decided to spin off FundWell and create a separate entity in 2011. During 2012, Chinwe and her co-founder were running the two businesses while an additional $300,000 in profits from the consulting firm were used to fund FundWell. Ultimately the decision was made that one of the co-founders would stay on to run O-H Community Partners, while the other, Chinwe, would focus on growing the new venture. To that end, she raised $400,000 in seed funding from angel investors in 2013. This round of funding allowed her to grow FundWell's client base of small firms from three thousand in December 2012 to seven thousand by December 2013. During that same time frame, the dollar volume of loan applications increased from $3 million to $6.4 million.

When asked if FundWell's location in the heart of Silicon Valley made it easier to raise that initial round, Chinwe laughingly responded, "Not at all!" In fact, several factors worked together to make fundraising a challenge. The first of these was the nature of FundWell's business. Although its loan-matching service is based on the use of technology, FundWell is not a traditional high-tech business founded by engineers or computer scientists. Thus, although Chinwe was able to get a number of meetings with potential funders, most of those discussions never advanced to the next level. A second factor was the Silicon Valley culture itself. Because entrepreneurship is such a prominent part of the ecosystem, funders are reluctant to say no to anyone, because you never know who might emerge as the next big success story. According to Chinwe, funders will meet with you and then meet with you again, and again, and again, a process that she refers to as "treading water." This leads us to the third factor, which Chinwe feels was her own failure to manage the funding process properly by being able to discriminate between serious funders and those who were just fishing. Rather than getting caught up in an endless loop of meetings to nowhere, Chinwe indicates that "You have to constantly be driving toward a close date in order to smoke out who's serious and who's not." She points out that it is difficult to exert this kind of pressure when you don't have a lead investor in place.

A fourth and final factor was the mismatch between Onyeagoro's expectations for the firm's stage of development and those of angel investors. Through her experience in raising the seed round, Chinwe found that angels had a much higher level of expectations for performance and progress than she anticipated would be required for a startup firm. "It was like dealing with Series A investors masquerading as angels." In spite of these challenges, Chinwe emphasizes that she learned valuable lessons from her seed round experience. When we spoke, she was planning to raise a Series A round in June of 2014, and felt that she was much better prepared.

In reflecting on Fundwell's first three years, Onyeagoro shared the following observations:

1. Traditional venture capitalists and angel investors base their decisions on "pattern recognition." In other words, they look for certain characteristics such as the quality of the management team, previous industry experience, and prior successful exits.

2. The entrepreneur needs to manage the fundraising process. It is like a campaign, and you don't necessarily know who will fund you and who won't. In light of that, "leave no stone unturned, and check your preconceived notions at the door."

3. It takes longer to raise capital than anticipated, and it costs money to do so. You need to develop and prepare presentations that will be letter- and picture-perfect, and you have to fly around the country to talk to potential investors. Be prepared for that and have a cushion of cash that will allow you to pay for these types of expenses.

4. Create an advisory board with credentials that will help you achieve your goals. Find individuals who can fill in the gaps in your own skill set. The advisory board is particularly valuable in terms of providing guidance and contacts during the early stages because the firm has not yet had time to develop its own track record and credibility.

5. Networking is essential, but some networking avenues are more productive than others. In Chinwe's case, she found that her most valuable sources of contacts were her advisory board and clients from her first business. Alternatively, "general networking" through angel investor events and boot camps was less productive.

Disruptive Technology Meets Angel Investing: The Emergence of AngelList

AngelList (https://angel.co) was developed by Naval Ravikant, an entrepreneur and investor, and Babak Nivi, an experienced venture capital investor. Their goal was to solve one of the most pressing problems in the entrepreneur's search for financial capital, the fragmentation and opacity of the angel investor market. Specifically, it is very difficult for entrepreneurs and angel investors to find and evaluate each other. In response to this unmet need, the two decided to launch Venture Hacks, a blog for entrepreneurs, in 2007. Once the blog was up and running, Ravikant and Nivi found that they were routinely asked for referrals to potential investors. As they responded to a growing number of these inquiries, it occurred to them that they could apply the same type of matchmaking and information-sharing techniques used on websites such as Craigslist, Facebook, and LinkedIn to angel investing (Nanda and Kind, 2013). Encouraged by the positive response to Venture Hacks, Ravikant and Nivi launched AngelList in 2012 with the goal of bringing entrepreneurs and angel investors together through an electronic marketplace.

The resulting AngelList platform is similar to popular social networking sites. Entrepreneurs can create a profile describing their leadership team and its qualifications, their product or service, progress or milestones to date, and proof of concept. When this has been done, AngelList applies an algorithm to screen firms in order to identify those that are most promising. Those firms, in turn, are "featured" on the AngelList website.

In like fashion, investors create a profile that includes information on their background, current portfolio, and anticipated amount of investments during the coming year. Only accredited investors, or those with a net worth in excess of $1 million, can participate on the site. Once approved for listing, each investor is provided with his or her own page, which includes featured companies, companies the investor is advising or following, and past and current investments. A valuable feature of the site is that it allows investors as well as entrepreneurs to "follow" each other. Thus, a somewhat inexperienced investor can "follow" an investor who has a track record for success and see what investments he or she is selecting. In addition to providing a forum for individual investors, AngelList also allows investors to establish "syndicates" as a way to raise and invest larger amounts of capital.

Ravikant and Nivi realized that the AngelList platform could also be used to serve a broader purpose than helping individuals who seek and provide funding. They noted that many startup ventures fail, leaving talented managers and workers without jobs. In turn, many startups that do succeed need the same type of talented managers and workers to help them grow. In response to this need, Ravikant and Nivi set up a talent-matching service on AngelList that allows available managers and workers to post their credentials for startup firms seeking employees with specific talents or experience.

AngelList's 2014 results are published on its website (https://angel.co). During that year, $104 million was raised from a total of 2,673 investors, providing funds for 243 startups. In addition to individual investors, 110 groups or syndicates invested through AngelList in 2014. In terms of its talent-matching service, 116,000 job seekers posted their qualifications and 8,000 firms sought employees through the site over the course of the year, yielding 207,000 matches.

As we write this chapter, AngelList is still too new for us to evaluate its full impact. In particular, it is unclear as to whether the AngelList platform provides broader access to growth-oriented women-owned firms or, alternatively, if its algorithms and screening process perpetuate the same type of structural barriers that have plagued women entrepreneurs in the angel and venture capital markets to date. A quick scan of the firms listed on the AngelList website reveals that the vast majority are headed by men, although a number show mixed-gender teams. It is our hope, however, that over time, the AngelList platform will serve as one more way to increase the visibility and potential of women-owned firms and to provide them with a broader array of alternatives for financing their growth.

Closing the Loop

In this chapter we have highlighted the critical role played by angel investors during the survival stage. At this point in the financial growth cycle, the firm may have products, services, and even revenue, but its sources of capital fail to cover its funding requirements. This is particularly true for growth-oriented firms that, by their very nature, consume larger amounts of capital. Angel capital often serves as a bridge between the entrepreneur's personal sources of capital and her ability to secure venture capital funding. In this sense, the entrepreneur's search for angel capital and the negotiations associated with obtaining it are valuable preparation for her subsequent pursuit of VC funding.

Angel investors are more idiosyncratic than venture capitalists in the sense that they often are motivated by personal as well as financial factors. Due to these mixed motivations, angels are also somewhat more patient and forgiving than VCs, who invest significantly larger amounts of capital and are responsible for delivering financial returns to their investors. Nevertheless, as Chinwe Onyeagoro's experience indicates, angel investors are becoming increasingly sophisticated and more like venture capitalists in their expectations and requirements. One factor that has contributed to this is a trend toward angel investor networks. These networks, such as the Golden Seeds Angel Network, are organized and led by experienced investment professionals like Jo Anne Miller. By pooling the financial resources of multiple investors, they are also able to provide larger amounts of funding.

As prior research has noted, women investors have traditionally been conspicuously absent from the angel investing space. This "gender divide" in angel investing has hampered women entrepreneurs' ability to raise angel capital. More recently, however, a growing number of angel investing networks are focusing specifically on funding growth-oriented women entrepreneurs. At the same time, these networks, such as Golden Seeds and Astia, are seeking out and developing high-net-worth women who have the potential to become angel investors. These are all positive developments for women entrepreneurs, because increasing the number of angel investors will also have the effect of increasing the pool of available angel capital. Similarly, because of the pattern of "homophily" that has been observed in angel investing, increasing the number of women investors will benefit women entrepreneurs in particular.

What Does This Mean for You?

The survival stage is just what it sounds like. Revenues are not yet sufficient to cover costs, and the firm is in grave danger of running out of cash to fund its daily operations and longer-term growth. At this point, also, the entrepreneur has typically exhausted internal sources of financing, including funds provided by the owner herself, friends, and family. In this chapter, our conversations with entrepreneurs Peggy Cross (Ecotensils) and Chinwe Onyeagoro (FundWell) and angel investor Jo Anne Miller (Golden Seeds) highlight some of the strategies that work for growth-oriented women entrepreneurs during this critical stage.

1. Cash goes out faster than it comes in. During the survival stage, revenues always come in slower and expenses go out faster than you anticipate. Once Peggy Cross developed her initial product, the Eco-taster, she encountered significant challenges in getting the product through the approval process of large companies. During this time she relied on personal sources of financing as well as capital provided by family and friends. She recognized, however, that additional external capital would be required to get her firm over the hump.

2. As FundWell's Chinwe Onyeagoro observed, "it takes longer to raise capital than anticipated and it costs money to do so." Onyeagoro stressed the need for planning and preparation and compared raising financial capital to managing a campaign. In light of that, she cautions new entrepreneurs to create a "cash cushion" to help them with the expenses and delays associated with raising capital.

3. The angel investing space is changing. Chinwe Onyeagoro alerted us to the changing expectations of angel investors. As angels have become more sophisticated, and as they have migrated toward angel networks, their funding behavior and expectations more resemble those of venture capitalists rather

than those of more traditional angel investors, many of whom invested for personal as well as financial reasons. In response to this trend, you need to be prepared to supply performance metrics and other measures of your firm's progress to date.

4. Build a strong team. Both Chinwe and angel investor Jo Ann Miller emphasized the qualifications of the entrepreneurial team and advisory board. As we discussed in Chapter 5, entrepreneurial teams provide several important advantages, including greater diversity in skills and experience combined with access to different networks and contacts. Prior research reveals that the majority of growth-oriented firms are, in fact, established by teams rather than by individuals. In light of that, the survival stage could be the ideal time for you to start building out your leadership team and advisory board, something that external providers of capital including angels and VCs will look at carefully.

5. Think big and take risks. After years of evaluating firms and working with entrepreneurs, Jo Anne Miller observes that women entrepreneurs often don't "think big enough." Thus, women don't raise enough financial capital to grow their firms to their full potential. Jo Anne advises women entrepreneurs to develop a long-term vision for their firm and what it can become. This vision will sustain you through your entrepreneurial journey, and it will help you avoid fixating exclusively on daily concerns and setbacks. An added benefit of having a long-term vision is that it forces you to think about your planned exit strategy early on. This is also something that you should be prepared to talk about when you start reaching out to external investors.

6. Consider all your options. One of our favorite quotes in this chapter is Chinwe Onyeagoro's advice that entrepreneurs "leave no stone unturned." We could not have put it better! Consistent with this advice, we have included information on incubators and accelerators in this chapter. Both share the mission of working with early stage firms and helping them acquire the resources they will need to survive and grow.

7. Perfect your pitch. Accelerator programs typically culminate in a "pitch event" or "demo day." This provides an opportunity for entrepreneurs who have participated in the program to pitch their firm to potential investors. The pitch is a short presentation, typically accompanied by slides, that summarizes the unmet need, the way in which the firm will address that need

(the firm's value proposition), and the resources required to do so (Santinelli and Brush, 2013). Golden Seeds managing director Jo Anne Miller urges entrepreneurs to perfect and practice their pitch; to ensure that it is letter perfect. A pitch event represents a unique opportunity for growth-oriented entrepreneurs to capture the attention and interest of angel investors, who will see a number of pitches as a part of the event. Make sure that yours is memorable!

7

BRAVE NEW WORLD

Survival Stage Strategies

for Growth-Oriented Firms,

Part II

As we discussed in Chapter 6, the survival stage is often the "make or break it" point for growth-oriented firms. In this chapter we will focus on an important but often overlooked source that can provide funding or other types of support, the government. We also discuss some sources of support in the cities and regions around the country that can provide a number of different resources for you as you begin to scale your company. Although we have all heard the joke, "I am from the government and I am here to help you . . . ", in the case of growth-oriented firms, and particularly those firms that are developing new technologies, it is actually true.

Let's begin with a discussion of government programs and sources of support. These are available at the federal, state, and often local levels. Government at all levels has a history of supporting business creation, survival, growth, and success because of the economic benefits that come from a positive business environment. These benefits include things such as job creation, workforce development, tax revenues, strong communities and higher quality of life, and lower levels of crime. Growth-oriented firms are particularly attractive because of their job creation potential. New and growing firms are also an important source of innovative products and services. Finally, growth-oriented firms are more likely to be engaged in international trade and exporting, both of which contribute to economic growth. In light of these many benefits, it is not surprising that there are so many government programs providing support to growth-oriented firms. What is surprising is how underutilized many of these programs are, particularly in the case of women entrepreneurs.

Federal Programs

7(a) and 504 Loan Programs

The U.S. Small Business Administration (SBA) serves as one of our nation's workhorses in terms of developing and managing programs that benefit small and growing firms. The SBA defines a small business as one with five hundred or fewer employees, and most growth-oriented firms fall squarely into this category during their survival stage. In addition to information, advice, and assistance, the SBA has a variety of loan programs. The best known of these are the 7(a) lending program and 504 loans. The 7(a) loan program provides loans of up to $5 million through a large network of participating lenders in each state. The SBA guarantees between 75 percent and 85 percent of these loans, depending on loan size. To qualify, a firm must fit the SBA criteria for a small business and must have been turned down for loans by two different lending institutions. The second of these criteria is particularly valuable from the standpoint of a growth-oriented firm, which may not be sufficiently profitable to qualify for a traditional bank loan. Table 7.1 reveals that the SBA guaranteed $17.9 billion in 7(a) loans in FY2013.

Approximately 13 percent of this amount was for loans secured by women, a slight increase over the 12 percent in the previous year. 504 loans, the SBA's other major loan program, are provided through certified development companies (CDCs) for amounts up to $5 million for the purchase of real estate or equipment. More than $5.2 billion was guaranteed through this program in 2013. Of this amount, women-owned firms received $709 million, or 14 percent, of the total, an increase of two percentage points over the previous year, and one percentage point over 2011. These statistics reveal that, although women represent roughly one-third of business owners in the United States, they received only one-seventh of loans made through the 7(a) or 504 programs. This suggests that women entrepreneurs, for whatever reason, are not taking full advantage of these important sources of financing.

TABLE 7.1. SBA Loan Programs (504, 7a), 2011–2013

		2011	2012	2013
7(a) Loans	All	$19,638	$15,153	$17,868
	Women	$2,367	$1,847	$2,323
	Women as a percentage	12	12	13
504 Loans	All	$4,845	$6,712	$5,227
	Women	$642	$786	$709
	Women as a percentage	13	12	14

Note: Dollars of gross loans approved (millions).
Source: U.S. Small Business Administration, 2014

Although the 7(a) and 504 programs are the SBA's largest and best-known loan programs, the agency has a number of other types of loan programs to support different small business needs. These include Patriot Express, which guarantees loans of $500,000 or less, a microloan program for loans of up to $50,000, and special 7(a) loan guarantee programs to support exporters. For further information on the broad array of programs and services available through the U.S. Small Business Administration, visit your district office or the SBA website at http://www.sba.gov.

SBIR Grants

SBIR grants (http://www.sbir.gov) represent a source of financing targeted toward technology-based firms in particular. The Small Business Innovation Research program was originally authorized by Congress in 1982 to assist technology-based companies in the development of new products. Today, the SBIR program involves eleven federal agencies, of which the Department of Defense is the largest. Over $2 billion in funding is available each year, and firms must submit an application in order to secure funding. SBIR grants are designed for technology-based firms having fewer than five hundred employees. The firm must be at least 51 percent U.S. owned, and all work under the grant must be done in the United States. SBIR grants are grants, not loans, so they do not have to be paid back. Further, an SBIR grant does not require the firm owner to give up any equity.

SBIR grants are awarded in three different "phases," and a company can received multiple grants. Phase I provides funding up to $150,000 to conduct a feasibility study on the new product. Phase II, during which the company conducts research and development to design a prototype, can be funded at a level of up to $1 million. Finally, Phase III is the commercialization stage. At this stage the company is expected to secure outside funding in order to further develop and commercialize the product. From the entrepreneur's perspective, the advantage of securing SBIR funding is not just the money, but also access to expertise and key contacts. Researchers have also pointed out that securing an SBIR grant is like a Good Housekeeping seal of approval in the sense that firms that receive these grants are in a better position to attract other funding sources (Lerner, 1999; Audretsch, 2002). These dimensions of SBIR funding are particularly valuable to women entrepreneurs, who often lack access to key contacts and networks. Thus, receiving an SBIR grant can open doorways not only to sources of financial capital but also to human and social capital. Deb Santy, director of

TABLE 7.2. NIH SBIR Grants, 2004–2013

FY	SBIR Phase	Woman-Owned Organizations			All Organizations			Women as a Percentage of Total		
		Number of Applications	Number of Awards	Total Funding	Number of Applications	Number of Awards	Total Funding	Number of Applications	Number of Awards	Total Funding
2004	Fast Track	31	2	$199,068	353	58	$9,374,708	8.8	3.4	2.1
2004	Phase I	506	88	$13,427,425	5,373	965	$149,124,493	9.4	9.1	9.0
2004	Phase II	95	31	$14,807,654	906	300	$154,000,661	10.5	10.3	9.6
2005	Fast Track	22	1	$100,000	199	28	$4,566,024	11.1	3.6	2.2
2005	Phase I	430	55	$8,578,422	4,740	778	$121,650,043	9.1	7.1	7.1
2005	Phase II	102	29	$13,939,050	979	312	$163,695,822	10.4	9.3	8.5
2006	Fast Track	21	4	$523,641	210	41	$6,794,013	10.0	9.8	7.7
2006	Phase I	427	71	$9,643,042	3,893	682	$112,211,352	11.0	10.4	8.6
2006	Phase II	114	48	$25,096,621	974	355	$189,931,647	11.7	13.5	13.2
2007	Fast Track	20	2	$199,934	253	41	$8,574,112	7.9	4.9	2.3
2007	Phase I	356	61	$16,515,429	3,020	656	$112,170,707	11.8	9.3	9.4
2007	Phase II	85	31	$16,356,926	760	278	$145,386,622	11.2	11.2	11.3
2008	Fast Track	34	6	$618,398	254	67	$14,086,309	13.4	9.0	4.4
2008	Phase I	398	69	$10,966,370	3,064	739	$128,473,317	13.0	9.3	8.5
2008	Phase II	86	41	$23,111,798	702	287	$160,436,070	12.3	14.3	14.4
2009	Fast Track	34	6	$1,314,448	280	54	$15,730,380	12.1	11.1	8.4
2009	Phase I	424	89	$17,039,959	3,365	654	$129,125,351	12.6	13.6	13.2
2009	Phase II	74	23	$11,890,885	741	262	$158,512,925	10.0	8.8	7.5
2010	Fast Track	67	7	$3,077,024	493	67	$16,795,150	13.6	10.4	18.3
2010	Phase I	590	62	$12,255,945	5,025	617	$129,374,385	11.7	10.0	9.5
2010	Phase II	95	27	$15,897,390	825	248	$146,872,962	11.5	10.9	10.8
2011	Fast Track	67	4	$855,746	454	41	$9,696,876	14.8	9.8	8.8
2011	Phase I	611	61	$12,593,892	5,195	544	$124,387,049	11.8	11.2	10.1
2011	Phase II	85	26	$16,356,484	757	203	$137,268,750	11.2	12.8	11.9
2012	Fast Track	42	6	$1,382,650	392	57	$13,985,802	10.7	10.5	9.9
2012	Phase I	549	68	$15,643,496	4,761	680	$156,413,844	11.5	10.0	10.0
2012	Phase II	81	29	$17,665,694	638	225	$155,043,890	12.7	12.9	11.4
2013	Fast Track	39	4	$1,072,553	347	49	$14,058,901	11.2	8.2	7.6
2013	Phase I	579	60	$13,600,453	4,150	497	$114,180,449	14.0	12.1	11.9
2013	Phase II	85	23	$17,816,383	597	183	$137,517,923	14.2	12.6	13.0

Note: Data drawn from the frozen FY 2013 PUB file as of 11/21/2013. Data on company ownership are self-reported.
Source: National Institutes of Health, Office of Extramural Research, 2014

Connecticut's SBIR program, notes that the program is both under-recognized and underutilized, particularly by women entrepreneurs (Coleman and Robb, 2012, p. 174). Table 7.2, which tracks SBIR grants awarded through the National Institutes of Health (NIH), confirms this observation. Although the percentage of applications, awards, and funding granted to women-owned ventures has increased dramatically since 2004, women still garnered less than 15 percent of each in 2013. Clearly there is room for further gains.

Government Grants and Contracts

Each year the United States government spends billions of dollars on federal grants and contracts for products and services that meet the agency's needs and priorities. For 2013, federal grants totaled $503 billion and contracts totaled an additional $460 billion (USASpending.gov, 2014). These awards are spread across the various agencies of the federal government. As an example, the Department of Health and Human Services, the Department of Transportation, the Environmental Protection Agency, and the National Science Foundation play an important role in awarding federal grants. Conversely, the Department of Defense, the Department of Energy, and the National Aeronautics and Space Administration are major providers of government contracts. These federal government grants and contracts often serve as an important source of funding for firms that are developing new technologies such as fuel cells or life-saving drugs, including those used to treat various forms of cancer or Alzheimer's. Grants such as these have been critical for growth-oriented entrepreneur Manon Cox and her firm, Protein Sciences, which is involved in the R&D-intensive process of developing new drugs and treatments. Her story is presented later in this chapter.

The Government as "Customer"

In addition to providing funding for firms developing new technologies or life-saving drugs, the federal government is a major purchaser of goods and services. Contracting for these products and services accounts for approximately 15 percent of the federal budget (Snider, Kidalov, and Rendon, 2013). Historically, the majority of these purchases have been made from large firms, which are typically owned by men. In recent decades, however, Congress has shown a growing desire to diversify its mix of contractors to better reflect the characteristics of the population. This has created new opportunities for women- and minority-owned firms.

In recognition of the fact that women-owned firms were dramatically underrepresented in sales of goods and services to the U.S. government, Congress passed the Federal Acquisition Streamlining Act in 1994, which set a goal of awarding at least 5 percent of the value of contracts to women-owned firms. In the ensuing years, that goal was never enforced or met, however, leading to the passage of the Small Business Reauthorization Act of 2000, which authorized a set-aside program specifically targeted toward women-owned firms. This was followed by a decade-long delay, but finally, in 2011, the SBA announced that it would implement a new Women-Owned Small Business Federal Contract Program in an attempt to reach the goal of 5 percent (McManus, 2012). In developing the rules for this program, the SBA commissioned a study that identified eighty-three industries in which women-owned firms were underrepresented. Within those industries, women were substantially underrepresented in a subset of thirty-eight industries (McManus, 2012), thus clearly documenting the need for a more aggressive approach. Finally in 2015, women-owned firms were awarded 5 percent of government contracts for the first time.

Some contend that the environment for government contracting may become even less hospitable for women in an era of federal spending cuts. They note that agencies, in the interests of efficiency and timeliness, have a tendency to go back to the "tried and true" large contractors whom they have used in the past, thereby creating fewer opportunities for women-owned firms that are not already a part of that network (Ivory, 2013). A Canadian study of small business concerns about federal contracting revealed that the greatest concerns on the part of small firms included (1) too much paperwork, (2) lack of awareness of opportunities, and (3) suspicion that the selection process favors insiders and larger firms (Orser, 2009, p. 17).

In spite of these challenges, government contracting provides significant opportunities for firm growth. Women entrepreneurs who wish to explore these opportunities further can visit the Small Business Administration website, which includes a section on contracting (http://www.sba.gov). The SBA website also includes a section titled "Local Assistance," which provides additional information on sources of support for entrepreneurs who want to do business with federal, state, or local governments. We also advise entrepreneurs to get on the email distribution list for their district SBA office as a way to learn about upcoming training, networking, and other opportunities. A recent email from the Hartford (CT) district office announced the following series of work-shops, all of which are free:

Government Contracting 101

Doing Business with the Federal Government

Access to Capital—Financing Your Business

Opportunities in Exporting—Export 101

The Benefits of Certification

Revenues are an important source of funding for growth-oriented firms, and one of the ways in which women entrepreneurs can increase their revenues is by becoming certified as a woman-owned or minority-owned firm. There are a number of benefits associated with becoming certified as a woman- or minority-owned firm. The SBA offers a path to certification for small women- and minority-owned firms through its 8(a) Business Development Program. This program is designed to provide a broad scope of business assistance to firms that are at least 51 percent owned or controlled by socially and economically disadvantaged individuals (http://www.sba.gov). Firms certified under the 8(a) program have additional opportunities for contracts at the city, state, and federal levels. Once certified, firms receive further guidance and information on how to engage in government contracting. For further information on getting certified as an 8(a) woman- or minority-owned firm through the U.S. Small Business Administration, contact your district SBA Office or go to http://www.sba.gov.

Similarly, the Minority Business Development Agency (MBDA) helps firms become certified in order to expand opportunities for revenue generation. The MBDA was established at the federal level in 1969 to support the needs of minority business owners. Currently, the agency is housed within the U.S. Department of Commerce and operates through a nationwide network of business centers and strategic partners. The MBDA provides assistance to business owners in a variety of areas, including access to financial capital and markets. It also helps firms become certified as minority-owned businesses and assists them in identifying opportunities for contracts in both the public and private sectors. For further information on obtaining certification as a minority-owned business through the Minority Business Development Agency or to find a regional office for the MBDA near you, go to http://www.mbda.gov.

Manon Cox and Protein Sciences

After spending eleven years at Gist-Brocades, a large Dutch bioscience company, Manon Cox was looking for an entrepreneurial opportunity of her own. Cox was well prepared for that next step, holding a PhD in molecular biology, genetics, and biochemistry from the University of Nijmegen in the Netherlands. During her time at Gist-Brocades, she held leadership positions in research and development, manufacturing, and business development. These roles provided her with a broad range of managerial experiences and allowed her to see how the process of conceiving, creating, and producing a new drug fit together. As a part of her management development program, her company also financed her enrollment in an Executive MBA program, which allowed her to sharpen her skills in the areas of finance and financial management.

Although Manon had planned to realize her entrepreneurial dream by launching her own bioscience firm, a ready-made entrepreneurial opportunity presented itself in the form of a small, struggling firm based in Meriden, Connecticut. Protein Sciences was founded by serial entrepreneur Dan Adams in 1983 with the goal of developing vaccines and biopharmaceuticals. The two met during Manon's time at Gist-Brocades, and Adams convinced Manon to join Protein Sciences as the director of business development in 1998. She advanced to the role of chief operating officer two years later. At the time, Protein Sciences had a total of thirty-five employees and multiple projects in the pipeline.

When Cox arrived, she was confronted with several challenges. The first was the difficulty of managing scientists who, by their nature, want to discover and develop new ideas. Cox found that her new firm had too many projects underway for its size, capabilities, and resources. A second, more serious challenge, was the fact that Protein Sciences had invested over $100 million in developing a cure for HIV. Ultimately these efforts did not bear fruit, and Protein Sciences found itself with over $11 million in debt and minimal revenues. In 2009 the firm's creditors filed a petition to force the company into bankruptcy to be liquidated in order to partially satisfy their claims. One of those creditors, Emergent BioSolutions, attempted a hostile takeover.

Manon opposed the takeover attempt, because Protein Sciences had just been granted "fast-track" status by the Food and Drug Administration for its Flublok vaccine. Unlike most flu vaccines, Flublok is not made by using viruses grown in eggs. Thus, it can be produced more rapidly and can be used by individuals who are allergic to eggs. Manon felt that Flublok had the potential to be a "breakthrough" product for Protein Sciences and that current shareholders would lose out if the takeover went through. In an attempt to intimidate Cox, Emergent sued her personally for her opposition to the takeover. To Manon's dismay, her board of directors would not back her up, so she had to hire a lawyer and defend herself in court. Ultimately the charges against her were either dismissed or settled. Protein Sciences was able to remain independent thanks to an eleventh-hour investment by a Japanese venture capital fund that allowed the firm to satisfy its creditors.

Reflecting on that period of time, Cox commented, "You know what they say, what doesn't kill you makes you stronger." And it did. As Cox explained, "The fact that I defended myself against a big and powerful company put me on the map. I became known as a force to be reckoned with."

The year 2009 proved to be a welcome turning point for Protein Sciences and for Cox. The Biomedical Advanced Research and Development Authority (BARDA) awarded them $147 million to help bring Flublok to market more quickly. Both the FDA and BARDA noted that Flublok has a competitive advantage over traditional flu vaccines because its proprietary technology offers the potential to ramp up the vaccine's manufacturing process faster in the event of a pandemic (Srinivasan, 2013). Thanks to the BARDA contract, Protein Sciences has been profitable since 2009. Other sources of revenue include sales of research antigens and antibodies to members of the scientific community and revenues from its GeneXpress division, which allows other firms to use the Protein Sciences research platform to develop their own products.

Cox notes that Protein Sciences could not have survived without government funding (Srinivasan, 2013). Access to private capital for bioscience firms is a challenge, because of uncertainties inherent in the drug development process. The timeline for developing a new drug or vaccine is also a long one, twenty years in the case of Flublok, and most investors are not that patient. To date, Protein Sciences has raised over $300 million in external funding. Revenues in 2012 were $32 million, and, at the time of our interview, Cox expected them to top $36 million for 2013. During that same year, the FDA granted final approval for the sale of Flublok in the United States.

Manon Cox's story highlights some of the qualities that have helped her succeed as a growth-oriented entrepreneur. First, she had a strong educational grounding in the fields of biology, genetics, biochemistry, and business. Coupled with that, she gained valuable industry and leadership experience in a large bioscience firm prior to joining Protein Sciences. These experiences provided the types of human and social capital that Manon needed to succeed in running an emerging bioscience firm. Manon's personal qualities in the form of resilience, courage, and mental toughness also helped her navigate through the turbulence around a hostile takeover attempt. In this sense, Manon demonstrated a high level of self-efficacy, or the belief that she could do the job and do it well. This strong sense of purpose and belief in herself guided her through a particularly difficult time when she was not getting a lot of support from those around her. Why is this important? It's important because as women we have a tendency to underestimate our capabilities. This tendency, in turn, can lead to doubts about whether we can execute a difficult task effectively. The lesson to be learned from Manon Cox is, first, to develop a strong set of capabilities in the form of education, experience, and social capital, and second, to believe in yourself once you have done so. This is easy to say, but sometimes hard to do, so one strategy would be to practice this approach to self-efficacy, first with small things such as individual tasks or challenges, before moving on to a bigger challenge such as launching and running a firm.

State and Local Programs

In addition to the various types of federal programs we have discussed, states and municipalities also compete for entrepreneurial talent and for the job-creating potential of growth-oriented firms. Since your authors are from opposite ends of the country, we will use our own states as examples, as well as one from the middle of the country. Similar programs can be found throughout the United States and globally.

Connecticut Initiatives

Faced with lagging job creation and slower than average economic growth in the wake of the "Great Recession," Connecticut's state legislature passed the 2011 Jobs Bill, which created a number of programs directed toward spurring economic growth through job creation. One of these programs, CTNext, specifically targets the role of entrepreneurship through the creation of an "Innovation Ecosystem." This ecosystem will connect entrepreneurial firms and their founders with mentors, collaborative work spaces, universities, vendors, suppliers, and other like-minded entrepreneurs in an attempt to facilitate the growth and scalability of new firms. As of October 2013, this program had provided resource connections to three hundred entrepreneurial ventures as well as thirty-two microgrants to new firms for research, development, and proto-typing (*Reinventing CT*, 2013).

Another measure included in Connecticut's 2011 Jobs Bill was the provision of $25 million per year in additional funding for Connecticut Innovations (CI) to support promising high-tech companies and help them scale their firms to achieve global reach. CI is a quasi-public agency established by the Connecticut General Assembly in 1989 as a state-funded investment firm capable of provid-ing both loans and venture capital to emerging high-tech firms. The additional Jobs Bill funding allowed CI to more than double its investment in early stage high-tech firms while increasing the number of companies in its venture port-folio from fifty-six to ninety-one. During this same time frame, sixty-three of those portfolio firms were provided with growth capital in the form of follow-on investments (*Reinventing CT*, 2013).

As an incentive to increase the level of angel investing, the 2011 Jobs Bill also expanded upon existing provisions for angel investor tax credits. Angel in-vestors are an important source of external equity for young, growth-oriented firms, and this measure lowered the investment threshold required to qualify for the tax credit from $100,000 to $25,000, thereby opening the door for many more investors. This change had the effect of quadrupling the number of angel investors during the first year after the change and more than doubling the amount of dollars invested (*Reinventing CT*, 2013).

Further information on the programs highlighted above as well as other state-level initiatives to stimulate business growth is included in the Con-necticut Department of Economic and Community Development's website at http://www.ct.gov/ecd.

The Midwest: Pipeline Angels

Since its founding in 2006 (beginning in Kansas), Pipeline Angels (http://www .pipelineangels.com) has built an elite network of entrepreneurial leaders who work as one to face business challenges, funnel opportunities to their peers, and build market-leading technology and life-sciences businesses together. As keystones of the regional business environment, Pipeline members are creating jobs, investing in their businesses and communities, and mentoring the next-generation of business leaders.

In 2010, Pipeline expanded to a regional nonprofit. Each year approximately ten to twelve new entrepreneurs are invited to join Pipeline as fellows. After an extensive selection process, new fellows participate in a unique and rigorous year-long business leadership development program that blends workshop modules, advice from national experts, and a deepening of the relationships among new and current Pipeline members. This introductory year-long program leverages a national network of business advisors at the forefront of their respective specialties who engage deeply with Pipeline, effectively extending the entrepreneurs' business networks nationwide.

California: The Venture Greenhouse

While Silicon Valley in the southern San Francisco Bay Area is world famous for entrepreneurship, Marin County in the North Bay is mainly known for plentiful open space, wide beaches, and beautiful parks (Muir Woods, Point Reyes, and so on). Nevertheless, there are several initiatives under way to promote more entrepreneurship north of the Golden Gate Bridge, one of which is the Venture Greenhouse (http://venturegreenhouse.biz).

The Venture Greenhouse is an established Marin-based business accelerator, helping promising entrepreneurs from the North Bay and Greater Bay Area launch and scale businesses that will make a significant disruptive impact on their chosen industry and market. Client companies are launching and growing innovative business models in a variety of market segments such as clean technology, energy, software, medical, consumer products and services, the Internet, and transportation. The common thread among client companies is that an element of their product, service, business process, or operations is changing the status quo of their industry or market to become more sustainable. Further, the Venture Greenhouse helps companies integrate resource-efficient strategies and processes to enhance revenues, increase bottom-line profitability, and make the company more attractive to investors and customers.

The Venture Greenhouse model is a milestone-driven, one-day-a-week, twelve-month acceleration program, which has been developed and refined over the past three years. More than just a business training curriculum, Venture Greenhouse provides entrepreneurs with an entire expert team of seasoned mentors, specialty advisors with deep domain expertise, access to funding, expert professional service providers, and MBA interns. They partner with the County of Marin, the California Small Business Development Center, the Marin Economic Forum, and many others.

In this section we have highlighted some of the entrepreneurial initiatives in the states we live and work in. What programs and sources of funding are available in your state or local community? A good place to start answering this question is the website for your state office of economic development. You should also check your town or region's Chamber of Commerce for programs, presentations, and networking events. Finally, are there chapters of organizations such as the National Association of Women Business Owners (NAWBO) in your region? These types of organizations will help you develop a network of other entrepreneurs and business owners who have faced many of the same challenges you will encounter as a part of your entrepreneurial journey. These individuals can serve as a valuable source of information and contacts while also providing emotional support and understanding when the going gets tough. Although we do not recommend "random networking," which can consume a lot of time to no specific end, we do recommend "strategic networking" to help you gain access to resources, information, and key contacts.

What Is an Entrepreneurial Ecosystem?

What do we mean by the phrase "entrepreneurial ecosystem"? The term *ecosystem* was originally developed in the 1930s by Arthur Roy Clapham, a young botanist at Oxford University, to describe the physical and biological components of an environment and their relationship to each other (Willis, 1997). British ecologist Arthur Tansley, also at Oxford, further developed the term to describe the interactive system established between a group of living creatures and the environment in which they live (Tansley, 1935). More recently, the notion of an ecosystem has been applied to entrepreneurship as a way to explain the interactive relationship between entrepreneurs and their environment (Brush, 2012). Elements of that environment can include universities that teach entrepreneurship and conduct leading-edge research, a vibrant business community, government support and encouragement for entrepreneurship and free enterprise, a legal system that protects business ownership and intellectual property, and a funding system that provides support for entrepreneurs attempting to launch and grow their firms. Babson College's Daniel Isenberg emphasizes that an entrepreneurial ecosystem must integrate individual elements such as leadership, culture, capital markets, and customers into a holistic system. When these elements work together, the whole is greater than the sum of the parts, and the resulting ecosystem can "turbocharge venture creation and growth" (Isenberg, 2010, p. 3). In a thought-provoking article published in the *Harvard Business Review*, Isenberg also provided a list of questions to help entrepreneurs assess

Do You Have a Strong Entrepreneurship Ecosystem?

How do you know if you have the essential elements of an entrepreneurship ecosystem in place? To help governments address that question, Babson College has launched a global action-research project, the Babson Entrepreneurship Ecosystem Project.

Below is a summary of the framework BEEP uses to assess the crucial elements in an environment, so that governments know where to focus their efforts. Each category represents a key component of a healthy ecosystem. Though not exhaustive, the sample questions listed below will help you gauge where you are.

Do public leaders:
Act as strong, public advocates of entrepreneurs and entrepreneurship?
Open their doors to entrepreneurs and those promoting entrepreneurship?

Do governments:
Create effective institutions directly associated with entrepreneurship (research institutes, overseas liaisons, forums for public/private dialogue)?
Remove structural barriers to entrepreneurship, such as onerous bankruptcy legislation and poor contract enforcement?

Does the culture at large:
Tolerate honest mistakes, honorable failure, risk taking, and contrarian thinking?
Respect entrepreneurship as a worthy occupation?

Are there visible success stories that:
Inspire youth and would-be entrepreneurs?
Show ordinary people that they too can become entrepreneurs?

Are there enough knowledgeable people who:
Have experience in creating organizations, hiring, and building structures, systems, and controls?
Have experience as professional board members and advisers?

Are there capital sources that:
Provide equity capital for companies at a pre-sales stage?
Add nonmonetary value, such as mentorship and contacts?

Are there nonprofits and industry associations that:
Help investors and entrepreneurs network and learn from one another?
Promote and ally themselves with entrepreneurship (such as software and biotechnology associations)?

Are there educational institutions that:
Teach financial literacy and entrepreneurship to high school and college students?
Allow faculty to take sabbaticals to join start-ups?

Does the public infrastructure provide sufficient:
Transportation (roads, airports, railways, container shipping)?
Communication (digital, broadband, mobile)?

Are there geographic locations that have:
Concentrations of high-potential and high-growth ventures?
Proximity to universities, standards agencies, think tanks, vocational training, suppliers, consulting firms, and professional associations?

Are there formal or informal groups that link:
Entrepreneurs in the country or region and diaspora networks—in particular, high-achieving expatriates?
New ventures and local offices of multinationals?

Are there venture-oriented professionals, such as:
Lawyers, accountants, and market and technical consultants who will work on a contingency basis, or for stock?

Are there local potential customers who are:
Willing to give advice, particularly on new products or services?
Willing to be flexible with payment terms to accommodate the cash flow needs of young, rapidly growing suppliers?

FIGURE 7.1. Do You Have a Strong Entrepreneurial Ecosystem?

Source: Isenberg, 2010

their own entrepreneurial ecosystem (Figure 7.1). As you review this list, how would you assess the entrepreneurial ecosystem in your community? What are the strengths? The weaknesses? How can you employ the components of this ecosystem to launch and grow your firm? Interestingly enough, the World Bank published a global set of "Doing Business" indicators for 189 different countries annually (*Doing Business 2015: United States*). These include factors such as the ease of starting a business, enforcing contracts, dealing with construction permits, and getting credit among others. Although we often think of the United States as a highly developed and entrepreneurial country, it is both revealing and thought-provoking to see how we stack up in these various metrics. As an example, we come in second out of 189 in the category of "Getting Credit." Our performance was considerably less impressive in the areas of "Starting a Business" (46th) and even "Getting Electricity" (61st). These metrics make it clear that, in spite of our developed-nation status, we still have work to do when it comes to the entrepreneurial ecosystem.

Local Initiatives to Help Develop an Entrepreneurial Ecosystem

Some of you may reside in communities such as Silicon Valley; Greater Boston; Boulder, Colorado; or Austin, Texas, where a strong entrepreneurial ecosystem is already in place. Others, however, may live in communities where an ecosystem is not yet fully developed. What can you as an entrepreneur do to stimulate the development of your community's entrepreneurial ecosystem in ways that will benefit your firm, the firms of other entrepreneurs, and the community overall?

In answer to this question, there is a growing number of activities devoted to nurturing entrepreneurial ecosystems throughout the nation and the world as entrepreneurship gains in popularity. Speaking from personal experience, we know that women are typically in the minority in terms of participating in these activities, so there are lots of opportunities for you as a growth-oriented woman entrepreneur to get involved and make a contribution. We have listed some of our favorites here, but you can do your own Internet search on entrepreneurship initiatives in your area. We're sure you'll find lots of activities, some of which suit your needs and interests. If not, why not start your own? Many of the examples we give below have a growing number of chapters across the globe. Why not start a chapter in your community?

1 Million Cups

1 Million Cups (1MC) (www.1millioncups.com) is a simple way to engage entre-preneurs in communities around the world. Each week, the 1MC program offers two local entrepreneurs an opportunity to present their startups to a diverse au-dience of mentors, advisors, and entrepreneurs. Presenters prepare a six-minute educational presentation and engage in twenty minutes of feedback and ques-tioning after they present. Entrepreneurs gain insight into possible ways they can improve their businesses, gather real-time feedback, connect with a community that truly cares about their progress, and walk away feeling like they have ad-vanced their businesses. The audience also learns a great deal from the presenta-tions. Whether this is through passively listening or deeply engaging with the entrepreneurs, there is a wealth of take-aways every week from these dynamic and diverse communities. The program takes place every Wednesday morning from 9:00 to 10:00 a.m. in locations all around the country. Visit the website's "Find an Event" page for a list of locations. Each city runs the program semi-au-tonomously, and participants gather in coffee shops, co-working spaces, and even TV stations. 1 Million Cups is a program run by entrepreneurs for entrepreneurs.

The Athena Foundation's PowerLink Program

The Athena Foundation's goal is to support, develop, and honor women lead-ers while inspiring women to achieve their full potential. Consistent with this goal, the foundation established its PowerLink program (http://www.athena international.org/athena_power_link_program.aspx) in 1992 in Pittsburgh, led by two businesswomen who recognized that women entrepreneurs often lack access to advisors and mentors. In response to this unmet need, the PowerLink program's goal is to create panels of volunteers willing to advise women busi-ness owners in their communities on issues that can help them achieve greater success. Since that time, the PowerLink program has expanded nationwide. To participate, a business must be at least 51 percent owned and actively managed by a woman. It must also have been in business for at least two years and have a minimum of two full-time employees. Annual revenues must equal or exceed $250,000 for retail and manufacturing firms, and $100,000 per year for service firms. Participating firms are paired with an advisory panel composed of indi-viduals with skills that match the firm's needs. According to a recent ATHENA study, firms that participate have experienced an average increase in sales of 88 percent and an average increase in full-time employees of 36 percent (http://www.athenainternational.org/athena_power_link_program.aspx).

Startup Grind

Startup Grind (www.startupgrind.com) is a global startup community designed to educate, inspire, and connect entrepreneurs. They host monthly events featuring successful local entrepreneurs, innovators, educators, and investors who share personal stories and lessons learned on the road to building great companies. Monthly fireside chat interviews, startup mixers, and annual conferences provide ample opportunities to connect with amazing startups and the people behind them, tap into a strong support network, form meaningful connections, and gain inspiration for the startup journey ahead. Startup Grind was begun by Derek Andersen and Spencer Nielsen in February 2010 in a small office in Mountain View, California, with an original goal of bringing together friends who would help each other that has spread across the world. It is now the largest independent startup community, actively educating, inspiring, and connecting hundreds of thousands of founders in more than two hundred cities around the world.

UpGlobal

UpGlobal (UP) (www.up.co) is a nonprofit dedicated to fostering entrepreneurship, grassroots leadership, and strong communities. Its mission is to make the world a more innovative and prosperous place, one community at a time. UP members believe that entrepreneurs are critical to driving a strong global economy and a better world. They help develop these entrepreneurs by supporting the grassroots leaders who are at the core of every strong entrepreneurial ecosystem. Every leader in the UP community understands the transformative nature of entrepreneurship and is committed to empowering others around them. These individuals catalyze progress, connect entrepreneurs and supporters, drive innovation, and provide tools for their communities. Startup Weekend and Startup Next are just some of their program offerings. They've become a global presence in over five hundred cities and have helped launch the entrepreneurial journey of over 150,000 aspiring entrepreneurs. UP aims to help create and sustain strong communities through programs, resources, and a powerful network of leaders. Their vision is a world in which every person has the opportunity to become an entrepreneur. Their mission is to improve the global human condition by amplifying the efforts of startup community leaders and their ability to create and sustain flourishing entrepreneurial communities around the world.

The Role of Universities

In addition to the types of organizations we have cited, universities are widely recognized as an essential component of the entrepreneurial ecosystem (Fetters, Greene, and Rice, 2010; Allen and Lieberman, 2010; Butler, 2010). Universities provide future entrepreneurs with educational credentials in a broad range of fields, a key element of their human capital. In addition, universities provide aspiring entrepreneurs with access to faculty conducting leading-edge research in areas such as life sciences, computer science, and engineering. Similarly, universities provide valuable resources in the form of laboratories, graduate assistants, and student interns, and links with area companies and organizations. As we noted earlier, many universities also operate entrepreneurial incubators that provide working space as well as other types of support services for new firms. Our next mini-case, featuring biotech entrepreneur Natalie Wisniewski, provides a great example of the important role universities play in helping new entrepreneurs develop their innovative products and services.

Natalie Wisniewski and Profusa, Inc.

Dr. Natalie Wisniewski is a co-founder and chief technical officer of Profusa, Inc., a startup pioneering real-time monitoring of body chemistries though nanotechnology, biomaterials, and smartphone platforms. Natalie and her team have been growing Profusa since its founding in 2008. They currently employ seventeen full-time employees but are not yet generating revenues.

When asked about her primary motivations for launching Profusa, Natalie mentioned an experience in graduate school when she tested an early monitoring device for two weeks. This experience made an impression on her, because she saw how powerful it could be: a device that could do analytics of a person's body and continuously track them over time. The entrepreneurial seed was planted at the time. Fast forward a decade, and technology had advanced to the point where the idea now seemed possible, so Natalie started a company to drive that vision forward.

Natalie and her two co-founders began with a minimal amount of money. Other than an incorporation fee, there were very few expenses, because they weren't paying themselves. Natalie did consulting on the side to pay her living expenses, and one of the other co-founders was wealthy and nearing retirement, so she didn't need to be paid a salary. The third co-founder had a husband who was working and could cover her living expenses. However, although the founding team did not require a lot of financial capital, there was a huge opportunity cost in terms of the money they could have been earning in jobs outside the company.

Early on there were technical hurdles. . . . people have been trying to do what we are doing since the 1960s. I did the research and studied the issue for my PhD. I understood why they failed and thought I had figured out a solution. We still believe we have the solution, but investors in this space have been burned in the past so when we came to the table, they were like oh, yeah right, another one. We've seen hundreds. . . .

Starting a new firm is never an easy prospect, but it can be even more difficult when you start in the midst of a recession. Natalie's team had to flex their creative muscles in order to find funding to propel their efforts forward during the tough economic times of 2009–2010. They succeeded in raising $7.6 million from the NIH and the Defense Advanced Research Projects Agency (DARPA), an agency of the United States Department of Defense that commissions advanced research. The non-dilutive nature of these sources of capital is one of the key advantages of grant funding. Nevertheless, Profusa still needed to convince investors, which was a challenge, even with the NIH and DARPA backing them up. When they were able to get human data, however, the funding picture changed. Natalie shared that prior to gaining access to human data she did eighty-six investor pitches without raising a penny.

Profusa's ability to secure financial capital was a driving factor in the founders' decision to grow the firm. Before that time, the team's validation came in the form of benevolence from a few professors. This allowed them to get data and demonstrate their proof of concept. This in turn allowed them to write more grants, which got them money to get more data. Backing from the NIH and DARPA was critical, not just in terms of the funding it provided, but also in terms of the firm's validation by outside experts. The fact that Profusa gained the support of major government agencies gave outside investors confidence and encouraged them to invest.

A series of things happened along the way that, if each hadn't happened, meant that we wouldn't get to the next step. One was a professor who was a guru in the field and in Seattle where one of my co-founders was. We went to him and asked if we could try some stuff in his lab and he was really supportive. My co-founder ended up stepping into his lab as a funded post-doc and was able to do the prototyping. Interestingly, our innovation makes use of a biomedical invention of his, so he was excited that we could use his invention in a new and novel way.

Natalie says that time and money continue to be challenges. There never seems to be enough time to do all the things that need to be done. Beyond that, there is never enough money to buy all the instruments required, hire all the people they need, or accelerate growth at the rate they want to.

As we take each step, we move on, we validate, we reconfirm, we build on the proof of concept. We are marching along in that regard. But we are producing something that is injected under skin, which means it's a Class 3 medical device, which is high risk, has high scrutiny, and regulatory barriers that other products do not. This makes it more time intensive and more cost intensive . . . there is nothing easy about raising money. It was hard to get terms we wanted—we had to take a convertible note with a cap. It stretched over time . . . nine months, like giving birth.

On a positive note, Natalie observed that the challenge of raising financial capital forced them to go more slowly and raise more funding from grants. This has actually turned out to be an advantage because, as noted, those funds are non-dilutive, allowing the founding team to retain a substantial amount of equity in the firm.

Closing the Loop

This chapter highlighted government funding and local sources of support. As we noted earlier, government funding is often overlooked and underestimated. In fact, however, government sources can serve as a critical link between the owner's internal sources of financing and her ability to attract external providers of either debt or equity. As our case studies on Protein Sciences and Profusa illustrate, this is particularly true for firms in industries with prolonged development cycles such as bioscience, energy, and defense. Similarly, state and local governments offer grants and loans as well as tax incentives and training support, particularly for firms that will create new jobs. Finally, certification provides a way for women entrepreneurs to get a seat at the table when it comes to contracts awarded at the federal, state, or municipal levels.

Although government funding sources are often more labor intensive from an application, documentation, and reporting perspective, they can make the difference between surviving and not surviving for growth-oriented entrepreneurs. Aside from that, receiving a government grant or loan may open doors to additional sources of funding, as illustrated in our mini-cases on Protein Sciences and Profusa. These examples show that raising capital is a process; it is not an isolated transaction, and each step in the process builds upon those that have come before.

As we have pointed out in this chapter, becoming involved in the local entrepreneurial ecosystem also allows growth-oriented women entrepreneurs to tap into a myriad of resources, not just financial capital. By participating in networking activities such as weekly events through 1 Million Cups or monthly events through Startup Grind, aspiring entrepreneurs gain opportunities to network with other entrepreneurs, as well as with potential mentors and investors. Accelerators are yet another option that can provide not only financial resources but also access to mentors and markets. Finally, Natalie Wisneiwski's story highlights the importance of resources and support that can be provided through colleges and universities. Natalie first developed the initial idea for her entrepreneurial venture as a graduate student with access to new knowledge, current technologies, laboratory space, and experienced faculty. Ten years later when she actually launched her firm, the professors she had worked with continued to be a source of knowledge, information, and support during the firm's early days.

What Does This Mean For You?

1. Make the time to visit your regional office of the U.S. Small Business Administration. Talk to one of the business advisors there about your firm, its needs, and potential contributions, and explore sources of financing and support that can help you grow your firm. These individuals are typically very familiar with your region's entrepreneurial ecosystem, so even if you do not qualify for SBA funding, they can often provide you with advice and contacts that will lead to other sources of support.

2. In like fashion, visit your state's Office of Economic Development and ask to speak with someone who is knowledgeable about funding programs for growing firms. Explore other types of incentives and programs such as tax credits, consultation, or training as well. As in the case of the SBA, OED representatives can often direct you to other resource providers in your community.

3. Get on the notification list for government grants and contracts for the types of products and services your firm is developing or provides. This list will include a lot of activities that are not relevant for your firm, but periodically you may see a gem that can help you take your firm to the next level. You need to be vigilant about scanning the list frequently, at least once

a week, because you are often given a limited amount of time to submit a proposal. If you do submit and you are rejected, review the comments and talk to the program officer to find out what you can do to submit a stronger proposal the next time around. The good news is that, once you get that first grant or contract, it will pave the way for others.

4. Get your firm certified as woman-owned or minority-owned. This is almost a no-brainer, and it will open doors to government contracts representing 15 percent of the federal budget. Currently, women-owned firms are vastly underrepresented in the area of government contracting, so agencies may be particularly attentive to bids submitted by women-owned firms. As in the case for grants, once you get your first contract, it will open the door for others.

5. Use Daniel Isenberg's list of questions (Figure 7.1) to map out your community's entrepreneurial ecosystem. The ecosystem approach highlights the dynamic nature of the entrepreneur's relationship with her environment. What elements of the ecosystem can you use to help grow your firm?

6. Colleges and universities are an important component of the entrepreneurial ecosystem. Explore the types of resources and support that are available through your alma mater or through a college or university in your community. As in the case of Profusa founder Natalie Wisniewski, a university can provide access to valuable resources in the form of advice and expertise, laboratory space, or labor in the form of graduate students doing research in the same area. A growing number of colleges and universities are also launching incubators, accelerators, and pitch events that provide access to potential investors as well as other resources.

7. If elements of your entrepreneurial ecosystem are weak or lacking, explore strategies for developing the ecosystem in ways that will benefit your firm, the firms of other entrepreneurs, and the community overall. In this chapter, we have listed several initiatives devoted to helping entrepreneurs develop their entrepreneurial ecosystem. You could join or start one of these chapters in your community. Alternatively, there may be other initiatives underway in your region that will also achieve this goal.

8

CROWDFUNDING

The New Kid on the Block

In this chapter we will focus on crowdfunding, an innovative funding mechanism that leverages the Internet and social networks in order to raise funds from a large number of investors, many of whom contribute small amounts. Over the course of the last decade, technological progress has allowed for the widespread adoption of crowdfunding for a broad range of purposes. Crowdfunding represents a disruptive innovation in that it enables the entrepreneur to establish a direct connection with potential investors, thereby bypassing financial intermediaries such as venture capital firms.

Initially, crowdfunding was utilized mainly in the creative arts. Today it is used widely by many different kinds of people for very different reasons. Entrepreneurs have joined the crowd, using this funding mechanism for things such as seed financing for startup costs, financing for the manufacturing and distribution of a product or prototype, or to purchase equipment or inventory in order to scale their businesses. Massolution, a research company specializing in crowdfunding solutions, indicated that crowdfunding platforms raised $16.2 billion in 2014, a 167 percent increase over the $6.1 billion raised in 2013 (Massolution, 2015). The growth in funding volumes continued to be primarily driven by lending-based crowdfunding, but significant annual growth in equity-based crowdfunding and increased adoption of newer hybrid and royalty-based models indicates that the allocation of funding volume across different models will be more widely distributed over the coming years (Massolution, 2015).

We are excited about this new phenomenon because it might have dispro-portionate effects on female entrepreneurs, who have typically been under-represented both in entrepreneurship and in funding entrepreneurs. Some of its supporters argue that crowdfunding has the potential to "democratize" the entrepreneurship and capital markets by serving as a means for women entre-preneurs as well as women investors to participate more fully (see, for example, Forbes.com, December 4, 2013; March 8, 2014; and March 26, 2014).

In fact, several research projects provide evidence of this democratization. A recent paper by Marom, Robb, and Sade (2014) found that women were more likely than men to reach their funding goals on the platform Kickstarter. Perhaps more interestingly, they found that women actually made up a larger percent-age of investors than entrepreneurs on this crowdfunding platform. They also found a clear trend showing that the share of women investors rises in instances where women play a more dominant role in venture teams (that is, two females is greater than one female, one female is greater than one male, female-male is greater than male-female, and one male is greater than two males). In almost every category women invested in more female-led projects, while the men chose to invest in male-led projects. Thus, getting more women involved on the invest-ing side seems to bode well for getting more funding to female entrepreneurs.

An examination of Kickstarter data by Meek and Sullivan (2015) found somewhat higher levels of equality in a narrow category. They identified all suc-cessfully funded crowdfunding campaigns in the United States between 2009 and 2012 on sustainably oriented agriculture businesses in the Food category. They found no significant differences in funding goals of men and women, nor in the amount of money raised. In addition, they further examined whether differences existed relative to men and women's firms that were still operating as of March 2015 compared to those that were not operating; again, they found no significant differences.

Jason Greenberg and Ethan Mollick (2014) examined why, all other things being equal, women are 13 percent more likely than men to succeed in raising their goal in a crowdfunding campaign. Using lab experiments and data drawn from Kickstarter, they found that women seemed to succeed in areas in which female investor concentration was low, rather than high. In a series of experi-ments, they demonstrated that a proportion of women exhibit "activist choice homophily"—showing a preference for female-led projects. For these activists who were interested in supporting other women, crowdfunding was a way of rectifying historical disadvantage.

Crowdfunding is categorized into different types, distinguished by what investors are promised in return for their contributions (Bradford, 2012). The donation model is when investors give money on a platform and receive nothing in return for their contribution. Although the contributor's motive is often charitable, the recipient's need not be. Other types are the reward model and the pre-purchase model. These two crowdfunding models are similar to each other, and often appear together on the same site. The reward model offers something to the investor in return for the contribution, but without interest or part of the earnings of the business. The reward could be small, such as a key chain, or it could be something with a little more cachet, like the investor's name appearing in the credits of a movie. The pre-purchase model is similar in nature, whereby contributors receive the product that the entrepreneur is making. For example, if the entrepreneur produces a music album, contributors would receive a copy of the album.

The lending model for crowdfunding is based on a loan, in which contributors are only providing the funds temporarily and repayment is expected. In some cases, investors are promised interest on the funds they loan. In other cases, they receive only their principal back. Crowdfunding can also be used to raise financial capital in the form of equity thanks to the 2012 Jumpstart Our Business Startups or JOBS Act. The equity model offers investors a share of the profits or an equity stake in the business they are helping to fund.

Reward and Pre-Purchase Models

Two of the more prominent crowdfunding platforms for reward or pre-purchase contributions are Indiegogo and Kickstarter. Indiegogo (http://www.indiegogo.com), launched in 2007, allows essentially anyone to raise money through crowdfunding for any purpose including projects, charities and social causes, or personal goals such as a trip or wedding. Indiegogo-funded projects tend to be relatively small, with an average goal of $3,700 (Barnett, 2013). In spite of that, however, 80 percent of Indiegogo's campaigns fail to reach their funding goal, reflecting the participants' lack of sophistication and the diverse nature of their funding requests.

For successful projects, Indiegogo charges a fee equal to 4 percent of the funds raised. The site offers Fixed Funding and Flexible Funding options. Under the Fixed Funding option, unsuccessful projects are not charged any fees, but all contributions must be returned. Under the Flexible Funding option, the participant may keep the funds raised in an unsuccessful campaign by paying a fee of 9 percent. Although this is a relatively stiff penalty for not reaching the funding goal, it does allow an entrepreneur the option of using whatever money she has been able to raise. In an interview with VentureBeat, Indiegogo co-founder Danae Ringelmann reported that women are well represented among those who succeed; 47 percent of the firms that reach their funding target are run by women (Farr, 2014).

Unlike Indiegogo, Kickstarter (http://www.kickstarter.com), launched in 2009, has specific criteria for projects and an all-or-nothing funding policy. In terms of funding criteria, Kickstarter projects must fall into one of the following categories: Art, Comics, Dance, Design, Fashion, Film, Food, Games, Music, Photography, Publishing, Technology, or Theater (Barnett, 2013). Anyone can donate, but only projects created in the United States, Canada, or the United Kingdom are eligible for funding. Funding requests are often geared toward the completion of a specific creative product, such as a book, CD, film, game, or app. Like Indiegogo, funding amounts tend to be modest, with a typical campaign goal of $5,000.

Due to its more rigid guidelines and criteria, Kickstarter participants have a higher success rate. Nevertheless, 56 percent of Kickstarter campaigns fail to reach their funding goals in sixty days, the maximum allowable duration for a campaign. An interesting study by Mollick (2013) finds that projects generally succeed by small margins, or fail by large ones. Social capital and preparedness are associated with an increased chance of project success, which suggests that quality signals play a role in project outcomes. He also found that geography appears to be linked to the success rates of projects.

Kickstarter charges a 5 percent fee for projects that do reach their funding goals. Those that do not pay no fees, but all funds are returned to the donors. From its launch in 2008 through to the beginning of March 2014, Kickstarter accounted for more than 57,000 successfully funded projects, and attracted over 5.7 million investors who collectively contributed over $1 billion.

Early stage fundraising through crowdfunding can help startups grow, perhaps even offering an alternative to the traditional pre-seed financing or a pre-stage to the current seed-funding solutions like angel investment, venture capital, or governmental support. In one study, Mollick and Kuppuswamy (2014) found that 90 percent of successful crowdfunding projects turned into ongoing ventures, many of these high-growth ventures. As an example, Oculus Rift raised about $2.5 million for a virtual reality (VR) headset designed specifically for video games. Oculus VR—the company behind Oculus Rift—went on to raise $16 million in a Series A round, and another $75 million in a Series B round before being acquired by Facebook for $2 billion (Wired.com, 2014).

• The Pebble Smartwatch and Crowdfunding

The Pebble Smartwatch (https://getpebble.com) was designed by Canadian engineer Eric Migicovsky while he was still a student at the University of Waterloo in Ontario. Eric noticed that he was continually pulling out his cell phone to check messages. It occurred to him that this would be much easier and less disruptive if the messages would just show up on his wristwatch. Together with several friends, Migicovsky developed an early version of the watch in the garage of their home. In 2011, the project was accepted into Y Combinator, a high-tech business incubator in California that provided seed funding, guidance, and key contacts. Eric attempted to raise additional funds through the traditional venture capital route with limited success. Assuming it was a long shot, he decided to try raising capital through the Kickstarter crowdfunding site (How He Invented the Smart Watch, 2013). Migicovsky launched his Kickstarter campaign on April 11, 2012, with an initial goal of $100,000, which he achieved within two hours. Migicovsky's firm, Pebble Technology, closed its funding campaign on May 18 after raising $10.2 million from 68,929 backers, making it the largest funded project in Kickstarter's history (Here's How the Pebble Smartwatch Became the Most Funded Project in Kickstarter History, 2014).

The Kickstarter funding enabled Pebble to begin its rapid-growth trajectory by producing and shipping watches on a larger scale. This set the stage for a Series A round of funding from Charles River Ventures for $15 million, raising the level of total external funding to $27.5 million. Over time Pebble added a number of features, including waterproofing, caller ID, a control for music played on a phone, and a variety of apps. Although earlier versions of the Pebble watch sold for approximately $150, the most recent version, the Pebble Steel launched in 2014, sells for $249 and is dressier and more stylish. While Migicovsky initially focused on developing the hardware for his product, today he is much more focused on software applications. The Pebble Appstore was launched in February 2014 to take advantage of this trend and features over a thousand different apps. Although Pebble has only sold about 300,000 smartwatches to date, Migicovsky is convinced that wearable devices are "the next big thing" (Burns, 2013). He was quoted in a recent *Forbes* article as follows:

> Now is the right time to be thinking about a smartwatch because the technology is
> there and people are ready for it. What we've shown with Pebble is that when you have

the right combination of cool features and watch options, that's when people are going to care about smartwatches. I'm sure that we'll see different types of hardware down the line, but ultimately, I think most of the developments are going to be software. That's the real value for the user (Adams, 2014).

Although the Pebble Smartwatch, created by a male entrepreneur, is the poster child of successful Kickstarter campaigns, a growing number of women entrepreneurs are also raising funds through this platform. In fact, Julie Uhrman, founder of video game console maker Ouya, raised $8.6 million, making it Kickstarter's third most successful campaign to date.

Debt Platforms

As in the case of donations, crowdfunding for debt is not a new phenomenon, and has traditionally been associated with the provision of small loans to microentrepreneurs, often in developing countries. The Grameen Bank, founded in Bangladesh by Nobel Prize–winner Mohammed Yunis, pioneered the idea of having individuals in a community pool their financial resources in order to make small loans to each other. This approach empowers community members and encourages them to be financially responsible for their mutual benefit. The success of the Grameen experience has led to wide replication of the microlending model in both developing and developed countries. Microlending organizations play an important role in responding to the credit needs of entrepreneurs who do not have access to more traditional sources of debt in the form of bank loans. Their firms are small and often new, and their loan requests are not big enough to make them profitable for banks. Further, many small borrowers have limited levels of financial literacy combined with nonexistent or poor credit histories.

• Jessica Jackley and Kiva

Like Yunis, American entrepreneur Jessica Jackley also took on the task of targeting the credit needs of unbankable firms by launching Kiva (http://www.kiva.org) in 2005. Kiva uses the power of the Internet to connect firms needing credit with thousands of small, individual lenders. Each entrepreneur develops a description of her company, which is posted on the website, often accompanied by pictures of the entrepreneur and her products or services. She also indicates how much money she is attempting to raise and what it will be used for. Potential lenders browse the site in order to select firms that they are willing to lend to. The Kiva website states,

> We are a non-profit organization with a mission to connect people through lending to alleviate poverty. Leveraging the internet and a worldwide network of microfinance institutions, Kiva lets individuals lend as little as $25 to help create opportunity around the world. (http://www.kiva.org)

Today, Kiva operates in seventy-three countries by channeling funds through local microfinance organizations that in turn make loans. To date, Kiva has provided $529 million in loans, primarily to women. Over 98 percent of these loans are repaid. Recently, Kiva started lending to business owners in the United States as well as those in developing economies.

Although microfinance organizations typically do not target the types of growth-oriented firms that we are focusing on in this book, they do provide debt capital to firms in the survival and early growth stages. Given the growing number of women who are receiving loans through these channels, it is entirely likely that some of them will eventually emerge as growth-oriented enterprises. In this sense, crowdfunding for debt capital can be viewed as another alternative, particularly for early stage entrepreneurs.

The first wave of online platforms for lending used innovative software and data metrics including social media interactions and Yelp reviews. These tools made it possible to assess the health of businesses and to make decisions on business loan applications. OnDeck (https://www.ondeck.com), established in 2007, was an early entrant in this space and has underwritten more than $900 million in loans. Kabbage (https://www.kabbage.com), founded in 2011, targets online merchants and lent $200 million in 2013 alone.

A more recent wave of online lending platforms has combined digital innovation and efficiency with true term loans. These online platforms offer a middle path between banks, which lend primarily to the most creditworthy businesses, and cash advance lenders, who target subprime candidates. Funding Circle (https://www.fundingcircle.com) provides loans up to $500,000, usually with rates between 10 and 17 percent, while Dealstruck (https://www.dealstruck.com) offers business loans of up to $250,000, rates from 8 to 24 percent, and terms of up to three years. Fundera acts as a matchmaker between small firms and alternative or non-bank lenders. Founded in February of 2014, Fundera helped over 850 firms secure a total of $42 million in loans over the course of its first eighteen months (http://www.fundera.com). Prosper (https://www.prosper.com) and Lending Club (https://www.lendingclub.com), which have made more than $4 billion in consumer loans, have also expanded into the small business lending market. Rising demand and increased visibility for the potential of crowdfunding has attracted other entrants as well. Daric (http://daric.com), a peer platform backed by a former Wells Fargo chief executive, opened recently, and Fundation (http://fundation.com), based in New York, offers terms comparable to those of peer-to-peer lenders using financial capital supplied by a partner (Garrison Investment Group). These new competitors are already influencing the online lending environment by forcing established players to adjust with offerings of bigger loans and better terms.

An important distinction between Kiva and these new crowdfunding platforms is in the rigor of their review process. Professional underwriters review all loan applications before they are posted to the platforms. Along with making additional loan funds available to small businesses, these platforms also provide investors with opportunities to earn an attractive return. Loan rates are based on the borrower's ability to repay, as in the case of bank loans. At present, for example, Funding Circle investors earn an average net return of 5.7 percent, which compares favorably to a number of other investment alternatives in our current low-interest-rate environment.

Community Sourced Capital (communitysourcedcapital.com), launched in 2013, is a lending platform with a slightly different model. CSC connects businesses to people in their community (and beyond) by providing technology, marketing, and administrative know-how to make borrowing money from those people possible. CSC refers to lenders as "Squareholders," and sets squares at $50 each. In 2013 they had thirteen completed campaigns, well over a thousand Squareholders, and just under $200,000 in loans provided to small businesses. As of 2014, they were bringing CSC to new communities around the country, expanding their team, and growing their community of borrowers by a factor of ten. One of us (Alicia Robb) met them at the Social Capital Markets (SOCAP) conference in 2012 and was so impressed she became a Squareholder in a vegan food company in Seattle (supporting vegan businesses is one of her passions). We also spoke with Jessika Tantisook, co-founder of Starvation Valley Farms in Washington State, who used CSC to raise funds for a juicer after being turned down by local banks. She raised about $12,000 on the CSC platform to buy the juicer, which allowed her firm to move from just selling cranberries into producing organic cranberry juice for sale. This first loan allowed Starvation Valley Farms to build a track record by rolling out a new product line, which in turn made it possible for them to secure a $100,000 loan from a local community development financial institution.

Equity Platforms

Although crowdfunding for donations and loans have both been around for a while, crowdfunding for equity is a new development authorized by passage of the Jumpstart Our Business Startups (or JOBS) Act in April 2012. This act provides a means for startups and small firms to raise equity capital through securities offerings using the Internet, thereby lowering costs. Currently, equity crowdfunding platforms are restricted to accredited investors (those individuals with more than $1 million in assets aside from their home, or $200,000 of income annually).

The initial entrant in the equity crowdfunding space was AngelList (https://angel.co), which we profiled in Chapter 6. Another major platform, Circle Up (http://www.circleup.com), is an equity crowdfunding platform that focuses on consumer products only. Investments typically range from $10,000 to $25,000, but can sometimes be as low as $5,000. Yet another platform, WeFunder (https://wefunder.com), is the closest to true crowdfunding, with investors making investments of as little as $100. WeFunder aggregates these small investors into one investment vehicle, rather than having hundreds or even thousands of individuals on the capitalization table. Targeted platforms are also beginning to emerge, such as Portfolia.com, which targets both female investors and women-led companies.

Massolution's 2015 crowdfunding report indicates that all types of platforms grew rapidly over the 2013–2014 period:

1. Lending-based crowdfunding grew 223 percent to $11.08 billion.

2. Equity-based crowdfunding grew 182 percent to $1.1 billion.

3. Hybrid-based crowdfunding grew 290 percent to $487 million.

4. Royalty-based crowdfunding grew 336 percent to $273 million.

5. Donation- and reward-based crowdfunding grew 45 percent and 84 percent respectively (Massolution 2015).

The JOBS Act and the SEC

The Securities and Exchange Commission (SEC) has the responsibility for developing rules governing the offer and sale of securities. Consistent with that, at the end of 2013 it issued proposed rules for securities issued through crowdfunding with a request that comments be submitted by the beginning of February 2014 (http://www.sec.gov). The SEC published their final rulings on Title III of the JOBS Act on October 30, 2015, which open up investing to non-accredited investors for the first time (Securities and Exchange Commission, 2015).

Title III allows companies to make securities offerings to non-accredited investors of up to $1 million within a twelve-month period, which means that for the first time, entrepreneurs can seek investors from the general public. Unlike the donation model described above, firms seeking capital through this new crowdfunding model can issue debt or sell ownership shares (equity) online to investors seeking a financial return. Several concerns have already been raised about restrictions imposed on equity crowdfunding under Title III. Some contend that the cap of $1 million over a twelve-month period is insufficient for rapid-growth firms. Similarly, Title III places caps on the amount that individuals can invest through crowdfunding. For those with incomes of $100,000 or more, there is a cap of 10 percent of annual income or net worth, whichever is higher. For those with incomes of less than $100,000 the cap is $2,000 or 5 percent of annual income or net worth, whichever is higher. Finally, concerns have been expressed about the potential for fraud and misinformation, particularly in light of the fact that crowdfunding may attract relatively unsophisticated investors who may be unaware of the risks associated with their investments (Korn, 2013).

To combat the risk of fraud and protect investors, Title III requires that crowdfunding transactions be conducted through an intermediary registered with the SEC. This can be either a broker-dealer or a funding portal. These intermediaries would be required to

1. Provide investors with educational materials.

2. Take measures to reduce the risk of fraud.

3. Make information available about the issuer and the offering.

4. Provide communication channels to allow discussions about offerings on the platform.

5. Facilitate the offer and sale of crowdfunded securities.

Similarly, funding portals would be prohibited from

1. Offering investment advice or making recommendations.
2. Soliciting purchases, sales, or offers to buy securities offered on their websites.
3. Imposing certain restrictions on compensating people for solicitations.
4. Holding, possessing, or handling investor funds or securities (Eyden, 2013).

In spite of its possible limitations and risks, Title III crowdfunding has the potential to open up new avenues of funding for growth-oriented entrepreneurs, particularly during the survival stage when funding options may be limited. To date, women entrepreneurs have been the major beneficiaries of raising capital in the form of donations and small loans through crowdfunding. Similarly, equity crowdfunding could also benefit women who are often not well represented in angel investor and venture capital networks. In effect, crowdfunding has the potential to "democratize" the private equity market by serving as a means for both women entrepreneurs and women investors to participate more fully. The Appendix lists some of the major crowdfunding platforms to date. It is anticipated that the recent approval of Title III crowdfunding for non-accredited investors will open the door to a flood of additional new entrants.

Platforms Focused on Women Entrepreneurs

Portfolia is currently the only crowdfunding platform raising equity capital that is focused on female entrepreneurs and female investors that we are aware of. Others, however, are raising capital for women entrepreneurs through reward and pre-purchase models. Let's take a look at how these various platforms work as well as the benefits they can provide for growth-oriented women entrepreneurs.

Portfolia

Portfolia (Portfolia.com) is an equity crowdfunding site that creates a social network of engaged investors around women-owned entrepreneurial ventures. Portfolia's digital platform makes it possible for individuals and affinity groups to discover and invest in private entrepreneurial companies in their areas of expertise and interest. Companies access both money and markets as investors engage their social networks and collective buying power for the company's competitive advantage and mutual long-term financial gain.

The Portfolia community scouts out growth-oriented women entrepreneurs who are creating the most exciting young companies. It searches for companies and teams that understand the importance of connecting with customers early in order to get feedback on products and services, to share the company story with friends and colleagues, and to provide growth capital by investing in the company. Most important, Portfolia looks for founding teams that have the expertise and commitment to deliver on their vision.

We spoke with Trish Costello, founder and CEO of Portfolia. At that time, Portfolia had launched its Beta version, and Trish was excited because early results supported her conjecture that, if we give women a place to come and be part of an investor community, they will invest. Trish used the company Shebooks as an example. Shebooks.net offers a curated selection of short e-books on the topics women care about most. Sold singly or by subscription and downloadable to tablets, smartphones, and e-readers, Shebooks are designed to be read in under two hours, perfect for busy women and their book clubs. The Portfolia platform attracted several successful women executives who invested equity for the first time in this company. Once these women and others like them became a part of the platform, they went on to invest in other companies as well. Trish is confident that we are just starting to see the tip of the iceberg, and that more and more women are going to be drawn into the investing scene.

MoolaHoop

MoolaHoop (Moola-hoop.com) is a reward-based crowdfunding platform created by women to help women leverage the "power of the crowd" to grow their businesses. MoolaHoop enables female entrepreneurs, business owners, and managers to garner financial support for their projects by reaching out to their customers through rewards in the form of special pricing on their products and services and unique experiences. MoolaHoop recognizes women's expertise in relationship-building and networking, and has created a secure web-based platform especially for female entrepreneurs to help them extend their own "crowd" of supporters in the form of existing and potential customers, professional networks, friends, and family. Launched on July 24, 2013, the MoolaHoop site marks the first step in the design and development of a robust ecosystem—the "Hoop"—to fund ideas and provide ongoing services to women business owners. As envisioned by company co-founders Brenda Bazan and Nancy Hayes, MoolaHoop will eventually grow through partnerships to offer a suite of resources supporting women-owned and women-led businesses, including access to funding sources, expert advice, education, and mentoring. Their target market is small businesses aiming to raise $10,000 to $20,000.

We spoke with Nancy Hayes, co-founder of MoolaHoop, about the challenges for businesses that are raising funding on these kinds of platforms, including hers. Nancy has more than thirty years of experience as a business leader and mentor in for-profit, nonprofit, and academic organizations. She also has an MBA with a concentration in finance. She shared that she and her partner have had to spend a lot of time prepping business owners for their crowdfunding campaigns. Thus, they have not been able to scale MoolaHoop as quickly as they had originally planned. According to Nancy, social media has served as an important vehicle for attracting both firms and investors to the platform. Although MoolaHoop targets small firms rather than high-growth ventures, it does provide an alternative source of funding for early stage entrepreneurs. As we have noted in this text, many women launch their firms with relatively modest goals. Once they actually get up and running, however, both their goals and their perceptions of their own capabilities and potential can change.

Plum Alley

Plum Alley crowdfunding is a way for women to raise money in large or small amounts to fund a specific project, product, or company. No ownership equity is given to the funder, but rather, the funder is given rewards, recognition, or products. On Plum Alley (PlumAlley.co), project creators usually have up to sixty days to raise funds.

The platform states that it takes this "all or nothing" approach for three reasons:

1. Psychology of a campaign: People want to be associated with success and many times will rally to contribute even more at the end of a campaign.

2. Honesty and transparency: In that you will do what you say you are going to do. Half a project is not what your supporters want.

3. Negative feel to campaigns that did not reach their goal. Future investors or supporters look at campaigns. You probably won't feel great explaining why your campaign fell short. We believe there is no reason to fail if your goal was set properly and if the campaign was organized and well run. That is why we built our site to guide you and demystify the process. We want you to reach success and not be on the defensive on why your campaign fell short (https://plumalley.co/faq).

Plum Alley emerged from a desire to support women entrepreneurs and innovators in a meaningful way. Deborah Jackson, founder of Plum Alley, realized that crowdfunding could serve as a means for encouraging women's innovation and increasing their access to financial capital. Deborah states, "Plum Alley exists for two reasons: to get more money to women's ventures and to increase the number of women and men who provide dollars to fund them. This isn't just a 'nice to have.' This is the way that our economy will grow and new jobs will be created."

Deborah has been recognized as a leader, entrepreneur, CEO, and funding expert by numerous groups and publications: TechCrunch 2014, Fast Company's League of Extraordinary Women 2012, *Forbes* magazine. Recently she was named as one of the hundred most prominent people in tech in New York, and her story was a chapter in the recent book *Innovating Women* (Wadhwa and Chideya, 2014).

Kathryn Moos, founder and CEO of Vrou, a company that infuses water with essential minerals, antioxidants, and electrolytes, used Plum Alley to raise more than $30,000 to test new flavors and build out an e-commerce site (http://www.vroulife.com). She exceeded her funding goal, and her products can now be found on the Vrou website and Amazon.com as well as in Whole Foods stores. Commenting on her experience with Plum Alley in a *Wall Street Journal* blog, Kathryn stated, "I don't know if it will ultimately solve the problem for women entrepreneurs that want to really scale their business, but we see this as an opportunity to start to really build upon our brand" (Murray, 2013).

Consistent with Moos' observation, although Plum Alley and MoolaHoop can serve small businesses, these platforms have not yet been used by companies that need to raise significant amounts of capital. Alternatively, equity platforms such as Portfolia and CircleUp provide larger amounts of capital for firms on a higher growth path. As an example, Willa founder Christy Prunier raised $1 million on CircleUp to fund her natural skincare company, while Meika and Jeffrey Hollender used CircleUp to raise $600,000 for their socially conscious condom company, which markets primarily to women and donates a part of its profits to improving women's reproductive health. These various examples illustrate both the accessibility and flexibility of crowdfunding as a financing strategy for women entrepreneurs, a growing number of whom are already using new and established platforms to raise financial capital for a broad range of business needs.

Closing the Loop

As we have noted in earlier chapters, early stage and survival stage financing can be a challenge for growth-oriented women entrepreneurs. Typically, women rely on internal sources of capital, including their own funds, family and friends, and bootstrapping, as major sources of early stage financing. These sources may be limited, however, due to women's lower level of earnings and wealth, thereby constraining the firm's potential for survival and growth. Those firms that reach the survival stage typically need to start reaching out to external investors or angels because they have exhausted the entrepreneur's early stage sources. This also poses a challenge for women entrepreneurs who are less likely to be a part of networks that would bring them in contact with potential angel investors, the majority of whom are men. In this chapter, we have focused on crowdfunding, an emerging source of early and survival stage financing that could be particularly beneficial to growth-oriented women entrepreneurs.

Crowdfunding is a relatively new source of funding used by an increasing number of growth-oriented firms to raise financial capital. As we have noted, rewards-based and pre-purchase models for crowdfunding have now been around for a while and have been used for innovative products such as the Oculus Rift virtual reality headset and the Bia Sport, the makers of which both went on to become full-fledged companies. Crowdfunding for debt is less established in the United States, but is rapidly gaining traction. Crowdfunding for external equity is very new, and is just beginning to emerge as a major financing strategy for firms that have exhausted the entrepreneur's personal sources of capital but are not yet ready for angel or venture capital funding. As with AngelList, which we profiled in Chapter 6, crowdfunding provides an opportunity for entrepreneurs to raise equity capital directly from multiple investors. This approach has the potential to benefit women entrepreneurs in particular, because it allows them to "tell their story" directly to investors rather than going through financial intermediaries who may have a bias toward certain types of industries, firms, and entrepreneurs. In addition, crowdfunding can serve as a means for unlocking the investing power of women who have played a more limited role in both angel and VC investing. This is good news for women entrepreneurs as well, because studies show that women investors are more likely to consider firms owned by other women. Thus, although growth-oriented women entrepreneurs will not get a free ride from women investors any more than they would from men, they are at least more likely to get on the radar screen. Early results suggest, in fact, that crowdfunding is helping to level the playing field for early stage financial capital for women. In turn, a growing number of women entrepreneurs and women investors are turning to crowdfunding platforms to raise financing and to support the growth of women-owned firms (Marom, Robb, and Sade 2014; Greenberg and Mollick 2014).

What Does This Mean for You?

What do you need to be aware of if you are considering crowdfunding as a source of financial capital?

1. First, determine what type of capital you want to raise through crowdfunding. Different platforms target firms looking for donations, loans, or equity. Remember that donations do not have to be repaid, but loans do. Similarly, lenders do not expect an ownership interest in your firm, but equity investors do.

2. Once you have decided on the type of capital, begin researching platforms that specialize in that particular type. How long has the platform been in existence, and what is its track record? Does the platform target particular industries or lines of business? What types of firms are listed on the site, and have they achieved their funding goals? What percentage of funded firms have women founders or women as a part of the founding team?

3. What are the platform's terms for firms raising capital? In other words, what will it cost you to raise financial capital from this source, and are there less costly platforms or other alternatives? As we discussed earlier, individuals raising funds through Indiegogo pay a fee of anywhere from 4 to 9 percent. Similarly, on lending-based platforms, what is the interest rate charged and are there associated fees? For equity-based platforms, what types of expectations do investors have in terms of receiving equity, oversight of the firm, and having a role in governance?

4. How much money can you actually expect to raise on the platform? Some platforms, particularly donation-based and lending-based platforms, focus on individuals or firms attempting to raise relatively modest amounts, that is, $5,000 or less. Although these platforms may address the needs of very early stage entrepreneurs, they are probably not appropriate for firms that are growing rapidly.

5. If you plan to raise equity capital from non-accredited investors through a crowdfunding platform, familiarize yourself with the terms and limitations imposed under Title III of the 2012 JOBS Act. One of the most important of these is that firms raising capital through this means are limited to $1 million within a twelve-month period. This doesn't mean that crowdfunding is unsuitable for high-growth firms, but it does mean that those firms that are scaling rapidly may have to supplement crowdfunding with other external sources.

6. As in the case of bootstrapping, do not over-rely on crowdfunding to the extent that you neglect to develop your network of potential funding sources for rapid growth. Crowdfunding is an exciting addition to the funding alternatives of early and survival stage firms. Nevertheless, high-growth firms that emerge from these stages will need large amounts of external financial capital to power them through their rapid-growth stage. This funding typically comes from venture capitalists who provide a mix of financial, human, and social capital. Thus, the growing popularity of crowdfunding does not negate the entrepreneur's need to develop and nurture relationships with potential upstream funding sources.

7. Explore crowdfunding platforms like Portfolia that target growth-oriented women entrepreneurs. These platforms are actively looking for high-potential women-owned firms to fund. As an added benefit, they are also more likely to attract women investors who want to support such firms. In this sense, platforms such as Portfolia bring together two previously neglected segments of the funding mix, women entrepreneurs seeking to grow their firms and women with the desire and means to invest.

8. Finally, explore the experience of other firms that have used crowdfunding in order to become aware of its strengths, weaknesses, limitations, and risks. As with most other funding strategies, there is no such thing as a "free lunch," so doing your homework up front can help you avoid unpleasant surprises. We are at the early stages of the crowdfunding "wave," so we all have a lot to learn.

9

LIFTOFF!

Financing Strategies for Scaling Up
and Managing Rapid Growth

A key challenge for growth-oriented entrepreneurs, once they have proven the viability of their business model, is scaling the firm to achieve significant size and scope. It is an even greater challenge for women entrepreneurs, because they are less likely to have prior experience at the most senior levels of large and growing firms. Similarly, there are as yet fewer growth-oriented women entrepreneurs who can serve as role models. Major sources of financing to achieve scale typically include venture capital, private placements of debt or equity, bank loans, and mezzanine or bridge financing. Prior research has revealed that growth-oriented women entrepreneurs experience greater difficulties in securing these important sources of external capital because to date they have not had access to the types of networks and contacts that provide them. Previous studies also suggest that when women entrepreneurs do secure growth capital, they often struggle with the negotiation process and raise amounts that are insufficient for their needs. In this chapter we will focus on the financing sources and strategies used by women entrepreneurs who have scaled their firms.

The Role of Venture Capital

In Chapter 6 we highlighted the importance of angel investor capital as a source of early stage financing. As we noted, angel investors play a critical role in the provision of external equity for early and survival stage firms. Angel investors may invest individually, or, increasingly, through the collective efforts of an angel investor network. In Chapter 6 we also discussed the development of new, online platforms such as AngelList that allow angel investors to connect directly with entrepreneurs and with each other. In each instance, the angel investor is investing his or her own money rather than someone else's. In contrast, venture capital firms are organized as financial intermediaries. They raise capital from investors, pool that capital, and invest it in growth-oriented firms (De Clercq, Fried, Lehtonen, and Sapienza, 2006). Typically, the partners in the firm invest their own capital along with that of their investors, but for the most part they are investing other people's money. Whereas angel investors have a rather diverse array of motivations, venture capitalists tend to be more focused on providing attractive financial returns to their investors. This typically occurs through the sale of portfolio firms or through an initial public offering.

From the entrepreneur's perspective, there are a number of advantages associated with venture capital funding. VC firms can provide large amounts of external equity, typically in excess of $1 million. In addition, they have the financial means to provide multiple rounds of funding to firms that achieve growth and performance targets (Mason and Harrison, 1999). Venture capitalists are also patient investors in the sense that they are willing to wait for as long as five to ten years for a firm to generate returns. This characteristic is particularly important for entrepreneurs in industries such as bioscience with long development cycles. Like angel investors, VCs accept the risk of investing in new, privately owned firms, and recognize that not all of their portfolio companies will yield a positive return. In light of the risky nature of their investments, VC firms anticipate a higher return for their investors from those portfolio companies that do succeed (De Clercq, Fried, Lehtonen, and Sapienza, 2006). Typically, VC firms co-invest with other VC firms as a way to minimize their exposure to individual firms (Mason and Harrison, 1999). This syndication approach provides an added benefit to entrepreneurs in that it provides additional sources of funding.

Figure 9.1 illustrates venture capital's roller coaster ride over the course of the last two decades. Both deals (upper line) and amounts invested (lower line) rose sharply during the dot-com buildup, peaking in the year 2000, and then dropped just as sharply during the ensuing dot-com bust. From 2004 to 2007 the industry recovered modestly, only to suffer another drop during the years of the financial crisis and Great Recession (2007–2009). When we interviewed entrepreneurs for our first book, *A Rising Tide*, several alluded to the virtual impossibility of raising VC capital during that time. Since 2010, however, the VC industry has seen yet another slow period of recovery. Figure 9.1 shows

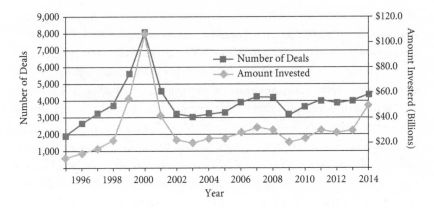

FIGURE 9.1. Venture Capital Deals and Amount Invested Over Time
Source: National Venture Capital Association Yearbook 2015

that although the numbers of deals and dollars invested have risen steadily, they have not yet regained their pre-financial-crisis levels. This observation has been confirmed by our more recent entrepreneur interviews, which have documented the continued challenges associated with raising venture capital in an improving but not fully healed economy.

Unlike angel investors, venture capital firms tend to focus on a fairly limited number of industries. These include software and technology, health care and bioscience, and growth-oriented segments of the retail or consumer services markets (De Clercq, Fried, Lehtonen, and Sapienza, 2006; Gompers and Lerner, 2001). This industry focus allows VC firms to develop specialized knowledge about products, services, and industries that are new and as yet untested, thereby ameliorating the problem of asymmetric or incomplete information. This specialized knowledge provides links to key contacts, industry experts, and other funding sources that can benefit their portfolio companies. Thus, venture capitalists are an important source of human and social capital as well as financial capital.

Table 9.1 highlights the two industries that venture capital firms have focused on in recent years. It illustrates that information technology accounted for almost 70 percent of deals and investment dollars in 2013. In contrast, firms in the second largest sector, the medical, health, and life sciences industries, represented 20 percent of deals and 23 percent of investment dollars. All other industries together accounted for roughly 10 percent of deals and less than 10 percent of investment dollars. Figure 9.2 provides a more detailed breakdown of VC investments in 2013 by industry sector.

Given the size of their investments and their relatively long investment time frame, it is probably not surprising that venture capitalists take a very "hands-on" approach to working with their portfolio companies. The VC firm takes seats on the firm's board of directors and monitors the firm's performance on an ongoing basis (De Clercq, Fried, Lehtonen, and Sapienza, 2006; Gompers and Lerner, 2001). This is partially to provide ongoing support and assistance, but it also allows the VC firm to evaluate whether or not the firm

TABLE 9.1. Venture Capital Investments in 2013 by Industry Group

Industry Group	All Investments			Initial Investment		
	Number of Companies	Number of Deals	Amount ($ Billions)	Number of Companies	Number of Deals	Amount ($ Billions)
Information Technology	2,360	2,784	20	1,009	1,009	3.5
Medical/Health/ Life Science	649	816	6.9	167	167	1.2
Non-High Technology	373	440	2.7	157	157	0.4
Total	3,382	4,040	29.6	1,333	1,333	5.1

Source: National Venture Capital Association, 2014

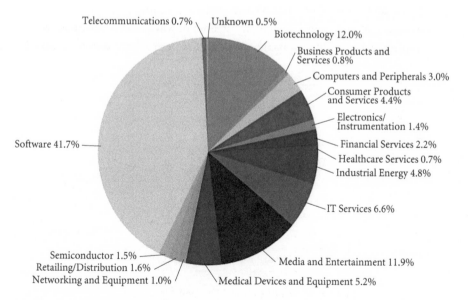

FIGURE 9.2. Venture Capital Investments by Industry
Source: National Venture Capital Association Yearbook 2015

merits continued funding. As firms progress through their rapid-growth stage and build out their infrastructure to support significant size and scale, venture capitalists provide additional value by helping to identify individuals to fill key managerial positions.

A Model of Venture Capital Investing

Entrepreneurship scholars Tyzoon T. Tyebjee and Albert V. Bruno (1984) presented and tested a model of venture capital investing activity using a sample of venture capitalists in three states (Figure 9.3). Their model consists of five sequential steps: (1) deal origination, (2) screening, (3) evaluation, (4) deal structuring, and (5) post-investment activities. In terms of deal origination, Tyebjee and Bruno found that the majority of deals (65 percent) came to the VC's attention through referrals from sources such as other VCs, prior investees, personal acquaintances, banks, and the like. This finding highlights the importance of the entrepreneur's social capital and the networks she is a part of.

Screening criteria included a number of considerations such as the amount of capital required, market sector, geographic location, and stage of financing. Tyebjee and Bruno found that VCs tended to have minimum and maximum amounts that they were willing to invest, both of which were higher than what an entrepreneur could reasonably expect to raise from angel investors. As noted

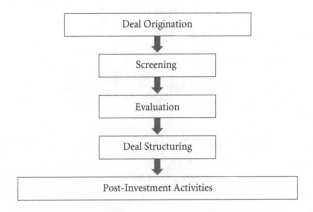

FIGURE 9.3. Venture Capital Decision-Making Process
Source: Tyebjee and Bruno, 1984

above, the VCs in this study specialized by industry, with roughly 75 percent focusing on technology-intensive markets. A number of the VC firms also had a geographic focus in order to facilitate regular meetings and monitoring of portfolio companies. Some of the more interesting findings from the Tyebjee and Bruno study were those relating to stage of financing. They found that VCs rarely provided financing for the nascent stage, making it necessary for entrepreneurs to rely on internal sources and angel financing for that stage. Alternatively, VCs provided financing for firms in the startup (45.6 percent), first-round expansion (22.2 percent), and second-round expansion (21.1 percent) stages. Subsequent studies by other researchers have also found that venture capital firms in general are moving toward later rather than early stage investments as a way to minimize risk.

In terms of evaluation, the VCs surveyed evaluated potential deals based on five characteristics:

Market attractiveness: the size, growth, and accessibility of the market as well as the extent to which there was an unmet market need.

Product differentiation: the entrepreneur's ability to create a product that is unique and can deter competition through such means as patents.

Managerial capabilities: the managerial skills and experience of the founding team as well as favorable references.

Environmental threat resistance: the extent to which the venture is resistant to environmental pressures such as obsolescence, changes in the economy, or competition.

Cash-out potential: the likelihood that the venture can achieve a liquidity event in the desired time frame.

Subsequent studies have confirmed the importance of these screening criteria (De Clercq, Fried, Lehtonen, and Sapienza, 2006; Fried and Hisrich, 1994; Mason and Harrison, 1999).

Although Tyebjee and Bruno did not collect data on deal structuring or post-investment activities from their sample of VCs, they did interview a smaller sample on these issues. Their feedback indicated the VCs typically took an equity position in their portfolio firms structured in the form of convertible preferred stock. Post-investment activities included board representation, management guidance, and business contacts.

Judy Robinett on "How to Be a Power Connector in Venture Capital"

Consistent with Tyebjee and Bruno's observations regarding the role played by VC networks, our next mini-case focuses on entrepreneur and corporate leader Judy Robinett, one of the nation's leading experts on helping leaders develop strategic relationships (http://www.judyrobinett.com). Robinett has more than thirty years of experience as an entrepreneur and corporate leader and has served as the CEO of both public and private companies and in management positions at Fortune 500 companies. She has also helped entrepreneurs and businesses access millions of dollars in funding. When we spoke with her about her role as an advisory board member for Springboard Enterprises and as a managing director for Golden Seeds, she had just returned from judging a Dolphin Tank event in San Francisco (https://sb.co/dolphin-tank/).[1] In her recently released book, *How to Be a Power Connector* (Robinett, 2014), Judy discusses the power of high-value, strategic connections. In the area of venture capital, these connections can be extremely important because, she says, "it's not just the details that cause investors to open their wallets. It's also the people who recommend the deals that open the doors that lead to funding." Judy cited a 2012 *Inc.* magazine study showing that social ties between venture capitalists and entrepreneurs seeking funding are actually more important in the funding decision than whether a prestigious VC firm has already committed to the deal (McGinn, 2012). This observation gives credence to why we need more women involved on both sides of the funding table. Judy spends a great deal of time mentoring female entrepreneurs and helping them make connections with angel and VC investors.

Women Entrepreneurs and Venture Capital

Prior research confirms that only a small percentage of venture capital financing goes to women-owned firms (Bosse and Taylor, 2012; Brush, Carter, and others, 2001). These studies also point out that challenges in attracting venture capital pose a significant risk to the ability of women-owned firms to survive, grow, introduce product and service innovations, and contribute to the economy. A number of theories have been posited for the gender discrepancy in VC financing. One is that women are less likely to launch firms in technology-based industries that are attractive to venture capitalists. Alternatively, they are more prone to start firms in retail and service sectors that are characterized by high competition, lower levels of profitability, and slower growth (Greene, Brush,

Hart, and Saparito, 2001). A second factor that has been cited is that women are less likely to be a part of the networks that would provide them with access to venture capital (Bosse and Taylor, 2012; Brush, Carter, and others, 2001). The venture capital industry remains male-dominated, particularly at the most senior decision-making levels. Similarly, women entrepreneurs are less likely to have previous entrepreneurial experience resulting in contacts with venture capital firms or other entrepreneurs who might refer them to VC firms (Greene, Brush, Hart, and Saparito, 2001). A third factor is the belief that women are less motivated to grow their firms and are more risk averse when it comes to the challenges and complexities of operating large firms (Bosse and Taylor, 2012; Cliff, 1998). Thus, they are less likely to launch firms that will ultimately achieve the types of harvest events and returns that venture capital investors look for.

In a study on the topic of women and equity capital, the Diana Project researchers (Brush, Carter, and others, 2001) surveyed women entrepreneurs who participated in the Springboard 2000 forums in an attempt to dispel some of the "myths" about women entrepreneurs and firm growth. These forums were designed to bring together growth-oriented women entrepreneurs and providers of angel or VC financing. Through this process, Professor Candida Brush and her colleagues found that the Springboard forums were attracting a substantial number of women who did aspire to rapid growth and needed equity capital to help them achieve that end. In fact, that year's forums attracted 1,700 applicants for 175 available slots (Brush, Carter, and others, 2001, p. 4). Findings from their study revealed that a high percentage of women who participated in the Springboard forums, 50 percent, had launched firms in technology sectors.

In contrast, the Diana Project team found it more difficult to dispel the "myth" about network access. Their findings revealed that although more women were gaining employment at VC firms, their percentage representation actually decreased from 1995 to 2000. Similarly, Dr. Brush and her colleagues found that an alarmingly high percentage of women who were employed in the industry simply left. This led the authors to conclude that the venture capital industry remained male-dominated and that women VCs did not stick around long enough to reach the more senior ranks of their organizations.

Intrigued by these results, the Diana Project researchers conducted a second set of studies focusing more specifically on women's involvement in the venture capital industry (Brush and others, 2004). Their findings confirmed the results of the earlier study. In particular, they found that women entrepreneurs' lack of connections with venture capitalists hampered their ability to secure funding from this source. This was particularly true in VC firms with no or limited representation of women in decision-making roles. In contrast, however, VC firms with women in those roles were much more likely to connect with and attract women-led firms. Although the women VCs did not give preferential treatment to women-owned firms, the fact that they were visible and had a role in the decision-making process led to more deals closed with women-led ventures. On the basis of their findings, Brush and her colleagues concluded that (1) more opportunities need to be created for growth-oriented women entrepreneurs to network directly with venture capitalists, and (2) more women VCs in visible, decision-making roles would increase deal flow and funding for women-owned firms.

In 2014, members of the original Diana Project team and others (Brush and others, 2014) revisited the issue of venture capital funding for women entrepreneurs by examining more recent data for the 2011–2013 time frame. Their findings revealed that 15 percent of firms receiving VC funding during that period had a woman on the executive team, compared with fewer than 5 percent in their earlier study. Although this percentage does not mirror the percentage of women who are entrepreneurs, it does represent important progress. Brush and her colleagues further noted that firms with women on the founding team were more likely to receive later-stage funding (21 percent) than those in the early (13 percent) or seed (9 percent) stages. Consistent with the industry focus of VC firms in general, investments in firms with women on the executive team clustered in the areas of biotechnology (25 percent), health care services (22 percent), IT services health care (17 percent), and consumer products (15 percent).

From the standpoint of the gender composition of venture capital firms, Brush and colleagues (2014) noted that the number of women partners in VC firms has actually declined since their earlier study using 1999 data, from 10 percent of partners to 6 percent. Nevertheless, they found that VC firms with women partners were twice as likely to invest in companies with a woman on the management team (34 percent versus 13 percent). Similarly, VC firms with women partners were three times more likely to invest in companies with women CEOs (58 percent versus 15 percent).

In spite of these impressive gains, however, Brush and her colleagues warn that there is still a significant gap in VC funding between firms with a women on the executive team and those without. Their findings revealed that only 2.7 percent of the companies receiving VC funding during 2011–2013 had a woman CEO, while only 14 percent had a woman in any type of executive position. Clearly there is more work to be done in creating a better balance of women in decision-making roles in VC firms as well as among women entrepreneurs who seek and obtain VC funding. Equipped with these findings and insights, let's see how one growth-oriented woman entrepreneur, Diana Hessan, navigated the uncertain waters of venture capital.

Diane Hessan and Communispace

Diane Hessan established Communispace (http://www.communispace.com) to revolutionize the ways in which companies connect and gain input from their customers and markets. This allows those firms to make the customer an integral part of the product design and development process. Remember the "old days" when companies got input from focus groups? A focus group is a group of typically six to ten customers or market representatives who discuss open-ended questions in a session led by a facilitator. This provides qualitative input on such issues as product design and delivery, customer satisfaction, competing products and services, and ideas for new product or service offerings. An obvious weakness of the focus group method, however, is that input is based upon a limited number of respondents. Enter Communispace, stage left!

Communispace, founded in 1999, works with companies to develop online "community groups" that provide ongoing input on their product and service needs and preferences. By using this approach, Communispace is able to gain an in-depth understanding of both the firm and its customers. Hessan refers to her firm as a "consumer collaboration agency," pointing out that it allows customers to co-create products and services. This approach has been transformational in that it moves the customer from the end of the value chain to the front of it.

Hessan originally founded Communispace with a dedicated group of approximately a dozen individuals. For the first year, they survived on sweat equity by working for free. A small amount of capital, less than $1 million, was also raised from angel investors and corporations. By June of 2000, Hessan had a business plan and a prototype for her firm, which allowed her to go after "serious money." She made the rounds of VC firms armed with her PowerPoint presentations but met with little success on the East Coast. Her corporate attorney recommended a venture capital firm on the West Coast, however, Dominion Ventures. Dominion signed on and brought in another VC firm, Women Growth Capital, based in the Washington, D.C., area. One of Diane's early angel investors also joined in, and these three sources combined provided

Communispace with $10.5 million in funding. This much needed financing made it possible for Communispace to develop its enterprise software, build out its product offerings, and prove its business model.

During the ensuing months, Hessan expanded the firm, hiring engineers and software professionals who could increase the number of service offerings. As the firm grew, it also consumed a lot of cash, and quickly. By November of 2001, Hessan needed to raise additional external capital. The timing could not have been worse.

It was an awful time to be raising money. It was right after 9/11, and no one knew what was going to happen with the economy or the financial markets.

Fortunately, the two VC firms that had already invested in Communispace stayed with them. Due to uncertainties in the marketplace, however, Hessan was only able to raise enough capital to get her through the next eight months. This brought them up to June 2002. By that time, the markets had settled down somewhat, and Hessan was able to raise another $1.1 million from the same two VC firms. Her final round of funding in the amount of $2 million also came from these two firms. At that point, Communispace was growing rapidly, and this final round was used to support that growth.

As we spoke, I commented on how unusual it was for Diane's firm to have stayed with the same two VC firms throughout the various stages of her firm's growth. I asked about the nature of her relationship with those VCs.

It was tumultuous and, at times, very difficult. Over that space of time the economy had some dramatic ups and downs, and Communispace also had its ups and downs. Nevertheless, they stayed with us and supported us at critical times in the firm's development. That's what really cemented our relationship. When we really needed them, they were there for us, not just with money but also with professional and emotional support.

In summarizing some of the key lessons learned from her experience with raising capital, Diane shared the following points:

First, financing is a long-term partnership, and you have to talk to that person every day for years. There are great partners, and there are terrible partners. You have to ask yourself, "Is this someone we want as a partner?" The answer to that question is more important than what they can provide in terms of money. Second, raise as much capital as you can in each round. It is very time-consuming to be out there raising money, and the more frequently you have to do it, the more time you take away from developing and growing your business.

In January 2011, Communispace was sold to the Omnicom Group, a large multinational advertising and marketing communication services firm. In describing the reasons behind this decision, Hessan explained,

We were doing very well at the time, and our customers were all Fortune 500 firms. We needed to be more global in order to satisfy their needs, and this was a way to get us there quickly. It was a win-win on both sides, and Omnicom has allowed us to retain operating control as long as we deliver the results.

When we asked if Hessan was able to realize the economic rewards that came with the sale, she indicated that she benefited "tremendously" as did the other members of the founding team and the two loyal VC firms that backed them. Hessan stayed on at Communispace after the sale and served as its CEO. In January 2014, she announced her successor as well as her intention of moving into the role of chairman (New Communispace CEO, 2014). This will allow her to focus on strategic issues facing Communispace and its industry going forward.

How Do Venture Capitalists Add Value?

Diane Hessan's story highlights the critical role played by venture capital at key points in her firm's development. A large part of that role was in providing financial capital that allowed the firm to grow. Other aspects of the relationship included advice, guidance, and emotional support, and a number of researchers have confirmed the multifaceted nature of the entrepreneur-VC relationship. From a financial perspective, VC firms are uniquely able to provide substantial amounts of external equity for an extended period of time. They are also able to use their vast network of contacts to bring in additional VC investors by syndicating the deal. From a strategic perspective, VCs provide a sounding board for entrepreneurs, thereby helping them guide the firm as it grows (De Clercq, Fried, Lehtonen, and Sapienza, 2006; Sapienza, Manigart, and Vermeir, 1996). The tendency of VC firms to specialize by industry allows them to develop an in-depth knowledge of the industry's structure, competitive dynamics, and key players. As financial intermediaries, VC firms also create and communicate information about new and informationally opaque firms through their screening, due diligence, and monitoring activities, thus alleviating the problem of asymmetric information for the firm's investors (Van Osnabrugge, 2000).

Entrepreneurship researcher Dirk De Clercq and his colleagues (2006) commented on the "disciplinary role" of VCs in establishing objectives, goals, and benchmarks for portfolio firms. These measures ensure that the entrepreneur stays on target and moves toward a harvest event in a timely fashion. Benchmarks also help to identify performance shortfalls that may necessitate managerial changes. This type of change can be particularly painful for an entrepreneur who may have started the firm with a small but loyal band of followers. One of the challenges of growth, however, is the need to create an organizational infrastructure to support that growth while also bringing in managers with talents and expertise to achieve it (Van Osnabrugge, 2000).

Consistent with this theme of "staying on target," VC firms also help successful portfolio firms prepare for and achieve a harvest event. Typically this is in the form of a sale or merger, as in the case of Communispace, or, somewhat less frequently, an initial public offering. Table 9.2 highlights the growth potential of a sample of well-known firms that have gone public, some with innovative business models and others with innovative technology-based products.

Correspondingly, Figure 9.4 illustrates the exit routes for a sample of over eleven thousand firms first funded in the years between 1991 and 2000. It shows that a minority of firms, 14 percent, actually reached sufficient size and scale for

TABLE 9.2. *Venture Capital–Backed Companies (Employment at IPO and Now)*

Employment at Companies Known for Innovative Business Models			
Company	As of IPO	Current	# Change
The Home Depot	650	331,000	330,350
Starbucks Corporation	2,521	160,000	157,479
Staples	1,693	89,019	87,326
Whole Foods Market, Inc.	2,350	69,500	67,150
eBay	138	31,500	31,362

Employment at Companies Known for Innovative Technology Products			
Company	As of IPO	Current	# Change
Microsoft	1,153	94,000	92,847
Intel Corporation	460	100,100	99,640
Medtronic, Inc.	1,287	45,000	43,713
Apple Inc.	1,015	76,100	75,085
Google	3,021	53,861	50,840
JetBlue	4,011	12,070	8,059

Source: *National Venture Capital Association Yearbook 2015*

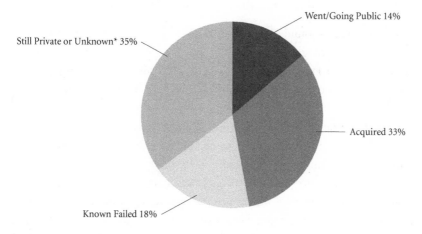

*Of these, most have quietly failed

FIGURE 9.4. Exit Funnel Outcomes of VC-Backed Companies

Note: Includes statistics from the PriceWaterhouseCoopers/National Venture Capital Association MoneyTree Report, based on data from Thomson Reuters.
Source: *National Venture Capital Association Yearbook, 2010*

an initial public offering. In contrast, roughly one-third of firms (33 percent) exited by being acquired by another firm. A similar percentage (35 percent) continued to exist as privately owned firms, while 18 percent of the sample was known to have failed. For these less successful portfolio firms, VCs also take a role in the liquidation of the firm and distribution of its proceeds.

A number of researchers attest to the emotional support provided by venture capitalists to entrepreneurs (Fried and Hisrich, 1995; Sapienza, Manigart, and Vermeir, 1996). Being an entrepreneur can be a lonely proposition, and the road to success is full of potholes and uncertainties. VCs who have guided other entrepreneurs through this process can encourage, support, and reassure first-time entrepreneurs in particular. Further, their industry experience and contacts can alleviate at least some of the uncertainties, thereby freeing up the entrepreneur to focus on developing her firm. Diane Hessan, the founder of Communispace, highlights the "relationship" aspects of her VC experience and cautions other entrepreneurs to think of it as "a long-term partnership" that will involve frequent interactions and tough decisions. In other words, financial support is important, but a good working relationship with your VCs is equally important for entrepreneurial success.

Maria Cirino from .406 Ventures

Maria Cirino is co-founder of .406 ventures, a venture capital firm that funds early stage technology companies. She started the firm in 2005 with Larry Begley and Liam Donohue, after having worked together for many years in operational and board settings. They shared the belief that entrepreneurs could benefit by working with venture partners who provided operational expertise along with capital.

Maria and her co-founders focus on finding talented entrepreneurs and helping them to build their companies. They share the belief that good partnerships are the key to good results, and that it starts by being fair to founders. They "work to achieve a balance of being an exceptionally strong advocate and a constructive sounding board. We are committed to direct, open, and honest communications not only with our entrepreneurs, but with our investors and business partners."

The name .406 ventures stems from the record batting average of .406 achieved by Boston Red Sox legend Ted Williams in 1941. His extraordinary vision and his selective hitting, only swinging at pitches within the strike zone that he knew he could hit best, inspired her and her co-founders to embrace a similar strategy in venture capital by focusing on industries they knew well and using a rigorous due diligence process to invest in high-potential companies with the greatest likelihood of producing hits.

We spoke to Maria about her experiences, both as a woman VC and as a VC investing in women entrepreneurs. She stated that she has witnessed that it is much more difficult for men to take critical feedback from women than the same feedback from men and notes that it is *their* issue, not yours. She has also seen women come up with ideas in meetings only to receive a lukewarm reception. Then, forty-five minutes later, a man comes up with the same idea and everyone thinks it's great. Maria shared that she was about seven months into the launch of her venture when she finally put her finger on something at her own firm: "In the structure of viewing all the deals and vetting them (we do six deals a year out of about a thousand that we see), I noticed my partners dealt with each other differently than they dealt with me." She observed that when the two other co-founders (both male) talked about deals, they used different language, and they were not as direct. Further, if Maria said she wasn't interested in a particular deal, they took more offense than if the other male partner had a negative reaction to the deal.

Intrigued, Maria tracked this behavior over a thirty-day period and then presented it to her male co-founders. She articulated it within the context of a data-driven conversation, hashing it out in a non-emotional manner.

They couldn't argue with my evidence . . . they were horrified. They apologized, said they really wanted to fix it, and they changed. The behavior stopped, and it's now been more than eight years since that conversation.

One thing that happened recently made her realize that some things haven't changed as much as she'd hoped. A VC friend of hers had a daughter who wanted to talk with her. Maria thought that the daughter wanted a job, but she already had one. What the young woman really wanted to talk to her about were some biases she'd experienced in college. This young woman had noticed that as a female, if she answered questions faster or more than men in her classes it made her extremely unpopular with the men. She noted that it really affected her socially, and she saw other women sitting back and laying low to give men the chance to look smarter. She was coming to Maria for advice on how to handle these attitudes and her own response to them going forward.

Maria told us that it was surprising to find out that among the handful of women she is closest to, most went to all-women's colleges, high schools, or both. She said she never appreciated the fact that doing so gives women the opportunity to *not* lean back at an early age. In fact, you could lean as far forward as you wanted to. And if you didn't answer, probably nobody else would either. She stated that "we need to see that naturally we lean back, and we need to proactively change that if we want to get places."

As a venture capitalist, Maria sees about a thousand deals a year, of which only about 6 to 8 percent are from women-led companies. She notes that confidence is a huge issue for women.

Women come in and say, thank you so much for your time; we really appreciate it. . . . We are not looking for money, we'd like some advice. Guys come in and say, you're low on our priority list; we've talked with ninety-seven VCs, and we expect ninety-six terms sheets by Monday so you better hurry up and get in.

"Men definitely walk into our offices expecting to walk out with a check." She notes that *neither* of these approaches is optimal. A couple of pieces of advice: You don't get what you don't ask for, so don't shy away from the ask. Take yourself seriously. If you don't take yourself seriously, no one else will.

Maria observed that men

have no compunction about saying, "This is what I'm good at. This is what I'm not good at. I need to hire person X and person Y to do A, B, and C." Women are more likely to say, "I can do those things . . . I'll do fifty thousand things. I can do this, save money, and do everything." It's okay to hire someone to do that even though you can. You need to scale bigger and faster. And you can do that by spending this VC funding on hiring great people and getting it done.

The Art of Negotiating

As we have discussed in this chapter, one of the challenges for growth-oriented women entrepreneurs is gaining access to networks of private equity providers that have previously excluded them. As our interview with Maria Cirino suggests, however, once they have gained access, women often face additional challenges in negotiating effectively for themselves and their firms. Prior research on gender and negotiation styles has revealed that women are less likely to initiate negotiations, particularly with males (Babcock, Gelfand, Small, and Stayn, 2006; Bowles, Babcock, and Lai, 2007), and when they do negotiate, they achieve less favorable outcomes (Stuhlmacher and Waters, 1999). Past studies tend to focus on how women fare in negotiating for salaries and compensation. More recently, however, new studies are adapting the theme of gender and negotiation to the realm of entrepreneurial finance in an attempt to determine if similar patterns emerge. In one such study, entrepreneurship scholars Frances Amatucci and Jeffrey Sohl (2004) found that women entrepreneurs did not ask for enough capital when they raised funds from angel investors. In this sense, their findings are consistent with earlier work done by authors Linda Babcock and Sara Laschever (2003) asserting that "women don't ask." The obvious risk of this approach is that firms launched with too little capital are less likely to survive, and those that do survive often struggle with growth. Similarly, a later study of women who raised VC financing found that they were less reluctant to ask for help and advice, precisely the areas in which VCs can add value (Nelson, Maxfield, and Kolb, 2009). These researchers point out that women often face a "double bind" in their attempts to negotiate. If they are forceful and aggressive, they risk alienating the other party. Conversely, however, if they are too self-effacing and compliant, they may not get the funding or terms that they want.

In a recent study incorporating the use of social media to locate and connect with growth-oriented women entrepreneurs, researchers Ethne Swartz, Frances Amatucci, and Susan Coleman (2016) focused on a critical piece of the venture capital process, term sheet negotiations. The term sheet is the formal "contract" between the entrepreneur and the VC firm that spells out the amount and conditions of funding. Key elements that are negotiated include (1) the value of the firm, (2) anti-dilution protection, and (3) board representation for the VCs and for the entrepreneur. In essence these terms specify how much firm ownership the entrepreneur will be able to retain, thereby directly affecting her future wealth, as well as how much her voice will count at the board level in determining the future direction of the firm. Preliminary results from this research yield important insights for women entrepreneurs seeking equity capital. In spite of the frequent criticism for the value of business plans, 90 percent of respondents did them, while 85 percent prepared financial statements. Sixty-four percent of respondents assembled industry forecasts to avoid being blind-sided by VCs who have a high degree of industry specialization. In terms of negotiating style, 53 percent of respondents characterized negotiations as primarily cooperative, while 31 percent characterized them as a mixture of cooperation and confrontational. Only a small percentage of respondents felt that the negotiations were primarily confrontational. In spite of this mix of negotiating styles, over 80 percent of respondents felt that they were treated fairly. It is worth noting that the lowest entrepreneur ratings occurred in the areas of trusting one's investors and feeling confident throughout the negotiation process. The study's authors concluded that these two findings suggest a lower sense of self-efficacy in the term sheet negotiation process on the part of women entrepreneurs. On the basis of these results, women appear to be less trusting and more concerned that they will be taken advantage of. Similarly, they have less confidence in their own ability to negotiate desired outcomes even though the majority raised all or most of the funding they sought. The participants in this study shared several "lessons learned" from their term sheet negotiation experiences.

1. First, establish strong and frequent lines of communication with the equity provider. As Diane Hessan pointed out, this is someone you will be talking to "every day."

2. Second, develop a deep knowledge about your business and industry, including what makes the business model work.

3. Third, know when to walk away, because sometimes the money isn't right, the deal isn't right, or the people aren't right.

4. Finally, build your network and relationships with industry experts and others who can provide information or support as you move through the process. Prepare yourself, and know your stuff, because your best defense is being competent and well informed.

Closing the Loop

In this chapter we have focused exclusively on venture capital, which serves as a key link to size and scale for high-growth firms. Although only a small percentage of firms actually receive VC funding, those firms are important, because they are the subset of all firms most likely to produce innovative business models; new products, particularly in the areas of technology and life science; and a significant number of jobs. Venture capitalists are "value added" investors in the sense that they provide not only substantial amounts of financial capital, but human capital in the form of expertise and social capital in the form of key contacts and networks as well. They serve as a critical piece of the puzzle for growth-oriented entrepreneurs who seek that gold ring of exit options, an initial public offering.

Prior research conducted by the Diana Project researchers (Brush, Carter, and others, 2001; 2004; Brush, Greene, and others, 2014) and by ourselves in our earlier book, *A Rising Tide* (Coleman and Robb, 2012) document the challenges of women entrepreneurs seeking venture capital funding. The venture capital industry remains heavily male-dominated, and women have struggled to break into this space both as entrepreneurs and as investors. More recently, however, the tide has begun to turn thanks to the success of a growing number of high-profile women entrepreneurs such as Spanx' Sara Blakely and Zipcar's Robin Chase. Organizations such as Springboard Enterprises and Astia have also played a key role in helping high-growth women entrepreneurs prepare for and secure venture capital funding.

As our entrepreneur interviews indicate, however, the process of seeking out and subsequently living with venture capital is not for the faint of heart. Although venture capital firms have the potential to provide significant amounts of funding, they have high expectations for their portfolio firms in terms of performance and the ability to achieve designated benchmarks. Although VCs care about the ultimate success of their entrepreneurs, they care even more about their own ability to deliver financial returns to investors. Thus, in exchange for funding, they also take a key role in ownership and control of the firm as it moves through its growth cycle. In many ways this is an advantage, because VCs, thanks to their industry specialization, can provide industry knowledge, expertise, key contacts, and access to needed resources. The downside of all this is that the entrepreneur may find herself sharing ownership and control with VCs whose goals are not completely consistent with her own. Diane Hessan's experience with VC funding for her firm, Communispace, illustrates the often turbulent nature of the entrepreneur-VC relationship. As our interviews point out, however, many of our growth-oriented entrepreneurs find a way to live with this in order to achieve their long-term goals for firm growth and eventual harvest. That emotional transition from sole or team ownership and control to more broadly shared ownership and control is a necessary part of their entrepreneurial voyage.

What Does This Mean for You?

As we close out this chapter, we would like to finish with a few take-aways for growth-oriented women entrepreneurs who anticipate seeking venture capital as a part of their funding mix.

1. First, develop a longer-term vision for your firm and your own goals for harvesting value. This will help determine if venture capital is an appropriate funding source for you. Similarly, it will help you absorb some of the funding, ownership, and control trade-offs that accompany this type of funding.

2. Second, find ways to develop a network that will provide you access to venture capital funding. If you have prior entrepreneurial experience, you may already have some of these contacts. Alternatively, if you are a first-time entrepreneur, organizations such as Springboard Enterprises, MergeLane, Emerging Women, and Astia can provide valuable contacts and preparation.

3. Seriously consider launching as part of an entrepreneurial team. This is a strategy that we have observed in a number of firms we have included in this book, including the Gilt Groupe and Communispace. Team ownership broadens your range of human and social capital, since different members of the team come with different types of expertise, experience, and contacts. In the case of the Gilt Groupe, one of their team members was a serial entrepreneur who already had a network of industry and venture capital contacts.

4. Prepare thoroughly for your venture capital interactions. By that we mean become an expert on your industry and your firm. This knowledge helps level the playing field, because although VCs may be industry experts, no one knows the ins and outs of your firm and its business model better than you do.

5. Seek advice from other entrepreneurs who have secured venture capital funding to learn how the process works. There is no reliable "instruction manual" for VC funding, so one of the best ways to prepare is to learn from others who have gone before you.

6. Develop and practice your "pitch" and anticipate the types of questions you may be asked. Throughout this process, your best defense is knowing your stuff inside and out.

7. Do your homework on VC firms. As Diane Hessan pointed out, venture capital funding is a close and long-term relationship that will have its ups and downs. Money is an important part of that relationship, but the ability to work together over time, shared goals, and trust are just as important.

8. Consistent with the theme of "doing your homework," look for venture capital firms that fund companies like yours. Several of our entrepreneurs have pointed out that VCs tend to have a company profile in their heads, and if your firm does not match up with that, they are unlikely to provide funding. In light of that, look for firms that have funded companies in your industry sector. Similarly, look for firms that have funded women-owned firms or firms in which women play a key role within an entrepreneurial team. Fortunately, there are a growing number of VC funds that either focus on women-owned firms or include women-owned or women-led firms in their portfolios. Our parting gift to you as we leave this chapter is a list of venture capital funds with either women partners *or* a track record of investing in women, which you can find in the Appendix.

10

GOING FOR GOLD

Harvesting Value

In Chapter 9 we examined strategies for securing venture capital as a means for achieving rapid growth, using the experience of Diane Hessan, one of the co-founders of Communispace. Once a company has achieved significant size and scope, the entrepreneur is in a position to "harvest value." Harvesting value refers to the means by which the entrepreneur achieves liquidity and financial gain in return for her investment of time, talent, and capital. The two best-known strategies for harvesting value are an initial public offering or sale of the firm, as in Diane's case. This chapter will address the strategies for pursuing these two paths as well as the financial and other considerations that the entrepreneur needs to be aware of. The topic of harvesting value is particularly suited to a discussion of growth-oriented women entrepreneurs, because it is typically only growth-oriented firms that actually go through the IPO process. Similarly, although a number of small or mid-sized firms may go through the process of being sold, the financial complexity and the potential financial rewards for selling a growth-oriented firm are much greater.

Among other issues, we will discuss the strategies for selecting and working with an investment bank and steps in the IPO or firm sale process as well as the nature of the entrepreneur's involvement in that process. What factors differentiate between these two possible outcomes, and how can women entrepreneurs prepare themselves? These topics are particularly relevant for our readers, because, compared with men, only a small number of growth-oriented women entrepreneurs have gone through the IPO or sale process. This chapter provides us with an opportunity to share their experiences and lessons learned.

Bank Loans and Banking Relationships

Before we begin, however, we need to digress briefly in order to introduce and discuss bank loans, another important source of financing for growth-oriented firms. Unlike equity providers, who readily embrace risk, banks are highly risk averse and typically do not make loans to startups or firms that have not yet achieved profitability. Thus, bank loans play a larger role at later stages of the firm's development. The exception to this rule is bank loans made to the entrepreneur herself rather than to her firm. These personal loans are often used for early stage financing and can take the form of credit card debt, home equity loans, or other loans secured by personal collateral such as the entrepreneur's home or personal guarantees. This practice illustrates what the University of Florida State University's James Ang (Ang, Lin, and Tyler, 1995) referred to as the "lack of separation" or the blurring of lines between the entrepreneur's personal finances and those of her firm. Women entrepreneurs are particularly vulnerable to this risk, because they are more heavily dependent on personal rather than external sources of debt.

In contrast, loans made directly to the business rather than to the entrepreneur are governed by the "5 C's of Credit" (Ross, Westerfield, and Jordan, 2014). These are capacity, capital, collateral, conditions, and character. Capacity refers to the borrower's ability to repay the loan and is often determined by an assessment of the firm's financial health and cash flows. Capital refers to the entrepreneur's financial commitment and reflects the fact that most providers of external capital want to make sure that the entrepreneur has put her own capital at risk before asking others to do so. Collateral consists of assets such as buildings, facilities, equipment, inventories, vehicles, and the like that can be pledged in the event that the borrower does not repay the loan. Collateral has the effect of reducing the lender's level of risk and thereby increasing her willingness to lend. In addition to the internal factors, lenders also consider the condition of the economy and the firm's industry. Thus, loans are more plentiful during a healthy economy than during a period of economic adversity such as we experienced during the Great Recession in 2008–2009. Last but not least, lenders consider the entrepreneur's character or reputation, including her credit history and track record for repaying past loans.

June Ressler, president and CEO of Cenergy International, has used bank loans as her primary source of external financing since the firm's earliest days. Her story illustrates the importance of finding a bank that understands the nature of her business and is prepared to support rapid growth.

June Ressler and Cenergy
International Services LLC

June Ressler was working as an attorney in Pittsburg when her husband, a drilling engineer, accepted a position in New Orleans. The family, which included three children, made the move. Since June's children were still relatively young and trying to adapt to a new community, new schools, and new friends, June decided to explore opportunities that would allow her to work out of her home. Given her familiarity with the oil industry, she saw an opportunity in the area of workforce solutions for firms operating in the energy field, and in 1996 Cenergy was born!

June launched and operated Cenergy (http://www.cenergyintl.com) from her home and financed the early stages of the firm's development with her savings. This approach allowed her to begin generating revenues and earnings relatively quickly, paving the way for a bank line of credit. June noted that her industry is highly competitive with a number of established players. To gain market share, she took a somewhat lower percentage on placements at the beginning. This initial strategy worked for her, because she was able to keep costs low by working from home. Cenergy grew rapidly, adding a number of the major oil and gas companies as clients. By 2001, the firm had outgrown its "home office" status and moved into new quarters in New Orleans' Central Business District.

Cenergy's website states,

> We provide specialized energy personnel, safety solutions, inspection solutions, logistics and vendor management support. We provide logistics assistance by meeting our clients' planning, dispatching and tracking needs for marine, air, and ground transportation. (http://www.cenergyintl.com)

Cenergy works with client companies to place both production personnel (engineers, project managers, geologists, rig supervisors) and support personnel (administrators, IT professionals) throughout the world. The firm prides itself on being an industry leader in safety, and has consistently led the oil and gas industry in safety performance (http://www.cenergyintl.com).

In 2005 Hurricane Katrina devastated New Orleans as well as the Cenergy office, forcing the firm to relocate to nearby Lafayette, Louisiana. In spite of the turmoil, Cenergy continued to grow, actually doubling its number of employees in the months after the hurricane. June was eventually able to reopen the New Orleans Office, but also decided to maintain the Lafayette office as well in order to serve her growing client base (Bradford, 2012).

June describes her approach as "very client oriented," a factor that has contributed to Cenergy's success. She never says no to clients, but rather listens to their needs and finds a way to make it happen. Clients appreciate that, and it has led to repeat business and word-of-mouth referrals for new clients. When questioned about the challenges of being a woman in the male-dominated oil and gas industry, June shared that it was a bit of a struggle at first until she was able to prove what her firm could do. Thanks to her track record of success and reputation, however, it is not an issue any more.

As the firm grew, June realized she had outgrown her current bank. Although June had a great relationship with that bank, they could not accommodate the credit needs of her firm that was doubling in size every year. June believed it was extremely important to pay her consultants promptly in order to ensure Cenergy's access to top-quality people. The firm's bank line of credit allowed them to achieve this goal while waiting for payment to come in on invoices. One day, however, June got a call from her comptroller telling her that they could not make payroll because the firm had reached the limit on its line of credit. June immediately got on the phone with her bank, asking them to raise the limit. Their response was "Absolutely not!" and June had to cover the payroll shortfall with her own savings.

At that point, June knew it was time to make a change. As the sole owner of Cenergy, she did not want to take on additional partners or investors, so she needed to find a bank that could accommodate the firm's growing need for financial capital. Through her personal network, she made contact with a much larger global bank that responded immediately. Impressed by the bank's responsiveness and desire to help her firm grow, June switched her line of credit from her original bank to the new one and has been with them ever since. This relationship is particularly important, because June uses no external equity, and her bank line of credit is her only source of debt. When asked about her experience with the new bank, June responded,

It has been a dream. They are very proactive and will call me in anticipation of our needs. They understand our firm and have been very supportive of our growth.

In 2007 June moved her firm to new headquarters in Houston, Texas, the center of the oil and gas industry. In doing so, she hired a new chief financial officer whom she described as "horrible" and prone to spending large amounts of money, a practice that conflicted with June's commitment to lean management. She ended up hiring two comptrollers to try to counteract the damage, but even that wasn't enough. Eventually, June had no choice but to fire the CFO, whom she replaced with "an amazing woman CFO" who is still with the firm today.

The Houston move coincided with the onset of the financial crisis and Great Recession. In anticipation of a downturn, June braced herself to begin downsizing. Her lean strategies served her in good stead, however, and the effects of the economic downturn were not as severe as she had anticipated. In fact, she was actually able to acquire some top-notch employees when some of her competitors were forced to downsize:

The recession didn't stop our growth, but instead of 30 percent, it was 5 percent. . . . I mapped out my ability to be scalable, down or up. I could scale down and we could hit the ground running. But we didn't. We ended up identifying some key management people who were suddenly available. I started interviewing and got some really good people. (Bradford, 2012)

In 2012, when June's youngest child graduated from high school, June moved from New Orleans to Houston. By 2014, Cenergy employed approximately eighty individuals as well as an additional six hundred "field consultants" who are hired to serve the needs of client companies. The consultants work both onshore and offshore in seventeen countries and on every continent but Antarctica (http://www.cenergyintl.com). Revenues are in the range of $300 million per year, and June is still the sole owner of the firm.

In 2014, Cenergy was included in *Inc.* magazine's list of the five thousand fastest growing firms in the United States for the ninth consecutive year (http://www.cenergyintl.com). June has also been personally recognized for her entrepreneurial leadership by Ernst & Young, which named her as their 2012 Entrepreneur of the Year for the Gulf Coast Region. In addition to these and other accolades, June serves on the National Petroleum Council, a group that advises the president on energy-related matters.

One of your authors recently spoke with June again in March 2015, to ask about how Cenergy was weathering the downturn in the oil and gas industry. June's response was both upbeat and proactive, qualities that we have come to expect from her:

As the CEO, I have to have the mind-set that it will all turn out OK. We are in an industry that goes through cycles, and I have been through three downturns prior to this one. I feel confident, because our business model is highly scalable. It needs to be that way, because whether or not our client companies hire consultants is out of our control.

June also talked about strategies she is developing to diversify her revenue stream in ways that will make Cenergy less vulnerable to industry ups and downs.

We actually started to see signs of a downturn back in 2013 when some of the big majors (oil companies) started cutting back in anticipation of lower demand. At that time, about 80 percent of our revenues came from placing consultants, and we were heavily dependent on business from two of the big firms. Because of the industry layoffs, I was able to hire some great new salespeople who could go after smaller firms that we had not previously done business with. This created new opportunities for us and helped us reduce our reliance on revenues from a few large firms.

We have also started to diversify into other related lines of business that are not as vulnerable to industry fluctuations. As an example, we took a 51 percent position in a firm that specializes in safety and safety training, something that has to be addressed whether the industry is up or down. We are in the process of developing similar opportunities. There are a lot of good small businesses out there that have great products but don't know how to market them or invoice for them. That's where we can add value.

When questioned about strategies that have helped her firm become and remain so successful, June shared the following:

1. Stay as lean as possible. The oil and gas industry is cyclical with its ups and downs. By practicing lean management strategies, you are in a better position to weather the downturns.

2. Retain as much equity as possible. This allows you to control how the company is operated as well as its future direction. In addition, if you are looking to make acquisitions, it is easier to do that if you hold all the equity.

3. Learn your financial lessons. In particular, learn how to read the balance sheet and income statement and keep an eye on them.

4. Don't be afraid to take chances, because that's where a lot of your opportunities will come from. June describes herself as "absolutely a risk taker; more than most."

5. Develop networks and resources that will enhance your skill set. June does not have a business degree, but her participation in the Women Presidents' Organization has helped her learn a lot about strategy.

When questioned about her goals going forward, June stated that she wants to continue to grow the firm and sees "incredible opportunities every day." As an example, she noted that safety and compliance are becoming increasingly important in the industry she serves, and she could see herself buying a couple of small companies specializing in those areas. Longer term, a merger with other firms that might ultimately lead to an IPO is not out of the question.

- ## The Women Presidents' Organization (https://www.womenpresidentsorg.com)

The Women Presidents' Organization (WPO) is a nonprofit organization for women presidents of multimillion-dollar companies. It was created to improve the business conditions for women entrepreneurs and to promote the acceptance and advancement of women business owners in all industries. Currently, there are approximately 120 WPO chapters operating in the United States and abroad. Each chapter consists of roughly twenty women presidents who take part in professionally facilitated peer advisory groups. These groups are designed to bring out and share the collective wisdom and experience of their members, thereby facilitating business growth. A recent study conducted by the WPO and sponsored by Key Bank noted that access to capital is still the main concern for women-led firms in the United States. This, in turn, leads to concerns about women's ability to grow their firms. WPO president and founder Marsha Firestone commented on the study, noting that women receive less than 10 percent of small business loan funding and an even smaller percentage of venture funding (Persaud, 2014). Alternatively, women are heavily reliant on personal savings, personal debt, and loans from family and friends. In spite of the impressive performance of women-owned firms, Firestone observed that stereotypes about the nature of women's entrepreneurship persist: "I think the bias that women don't grow substantial businesses that generate increased revenue and employment is programmed into the DNA" (Persaud, 2014).

In spite of these stereotypes, however, members of the WPO had average revenues of $13.2 million in 2014. Similarly, member firms each employed ninety-two workers on average during that same year (https://www.womenpresidentsorg.com). One of the WPO's annual highlights is the publication of its annual list of the "50 Fastest-Growing Women-Owned/Led Companies." June Ressler, founder of Cenergy, was number 4 on the 2014 list.

The Borrowing Experience
of Women-Owned Firms

Prior research on the borrowing experiences of women entrepreneurs is mixed. Several studies have found no difference between women and men in terms of loan approvals when they controlled for factors such as firm size, industry, and credit quality (Cole, 2008; Orser, Riding, and Manley, 2006; Treichel and Scott, 2006; Vos, Yeh, Carter, and Tagg, 2007; Watson, Newby, and Mahuka, 2009). Nevertheless, some studies have found that although women are just as likely to be approved for loans, they are less likely to apply (Cole and Mehran, 2009; Treichel and Scott, 2006). These conflicting findings have given rise to a debate as to whether women's lower reliance on external debt in the form of bank loans is a function of supply or demand factors.

Supply factors include discriminatory practices on the part of lending officers or less overt behaviors that discourage women from applying for loans. Although studies conducted in developed economies have found little evidence of overt discrimination, women still report greater difficulty with the lending process (Constantinidis, Cornet, and Asandei, 2006; Orser, Riding, and Manley, 2006). This is consistent with the findings of a British study conducted by researcher Sara Carter and her colleagues (2007) revealing subtle differences, by gender of the applicant, in the criteria used to evaluate loans. These differences were even more pronounced when the lending process itself was evaluated. In contrast, demand-side factors suggest that women entrepreneurs are less likely to ask for loans, and when they do, they apply for smaller amounts. This is consistent with the contention that women underestimate the potential of their firms, don't "think big" enough, and, as a result, don't ask for enough money.

A recent article by your authors (Coleman and Robb, forthcoming) examined the credit market experiences of a cohort of entrepreneurs using data from the Kauffman Firm Survey. This survey comprises a sample of over four thousand U.S. firms launched in 2004 and tracked through the year 2011. Questions concerning loan applications were added to the survey in 2007. Table 10.1 provides a summary of borrowing experiences, by gender, for the years 2007–2011, a period that included the financial crisis and Great Recession. Data are provided for (1) all firms, (2) high-growth-potential firms (HGP), and (3) the top twenty-five firms ranked by employment.

Table 10.1 reveals that, although women-owned firms on average were less likely to apply for loans than men, their application rates were similar for high-

TABLE 10.1. Credit Market Experiences, 2007–2011

		All		High-Growth Potential		Top 25	
	All	Female	Male	Female	Male	Female	Male
New Loan Apps							
2007	12.3%	9.8%	13.3%	30.9%	29.5%	44.9%	25.8%
2008	12.6%	10.4%	13.6%	27.3%	28.1%	32.3%	24.8%
2009	12.0%	10.2%	12.5%	29.0%	29.2%	19.4%	40.4%
2010	11.2%	8.3%	11.9%	15.2%	26.1%	19.1%	36.0%
2011	10.5%	9.9%	10.8%	17.5%	23.6%	10.3%	48.2%
Did Not Apply for Fear of Denial							
2007	15.9%	16.8%	15.6%	14.5%	15.6%	24.4%	0.8%
2008	19.2%	21.1%	18.2%	29.2%	19.2%	27.8%	25.9%
2009	20.5%	22.7%	19.4%	39.2%	18.7%	47.7%	8.6%
2010	18.6%	19.8%	17.3%	31.5%	15.0%	37.5%	18.6%
2011	18.0%	20.0%	17.1%	31.3%	17.6%	37.3%	0.7%
Always Approved							
2007	71.3%	74.0%	70.3%	68.4%	84.4%	51.0%	95.4%
2008	65.2%	56.7%	67.6%	47.6%	69.9%	59.8%	82.3%
2009	60.9%	54.9%	63.0%	37.1%	71.0%	*	81.8%
2010	61.3%	56.3%	64.4%	45.6%	74.3%	*	78.0%
2011	68.4%	58.6%	73.2%	56.3%	82.7%	*	92.7%

Note: * Sample size too small.
Source: Kauffman Firm Survey microdata, 2012

growth-potential firms for the years 2007–2009 before dropping sharply in 2010–2011. The top twenty-five women-owned firms actually had higher loan application rates than men for 2007 and 2008, but also dropped sharply in 2009–2011. In contrast, the loan application rates of the top twenty-five men-owned firms rose during those years. Table 10.1 also shows that the fear of being denied for a loan rose significantly for high-growth-potential and top twenty-five women during the years 2009–2011 while remaining relatively stable for men. It appears that this fear was somewhat justified, because women were less likely to have their loans approved than men. This was particularly true for high-growth-potential and top twenty-five women.

The findings reported in Table 10.1 suggest that women in general, and high-growth-potential women in particular, experienced greater difficulty in securing loans during the crisis years. Although their lower level of loan applications and greater fear of denial may suggest a higher level of risk aversion during this period of economic turbulence, their lower levels of loan approvals also suggest supply side problems for growth-oriented women entrepreneurs. Multivariate analysis using this same data confirmed many of these findings. Controlling for other firm and owner characteristics including credit quality, women exhibited loan application rates that were similar to those of men. Nevertheless, our multivariate results suggest a greater unmet credit need among women, because women were significantly more likely to refrain from applying for loans because they believed they would be denied. Similarly, women were less likely to be approved for loans than men, although the difference was only significant in one out of five years when we controlled for other variables.

What does all this mean? Essentially, it means that the riddle of credit availability for growth-oriented women entrepreneurs has not been fully solved. Although demand-side factors such as a higher level of risk aversion, particularly in the wake of the financial crisis, may have played a role in women's lower usage of external debt, it appears that demand-side issues alone cannot explain the differences between women and men. Alternatively, our analysis suggests that growth-oriented women entrepreneurs may have suffered disproportionately from the contraction of credit that accompanied the recent financial crisis and ensuing recession.

Helen Greiner and iRobot

Helen Greiner was well prepared for the launch of her growth-oriented, high-tech firm iRobot. She held an undergraduate degree in mechanical engineering and a master's degree in computer science, both from MIT. After graduation, she held positions at NASA's Jet Propulsion Laboratory and the MIT Artificial Intelligence Laboratory (*Encyclopedia of World Biography*, 2014). As a child, Greiner was inspired by the movie *Star Wars*. She was particularly fascinated by the capabilities and even the personality of the robotic character R2D2. It was the beginning of a lifelong love affair with robots and their potential.

In 1990, Greiner launched her firm together with two co-founders whom she met at MIT. Initially the firm was called IS Robotics and operated out of the apartment of one of the founders. The three started out building robots for university researchers that were sold for approximately $3,000 each, working eighteen-hour days and maxing out their credit cards. Their first big break came in 1993 with a government contract from the Department of Defense and the Office of Naval Research to design an underwater minesweeper. Shaped like a crab, the sweeper, which was named Ariel, was programmed to detect mines, place explosives to destroy them, and scurry away before they blew up. This project allowed the team to move into headquarters in Somerville, Massachusetts, and to hire some engineers. At the same time, they changed the firm's name to iRobot, taken from a book of short stories written by Isaac Asimov. Although the bulk of iRobot's business continued to be focused on military applications, the firm also diversified into nonmilitary work. One such project involved designing a robot that could travel underground to make repairs in oil-well bores for Baker Hughes, an oil service company.

iRobot's second big break, also in the form of a military contract, came in 1995 when the Department of Defense commissioned the firm to develop what became one of its premiere products, the PackBot, a small tank-like robot designed to scope out areas too dangerous for soldiers. The PackBot weighs approximately forty pounds and is designed to be portable. It is able to climb stairs, navigate challenging terrain, and, if knocked over, use flippers to get itself back up. PackBots were used after the attack on the World Trade Center in New York to make sure that structures were sound and safe for entry. They were also first used in combat in Afghanistan to search caves in order to detect booby traps. Similarly, PackBots were used in Iraq to search buildings, vehicles, and airfields for booby traps, mines, and harmful gases.

In spite of her success in the military and industrial sectors, Greiner still cherished the goal of breaking into the consumer market with applications that would be both practical and affordable. To that end, iRobot partnered with the toy company Hasbro to develop a robotic doll that began selling in 2000. Although reasonably priced, the doll's price tag of close to $100 was still a stretch for most families, and ultimately, only about 100,000 were sold. This experience paved the way for other products, however, and in 2002, iRobot launched a robotic vacuum cleaner called the Roomba. This appliance is shaped like a disk and weighs about five pounds. It runs on rechargeable batteries and propels around the room in circles, bouncing off obstacles as it encounters them. When it has finished vacuuming, it beeps in true R2D2 style and turns itself off. The Roomba has sold well, benefiting from a fairly considerable amount of publicity. Oprah Winfrey named the Roomba as "one of her favorite things," and it also received the seal of approval from *Good Housekeeping*.

By 2004, iRobot had 120 employees and multiple contracts in the academic, industrial, military, and consumer sectors, making it the largest privately owned robotics company in the world. In spite of this impressive growth, the founders held fast to the entrepreneurial spirit that had sustained them through the tough years, pledging to "build really cool stuff; to make money; to have fun; and to change the world" (*Encyclopedia of World Biography*, 2014).

Going Public and the Investment Banking Process

Entrepreneurs have several options for harvesting value. These strategies have important financial and psychological implications for the entrepreneur herself and for her investors. One option, more appropriate for smaller firms, is to limit growth by channeling cash flows to the owners rather than investing them in the firm. This strategy may be appropriate for entrepreneurs who no longer wish to run the firm themselves but have no obvious successors or buyers (Petty and others, 1994). A second strategy is a management buyout (MBO), whereby the managers of the firm buy out the ownership rights of the founding entrepreneur, typically using a fairly substantial amount of debt. In other instances, employees actually "buy" the firm through an Employee Stock Ownership Plan (ESOP). This involves having the firm set up the ESOP and allowing employees to invest in the stock, which is held in a trust. The effect of both of strategies is to keep the stock of privately held firms in "friendly" hands, thereby protecting the jobs and financial well-being of managers, employees, or both.

Strategies four and five are much more appropriate for the types of growth-oriented firms we address in this book. Accordingly, the fourth strategy is merging with or being acquired by another firm. This strategy may be employed as a way to secure resources from a larger, established firm, as in the case of the acquisition of Communispace by Omnicom. In other instances, sale of the firm serves as a means whereby the entrepreneur and other inside investors achieve liquidity and realize financial gains. As Communispace co-founder Diane Hessan put it, both she and her VC investors benefited "tremendously" when the firm was sold.

The fifth and final strategy is an initial public offering (IPO), which involves converting from private to public ownership through the sale of stock, which is then listed on an organized exchange. In baseball parlance, doing an IPO is the equivalent to "going to the bigs." Prior research reveals that women-owned firms are less likely to harvest value through either sale of the firm or an IPO. Of the companies that went public between 1996 and 2013, only 3 percent were led by women, according to sociologist Martin Kenney and economist Donald Patton, and just two of eighty-two "emerging-growth" businesses that went public last year had female chiefs. Kenny attributes this to structural factors rather than discrimination (Kenny and Patton, 2015). Nevertheless, in a recent paper using a sample of MBA students, Lyda Bigelow and her co-authors constructed a simulated IPO, manipulating the gender demographics of the top management team. They found that, despite identical personal qualifications and firm financials, female founders and CEOs were perceived as less capable than their male counterparts, and IPOs led by female founders or CEOs were considered less attractive investments (Bigelow, Lundmark, Parks, and Wuebker, 2014). These results led Bigelow and her colleagues to conclude that women experience disadvantages in their attempts to attract growth capital, even controlling for other variables. Colorado State's Dawn DeTienne and her colleagues suggest that the IPO gap between women and men may be due to different attitudes toward growth on the part of women entrepreneurs (DeTienne, 2010). Nevertheless, as we have illustrated in this book, an increasing number of women entrepreneurs are embracing growth-oriented entrepreneurship. In light of this trend, it is not unreasonable to anticipate that more women founders will experience significant harvest events in the form of a company sale or merger or an IPO going forward.

Reasons for "Going Public"

"Going public" is the ultimate brass ring of harvest options. When a firm goes through an initial public offering (IPO) it shifts from being privately owned by the entrepreneur, investors, and other insiders to being publicly owned and traded on a major exchange such as the New York Stock Exchange or Nasdaq. Firms go public for a number of reasons, including greater visibility for the company and its products. A primary reason for going public, however, is the opportunity to access large amounts of equity capital through the sale of stock (Petty and others, 1994). Going public also allows the entrepreneur to realize the significant financial returns for her years of hard work (DeTienne, 2010).

There are a number of advantages associated with going public. As just noted, it serves as a means for raising large amounts of equity capital that can be used to fund further growth, research and development, and the introduction of new products and services, all of which are vital for growth-oriented firms. An IPO also provides current stockholders, typically the entrepreneur and other insiders, with an opportunity to diversify their personal financial holdings while also liquidating some of those holdings. This increased wealth allows entrepreneurs to launch other new ventures, invest in other entrepreneurial firms, engage in philanthropic endeavors, or just enjoy the good life.

An important benefit of going public is that it establishes a value for the firm. Any student of entrepreneurial finance knows that it is extraordinarily difficult to value privately held firms, because their stock is not traded on an organized exchange. In contrast, the stock price of publicly traded firms is widely publicized and updated on an ongoing basis. The value of the firm is simply the stock price multiplied by the number of shares outstanding.

From a marketing perspective, publicly owned firms tend to attract a greater amount of attention in the media and among financial analysts. This in turn raises awareness and demand for their products and services. Finally, going public can make it easier for the firm to raise other sources of capital. Once a firm is publicly owned, it typically has access to a full range of debt and equity alternatives. As an added advantage, the cost of financial capital is lower for publicly rather than privately owned firms, because public ownership addresses many of the issues associated with asymmetric or incomplete information about the firm and its financial prospects.

When we examine this list of advantages we might well ask why everyone doesn't just go public.

The Downside of Going Public

Well, as you may imagine, every coin has its flip side, and there are some important disadvantages with being publicly owned as well. The first of these is the loss of control on the part of the founding entrepreneur. Up until the time of the IPO, the entrepreneur can largely control or choose the other individuals or groups such as VCs that invest in her firm. Once the firm is publicly owned, however, anyone can buy or sell the stock. Although the founding entrepreneur often continues to be a major shareholder, she no longer has a majority stake in the firm. Similarly, her ability to control the future direction of the firm is diminished, because other stockholders also have a voice.

Another disadvantage of public ownership comes in the form of requirements for disclosure and information sharing with the Securities and Exchange Commission, which regulates publicly held firms in the United States (Kroll, Walters, and Le, 2007). Publicly held firms are required to file quarterly and annual reports with the SEC. These reports are readily available on the SEC website, so any interested party can access detailed information about the firm's performance and financial statements. Similarly, publicly held firms are required to provide shareholders with quarterly and annual reports. An annual meeting for shareholders must also be held to allow stockholders to question management on issues of firm performance and to vote on important issues. The entire process of managing investor relations can be time-consuming and sometimes contentious.

In addition to these various reporting requirements, publicly owned firms face more rigorous requirements for financial governance, reporting, and accountability. The Sarbanes-Oxley Act, passed in 2002, was a response to a series of accounting scandals involving major firms such as Tyco, WorldCom, and Enron. As a result of these scandals, thousands of investors lost money and thousands of employees lost jobs when these firms collapsed. Sarbanes-Oxley mandates greater financial disclosure for publicly held firms, thereby raising costs for financial systems and controls, financial audits and other services obtained from major accounting firms, and staff increases in the accounting area. All told, it is probably easier and less costly for a firm to remain privately owned. This is not an option, however, for firms seeking both significant size and scale and the financial capital to support those aspirations.

What Is the Right Time for Doing an IPO?

Typically, a firm's decision to go public is governed by several major considerations. The first of these is the extent to which it needs a large amount of external equity to satisfy its goals for growth and expansion (Petty and others, 1994). Thus, firms that do not seek growth have no need or reason to go public. A second major consideration is the extent to which the firm has achieved major benchmarks such as the sale of products and services, the generation of revenues, and, in many instances, profitability. In other words, the firm has to demonstrate that it has "arrived" in the sense of being an established entity with continued prospects for growth and profitability. A third consideration is the desire of the entrepreneur or other investors to harvest value through a liquidity event such as an IPO or sale of the company (DeTienne, 2010). This is typically an important consideration when the firm has used venture capital as a source of financing. Although VCs are patient investors, their ultimate goal is to provide a financial return to their investors within a reasonable time frame. From their perspective, the "big wins" come when one or more of their portfolio firms go public. A final consideration is the condition of the stock market in general and the stock market for the firm's industry sector in particular. Entrepreneurs prefer to go public when the stock market is healthy, because they get better valuations for their firm. Alternatively, firms that attempt to go public during stock market slumps raise less capital and run the risk of having to pull their offering due to low demand.

The IPO Process

When a company has made the decision to go public, it typically engages the services of an investment bank to assist with the process (Petty and others, 1994). In selecting an investment bank, the entrepreneur would research and evaluate the investment bank's experience, reputation, and track record with firms in its industry. This is where VC investors who serve on the firm's board can provide valuable contacts and expertise, since they have worked with various investment banks when other firms in their portfolio have gone public (Certo, Covin, Daily, and Dalton, 2001). The entrepreneur also needs to evaluate the bank's mix of institutional and retail clients to ensure that it has access to the large institutional buyers who will participate in the IPO as well as retail clients who can serve as both buyers and sellers in the post-IPO market. This post-IPO support in the form of a broad client base as well as reputable analysts who will track and issue reports on the company and its stock are important considerations.

Once chosen, the investment bank plays an important role in the IPO process. One of its major responsibilities is to assist the firm in developing the registration document, or S-1, required by the SEC. The S-1 describes the company, its products and markets, management, factors, and characteristics of the offering. The S-1 also addresses risks related to the business and provides financial statements. Similarly, the investment bank assists in developing the firm's prospectus, which includes information about the firm, its industry and products, and financials. The prospectus is provided to potential investors to help them learn about the firm and determine if they want to participate in the offering.

Organizing the "road show" is another key task for the investment bank. The road show involves both national and international presentations to large institutional investors such as mutual fund managers, pension fund managers, and endowment fund managers, who have the potential to purchase significant blocks of stock in the IPO. The entrepreneur and her CFO prepare the presentation with the help of the investment bank, and this same presentation is given at each stop on the road show to ensure consistency. Road show participants may also ask questions about issues that are not covered in the presentation or areas in which they would like more detail. In addition to its role as a "selling opportunity," the road show is important because it provides the investment bankers with a sense of the market's demand for the firm's stock. This, in turn, will help them determine an offer price. The higher the price, the greater the amount of capital raised. If, however, the price is set too high, there is a risk that the offer will be undersubscribed, meaning that the firm will raise less capital than anticipated. This is definitely not what you want to have happen, because many of the costs associated with an IPO are fixed and have to be paid whether the offering is successful or not. An undersubscribed offering also sends a negative signal to the market that may depress future demand for the stock. All in all, setting the "right" price is a delicate balance.

iRobot's Initial Public Offering

iRobot's growth and success in its various markets began to garner considerable recognition for Greiner and her co-founders. In 2002, Helen was named as one of the "Innovators for the Next Century" by MIT's *Technology Review*, and in 2003 she was included in *Fortune* magazine's list of "Top 10 Innovators Under 40" in the United States. Riding this wave of national recognition combined with the gradual stock market recovery after the dot-com bust in the early 2000s, Greiner and her co-founders concluded that the timing was right for an initial public offering. At the time, Greiner felt that iRobot was just beginning to take off, and that there were many opportunities for new products and new applications. The capital raised through an IPO would provide the funding required to take the firm to this next level.

As a first step, the founders began to interview investment bankers. They wanted to find a firm that understood and appreciated the potential of their business and products. Greiner also emphasized the importance of compatibility, shared goals, and the ability to communicate. The firm ended up selecting two firms, Morgan Stanley and J.P. Morgan, to lead the offering. Greiner commented that although going with one firm is the "normal" practice, they felt that they would get a broader perspective and complementary types of expertise by using two. These two co-leads, in turn, put together a syndicate that included three other investment banks.

The first major shared task was the creation of the S-1. Greiner describes this as an arduous and time-consuming process involving the investment banks, management, the board, attorneys, and accountants:

There was a lot of back and forth between the various parties, each of which had a somewhat different perspective.

Following the completion of the S-1, Greiner and her colleagues embarked on the road show to present iRobot as an investment opportunity to large institutional investors.

We started in Europe to make sure that we have our firm's story straight and to field test our presentation so it would be letter perfect. The presentation is very important, because you give the same presentation at every session. Questions from the various investment groups may vary, but the presentation itself has to be the same.

Greiner shared that their investment bankers organized the road show and handled every aspect of logistics to ensure that each presentation would be top-notch.

We traveled on a private plane, which was really neat. No checking in and waiting in lines at airports, nothing like that. You just get to the airport and walk onto the plane. They even checked on our hotel rooms prior to arrival in every city to make sure they were ready and had everything we would need. It makes sense, because each presentation was so important, and you don't want to blow one of them because your CFO didn't sleep the night before because of a problem with the hotel or his room.

Following the European round of presentations, the team returned to the United States, where they gave an additional sixty presentations to investor groups. Greiner describes it as a whirlwind tour, noting that on one day they gave presentations in three different states. At one point, the group found themselves with a free weekend in California, and the founders decided they wanted to take a break by going rock-climbing.

Our investment bankers even arranged that, but I think that they were petrified the whole time that one of us would fall and disrupt our schedule by breaking something!

Eventually the group concluded its odyssey in New York. The response to the road shows was very positive, and the deal ultimately priced at $24 per share, $1 above the target range. On November 15, 2005, iRobot went public on Nasdaq with an offering of 4.9 million shares of common stock priced at $24 per share. The offering was twenty times oversubscribed, and Greiner describes it as "a picture perfect IPO." Greiner and her colleagues opened the stock exchange that day and thus had the opportunity to track the stock's performance from that first opening bell. After that, they took yet another private plane to Boston for what Greiner describes as "the party to end all parties."

Researcher Dawn DeTienne, who has written extensively on the topic of entrepreneurial exits, argues that an initial public offering is not only a financial event for the entrepreneur, her firm, and the economy overall, but also a psychological event (DeTienne, 2010). Prior to the IPO, firm ownership and control are held by a small group of inside investors including the entrepreneur, key managers and employees, and investors such as VC firms. Although the entrepreneur does not necessarily hold a majority stake in the firm, due to dilution experienced through successive infusions of funding from her VC investors, she still has a significant share and plays a dominant role in decision making and management. With the IPO, however, that ownership and control become much more widely dispersed as large institutional investors and subsequently retail investors enter the picture. Thus, the IPO often serves as a gateway to a more mature and professionally managed stage for the firm (Certo, Covin, Daily, and Dalton, 2001; Kroll, Walters, and Le, 2007).

At that point, if the firm has not already done so, it needs to establish an infrastructure with its associated systems and controls to support further growth. Similarly, professional managers with expertise in the various functional areas are brought in to manage the day-to-day operations of the firm. This transition may leave the founding team who started out doing everything themselves a bit at loose ends. DeTienne argues, however, that growth-oriented entrepreneurs are much more likely to anticipate and plan for an exit strategy early in the life of their firm. Thus, they are more prepared to give up a portion of equity ownership and the control that goes with it in exchange for an opportunity to acquire the financial resources that will allow them to achieve both firm and personal goals.

This observation was confirmed in our interview with iRobot founder Helen Greiner. When asked how the transition from private to public ownership affected her personally, she responded that she accepted that as a part of the entrepreneurial process. Further, she had anticipated that her role in the firm would change and evolve as the firm moved through the various stages of its life cycle. As an example, when the decision was made to take iRobot public, Helen held the role of chief operating officer. She relinquished that role with its day-to-day operating responsibilities and moved into the role of CEO in order to focus on the IPO process. Following the IPO, she remained on as CEO for an additional three years before giving up that position to become a member of the board. After three years on the board, she again stepped down and currently has no involvement with the firm aside from holding its stock. As she puts it, "I was only in my forties at the time of the IPO, and I wanted to move on to the next thing."

Helen's "next thing" is a new high-tech entrepreneurial startup named CyPhy Works, which is in the process of developing unmanned aerial vehicles, otherwise known as drones.

The JOBS Act: An Update

The challenges faced by new, young, and growing firms in accessing the capital they need to start and grow their businesses have been widely documented. The United States took a significant step toward easing various securities regulations to encourage greater funding of small and young firms in the spring of 2012 with the passage of the Jumpstart Our Businesses Startups (JOBS) Act.

Typically, companies that are seeking to raise funds through the sale of securities must either register the securities offering with the SEC (which is very costly) or rely on an exemption from registration. Most of the previous exemptions from registration prohibit the general solicitation. However, Title II of the JOBS Act allows companies to do a general solicitation through the Internet or other avenues, provided they follow the rules and guidelines of Rule 506 of Regulation D and only make an offering to "accredited" investors. The act defines an accredited investor as anyone who meets certain income ($200,000 a year for three years prior to securities purchase) or net worth ($1,000,000, not including principal residence) thresholds.

The commissioners of the U.S. Securities and Exchange Commission voted unanimously in April 2015 to adopt final rules implementing Title IV of the JOBS Act, often referred to as Regulation A+. While crowdfunding has shown to be a successful route for many entrepreneurial firms in raising capital (debt, equity, or rewards-based), this new ruling will allow companies with serious growth potential to raise up to $50 million from unaccredited (and accredited) investors through offering stock directly to the general public, rather than having to raise venture capital or other institutional capital. This $50 million cap far exceeds the average level of funds being raised by individual firms through the various crowdfunding platforms.

The new rules update and expand Regulation A, an existing exemption, which previously allowed companies to raise $5 million from investors without going public. The *preemption* of state-by-state Blue Sky laws that required companies to also be reviewed and approved by individual state regulators before issuing shares to the public resulted in its infrequent use since its creation in 1934. Now, companies raising capital under the regulation will no longer need to register with each individual state where they are seeking to raise capital, which makes it a far more efficient and less costly process.

This new ruling will allow private companies to enter the public market at a much lower cost than a traditional IPO. In addition, the regulation opens up new investment opportunities to both accredited and non-accredited investors (the latter group will be limited to investing up to 10 percent of their net worth). This should be a win-win for both companies and investors. Companies now can access capital by soliciting from a far wider audience, while investors now have an increasing number of investment choices.

Regulation A+ also provides investors with liquidity, as the shares are freely tradable upon their issuance. This liquidity and greater transparency sets Regulation A+ apart from Regulation D and Rule 506—with no mandatory disclosure, no dollar limitation, and a holding period of one year. Another attraction is the self-certification of accredited investor status. Unlike Rule 506(c) under Title II of the JOBS Act, investors will be able to self-certify their income or net worth for purposes of the investment limits, so there will be no burdensome documentation required to prove income or net worth.

Closing the Loop

In this chapter we have focused our attention on strategies for harvesting value. Historically, women entrepreneurs are less likely than men to have harvested value through the sale of their firm or an IPO. This is not surprising in light of the fact that women traditionally have launched smaller and less growth-oriented firms. More recently, however, a new cohort of growth-oriented women entrepreneurs like iRobot's Helen Greiner and Communispace's Diane Hessan has gained valuable experience and visibility through successful harvest events. These events, in the form of IPOs or sale of the firm, have provided the financial resources required for further growth as well as the development of new products and services. They have also increased the personal wealth of the entrepreneur, thereby allowing her to pursue other entrepreneurial opportunities or to assume a broader leadership role within her industry. In this sense, harvesting value is not the end of her entrepreneurial journey but rather a temporary harbor that allows her to chart the next stage of her course.

This chapter has provided several insights into harvesting value for our intrepid growth-oriented women entrepreneurs. First, planning for an entrepreneurial exit is an integral part of the entrepreneurial process, particularly for growth-oriented entrepreneurs. In light of that, women launching growth-oriented firms need to see "the big picture," and that picture needs to include their desired method for harvesting value. As with other key decisions, the harvest option will help to determine the types of financial capital that are appropriate. As an example, entrepreneurs who do not anticipate selling their firms or going public are not typically candidates for venture capital funding.

Although only a few firms harvest value through an initial public offering, those firms tend to receive the greatest amount of attention, because they tend to be the largest and most successful. Our case study of iRobot profiles a highly successful IPO in which all the pieces of the puzzle miraculously came together for a positive outcome. It doesn't always work that smoothly, and Helen Greiner herself pointed out that, in spite of the relative ease of their IPO, iRobot went through a lot of tough times before it got to that stage, leading the founders to wonder if the firm was actually going to make it.

An additional topic covered in this chapter is the changing nature of the entrepreneur's role as the firm makes the transition from private to public ownership. During the firm's early days, the entrepreneur often serves as a Jack (or Jill!) of all trades. As we have noted, however, an IPO comes with a number of leadership and regulatory changes, not the least of which are changes in ownership and control. Although the entrepreneur may still hold a significant amount of stock, she no longer controls who the other shareholders are. This is a normal and even healthy part of the IPO process, but it can be a difficult transition for an entrepreneur who has nurtured her firm and worked with key employees from the earliest days.

Last but certainly not least, we have focused on the wealth-creating potential of a successful harvest event in this chapter. This is an important consideration because it harkens back to Chapter 1, in which we asked the question, "Why growth?" Although entrepreneurs benefit financially from any of the five harvest options we have detailed in this chapter, the biggest financial returns come from doing an IPO. This is true not only for the entrepreneur herself, but also for other insiders such as managers, key employees, and investors such as venture capitalists. Although we all know that money doesn't necessarily buy happiness, it does give women a broader range of opportunities and choices. Those post-harvest choices will be the focal point of our next chapter.

What Does This Mean for You?

In Chapter 10 we have explored harvest options for growth-oriented women entrepreneurs using the example of Helen Greiner and her firm, iRobot, which went through a highly successful initial public offering. Helen's experience provides valuable insights into the IPO process as well as strategies that contribute to a positive outcome.

1. Identify your most likely harvest option during the earliest days of your firm. Your planned harvest event will help determine the ultimate size of your firm as well as its financial sources and strategies. As an example, an entrepreneur who aims for an initial public offering will use a different financing mix than that of an entrepreneur who plans to sell her venture to managers or employees at some unspecified future date.

2. Build an organizational infrastructure to support your firm's growth. During a new venture's early days, the entrepreneur and her founding team find themselves doing a bit of everything. As the firm grows, however, it is important to create an organizational structure, including people, systems, and controls, that supports that growth.

3. Pick your advisors carefully. The process of doing an IPO is complex and time consuming; the entrepreneur will need advisors such as venture capitalists and investment bankers who have expertise in this area. In addition to their financial expertise, Helen Greiner stressed the importance of "compatibility, shared goals, and the ability to communicate."

4. Recognize the fact that your role will change during the IPO process. Prior to the IPO, many entrepreneurs are heavily involved in managing or supervising the daily operations of their firm. During the IPO process, however, the entrepreneur needs to step back from day-to-day operations and focus on working with the firm's investment bankers and communicating its achievements and prospects to potential investors.

5. Understand and accept the implications of public versus private ownership. From the entrepreneur's perspective, her share of ownership and control will be diminished through the issuance of additional shares of stock. Although she will continue to have an important voice in the firm's management and direction, this may lessen over time as the firm shifts from "entrepreneurial mode" to "mature firm mode." This inevitable transition can be difficult for entrepreneurs who have nurtured a firm from its earliest

beginnings, and it helps explain why successful entrepreneurs like Helen Greiner are already thinking about "the next best thing" even as their most recent venture enters its maturity stage. With this in mind, we will now move on to Chapter 11, which helps answer the question, "Is there life after an IPO?"

11

NO REST

Life After Harvesting Value

Once the entrepreneur has harvested value through an IPO or sale of her company, the firm typically has access to a much broader range of financing alternatives, including funding from the public debt and equity markets. Post-IPO, financial strategies shift over time from managing growth to managing operations and profitability. This new set of tasks often entails replacing the original entrepreneur and her team with individuals who will take over the management of the firm as a going concern. One of the key issues for the entrepreneur is her role going forward. In this chapter we will discuss some of the financial strategies women entrepreneurs use to manage this period of transition. Some remain with the firm as a member of the board of directors. Others choose to deploy their newly acquired wealth to launch new entre-preneurial ventures, to take leadership roles within their industry, to pursue philanthropic goals, or to invest in other firm startups.

We will illustrate that this is typically not an abrupt shift from one role to the other. Rather, growth-oriented women entrepreneurs often make the transition from one type of leadership role within the firm to a broader leadership role both within the company and beyond. As an example, a woman entrepreneur might shift from managing day-to-day operations to serving in the capacity of CEO or some other leadership position as the firm grows. Similarly, post-IPO, she may become a major shareholder and member of the board of directors. Simultaneously, her experience in launching and growing a successful firm can lead to board positions for other firms or the role of an industry leader. Finally, her accumulated wealth may open the door to the pursuit of philanthropic goals or becoming an active investor in the firms of other growth-oriented women entrepreneurs. This sequence of activities or "virtuous cycle" takes our growth-oriented entrepreneur from being a recipient of human, social, and financial capital to the point at which she is able to become a major contributor in each of these areas. In doing so, she has opportunities to create a type of positive ripple effect on her firm, her industry, her community, and the economy overall.

Round Two:
Launching New Entrepreneurial Ventures

Once bitten by the entrepreneurial bug, many entrepreneurs find themselves planning for their next venture even as they prepare to harvest value from the first. From a public policy perspective, this is indeed a good thing, because the economy benefits from this recycling of entrepreneurial talent. An editorial in the *Wall Street Journal* (Malone, 2014) observed that large, established firms like Facebook, Cisco, Yahoo, and even Apple are no longer a primary source of new products, services, and technologies. Instead, these innovations emerge in newer, smaller firms that grow "exponentially." Thus, a current innovation strategy for many larger firms is to purchase such firms and the talent that comes with them. The author concludes that

> it may be time to stop waiting for famous tech companies to roll out the hot-test new product and start investing in startups that can sell their innovations to big companies. Tech appears to be evolving into a different kind of field: one that is, paradoxically, more static at the top but also more dependent on entrepreneurship than ever before. (Malone, 2014, p. A13)

Several of the entrepreneurs that we interviewed for this book are well on the way to launching a second firm. Chinwe Onyeagoro, co-founder of FundWell, used the proceeds from her first firm to help launch her second. Her entrepreneurial experience played a key role in preparing her for the challenges of raising capital for her second firm. Simultaneously, that prior experience helped her expand her network of individuals who could provide contacts to help her raise capital for FundWell. Helen Greiner put the proceeds of her iRobot IPO to work in launching CyPhy Works (http://www.cyphyworks.com), a startup focused on the development of unmanned aerial vehicles (UAVs) or drones. These vehicles can be used to help military and police personnel investigate the interior of buildings without sending people in. Thus, the UAVs can be used to search for survivors in natural or man-made disasters. They can also be used to inspect bridges, buildings, and other types of structures for safety and soundness. In addition to putting in her own capital, Greiner was able to raise $3 million in venture capital financing for CyPhy (Kirsner, 2012). More recently, she raised an additional financing round of $7 million from a combination of VC and angel investors. This is not surprising, given that there is nothing an investor likes more than an entrepreneur who has already proven she has what it takes to succeed (Hsu, 2007; Zhang, 2011). This most recent round will allow CyPhy to expand into additional sectors, including agriculture, mining, construction, oil and gas, and insurance (http://www.cyphyworks.com). Like Onyeagoro and Greiner, our next featured entrepreneur, Jenny Mather, was able to use capital gained from the sale of her firm, Raven Biotechnologies, to launch her new firm, CanFel. In addition to financial capital, however, she also gained important insights into the fundraising process and dynamics from her experience with Raven. These have helped her become a better-informed and prepared entrepreneur this second time around. As the saying goes, knowledge is power.

Jennie Mather and Raven Biotechnologies

Raven Biotechnologies was founded in 1999 with the goal of developing mono-clonal antibody therapeutics for the treatment of various types of cancer. Founder Jennie Mather was well prepared for her foray into biotech entrepreneurship, having spent a number of years as a staff scientist for Genentech. While there, she had the opportunity to work in both the scientific realm of drug development and the manufacturing side of drug production. This fairly unique combination of skills served her well when she launched her own firm.

Dr. Mather described the challenges of raising capital for a biotechnology firm engaged in the development of new drugs and treatments. First, the development cycle is very long, typically in excess of ten years, due to regulatory requirements for clinical trials and approvals. During this time frame, the firm consumes large amounts of capital while generating minimal or no revenues. These regulatory requirements pose another challenge, because they have dramatically increased costs as well as the time required to receive approval. Mather contends that

the funding model for biotechnology is broken. In 1999 when Raven was launched, it took somewhere between $50 million and $100 million to develop a new treatment. Today, the

amount of financial capital required has climbed to a range of $500 million to $1 billion.
The regulatory burden and the costs that it imposes has reached the point where it is both
unrealistic and unmanageable. It is also serving as a major impediment in the launch and
development of new firms capable of developing life-saving drugs and treatments.

Initially Jennie and her co-founder funded Raven using their own financial resources. They worked without taking salaries and bootstrapped to minimize
startup expenses. Subsequently, however, Raven went through four rounds
of external funding. Dr. Mather noted that, as the economic environment
changed, the nature of her fundraising experience also changed dramatically.

The first investment round of $1.3 million was raised in 1999 from two ven-
ture capital firms. Jennie noted that her credentials and contacts from Genentech were a key factor in securing this round of funding. She also observed that
she probably did not raise enough money during that first round. Given the
amount of time and energy it takes to secure funding, she should have raised a
larger amount.

By raising too little in her first round, Jennie had to go back out for funding
again at the end of 2000. At that point, she raised a larger amount, $20 mil-
lion, also from VCs. In spite of her relative inexperience as a new entrepreneur,
Dr. Mather described the funding environment during that initial 1999–2000
time frame as relatively favorable. All that changed, however, after 9/11. The
third round of funding was particularly difficult, because it came immediately
after 9/11 and, according to Jennie, "took forever to close." The fourth and last
round of funding (Series D) closed in October of 2005 for $48.5 million. Dur-
ing that final round, investors actually approached Raven instead of the other
way around. As an added advantage, some of the VCs who had already invested
provided assistance in identifying additional investors. In total, Raven raised
$115 million over the course of the four rounds.

In 2008, Raven Biotechnologies was bought by MacroGenics. When asked if
she benefited financially from the sale, Jennie responded that most of the proceeds went to investors who had participated in the last two rounds of funding
(Series C and D) rather than to the early stage investors including herself and
employees who had been with the firm from its earliest days. Due to the more
adverse funding environment after 9/11, later-stage investors demanded and received "preferences" of two to three times. This had the effect of squeezing out
those who had participated earlier. Jennie tried to convince the VCs to set aside
10 percent of the proceeds from the sale for the early stage investors, but they
were not willing to do so. She pointed out that this is becoming an increasingly

familiar pattern for firms relying on multiple rounds of VC funding. Large VC funds hold off investing until the later rounds, demand preferences, and walk away with most of the returns associated with a liquidity event.

Fortunately, most of the employees from Raven, including Jennie, were kept on and given jobs at MacroGenics. Further, they received stock in MacroGenics as a part of their compensation, and benefited in that way when MacroGenics went public in 2013. These were hard lessons for Jennie, who viewed the company and her employees as family. She prided herself in creating a positive environment and culture at Raven that energized her employees and empowered them to achieve impressive results with a relatively small number of people. One of the reasons she is currently taking the plunge and launching a new biotechnology firm, CanFel Therapeutics, is to re-create that culture and the results that accompanied it.

In thinking about her Raven experience, Jennie admits,

I was naive. One out of four or one out of five drug treatments actually works, so I wanted to build an efficient platform for developing treatments. The board, composed primarily of VCs, had very different objectives. They wanted to develop one success that would enable them to get out.

Jennie summarized lessons learned from her VC process as follows:

1. Get someone on your team who has a business versus pure science background. You need to understand the role that VCs play and what their motivations are.

2. If at all possible, choose a lead investor that you personally get along with. You want to have a sense of mutual respect, trust, and support.

3. Get some big money behind you early on. You want to attract funds that are capable of doing two or three rounds.

4. Given the amount of time it takes to raise money, raise as much as you can when you do a round of funding. I underestimated my needs early on and had to go back out for a second round almost immediately after closing on my first.

Currently, Dr. Mather is the senior vice president for stem cell research at MacroGenics. She is also in the process of launching her second biotech firm, CanFel Therapeutics (http://www.canfeltherapeutics.com). Her goal for this second venture is to circumvent some of the regulatory challenges she encountered the first time around by focusing on developing treatments for cats and dogs. She points out that as health care for pets is improving, they are also living longer. Thus, approximately 50 percent eventually die of cancer, just like humans. With CanFel, Jennie plans to develop an efficient platform for the discovery on antibodies that can be used in animals. These findings can, in turn, be applied to human subjects. Her goal is to get multiple antibodies into clinical trials, thereby positioning CanFel to go directly to large pharmaceutical firms that have animal health units. By establishing partnerships with these large firms, Jennie can get the funding required to grow her firm.

Thus far CanFel's major source of financing has been funding provided by Dr. Mather and her co-founder. In addition, they have bootstrapped to buy used and broken equipment that can be fixed. They have even turned to crowdfunding, raising $20,000 on Indiegogo that allowed them to buy two pieces of used equipment on eBay. At the time of the interview CanFel had two full-time employees, Jennie and her co-founder. Three ex-Raven employees were helping out part time and waiting to be hired.

Mather's experience highlights the fact that the entrepreneur's personal interests and priorities may not be entirely compatible with those of her investors. This is particularly true in the case of venture capitalists whose main priority is to provide returns to their investors. Several of our entrepreneurs have cautioned that it is important to "know where your investors are coming from," since you cannot simply assume that your own priorities are the same as theirs. Serial entrepreneurs have an inherent advantage in dealing with these types of situations, because, like Mather, they have seen it and been through it before.

Leadership Roles in the Firm and Beyond

As her firm moves through the various stages of the life cycle, it is not uncommon for the founding entrepreneur to assume different roles. Initially, during the earliest stages, she is what my grandfather used to refer to as "chief cook and bottle washer," meaning that she essentially does everything, because she cannot yet afford to hire additional people. As we have shown through our case studies, this is one powerful reason for founding teams, a strategy that provides diverse talents, networks, and some extra sets of hands for dividing up the types of tasks that need to get done. As the firm evolves and begins to generate revenues the entrepreneur begins to build out her leadership team and create an organizational infrastructure to support future growth. This is the point at which she needs to start delegating tasks, so her primary role shifts from doing everything herself to choosing and managing the right people to help her do them. Thus, as the firm grows, the entrepreneur typically assumes the COO or CEO title, or both. As the firm prepares to harvest value, however, the entrepreneur often shifts away from daily operating responsibilities and focuses on more strategic CEO-level responsibilities in order to get the company ready for its IPO or sale. Although many entrepreneurs may remain in the CEO position for a period of time post-harvest, they eventually move out of that role as well to become board members or stockholders. In this maturity stage, the growth rate in revenues slows and management's focus shifts from rapid growth to managing operations in ways that will maximize returns. As noted above, this shift provides an opportunity for the entrepreneur to diversify her talents and interests into other areas, including that of assuming a broader leadership role within her industry and the economy overall. These leadership roles have the advantage of drawing additional attention to the firm as well as its products and services, thereby helping to increase awareness, market share, revenues, and profits. They also provide a means whereby the entrepreneur can shape public policy in the form of government support, legislation, and regulations affecting her industry.

As an example, Manon Cox, president and CEO of Protein Sciences, was named as one of eight "Women in Innovation" by the Connecticut Technology Council in 2014. As the leader of a growing firm that is adding employees, she has also had the opportunity to host elected officials including Governor Dannel Malloy and U.S. Congresswoman Elizabeth Esty at her facility in Meriden, Connecticut (http://www.proteinsciences.com). The state of Connecticut is working diligently to develop a world-class bioscience sector, and Protein Sciences is exactly the type of firm that its elected officials want to attract and nurture. Robotics pioneer Helen Greiner has received numerous awards for her leadership in the area of technology innovation, including the Association for Unmanned Vehicle Systems International's prestigious Pioneer Award. In 2007 Greiner was also inducted into the Women in Technology International Hall of Fame. In April 2014, she was named a Presidential Ambassador for Global Entrepreneurship (PAGE) by President Barack Obama. In that capacity, she will work with other successful business leaders to help develop the next generation of entrepreneurs. In a press release announcing this honor, Greiner stated,

> I was lucky to have come as a child to the U.S., a place of limitless opportunity where you can follow your passion, create cool products and good paying jobs.
> I am thrilled to be a member of PAGE because I am passionate about entrepre-

neurship. I will use the position to promote the creation of scalable technology companies to improve quality of life, employment, employee growth, community prosperity, and social good. (http://cyphyworks.com)

As we have shown through our examples of Manon Cox and Helen Greiner, one way for entrepreneurs to become recognized as leaders is through awards or designations made at the state, national, or even international levels. Each state has its own recognition program for innovators and business leaders. In addition, there are a number of organizations that recognize the contributions of entrepreneurs at a national level. As an example, each year *Forbes* magazine creates a "World's Most Powerful Women" list which includes women representing many sectors and types of activities. The 2013 list included two of the women entrepreneurs we started off with in Chapter 1, Spanx founder Sara Blakely and media entrepreneur Oprah Winfrey. Similarly, *Enterprising Women* magazine creates a list of "Enterprising Women of the Year." This award recognizes women from around the globe and is divided into different categories. Cindy Monroe, founder of Thirty-One Gifts (http://www.thirtyonegifts.com), a firm that manufactures and sells handbags, totes, and other organizational items for women, was recognized in the "More than $25 million in annual sales revenue" category in 2014. Her firm has also been named as one of the top twenty global direct-selling firms by *Direct Selling News*. Cindy's firm is a great example of the type of "explosive growth" experienced by fast-growing firms, with sales increasing from $100 million in 2010 to over $700 million in 2012.

Two national organizations, the National Association of Women Business Owners (NAWBO) and the Women Presidents' Organization (WPO) also recognize leading women entrepreneurs on an annual basis. Kathy Mills, founder of Strategic Communications (http://yourstrategic.com), a firm specializing in voice, video, and data communications systems, was listed as number 1 on the WPO's 2013 list of "Fastest 50 Growing Companies" and as number 2 the following year. Cenergy (http://www.cenergyintl.com), founded by June Ressler and described in Chapter 10, was also listed as one of the top five firms on the WPO list in both years. Ressler serves as a great example of women who are launching and growing highly successful firms in previously male-dominated sectors.

Two of the major national accounting firms, Ernst & Young and PricewaterhouseCoopers, both recognize entrepreneurs in various categories on an annual basis. These are prestigious awards and, like the other awards listed, provide added visibility and stature to the entrepreneurs who receive them. According to Ernst & Young's Entrepreneur of the Year website (http://www .ey.com), 1,500 entrepreneurs were nominated in 2014. Their firms employed over 700,000 people and generated revenues in excess of $253 billion. Cindy Monroe, our Thirty-One Gifts founder, was a regional winner of Ernst & Young's Entrepreneur of the Year Award in 2011, as was June Ressler, founder of Cenergy, in 2012. Similarly, Jennifer Maier, the founder of WDS (http://www .womends.com), was selected as an Ernst & Young Entrepreneur of the Year award winner in 2012. WDS, which stands for Women's Distribution Services, is a national warehousing and distribution company serving the manufacturing, medical, and technology industries. WDS is certified as a woman-owned business, a designation that has helped the firm increase its revenues by providing services to national food processors in the areas of warehousing, distribution, and inventory management.

A number of women entrepreneurs, like Manon Cox and Helen Greiner, have parlayed their firm's growth and success into roles that allow them to develop "political capital" by shaping public policy as well as legislation and regulations affecting their own industries. June Ressler is one of the founding partners of Women Impacting Public Policy (WIPP), a national organization that advocates on behalf of women-owned businesses in the development of legislation and economic opportunities. She is also a member of the previously mentioned Women Presidents' Organization (WPO), another national organization, which has as its goal "to improve business conditions for women entrepreneurs and to promote the acceptance and advancement of women entrepreneurs in all industries" (http://www.womenpresidentsorg.com).

The examples we have provided here, in addition to many more, provide ample evidence that successful growth-oriented women entrepreneurs evolve over time beyond the boundaries of their firm and industry to become leaders and decision makers in a broader sense. Their achievements, and the visibility that comes with it, provides them with stature, influence, and power at national and even international levels. This evolution, in turn, provides new opportunities for entrepreneurs to pursue their personal passions, for example, in Helen Greiner's case for robotics and "doing good" on a much larger stage. Like Helen, biotech entrepreneur Sue Washer is passionate about the treatments her current firm is developing to treat severe diseases of the eye. A recent IPO that provided funds that will help propel the firm toward commercialization also got Sue thinking about her own next steps.

Sue Washer and Applied Genetic Technologies Corporation (AGTC)

Sue Washer joined AGTC (http://www.agtc.com), a biotech firm devoted to developing treatments for eye disease, in 2001 after accumulating valuable experience in both major pharmaceutical firms (Abbott Labs, Eli Lilly) and startups. In addition to her professional experience, Sue had an undergraduate degree in biochemistry from Michigan State as well as an MBA from the University of Florida. Her strong educational and business background made her a particularly attractive candidate to lead AGTC, a firm founded by five scientists. At the time, Sue was AGTC's third employee aside from the founders themselves (Rumbaugh, 2010).

AGTC was founded in 1999 with technology developed at the University of Florida with the goal of creating gene therapies that can be used to treat patients with severe eye diseases that can lead to blindness. The company's acronym, "AGTC," represents the first letters of the four bases in DNA, adenine, guanine, thymine, and cytosine. The venture began conducting research in the university's biotechnology incubator in Alachua, which provided support, equipment, and office space. Sue's task was to take AGTC beyond the incubator stage and transform it into a firm capable of conducting and commercializing world-class research on diseases of the eye. Consistent with that goal, Sue helped AGTC raise a second round of VC funding in 2003 totaling $15 million (Rumbaugh, 2010). This was followed by additional VC rounds over the course of the next decade, as well as grants from government sources. During this period of time, Sue took the lead in raising a total of over $90 million for the firm. Simultaneously, as AGTC evolved and grew, she was responsible for developing the firm's infrastructure, including recruiting an experienced and well-qualified management team.

As the economy and the stock market slowly emerged from the shock of the Great Recession, Sue and the AGTC board made the decision that it was time to take the next step by exploring the possibility of an initial public offering. An IPO would provide a significant amount of external equity capital while also increasing visibility for the firm and its technologies. When we spoke with Sue, we asked her to describe her experience with the IPO process as well as her role within the context of that process.

The initial public offering is a very proscribed process; there are specific steps that everyone goes through. One of the things you have to make sure of, however is that your supporting staff, both internal and external, are well qualified and on board. External mem-

bers of the team include your accounting firm, legal advisors, and the members of your banking team. It is very important that those individuals have experience in dealing with publicly held firms and firms that have gone public. In our case, I had not gone through an IPO before, but our accountants, lawyers, and investment bankers had.

One of the key roles for the banking team is to oversee filings required by the SEC and to set up and manage the road shows that serve as a means for assessing the demand for the offering, identifying investors, and establishing an offering price. As CEO, Sue's role was to drive the IPO process and to ensure that all of the key players were on board.

Since we are developing emerging technologies, we were also eligible to do a series of "testing the waters" meetings to help evaluate the level of interest in our firm. We actually did 105 of these, and they were very helpful. Subsequent to that, we did the road show for major investors in the U.S. and abroad. During that time, our banking team took orders.

AGTC went public on March 27, 2014, at a price of $12 per share, raising approximately $52 million. Currently the firm trades on the Nasdaq stock exchange under the symbol "AGTC." Several months later, AGTC did a second public offering of stock that raised an additional $34 million. Although Sue was very pleased with the outcome, we asked if there was anything she would do differently if she had to do it again.

If I had it to do again, I would do even more homework up front, particularly on the banking team. We did a lot of homework this time, but I would do even more, because we had to make a few changes, and did not end up with the same team we started out with. Ultimately, however, we ended up with a great banking team, and our IPO went great. For us, doing the IPO when we did was absolutely the right thing to do. As a life sciences company, we require a lot of resources, and you cannot fund a company like ours with just VC money. We needed to go public to raise the funds required for commercialization. An added benefit is that, as a publicly held firm, AGTC is much more visible. A lot more people know who we are, and that helps with partnerships and licensing.

We asked Sue if her role has changed significantly since the IPO.

We are still a small cap company, so we are not as visible as companies like Google or Abbot Labs. Prior to the IPO, I was interacting with VCs and raising money. I was also working with our board of directors and our partners. Now that we are publicly owned, I am still interacting with our investors or stockholders to communicate direction and strategy. One of the differences I have become aware of is that I have to be really careful about *timing and consistency when I disclose information. It is a much more structured process in that everyone has to have access to the same information at the same time.*

In terms of priorities going forward:

My biggest priority is to drive our technology through to commercialization. My goal is to get these treatments into patients' hands.

In spite of her demanding schedule, Sue has already found ways to give back by sharing her expertise and mentoring others. She is currently a mentor for aspiring entrepreneurs at the University of Florida's Center for Entrepreneurship, BioFlorida, and the Gainesville Chamber of Commerce. She has also served as a judge on numerous business plan competitions. Longer term, Sue can also see herself investing in other entrepreneurial ventures as well.

Pursuing Philanthropic Goals
Women as Philanthropic Entrepreneurs

The subject of "doing good" brings us to a third possible post-harvest outlet for growth-oriented entrepreneurs. As we discussed in Chapter 10, harvesting value through an IPO or sale of the company allows the entrepreneur to realize the wealth that she has created in launching and growing her firm. Other entrepreneurs, such as Sara Blakely at Spanx and Oprah Winfrey with her vast media holdings, accumulate significant wealth even prior to harvesting value. A growing number of these successful women entrepreneurs are channeling some of that wealth into making the world a better place by targeting specific social or environmental needs. It would seem that giving comes naturally to women. A 2010 report published by Indiana University's Center on Philanthropy found that households headed by single females are more likely to give to charity and give at a higher level than their male counterparts at all income levels (Mesch, 2010). A subsequent study focusing on the baby boom generation had similar findings (Mesch, 2012). In that study, baby boomer women in the top 25 percent income category actually gave over 1.5 times more than men, controlling for other variables.

Seeking to harness the giving power of women, sisters Swanee Hunt, ambassador to Austria from 1993 to 1997, and Helen LaKelly Hunt launched a campaign called Women Moving Millions in 2005 (http://www.womenmovingmillions .org). Their goal was to attract women capable of providing gifts of $1 million or more to create a fund for the advancement of women and girls. Between April 2007 and April 2009, the sisters raised a total of $182 million from 102 separate donors. These funds were then channeled through the Women's Funding Network (WFN) into forty-one of the network's member funds around the world. To date, over 200 donors have pledged in excess of $300 million. The Women Moving Millions Vision Statement states that

> Women Moving Millions is a community of individuals who have made gifts and pledges of one million or more to organizations/initiatives promoting the advancement and empowerment of women and girls. We believe that women and girls are the single best investment towards creating healthy societies, economic growth, and global stabilization. What is good for women is good for everyone. (http://www.womenmovingmillions.org)

Women as Social Entrepreneurs

Social entrepreneurship refers to the creation of organizations or firms that create social as well as economic value (Coleman and Kariv, 2016). Typically these social ventures address unmet social needs in the areas of health, poverty, hunger, education, social justice, and the environment, often on a global basis. Although social entrepreneurship is relatively new as a field of study, emerging research suggests that women entrepreneurs play an important role. Although men are twice as likely to become commercial entrepreneurs as women, the gap between women and men in the area of social entrepreneurship is much smaller (Terjesen, Lepoutre, Justo, and Bosma, 2012, page 21). Wendy Kopp, the founder of Teach for America, is one example of a social entrepreneur who has successfully achieved significant size and scope for her organization. Teach for America places enthusiastic and energetic recent college graduates into some of the nation's worst-performing schools to connect with and inspire their students (http://www.teachforamerica.org). Results reveal dramatic improvements in test scores for those schools that participate. Kopp is currently building upon her model for success in the United States by expanding globally through a program called Teach for All.

Another social entrepreneur that we are particularly fond of is Jane Chen, co-founder of Embrace, a firm that produces portable baby warmers for newborns suffering from hypothermia (http://www.embraceglobal.org). Chen and her co-founders developed the Embrace Baby Warmer as part of a class project while they were still students at Stanford University. They learned that over one million premature and underweight babies die each year from birth complications and hypothermia because they do not have enough body fat to keep themselves warm. Ninety-eight percent of these are in developing economies where mothers do not have access to hospitals or incubators, which are relatively costly. Unlike traditional incubators, the sack-like Embrace Baby Warmer is portable and can be distributed and used in remote locations. It can also be re-used, and, once charged, will provide warmth for four to six hours. Equally important, the Embrace warmer costs only a fraction of what hospitals pay for incubators, thus making it economically feasible to purchase and distribute the warmers in developing nations. Currently, the Embrace Baby Warmer is in use in eleven different countries, including Uganda, Afghanistan, India, China, and Guatemala. To date, the warmer has been used to preserve the lives of over fifty thousand premature or low-birth-weight babies.

In addition to their growing influence within the field of social entrepreneurship, women who launch growth-oriented commercial ventures are also pursuing philanthropic goals by donating their time, talents, and substantial amounts of funding. Fashion designer and entrepreneur Tory Burch launched the Tory Burch Foundation in 2009 with a goal of supporting the economic empowerment of women entrepreneurs in the United States through a combination of loans, networking programs, and mentoring support (http://www.toryburch foundation.org). In 2014 the foundation partnered with Bank of America to launch Elizabeth Street Capital, a program designed to provide both financing and support to early stage women entrepreneurs (Desai, 2014). This initiative was named after the location of Burch's first boutique in New York City. Since that time, Tory Burch has expanded to become a global brand with a presence in over fifty countries worldwide. The firm generated revenues in excess of $800 million in 2013, and Burch herself is estimated to have a net worth of over $1 billion (Inverso, 2014). Recent research conducted by Barclays Wealth Management found that women are becoming increasingly important donors in their own right and that they donate a larger percentage of their wealth to charity (*Tomorrow's Philanthropist*, 2009, p. 8). This suggests that as the number of successful growth-oriented entrepreneurs like Tory Burch grows, these women will play a greater role in providing support to nonprofits, foundations, and organizations supporting the development and empowerment of girls and women.

Closing the Loop

In this chapter we have discussed some of the possible "next steps" for women entrepreneurs who have grown their firms to significant size and scale or who have harvested value through a sale, merger, or IPO. One of the most attractive

options for many of these high-achieving women is to launch yet another entrepreneurial venture using lessons learned from their first entrepreneurial experience. The second time around, these experienced entrepreneurs, like Jennie
Mather, know a lot more about the entrepreneurial process as well as the potential bumps in the road. Similarly, entrepreneurs like Chinwe Onyeagoro have a
well-developed network of contacts, advisors, and potential funding sources. In
terms of financial capital, successful entrepreneurs have had an opportunity to
accumulate wealth through their earnings or through the sale of shares. Thus,
they have a nest egg (often substantial) that can be used to help fund a new
startup. That's not to say it's easy the second time around, but some of the first-
time challenges in the areas of human, social, and financial capital may be more
manageable thanks to the resources the entrepreneur has acquired through the
process of launching, growing, and harvesting her first firm.

As we have shown in this chapter, women entrepreneurs can also choose to
evolve into leaders and role models. The success of their firms leads to greater
visibility, and with that visibility comes increased opportunities for recognition
and involvement in their industry or the economy on a larger scale. Most of the
women entrepreneurs we have chronicled in this book have received numerous
awards and accolades. Often, these have opened doorways to new types of leadership opportunities, such as Helen Greiner's designation as one of President
Barack Obama's Presidential Ambassadors for Global Entrepreneurship and
June Ressler's role as one of the founding partners of Women Impacting Public
Policy (WIPP). Greater visibility also increases awareness for the company and
its products and services, thereby facilitating further growth and expansion. An
added benefit of visibility is that it serves as a source of political capital. Successful growth-oriented entrepreneurs and their firms are front and center on
the radar screens of elected officials and policy makers because of their potential to generate new jobs, the often innovative nature of their products and services, and their greater likelihood of involvement in international trade. Each
of these contributions provides benefits to a local, state, or national economy,
and public officials are eager to nurture firms of this type.

A third potential route for successful women entrepreneurs is the opportunity to share their wealth, time, and talents with others. Recent research suggests that women are more philanthropically inclined than men, which bodes
well for the next generation of growth-oriented entrepreneurs who will have
the potential to support social and environmental causes that will improve the
lives of others. Some of these highly successful women like fashion designer

Tory Burch have chosen to focus their philanthropic efforts on helping other women entrepreneurs get started. In this sense, Burch provides us with an example of the "virtuous circle" that we referred to earlier in this chapter, whereby women entrepreneurs who succeed pay it forward to others who follow in their footsteps. Burch's example also provides us with an ideal segue into our final chapter, where we focus on a fourth potential route for successful women entrepreneurs, the opportunity to invest in other women-owned firms.

What Does This Mean for You?

This chapter shifted attention from launching and growing the entrepreneurial firm to next steps for entrepreneurs who have moved through the survival and rapid growth stages of the entrepreneurial process. In some instances, these entrepreneurs have been able to harvest value through sale of their firm or an initial public offering. In other instances, firms that remain privately held have also generated significant wealth for their founders. What comes next for entrepreneurs who have achieved this level of success? As our interviews and research illustrate, many such entrepreneurs follow one or a combination of three different pathways that can be characterized as (1) do it again, (2) give back, and (3) help others. Which of these pathways is right for you?

1. Some of our entrepreneurs who have harvested value channel their passion, experience, and wealth into launching a new venture. Do you feel that your entrepreneurial work is not done yet? Do you love the challenge and exhilaration of starting something new and making it grow? If so, you have the makings of a serial entrepreneur or someone who channels her entrepreneurial energy into new directions.

2. Other entrepreneurs are prompted to give back to their community, their industry, and the economy overall as well as to other aspiring entrepreneurs. Think about your own entrepreneurial journey, the lessons you have learned and the skills you have acquired. How can you share this valuable human capital with other women who are launching their own firms? Never underestimate how valuable your knowledge, time, and attention are to those who are just getting started. What are some of the things you can do to share your expertise? You can start by mentoring entrepreneurship students at a local college or university and judging pitch events and business plan competitions. You can also join a local entrepreneurship organization that will undoubtedly include both nascent and early stage entrepre-

neurs who need advice and guidance. Similarly, join and become active in your local Chamber of Commerce or industry association. This will provide opportunities for you to mentor and share your experience with other entrepreneurs in your field.

3. A third potential path for women entrepreneurs who have successfully scaled their firms, thereby achieving significant levels of personal wealth, is to pursue philanthropic goals. As we have shown in this chapter, women are more philanthropically inclined than men. Thus, as more women make financial gains through growth-oriented entrepreneurship, we would also anticipate that they would take a larger role in addressing the unmet needs of their communities, their nations, and their world.

Although most of the women entrepreneurs whom we interviewed for this book were still too busy launching, growing, harvesting, or managing their firms to move to that next stage, several were thinking about it. As you plan your own entrepreneurial journey, what causes or unmet social needs touch you most deeply? Will you be willing to devote your time, energy, considerable talents and experience, and your personal wealth to furthering these causes? Are there organizations or groups you can become involved with now to start learning about and contributing to, even in small ways, a cause that you are passionate about? Alternatively, are you willing to launch an initiative targeting your cause on your own or with others?

12

LET THE CIRCLE BE UNBROKEN

Women Investors

In Chapter 11, we explored various "career paths" for women entrepreneurs who have succeeded in growing their firms to significant size and scale. These included launching another entrepreneurial venture, being recognized as leaders in their industries or the business community, or using their accumulated wealth to pursue philanthropic goals. From the standpoint of financial strategy, one of the most exciting dimensions of women's growth-oriented entrepreneurship is that successful women entrepreneurs have the opportunity to use their post-harvest wealth to become angel or VC investors, thereby promoting the launch, development, and growth of additional women-owned firms. In this chapter, we will describe the motivations and experiences of women who have made the shift from entrepreneur to investor. We will also discuss some of the support services and programs that are helping women learn how to evaluate and select companies for investment. A central premise of this book is that for growth-oriented entrepreneurs to succeed they need the example, encouragement, and support of other growth-oriented entrepreneurs.

Changes in the Investing Landscape

Let's first examine the landscape for these types of equity financing through the lens of angel and VC investors. Angel investors are individual investors who invest their own money into business ventures. These are typically high-net-worth individuals who seek attractive investment opportunities. An angel investor can also be someone with a particular interest in or affinity for specific industries, such as entertainment, communications, or biotech. Traditionally, the angel investor market has been highly fragmented, and entrepreneurs have found angel investors by using some variation of the pick-and-peck approach. More recently, however, angel investors have been organizing into angel groups and networks (http://www.angelinvestorforum.com), which facilitate the exchange of information and allow groups of angel investors to make larger investments than would be feasible for individuals.

• The Angel Capital Association

The Angel Capital Association (ACA)(http://www.angelcapitalassociation.org) is a professional and trade association supporting the success of angel investors in high-growth, early stage ventures. The ACA provides professional development, an industry voice, public policy advocacy, and other benefits and resources to its members. Its membership consists of more than two hundred angel groups and platforms and more than twelve thousand individual accredited investors. Their annual summit offers women investors an investment training opportunity in a pre-summit workshop, as well as networking opportunities with other female investors in specially hosted happy hour events.

As noted in Chapter 2, women have made tremendous gains in education and the workplace in recent decades. These gains have translated into higher levels of both human and financial capital. Human capital refers to education and experience. As more women earn college and graduate degrees, and as more gain access to the senior ranks of corporations, they develop knowledge and skills relevant for launching and managing large, growth-oriented firms. Similarly, these educational and workplace gains have translated into higher earnings and accumulated wealth that can be invested in such firms. Sohl and Hill (2007) point out that successful entrepreneurs who have cashed out through an IPO or company sale represent a high percentage of angel investors. As more women launch growth-oriented firms and reap financial rewards from a successful harvest event, these "entrepreneurial graduates" will also increase the ranks of potential women investors.

Table 12.1 reveals some interesting statistics about the top wealth holders in the United States. Surprisingly, women made up 43 percent of top wealth holders in both 2004 and 2007, compared to 57 percent for men. This find-

TABLE 12.1. Top Wealth Holders

| | 2004 | | | 2007 | |
Characteristics of Top Wealth Holders	Percentage of Total Top Wealth Holders	Percentage of Total Wealth	Characteristics of Top Wealth Holders	Percentage of Total Top Wealth Holders	Percentage of Total Wealth
Size of Net Worth (Males)			*Size of Net Worth (Males)*		
Under $1.5 million	19.5	4.7	Under $2.0 million	19.6	3.9
$1.5 - $2.0 million	27.3	12.6	$2.0 - $3.5 million	44.0	21.6
$2.0 - $3.5 million	31.0	21.3	$3.5 - $5.0 million	15.9	12.5
$3.5 - $5.0 million	9.1	10.0	$5.0 - $10.0 million	12.5	16.1
$5.0 - $10.0 million	8.5	15.3	$10.0 - $20.0 million	5.1	13.2
$10.0 - $20.0 million	2.9	10.6	More than $20.0 million	2.9	32.8
More than $20.0 million	1.7	25.4	Total	57.6	59.4
Total	57.0	57.5			
Size of Net Worth (Females)			*Size of Net Worth: (Females)*		
Under $1.5 million	25.0	5.4	Under $2.0 million	24.5	4.0
$1.5 - $2.0 million	23.1	10.6	$2.0 - $3.5 million	39.8	19.0
$2.0 - $3.5 million	29.9	20.3	$3.5 - $5.0 million	14.4	10.9
$3.5 - $5.0 million	8.4	9.2	$5.0 - $10.0 million	12.8	16.0
$5.0 - $10.0 million	8.7	15.6	$10.0 - $20.0 million	5.4	13.4
$10.0 - $20.0 million	3.0	10.9	More than $20.0 million	3.1	36.7
More than $20.0 million	1.9	27.9	Total	42.4	40.6
Total	43.0	42.5			
Size of Net Worth: (Both Sexes)			*Size of Net Worth: (Both Sexes)*		
Under $1.5 million	12.2	3.7	Under $2.0 million	12.9	3.7
$1.5 - $2.0 million	33.0	15.4	$2.0 - $3.5 million	49.7	25.4
$2.0 - $3.5 million	32.4	22.5	$3.5 - $5.0 million	18.0	14.8
$3.5 - $5.0 million	9.9	11.1	$5.0 - $10.0 million	12.1	16.3
$5.0 - $10.0 million	8.2	14.9	$10.0 - $20.0 million	4.7	12.8
$10.0 - $20.0 million	2.8	10.3	More than $20.0 million	2.7	27.0
More than $20.0 million	1.5	22.0			

Source: Internal Revenue Service, July 2008; January 2012

ing conflicts somewhat with our earlier discussion about women's challenges in achieving the senior ranks of corporations and financial rewards that go with them. Wealth can be accumulated through other means, however, including inheritance and marriage, and these figures reflect those additional sources as well as wealth that is earned. Table 12.1 also shows that the levels of wealth are spread across the various categories from lowest to highest for women just as they are for men. Although men tend to be somewhat more heavily concentrated at the highest levels of wealth ($10 million-plus), women are also well represented at those levels. It is noteworthy that although the mix of wealth levels between women and men is fairly similar in 2004, it diverges somewhat in 2007, with men being more heavily concentrated at the highest levels as measured by dollars. At that point, 50.1 percent of top wealth holding men were in the $10 million-plus categories versus 39.8 percent of women. This divergence could reflect men's more aggressive investing strategies for the period of 2004–2007 prior to the financial crisis. Whatever the case, Table 12.1 illustrates that women represent a significant portion of top wealth individuals in the United States, and are thus well equipped financially to serve as angel or venture capital investors.

Women in Angel Investing

Females historically have made up less than 15 percent of the angel investors in the United States (Padnos, 2010; Harrison and Mason, 2007). The University of New Hampshire's Center for Venture Research estimated that women angels represented 26.1 percent of the angel market in 2014, which is a 34.5 percent increase over 2013, when women only represented 19.4 percent of the market, which was itself a significant increase from the 12.2 percent number from 2011. Women-owned ventures accounted for 36 percent of the entrepreneurs that were seeking angel capital and 28 percent of those entrepreneurs that received angel investment in 2014 (Sohl, 2015).

Given the growing number of women with sufficient human and financial capital to invest in growth-oriented firms, we might ask ourselves how the behaviors of women angels are the same or different from those of men. In particular, we might ask how behavioral differences affect the funding prospects of women-owned firms. To this purpose, the University of New Hampshire's Jeffrey Sohl and Laura Hill (2007) conducted a fairly extensive survey of angel groups in the United States. They designated those groups with women representing at least 25 percent of their membership as "women-dominated."

Sohl and Hill found that these women-dominated angel groups were smaller in size than male-dominated groups and made fewer investments on average. Consistent with the theme of homophily, however, they found that over 30 percent of the firms presented for consideration in the women-dominated groups were owned by women, compared to an average of 12 to 13 percent for male-dominated angel investor groups. Thus, as one would anticipate, angel groups with a higher representation of women tend to attract and consider a higher percentage of women-owned firms. Similarly, Sohl and Hill found that women-dominated angel investor groups devoted a higher percentage of their investments to women-owned firms (13.3 percent versus 6.6 percent) for 2003.

In terms of motivation, Sohl and Hill found that women angel investors were driven by a combination of financial and nonfinancial considerations. As with angel investors in general, financial motivations include the desire to gain access to attractive investment opportunities, a desire to co-invest with experienced investors, and a desire to earn an attractive return on one's investment. Nonfinancial motivations include a desire to assist women entrepreneurs, a sense of social responsibility in investing, and a desire to increase access to capital for women entrepreneurs (Sohl and Hill, 2007). We'd like to highlight one such angel investor, Elizabeth Kraus, who went from being an angel investor herself to founding an impact angel group in Boulder, Colorado.

Elizabeth Kraus—
Impact Angel Group and MergeLane

Elizabeth Kraus is a Boulder entrepreneur and angel investor and co-founder of the Impact Angel Group, an angel investment group equally dedicated to making a difference and realizing a return. Prior to founding the Impact Angel Group, Kraus ran her own startups, myUsearch.com and Take it OUT! Fitness, and spent a lot of her time convincing smart people that investing for social and environmental impact wasn't just "feel good" investing but was "real" investing. She has also been very active in state and national efforts to improve the entrepreneurial ecosystem and mobilize angel investors. Recently, Elizabeth moved the Impact Angel Group under the wings of the San Francisco–based Investor Circle group, so she could focus on her most recent startup, MergeLane (http://www.mergelane .com), an accelerator targeting female entrepreneurs with high growth potential.

When we asked Elizabeth why she started an angel investor group she said that she found angel investing complicated, and the one angel group in Boulder was going through a transition, so there wasn't any large active angel group in the area. Adding impact investing onto angel investing made it even more complicated, but there were no local groups with this focus. Many of the people she spoke with expressed an interest in impact investing, so she saw a need and started a group. She ran the Impact Angel Group as a loose network for about five years and then as a formal membership organization for two more years before moving it under the arm of Investor Circle. She noted that the Impact Angel Group had 35 percent women members when this change occurred. When we asked Kraus if she thought the higher than average female participation was due to the focus on impact or because the founder of the group was a woman, she replied,

I actually think it was less the impact and more that I was a woman. A lot of women don't think they could be angel investors—they don't have it in their consciousness that they could be . . . and when they saw me being active and vocal—I think it encouraged more women to participate.

We also discussed strategies for encouraging more women to become active as investors. Some of Elizabeth's recommendations included the following:

1. On a macro level, the biggest impact for getting more women on the investing side is to create more women entrepreneurs, because entrepreneurs are more likely to invest in other entrepreneurs and the risk profiles of entrepreneurs match well to investing.

2. Highlighting women investors . . . every time there was an opportunity to talk about angel investing, I made sure women were speaking there, and that also brought more women. . . .

3. Any efforts to educate people outside of the startup community about angel investing would attract both men and women . . . and it would recruit investors that aren't entrepreneurs.

Kraus also provided the following advice for women who are just getting started as angel investors:

1. Look at twenty opportunities before making an investment. You will start to see patterns and begin to understand differences in quality.

2. Determine whether you're going to be an angel in just a few investments per year, taking an active role in each (and in an industry you understand), or you are going to make ten-plus investments and not be as involved before or after

the investments. These are two very different strategies—-invest in what you understand with a deep involvement before and after versus having enough investments that it has diversified the risk enough so that the numbers make sense. The biggest chance at failure is if you do something in between. Five a year and not deep enough and not diverse enough usually doesn't work.

3. Spend just as much time building relationships with other investors as you do getting to know companies. One of the best ways to do due diligence is to invest time in people that are investing and learning through these relationships.

Additional Organizations That Provide Training for Women Investors

While many angel groups offer educational opportunities, there are several organizations and programs that specifically focus on women who want to become angel investors and are looking for training, mentoring, or groups to work with in investing.

Golden Seeds

Golden Seeds (www.goldenseeds.com) was founded by Stephanie Newby after a long and successful Wall Street career. Her primary goal was to raise substantial capital for women entrepreneurs, who were, at the time, receiving less than 5 percent of venture capital investment dollars. She also wanted to empower both women and men to become active venture investors, by providing a venue where they could learn and work together on their investments. Golden Seeds' first investments occurred in 2005. Since its founding, it has evaluated over two thousand companies and has invested over $60 million in more than sixty companies. In addition, Golden Seeds has attracted over 275 members, managed three venture funds, and expanded nationwide. It offers a training program for potential new angel investors and provides classes for both members and nonmembers.

37 Angels

37 Angels (http://37angels.com) gets its name from the fact that 13 percent of angel investors are currently women and the founders want that number to be 50 percent. 37 Angels activates the untapped capital and experience women can bring to investing in male and female-led ventures by sourcing high-potential

deals and coordinating due diligence for members to invest in deals between $50,000 and $150,000. It also offers a unique training program to educate novice angels in the fundamentals of investing in young companies.

The first part of the training consists of an intense boot camp with eight to ten other women. In the boot camp, participants learn how to source, select, conduct due diligence on, value, and invest in early stage startups through workshops, hands-on applications, and case studies. Then they apply what they have learned to a real investment. 37 Angels looks at more than two thousand companies a year and curates the best companies to share with its network at its pitch forums, which take place five times a year. New investors are assigned an experienced investor who serves as a mentor. Participants also have opportunities to network with other investors at startup events organized by the 37 Angels team.

Pipeline Angels

The Pipeline Angels (www.pipelineangels.com), formerly the Pipeline Fellowship, is an angel investing boot camp for women, working to increase diversity in the U.S. angel investing community and create capital for women social entrepreneurs. The three main components of the program are education, mentoring, and practice. Since its April 2011 launch, Pipeline's angel investing boot camp has trained over eighty women, who have committed more than $400,000 in investment. In that time, the Pipeline network has expanded from New York City to Atlanta, Austin, Boston, Chicago, Los Angeles, Miami, San Francisco, Seattle, and Washington, D.C.

The Pipeline Angels program is six months long and requires two full days per month for six months. Each participant commits to investing at least $5,000 in the same women-led for-profit social venture at the end of the program. Pipeline Angel alumnae have continued to invest in startups, joined later-stage angel networks, and created their own angel groups, unleashing capital beyond the Pipeline Angel investment commitment. I spoke to a recent alum from the program who, with five of her cohort colleagues, is writing a book aimed at getting more women into angel investing!

Astia Angels

In 2013, Astia launched Astia Angels (http://astia .org/astia-angels), a global network of female and male angel investors that invests in growth-oriented women-owned firms that participate in the Astia program. These investors are actively involved in Astia's screening and development programs and enjoy several important advantages as Astia Angels. First, they get early exposure to a cohort of high-growth firms that have been through a screening, coaching, and mentoring process, thus ensuring high-quality deal flow. Second, they become engaged in post-investment activities and programs designed to help their portfolio companies succeed. Finally, since Astia now operates in thirty-two countries, they have opportunities to participate in events, programs, and investments that are sourced globally as well as in the United States.

Women in Venture Capital

Whereas angel investors invest their own money, venture capitalists invest someone else's money. A venture capital fund is a professionally managed pool of funds that is invested in potentially high-growth business ventures. High-net-worth investors or organizations, such as college endowment funds or pension funds, invest in VC funds, which are managed by a professional manager or management team. The team selects the firms in which to invest, monitors their progress, and eventually "harvests value" for those companies that succeed, either through an initial public offering or through selling the firm to another company. If a VC firm has a portfolio of twenty different companies, it can be the case that only one or two are highly successful. However, those one or two highly successful firms can more than compensate for the losses experienced from the other eighteen.

Venture capital investing is a risky business, and there is a high failure rate for portfolio companies. Thus, venture capitalists expect a high return on their investment, and they are interested in precisely the types of firms we are discussing in this book, those with the potential for rapid growth. Rapid-growth firms can go from being very small to being very large within a relatively short span of time. At that point, they become candidates for an initial public offering (IPO) or acquisition by a larger firm, thereby providing a return to the entrepreneur and her VC investors.

As we noted in Chapter 9 (Figure 9.1), the number of deals and the amounts being invested in venture capital are far lower than the peak in 2000 and still lower than the pre-recession years of 2007 and 2008. There are currently very few women founding partners for VC firms, and the percentage of women in the VC industry has actually declined since the financial crisis and Great Recession (2007–2009). The National Venture Capital Association (NVCA) and

Dow Jones VentureSource conducted the 2011 Venture Census survey, which examines the demographic composition of the U.S. venture capital industry. According to survey results, the percentage of VC investors that were women was 11 percent, down from 14 percent in 2008 (National Venture Capital Association, 2014). A more recent Babson Study (Brush, Greene, Balachandra, and Davis, 2014) found that the total number of women partners in venture capital firms declined significantly from 1999 to 2013, going from 10 percent to 6 percent. In fall 2014, only 139 of the 500-plus venture capital firms had any women partners.

The Forbes Midas List ranks the top one hundred tech investors each year, prioritizing newer, bolder, and earlier bets. In 2013, three women made the Midas List— Jenny Lee at GGV Capital, Mary Meeker at Kleiner Perkins Caufield & Byers (KPCB), and Theresia Gouw at Accel Partners. Lee first got onto the list in 2012 at number 94 and advanced to number 36 in 2013, largely driven by the recent IPO of Sinosun Technology. Meeker, who first appeared on the list in 2012 at number 42 (moving to the VC world after thirty years on Wall Street), is a leader of KPCB's digital growth strategy and ranked number 47 in 2013. Gouw has been on the list since 2011 and was ranked number 82 in 2013. In 2014, four women made the top one hundred. Mary Meeker moved up to number 21, the highest-ranked female. Ann Lamont came in at number 46, while Jenny Lee and Theresia Gouw dropped to number 52 and number 98 respectively. In 2015, five women made the list, and for the first time a woman was in the top ten (Jenny Lee, GGV Capital, number 10). Mary Meeker at KPCB was ranked number 15, Rebecca Lynn came in at number 23, while Ann Lamont and Beth Siedenberg were numbers 49 and 91 respectively. So while it appears women are making progress, it seems slower than ideal.

In one interesting development, Silicon Valley venture capitalists Jennifer Fonstad (DFJ) and Theresia Gouw (Accel Partners) stepped down as partners in their respective VC firms to launch their own VC firm, Aspect Ventures. When asked if their old firms' male culture frustrated them and led them to go off on their own, Fonstad stated that her industry's culture has been challenging at times and mentioned that she's experienced some of the "penalties women take for being aggressive and tough" that were highlighted in Sheryl Sandberg's book *Lean In*. For her part, Gouw asserted, "It's not so much about running from a place as running to a place. . . . By being more visible and showing we can do this, maybe women will become more confident to be entrepreneurs and investors themselves" (Sellers, 2014). Let's hope so!!

How do we get more women into the VC world? Jenny Lee suggests that "creating more opportunities at the associate entry level and more support in the form of women associations for female investors already in the industry would be steps forward," while Beth Seidenberg, a partner at KPCB, said, "Women need to see role models in the profession to know what is possible. . . . The first thing we need to do is fix the top of the funnel. We all need to encourage more women to go to school and train in engineering. We need broad outreach to universities and to encourage women to learn technical skills" (Slade, 2014).

A recent blog on INC.com by Lauren Leader-Chivee titled "America Loses When VC Money Ignores Women" (2013) highlighted some research findings from the Center for Talent Innovation, a New York–based think tank that she heads. Their study found that ideas and innovations from women, people of color, LGBTs, and even Gen Ys are *half as likely* to win the same support and backing as their straight, white male counterparts. It seems that having something inherently in common with the funder, decision maker, or investor makes an enormous difference, since 56 percent of decision makers don't value ideas they don't personally see a need for, even when evidence suggests that it's a good, marketable idea. This is troubling, given that venture capitalists, who are mostly men, are the ones providing so much of the seed funding to get ideas into the marketplace!

In terms of women's representation within the venture capital industry, Gompers and colleagues (2014) used VentureSource data on all venture capital investments made between 1975 and 2003 to find that 79 percent of the VC firms had no female investors. Of those firms that had a female investor, the vast majority (126 out of 169) had only one. In total, their sample included data on 3,225 male venture capitalists and 212 female venture capitalists, with females representing just 6.1 percent of the sample.

As a side note, an important finding from the research by Gompers and colleagues (2014) was that female venture capitalists had investment performances that were approximately 15 percent lower than their male colleagues, all else being equal, and that this effect was *largely attributable to a lack of contribution to performance from a female venture capitalist's male colleagues within their firm.* That is, women venture capitalists did not benefit, on average, from having good colleagues in the firm in which they worked, while male venture capitalists did. In addition, in survey responses and one-on-one interviews with a number of female VCs, these researchers found that the women in the sample felt that they were certainly at a disadvantage relative to their male colleagues. The women felt their advancement was hampered by a number of factors, including informal interactions and mentoring with and by their male colleagues, as well as gender biases by entrepreneurs (who are mostly male) in their perception of investors. Following are a few quotes from their study:

One senior partner at a firm with multiple female partners (a rarity!) stated, "The VC world is definitely gender biased. Women rarely rise to partner and if they do, they are generally the smaller funds. The VC world operates as an old boy network with women at a distinct disadvantage."

A female general partner in a New England–based venture fund stated, "Entrepreneurs just don't take me as seriously as my male counterparts. My questions get less attention when the companies present in front of the partnership. I feel that being a woman lowers the perceived quality of my contribution."

An associate at a U.S. venture capital firm with multiple offices stated, "As the only woman in my firm, I am often inadvertently excluded from a variety of social gatherings including 'guys' weekends. While I do not feel that I am explicitly excluded, the effect is to spend less time with my partners."

Other recent data and research show these situations persist. An examination of U.S.-based VC firms that have raised a minimum of one fund of at least $200 million (since 2009) yielded a total of ninety-two VC firms. The study found that only 23 of the 542 partner-level VCs identified in these firms were female, or 4.2 percent, which is even lower than the 4.6 percent of female CEOs among the Fortune 500. Of the ninety-two firms, only seventeen had one or more senior female partners. Of those seventeen, just five firms had two or more senior female partners. Of those five, only one firm (Scale Venture Partners) had at least three senior female partners (Primack, 2014). We spoke to one of those women, Kate Mitchell, about the situation of women in VCs.

Kate Mitchell: Scale Venture Partners

Kate Mitchell is a co-founder and partner of Scale Venture Partners (http://www.scalevp.com), a Silicon Valley–based firm that invests in early-in-revenue technology companies that seek to scale. Kate is also past chairperson of the NVCA and remains active in policy matters that have an impact on entrepreneurship, startups, and innovation. She chaired the IPO Task Force, whose recommendations to reform the IPO market were included in the recently enacted JOBS Act. Kate received the 2013 National Venture Capital Association (NVCA)

Outstanding Service Award for her policy work on behalf of the venture eco-system. She was asked to rejoin the board in late 2014 and take part in a task force aimed at addressing the lack of diversity in the venture capital industry.

Kate wasn't the first chairperson of the NVCA; there were two women before her. However, it had been quite a long time since there was in a woman in that role, so she was the first in many years. She said she was on a panel with seven other women in various senior roles (entrepreneur, CTO, CEO, and so on) and noted that only one of the panelists hadn't gone to an all-girls school as a student. She thinks there is something to this. In an all-girls school, the best scientists, the best athletes, the best students, and so on are female, so girls see what is possible. Another commonality among the group was being one of several daughters. Having peers who are also role models can also expand one's horizon on what is possible. Kate noted that many of the men who have been supportive and who have been involved with the issue of diversity—that is, the ones asking questions and seeking answers—are often men who have wives with equivalent jobs or who have daughters that they want to see achieve great things. She insisted that men needed to be part of any solution to this continuing problem.

Kate shared that about seven years ago, an Indian immigrant came in to pitch to the company. In that instance, it just happened that the three at the table all were women, leading the entrepreneur to comment, "I haven't presented to one woman let alone three. This is weird and good. It tells me you are open-minded and that you are going to look at me by my merits." Kate said she's proud that the presence of women stands out in her firm and reinforces the fact that they are committed to diversity.

Having so few women on the funding side matters. Women entrepreneurs continue to report challenges in being taken seriously when pitching to VC firms (we highlighted some of them in our last book, *A Rising Tide*). Jules Pieri, co-founder and CEO of the Daily Grommet online marketplace, recently posted this experience:

> It often feels like a 1969 office scene when you visit a VC in their native environment. The offices are swish and modern, but the workforce looks like the cast from Mad Men, diversity-wise. The only women you see moving along the corridors are serving admin roles (i.e., coffee) or are 26-year-old associates who are just passing through. One VC I visited made me seriously question my ambition to fund a startup. He was friendly enough. But the office walls were covered with endless pictures of all-male startup teams, and after hearing my pitch he asked, with a vapid grin, "So do you work out of your home?" I had

15 employees. I had impressive angel investors backing me. This was my third startup experience. Seriously? Did I work out of my HOME? And this is a relatively young VC, so he gets no free pass for being over the hill. (Pieri, 2013)

Because women are so few and far between on the funding side, it's often the case that a female VC is the only woman in the firm. That can make it socially challenging to do some of the out-of-office networking that is necessary to land deals. A recent, rather high-profile lawsuit brought some of these issues to light. Venture capitalist Ellen Pao filed a lawsuit in 2012 accusing her supervisors of penalizing her professionally because she spoke up about being sexually harassed by a colleague. As we were writing this book, the verdict came in (March 2015), and Pao lost the case against her former employer, the venture capital firm Kleiner, Perkins, Caufield & Byers (Reader, 2015; Friedman 2015). Although Pao lost the lawsuit, publicity around the case provided outsiders an inside look at what women in venture capital face on a regular basis. The trial revealed that Pao's firm held weekend ski trips from which women were excluded, dinners that women weren't invited to, and meetings at which women were seated at the back of the conference room. Managing partner John Doerr even acknowledged inequity at the firm in an internal email that was shared during the trial:

My concern goes beyond Ellen. I'm concerned with inequities in our partnership inconsistent among our practices with regard to "up and out"—I don't know how a junior partner could have a better year than Ellen did, measuring results, profits, increase in value—except for her clash with Randy. And honestly I think they both behaved badly. (Reader, 2015)

A recent study conducted at Stanford University found evidence of subtle gender bias in the VC evaluative context, specifically that women entrepreneurs without technical backgrounds were evaluated as having less leadership ability than their men counterparts. If funded, these women also received significantly lower amounts of capital than technical women, technical men, and nontechnical men entrepreneurs (Tinkler, Ku, Whittington, and Davies, 2014). The study's authors found that having a trusted social tie with the evaluator was more important for women entrepreneurs than for men. Thus, women need indicators of potential in the form of connections to key players and technical backgrounds more than men do in order to achieve legitimacy as entrepreneurial leaders and instill confidence in their evaluators about their abilities.

We thought Rachel Braun Scherl made a perfect case study for this chapter because of her experience with raising venture capital for a woman's product in the area of female sexual satisfaction. You would think that would be right up men's alley, right? Wrong! The lead investors for both of their institutional investors were—you guessed it—women.

Rachel Braun Scherl and Zestra

Rachel Braun Scherl and Mary Wallace Jaensch were business partners for more than a decade before they launched Semprae Laboratories, Inc. Their flagship product was Zestra Essential Arousal Oils (http://www.zestra.com), a patented blend of botanical oils and extracts, clinically proven to improve desire, arousal, and satisfaction for 70 percent of women. It is topically applied, works within minutes, and is available online and in leading retailers without a prescription. We'll let Rachel tell you her story:

When we started Semprae, we had been successfully running a strategic marketing consultancy for twelve years, focused on driving growth in the health care and consumer products space. Then, on what appeared to be an innocuous day in 2008, a venture capitalist who had never ever shared a business plan with me in twelve years gave me a business plan and uttered the words that will live in infamy, "You and Mary should run this business." That is the moment Mary affectionately refers to as "the moment we got pulled down the rabbit hole." Looking back, it is quite clear; we were blissfully naive enough that we had no idea what was coming.

As we started to look at this area of female sexual satisfaction, we saw an enormous, untapped market, limited available solutions, no established leader or source of information, and underneath it all, this little engine that could. Zestra was a product that actually worked, in clinical tests, in consumer experiences, and surprisingly in one of the few areas that women over thirty-five didn't seem to talk about, even with their best friends and mothers. Even better, it was in an area that we had worked in for many, many years; products and services driven by women, whether it was skin care, fertility, menopause, menstruation, or disease prevention. As we like to say, Mary and I had dealt with women from the tops of their heads to the tips of their toes. We believed that businesses focused on marketing to women fell in our sweet spot.

We thought the business plan and marketing strategy were going to be the easy parts, since that was what we had been doing together for years on behalf of our clients: communicating the market opportunity, defining their business model, demonstrating the growth model, conducting the competitive analysis, and so on. So we did what we knew how to do—we hit the computers—we created presentations; our presentations had presenta-

tions; our spreadsheets had spreadsheets—we had back-up and front-up. We felt ready for any question thrown our way.

And then we started to look for financing. It was at this point that reality sunk in. Our decisions and points of view were tested, questioned, refined, challenged, and re-created time and time again. And with that, most of the time, we were in rooms of men talking about female sexual satisfaction and female body parts whose names are often not said aloud, especially in mixed business company. There was so much discomfort over this discussion. Men didn't seem to know how to deal with it. They would tell us, "my wife loves it, but I'm not comfortable in this space." We spoke with more than a dozen smart VCs with whom we had personal relationships, and we were in an area that was exploding. Yet, funding was incredibly hard to come by.

A blog post from Forbes.com highlighted our experience, which was titled "Double Standards in Funding Sexual Satisfaction" [Ellevate, 2011]. We were shocked that despite the enormous business opportunity, significant size of market, and strong team experience and skills, there was often a "good reason" not to invest. Typical reasons included the following:

1. Women aren't really interested in these types of benefits. They won't buy products for enhanced sexual satisfaction.

2. It's all in their head. How could a topical product solve those kinds of problems?

3. Women won't buy this type of product online. Have you ever considered a retail strategy?

4. What will we tell our Limited Partners?

So despite our personal experiences talking to women, becoming the most popular people at every social event we attended, and being rushed at the end of focus groups for samples (as close to being rock and roll heroes as we will ever be), we struck out with money people. In fact, we would often bet on how long it would take during our presentations for one of two things to happen:

1. Someone would ask, "Great that it does something for women, but what does it do for men?"

2. Someone would make an off-color joke.

The longest time any potential funding group achieved was one hour, before the words "clitoral engorgement" forced the partners to hold up their hands in surrender. Finally, after many trips, crisscrossing the country and visiting different groups, we ultimately raised about $20 million from two VC firms. The lead investors of both funds were women.

After growing Semprae in the United States, we agreed with the board to seek a strate-gic partnership to accelerate growth. After a comprehensive review, the decision was made to sell Semprae to Innovus Pharmaceuticals in December 2013. Innovus has male sexual health products as well as a network of global distribution relationships, which are very important to ongoing growth. I assisted in the transition and still advise on issues, includ-ing the original clinical trials as well as marketing experience and other new initiatives.

Given her experience, Rachel also shared some important insights for po-tential entrepreneurs as they launch firms seeking equity financing.

Whatever you think is going to happen is probably not, so you need to be prepared for the unpredictable. There will be problems and challenges, some to your detriment. And no matter how hard you think it will be, it's harder. Some people think entrepreneurship is a way to achieve flexibility, but if you are VC backed it doesn't open up a whole world of flexibility. Being able to capitalize on it is not there yet. That process of getting there is re-ally hard and really time consuming. Hourly, weekly, monthly, you have to make choices, which really involve quite a lot of sacrifices. Work-life balance? What is your definition? I took a red-eye to be home for my daughter's prom. From my class of Stanford MBAs, only four of the twenty have worked full time since business school. That's it. That's indicative of how hard it is. Three of the four have children, myself included. My advice? You really can't lose your sense of humor or your primary coping mechanism. I always joked that I was doing God's work (thank you God from one woman's testimonial). . . .

Closing the Loop

In this chapter we have highlighted the increasingly important role of women, not only as growth-oriented entrepreneurs, but also as investors in growth-oriented firms. Although the angel and venture capital markets have been and remain male-dominated, women are making inroads both as investors and as recipients of funding. This is important from the perspective of women en-trepreneurs, because women angels and VCs are more likely to consider in-vesting in a woman-owned firm. This is not to suggest that women investors evaluate firms owned by women more leniently, but rather that they are more open to women as leaders as well as the types of firms they start. This trend has benefited from the emergence of organizations such as Astia, Springboard Enterprises, Golden Seeds, 37 Angels, and the Pipeline Angels, which provide educational training programs to prepare women and link women angel inves-tors with entrepreneurs seeking financial capital.

In spite of these gains in angel investing and funding, women have had a harder time cracking into the venture capital market. Venture capital firms are even more male-dominated than angel networks, and VC investors have a tendency to gravitate toward entrepreneurs who look, sound, and think like them. In other words, other men. Research conducted by the Diana Project researchers (Brush, Carter, and others, 2001; 2004) revealed that there are very few women in decision-making roles in venture capital firms, posing a significant barrier for women entrepreneurs. As in the case of the angel investor market, however, a small number of intrepid women VCs are paving the way by earning a place on the industry's Midas List, thereby increasing their stature and credibility within the industry. A growing number of women VCs are also leaving established firms to start their own funds as a way to gain greater power in the decision-making process. Both of these trends bode well for women entrepreneurs and increase their chances for being able to tell their story to VCs who will actually listen.

Rachel Braun Scherl, co-founder of Semprae Laboratories, created Zestra, a product that enhances sexual arousal in women, but got nowhere when she tried to pitch her firm to male VCs who were alternately disinterested, bored, or embarrassed. It took a couple of VC firms headed by women to recognize Zestra's market potential. Their investment in Rachel's firm eventually led to a successful harvest event in the form of Semprae's sale to a larger, global company. Rachel's experience confirms prior research suggesting that women angels and VCs are more likely to consider and fund firms headed by women. As the number of growth-oriented women entrepreneurs increases, this is why it is so important to also increase the number of women investors.

The emergence of organizations such as Astia, Springboard Enterprises, and others we have mentioned combined with the stories from Elizabeth, Kate, and Rachel serve as bright spots on the horizon for growth-oriented women entrepreneurs. As the pool of potential investors becomes more diverse, the types of entrepreneurs, firms, and products those investors consider and fund will also become more diverse. The tide's been out for women seeking equity financing for a long time, but the good news is that it's starting to come in at last. Can you hear the waves?

To end with a quote from Jules Pieri, founder and CEO of the Daily Grommet,

> The fundamental roadblocks to the success of more high potential enterprises founded by women entrepreneurs are inadequate access to capital and lousy media coverage of potential role models. (Pieri, 2014)

Let's create a The Next Wave of high-growth companies started by women, invested in by women, and highlighted by women. Let's create the momentum needed to really shift the current numbers onto a new trajectory, one that is more inclusive of women and one that is led by women.

For our own part, we have created a new initiative focused on increasing the diversity in entrepreneurship and investing (http://nextwave.ventures). The first effort around that is a learning-by-doing investor fund for new women angel investors named after our first book, *A Rising Tide.* We brought together ninety-seven women: nine experienced angel investors and ninety new or emerging angel investors in a fund that will make six to eight investments over the course of a year. The experienced angels will lead the deals and due diligence, while also mentoring new investors. New angels will be able to experience the entire process by investing in six to eight deals that are geographically dispersed across the United States, as well as having diversity across industry sectors. Training and mentoring will occur online as well as through regional meetings and an annual summit. Keep an eye out for the Rising Tide Fund (and the Rising Tide Europe Fund that brought together ninety women investors from twenty-five countries!) and the Next Wave Fund, which will follow these initial funds. We hope the opportunity for women to learn about investing through a diversified portfolio and ongoing mentoring, training, and education will help us launch the next wave of women investors!! Join us!

What Does This Mean for You?

This chapter represents a call to action for women who are willing and able to invest in the entrepreneurial ventures of other women. As we have shown throughout this book, women continue to face a variety of obstacles in their attempts to secure external sources of both debt and equity capital. Similarly, women tend to have smaller amounts of personal financial capital and other resources that they can draw upon. This combination of factors makes it particularly important for us to develop the investing knowledge, capabilities, and experience needed to equip the next generation of women investors. What can you do to help move the needle?

1. If you have never invested in an entrepreneurial venture, get started on a small scale. Last Christmas, one of your authors and her family decided to give each other a shared "gift" of investing in some of the women entrepreneurs on the Kiva website. The Sunday before Christmas, after a lovely meal,

we sat together in front of the widescreen TV and scrolled through different entrepreneur profiles, eventually selecting three women entrepreneurs from three different countries. We invested a relatively modest amount in the form of loans to each woman's business. Within three months, all of our entrepreneurs repaid us, and we currently have a positive balance in our Kiva account waiting for us to select additional entrepreneurs. Kiva is just one example of a platform that allows individuals or groups to invest small amounts of financial capital in women-owned entrepreneurial ventures. There are a growing number of other platforms focusing on small and emerging firms in a broad range of industries located in either the United States or other countries. Take a look at the companies featured on these platforms and read about the entrepreneurs who launched them and their goals. They are inspiring in so many ways, and, frankly, very hard to resist.

2. Exploit the potential of crowdfunding as a means for investing in growth-oriented firms. As we have noted, although crowdfunding for donations and loans has been around for some time, crowdfunding for equity is relatively new and was authorized as a part of the 2012 JOBS Act. In response to that legislation, a number of equity-based crowdfunding platforms have emerged, including some such as Portfolia, MoolaHoop, and Plum Alley, that focus on growth-oriented women entrepreneurs. Although equity crowdfunding was originally limited to accredited investors, or those with a net worth of at least $1 million or annual income of $200,000, the JOBS Act will dramatically increase the number of potential investors, because new regulations will open up equity investing through crowdfunding to non-accredited as well as accredited investors. Should you decide to pursue the equity crowdfunding route, research different platforms carefully to familiarize yourself with the types of firms the platform invests in, how long it has been in existence, and its track record. If you want to consider women-owned firms, what percentage of firms listed on the site have women founders or women as a part of their founding team? Platforms that list a relatively healthy percentage of women-owned or women co-founded firms on their sites are likely to attract more of the same as well as a greater number of women who want to invest in such firms.

3. We need more women venture capitalists in decision-making roles. If you are a woman contemplating a career in venture capital, scrutinize the gender composition of partners in firms that you consider joining. Are women represented in decision-making roles, and if so, how many women? The

greater the number of women in leadership positions, the greater your chances for having your voice heard and advancing your own career. Similarly, when you join a VC firm, find a mentor (male or female) who is an "insider." Ask your mentor to help you navigate the waters and gain access to informal types of events and communications that women are often excluded from. In like fashion, work with your mentor to lay out a career path and milestones, and develop a plan for achieving them. Ask her or him to provide guidance on the firm's unwritten rules as well as its unadvertised opportunities.

4. If you are a woman VC in a decision-making role within your firm, exert your power and influence to encourage the firm to consider other qualified women for associate and partner positions. For many years women viewed career advancement as a zero sum game, believing that there's only room for one woman at the top, and if it's you, it's not going to be me. As we have highlighted in this book, there's room for plenty of women at the top and at every stage of the trajectory leading there. Within the context of VC firms and investing, prior research shows that if women VCs are a small minority of decision makers, they are less likely to speak up to encourage the firm to consider women-owned firms. Alternatively, in firms where there is a stronger representation of women, there is a greater likelihood of both considering and investing in women-owned firms.

5. Another alternative for women VCs would be to join one of the growing number of venture capital firms such as Aspect Partners or Illuminate, founded by Cindy Padnos. Although many of these firms do not invest exclusively in women-owned firms, they do actively seek them out for consideration. Further, due to the nature of their funding profile, these firms tend to provide a better gender balance for women associates and partners, making it less likely that they will be sidelined and ignored.

6. If you are a woman investor who has accumulated a significant amount of wealth through your entrepreneurial or career success, consider becoming an angel investor and channeling some of that wealth toward new, growth-oriented women entrepreneurs. If you have prior entrepreneurial experience, you are probably already very familiar with the fundraising and investing process. It is also very likely that you have a good sense of what types of firms are most likely to succeed. Alternatively, if you have acquired your wealth through other means, there are a growing number of programs

and organizations to help women learn about the process of evaluating and investing in entrepreneurial firms. We have highlighted a few in this book, including Springboard Enterprises, Astia Angels, Golden Seeds, 37 Angels, Pipeline Angels, and the Rising Tide program. The Kauffman Fellows Program is a VC training program with high participation by women. As we have illustrated, successful women entrepreneurs are already giving back in a variety of ways that include serving as role models; mentoring aspiring entrepreneurs; and offering financial support for programs that focus on developing the talents, opportunities, and potential of women and girls. In light of that, investing in new, women-owned firms is a logical next step, and part of the "next wave" of initiatives directed toward supporting women who want to grow their firms.

We hope that you will join us on this journey!

APPENDIX: RESOURCES

Angel Investing
Venture Capital Investing
Crowdfunding Resources
Accelerators and Business Training Programs
Entrepreneurship Groups/Entrepreneurship Ecosystem
Resources for Financial Documents and Templates
Other Resources

ANGEL INVESTING
Women Focused

Next Wave Venture's Rising Tide Fund and Angel Training Program
(http://nextwave.ventures)
The goal of Next Wave Ventures is to drive diversity in high-growth entrepreneurship and angel investing by increasing the participation of underrepresented groups. The first initiative of Next Wave Ventures is the Rising Tide Fund and Angel Training Program, which seeks to narrow the gender gap in angel investing by providing women the education and training they need to become sophisticated angel investors, while offering them a unique learning opportunity that allows them to build a diversified portfolio of investments, receive mentoring by women who are experienced angel investors, and access a diversified online education and training program as well as opportunities for local, regional, and national events. The Rising Tide US Fund I is in partnership with Portfolia, while the Rising Tide Europe Fund I is in partnership with Go Beyond Investing and the European Business Angel Network. Future programs will focus on vegan investing, disrupting animal agriculture, social impact investing, investing in emerging markets, and minority investors.

Astia Angels (http://astia.org/astia-angels)
In 2013, Astia launched Astia Angels, a global network of female and male angel investors that invests in growth-oriented women-owned firms that participate in the Astia program. These investors are actively involved in Astia's screening and development

programs and enjoy several important advantages as Astia Angels. First, they get early exposure to a cohort of high-growth firms that have been through a screening, coaching, and mentoring process, thus ensuring high-quality deal flow. Second, they become engaged in post-investment activities and programs designed to help their portfolio companies succeed. Finally, since Astia now operates in thirty-two countries, they have opportunities to participate in events, programs, and investments that are sourced globally as well as in the United States.

Golden Seeds (www.goldenseeds.com)

Golden Seeds was founded by Stephanie Newby after a long and successful Wall Street career. Her primary goal was to raise substantial capital for women entrepreneurs, who were, at the time, receiving less than 5 percent of venture capital investment dollars. She also wanted to empower both women and men to become active venture investors, by providing a venue where they could learn and work together on their investments. Golden Seeds' first investments occurred in 2005. Since its founding, it has evaluated over two thousand companies, invested more than $60 million in more than sixty companies, attracted over 275 members, managed three venture funds, and expanded nationwide. It offers a training program for potential new angel investors. Angel Investing 101: An Introduction to Angel Investing and Angel Investing 201: Cap Tables and Term Sheets are open to non-members, and Angel Investing 301: Leading a Deal and Angel Investing 401: Boards and Exits are only open to members.

37 Angels (http://37angels.com)

37 Angels gets its name from the fact that 13 percent of angel investors are currently women and the founders want that number to be 50 percent. 37 Angels activates the untapped capital and experience women can bring to investing in male- and female-led ventures by sourcing high-potential deals and coordinating due diligence for members to invest in deals between $50,000 and $150,000. It also offers a unique training program to educate novice angels in the fundamentals of investing in young companies. The first part of the training consists of an intense training boot camp with eight to ten other women. In the boot camp participants learn how to source, select, conduct due diligence on, value, and invest in early stage startups through workshops, hands-on application, and case studies. Then they apply what's learned to a real investment. 37 Angels looks at more than two thousand companies a year and curates the best companies to share with its network at its pitch forums, which take place five times a year. Participants are assigned an experienced investor as a mentor and network with other investors at startup events curated by the 37 Angels team.

Pipeline Angels (www.pipelineangels.com)

Pipeline Angels, formerly the Pipeline Fellowship, is an angel investing boot camp for women, working to increase diversity in the U.S. angel investing community and create capital for women social entrepreneurs. The three main components of the program are education, mentoring, and practice. Since its April 2011 launch, Pipeline's angel investing boot camp has trained over eighty women, who have committed more than $400,000 in investment, and has expanded from New York City to Atlanta, Austin, Boston, Chicago, Los Angeles, Miami, San Francisco, Seattle, and Washington, D.C. The program is six months long and requires two full days per month for six months.

Women First Enterprise
(http://www.angelresource.org/en/Blog/2014/June/ARI-Launches-Women-First
-Enterprise.aspx)
The Angel Resource Institute's Women First Enterprise (ARI's WFE) caters to women in the early stage space by providing the appropriate training and exposure to finance and business realities. By addressing the specific pain points women face in the startup community, ARI's WFE will lead the female-driven movement by educating and mentoring women as they seek success in the competitive entrepreneurial industry. The WFE programs consist of lectures, panels, and interactive exercises with the audience as well as a question-and-answer period.

Isabella Capital Fund (http://www.fundisabella.com)
Isabella Capital Fund contributes intellectual and financial capital to early stage, women-led businesses.

Seraph Capital Forum (http://www.seraphcapital.com)
Seraph is a Seattle angel investor network that matches investors with women entrepreneurs.

Women Business Center of NOVA
(http://www.community-business-partnership-springfield-va.org/cbp-programs/
womens-business-center-of-northern-virginia.aspx)
The Women Business Center provides matchmaking service for women entrepreneurs and angel investors in Northern Virginia.

Women's Technology Network (http://www.witi.com)
The Women's Technology Network provides matchmaking service for technology-based women entrepreneurs and angel investors in San Francisco.

General

The Angel Capital Association (http://www.angelcapitalassociation.org)
The Angel Capital Association (ACA) is the leading professional and trade association supporting the success of angel investors in high-growth, early stage ventures. The ACA provides professional development, an industry voice, public policy advocacy, and an array of benefits and resources to its membership of more than two hundred angel

groups and platforms and more than twelve thousand individual accredited investors. The ACA website provides a listing of and links to angel investor groups and networks by geographic region at http://www.angelcapitalassociation.org/directory.

Angel Resource Institute (http://www.angelresource.org)
Founded in 2006, the Angel Resource Institute (ARI) is an innovative nonprofit that focuses on delivering education on proven best practices in angel investing to both entrepreneurs and investors, as well as delivering the most robust data trends in angel investing. The ARI Resource Center creates and acquires research, templates, investment experiences, and best practices for posting and use by angels, entrepreneurs, researchers, and the startup support community. The Resource Center can be used to discover new and useful information on angel investing trends, industry issues, and tools to help the efficiency and success of the investment and post-investment processes for early stage investors and entrepreneurs.

VENTURE CAPITAL INVESTING
Women Focused

Following are venture capital funds with either women partners *or* a track record of investing in women, as found at "The Ultimate Guide to Finding Women Investors," located online at https://medium.com/@joshuahenderson/the-ultimate-guide-to-finding-women-investors-2b95e632123b.

1. Women's Venture Capital Fund— A small fund focused on west-coast digital media and sustainability companies led by women—http://www.womensvcfund.com.
2. Illuminate Ventures—Founded by Springboard alumna Cindy Padnos—http://www.illuminate.com.
3. Aspect Ventures—Founded by Theresia Gouw and Jennifer Fonstad—http://aspectventures.com.
4. Cowboy Ventures—Founded by Aileen Lee—http://cowboy.vc.
5. Forerunner Ventures—Founded by Kristen Green—http://forerunnerventures.com.
6. Starvest Partners—Founded by Jeanne Sullivan and Deborah Farrington—http://www.starvestpartners.com.
7. Canaan Partners—Recognized for investing in women—http://www.canaan.com.
8. Scale Ventures—Recognized for the number of women partners—http://www.scalevp.com.
9. .406 Ventures—Co-founder Maria Cirino was one of our case studies for this book—http://www.406ventures.com.
10. Springboard Fund—Founded by Kay Koplovitz, Whitney Johnson, and Amy Wildstein to invest in women-led high-growth businesses, starting with Springboard alumnae.

Here are two additional venture capital firms that have recently launched:

1. Rivet Ventures—Founded by Shadi Mehraein, Rebeca Hwang, and Christina A. Brodbeck— http://www.rivetventures.com.

2. Merian Ventures—A U.S. and U.K. venture-investment firm based in San Francisco whose focus on "female entrepreneurs is more than a social statement. It is a clear objective to find, fund and profit from the rise in women-led innovation that has been largely overlooked by the investment community"—http://merianventures.com.

Following are some additional online sources of information for women seeking angel or VC funding.

Venture Valkyrie

(http://www.venturevalkyrie.com/category/women-in-venture-capital)
Venture Valkyrie provides articles and blogs on a range of topics related to entrepreneurship and the acquisition of capital. Valkyrie was a Marvel Comics superhero known for superhuman strength, stamina, and other warrior traits.

Global InvestHer (http://www.globalinvesther.com)

Global InvestHer is an online platform that provides information on the funding journey. Currently, it focuses on women entrepreneurs in North America and Europe but plans to expand to Latin America. Its funding focus is on women entrepreneurs from all industry sectors who are seeking seed capital up to Series A funding.

General

National Venture Capital Association (www.nvca.org)

As the voice of the U.S. venture capital community, the National Venture Capital Association (NVCA) empowers its members and the entrepreneurs they fund by advocating for policies that encourage innovation and reward long-term investment. As the venture community's preeminent trade association, NVCA serves as the definitive resource for venture capital data and unites nearly four hundred members through a full range of professional services.

Kauffman Fellows (http://kauffmanfellows.org)

The Kauffman Fellowship is a highly sought after two-year program dedicated exclusively to the world of innovation investing. While working full time at an investment organization (including venture, angel, accelerators, policy, corporate, and impact), fellows receive a structured curriculum with an individual development plan, executive coaching, facilitated mentoring, and peer learning and networking—all with a focus on giving back and on one's responsibility as an emerging leader in the industry.

CROWDFUNDING RESOURCES
Focused on Women

Portfolia (Portfolia.com)

Portfolia is an equity crowdfunding site that is creating a social network of engaged investors around entrepreneurial ventures. Portfolia's digital platform empowers individuals and affinity groups to discover and invest in private entrepreneurial companies in their areas of expertise and interest.

MoolaHoop (Moola-hoop.com)

MoolaHoop is a rewards-based crowdfunding platform created by women to help women leverage the "power of the crowd" to grow their businesses. MoolaHoop enables female entrepreneurs, business owners, and managers to garner financial support for their projects by reaching out to their customers, offering rewards in the form of special pricing on their products and services and unique experiences.

Plum Alley (PlumAlley.co)

Plum Alley crowdfunding is a way for women to raise money in large or small amounts to fund a specific project, product, or company. No ownership equity is given to the funder, but rather, the funder is given rewards, recognition, or products. Project creators have up to sixty days to raise funds.

General

Following are rewards-based crowdfunding and pre-purchase models.

Indiegogo

Indiegogo (IGG) is one of the most prolific crowdfunding sites of its type, with contributions to more than 200,000 projects in 196 countries. Founded in 2008 during an early wave of similar startups, IGG set out with the goal of "democratizing funding," initially for arts-related initiatives. It follows the "rewards" crowdfunding model, in which donors may receive perks in exchange for their contribution, but do not get an equity stake. IGG collects a 4 percent fee from campaigns that reach their funding goal; projects failing to hit their target may either refund donations or pay a 9 percent fee to IGG.

Indiegogo does not publish statistics showing the total amount of money raised to date. Nevertheless an analysis completed in 2013 by two independent researchers, based on data collected from individual project pages, estimated that donations from 44,000 IGG campaigns totaled approximately $170 million (IGG de-lists projects that fail to raise more than $500). In early 2014, IGG received a $40 million boost of new venture capital funding, bringing its total amount of investment received to $56.4 million.

Kickstarter

Kickstarter officially launched in 2009 after seven years of development, quickly becoming one of the largest sites in the crowdfunding sector; its website now receives more than three million page views a month on average. Kickstarter is oriented toward cultural ventures, with project creators permitted to seek funding among thirteen eligible categories: Art, Comics, Dance, Design, Fashion, Film and Video, Food, Games, Music, Photography, Publishing, Technology, and Theater. Kickstarter projects must be for-profit in nature, and based in the United States, Canada, Australia, New Zealand, or the Netherlands. Projects are vetted by Kickstarter staff before creators are allowed to proceed, in accordance with a series of eligibility rules. Pledges are accepted from anywhere in the world; 63 percent of total 2014 contributions originated in the United States.

Kickstarter is a rewards-based crowdfunding site, with contributors receiving merchandise or a unique experience in exchange for their pledge, but no equity stake in the project. Campaigns are "all or nothing," with no money exchange if the target amount is not met. Kickstarter charges 5 percent from projects that meet or exceed their funding goal; contributors cover a payment transaction fee of 3 to 5 percent. Since Kickstarter's launch in 2009, more than $1.5 billion has reportedly been pledged total to approximately 78,000 projects.

The next section features debt-based crowdfunding and peer-to-peer lending platforms.

Prosper

Prosper is a website where individuals can either invest in personal loans or request to borrow money—a peer-to-peer lending marketplace. It is operated by Prosper Marketplace, Inc., a San Francisco–based company founded in 2005, and was the first P2P lending platform in the United States. Prosper offers unsecured personal loans for up to $35,000, issued at fixed rates for terms of three or five years. Prosper has a transaction-based business model, taking a fee on its customers' transactions. Loan receivers pay an origination fee of 0.5 to 4.5 percent depending on the borrower's Prosper Rating (calculated by a custom algorithm that analyzes the borrower's credit report and financial information). Investors pay a 1 percent annual servicing fee. Prosper harbors over 2.2 million members and has funded over $2 billion in loans.

Lending Club

San Francisco–based Lending Club is a U.S. peer-to-peer lending company founded in 2006. It operates an online lending platform that enables borrowers to obtain loans and investors to purchase notes backed by payments made on loans. Lending Club is the world's largest P2P lending platform, having generated over $6.3 billion in loans. All Lending Club loans are unsecured personal loans and can be between $1,000 and

$35,000. Lending Club ascertains whether a borrower is credit worthy on the basis of credit score, credit history, desired loan amount, and debt-to-income ratio, and then assigns a credit grade determining payable interest rates and fees. The standard loan period is three years with a five-year period available at higher interest rates and additional fees. The loans, however, can be repaid at any time without penalty.

Daric
Based in Redwood Shores, California, Daric is a peer-to-peer lending marketplace that matches investors with borrowers. The company was incorporated in 2011, raised an angel round of funding in 2012 from Goldcrest Investments, and launched in 2013, cofounded by Greg Ryan, Vasant Ramachandran, and Cooper Dawson. Daric allows individuals to apply for loans up to $35,000 and small businesses to obtain loans up to $50,000. Daric takes a 1 percent service fee from the repayment, deducted from the investor's account. This fee is a fixed rate and is charged on any payment, whether regular, partial, or loan payoff. For borrowers, Daric claims an origination fee of up to 5 percent that varies depending on the size of the loan and financial history. While Daric grants a fifteen-day grace period for late payments, it also applies late-payment fees and unsuccessful payment fees on borrowers for every failed attempt to collect a monthly payment. The late-payment fee is the greater of either 5 percent of the unpaid amount or $15, while the unsuccessful payment fee is $15.

Fundation
Founded in November 2011 by Doug Gordon and Sam Graziano, New York–based Fundation is a direct-lending platform providing American small businesses with access to capital. Fundation aims to fill the gap between banks and merchant cash advances or cash flow loans and lends directly from its own balance sheet, taking the actual default risk of the loans it originates.

Fundation's loans are designed to serve mid-prime businesses for improvements or expansions and range from $50,000 to $500,000. Interest rates range from 8 to 25 percent, with a 1 to 3 percent origination fee. Fundation counts on its underwriting engine and team of lending experts to calculate default risk according to analyses of the industries from which loan requests originate.

Fundera
Fundera is an online platform that matches small business borrowers with potential lenders. It was launched in February 2014 by entrepreneurs Jared Hecht, Rohan Deshpande, and Andres Moran after Jared's cousin Zach could not get a bank loan for his thriving restaurant business. Through this experience, Jared learned how hard it is for small firms to get the financial capital they need, and Fundera was launched to address this problem. Through Fundera, businesses can apply for a variety of loan types and amounts including SBA loans, equipment financing, lines of credit, cash advances,

startup loans, term loans, short-term loans, and traditional business loans. Interest rates vary depending on the loan type, firm, and owner characteristics. When a loan closes, Fundera takes a fee of 1 to 3 percent. As of September 2015, Fundera had secured a total of $42 million in funding for over 850 small businesses.

OnDeck

OnDeck (first known as On Deck Capital) is a technology-enabled loan-financing platform for SMEs in the United States. It was founded in 2006 by Mitch Jacobs and headquartered in New York. OnDeck launched in 2007, using proprietary software to aggregate data about a business's operations and process that data with an algorithm that determines loan eligibility. OnDeck offers business loans ranging from $5,000 to $250,000, repayable over three to twenty-four months (in daily or weekly payments), and also offers businesses lines of credit of up to $20,000. It applies a fixed origination fee of 2.5 percent, and its APRs (including origination fee) are typically 36 percent. OnDeck provides loans to more than seven hundred industries based in all fifty U.S. states, with an average loan size of $45,000. Criteria for loan approval include having a business checking account, being in business for at least one year, and processing at least $3,000 in monthly credit card transactions or an equivalent average monthly bank account balance. OnDeck has financed over $1.7 billion in loans, serving over twenty-five thousand businesses.

Kabbage

Founded in 2009 in Atlanta, Georgia, by CEO Rob Frohwein, chairman Marc Gorlin, and COO Kathryn Petralia, Kabbage is an online financing technology and data company that lends money to small businesses and consumers. Advances from Kabbage range from $2,000 to $100,000, repayable over six months, and are based on an array of data factors such as business volume, business age, transaction volume, social media activity, and credit score. Fees are between 1 and 13.5 percent of the loan amount for the first two months, and 1 percent for each of the remaining four months. Kabbage's loan application process is 100 percent automated, and loans can be approved in a matter of minutes depending on the availability of complete data. In September 2014, Kabbage leveraged the same technology and data platform to launch Karrot—a service for personal loans. Serving over a hundred thousand small business owners, Kabbage has funded over $500 million in credit.

CAN Capital

CAN Capital (formerly Capital Access Network) provides capital to SMEs using its own real-time platform and risk-scoring models. Established in 1998, it is a pioneer and market share leader in alternative small business finance. Parent company of AdvanceMe and NewLogic Business Loans, CAN Capital has provided almost $4 billion in capital funding for more than 139,000 SMEs spanning over 540 industries. CAN

Capital provides loans between \$2,500 and \$150,000, with terms from four to twenty-four months and interest rates between 15 and 35 percent. Business financing eligibility is based on industry, time in business, monthly revenue, and credit score of the business owner, among other factors. CAN Capital also offers Merchant Cash Advances, in which a portion of a business's future card sales are acquired for an up-front lump sum. APRs range between 70 and 250 percent, with durations covering four to ten months.

Funding Circle

Funding Circle, co-founded in 2009 by Samir Desai, James Meekings, and Andrew Mullinger, is an online marketplace that allows savers to lend money directly to SMEs and was the first site to use the process of peer-to-peer lending for business funding in the United Kingdom. It now operates in the United States as well and has facilitated over £535 million in loans to small and medium-sized firms. On Funding Circle, investors browse businesses that have been credit assessed and approved for lending. Through an auction process that typically takes seven days, investors bid the amount of money they wish to lend and the interest rates they want to earn. After a business accepts a loan, monthly repayments are collected by Funding Circle and distributed to all the investors, who have usually bid small amounts on hundreds of different businesses to spread their risk. Funding Circle advertises a return of 6.3 percent after fees and bad debt. In the United Kingdom, loan lengths start at the six-month mark and go up to five years. Businesses can borrow between £5,000 and £1 million and pay a fee between 2 and 5 percent, depending on the size of the loan. An administration fee of 15 percent of arrears may be applied to repayments over seven days late.

Dealstruck

Dealstruck, a web-based peer-to-peer small business lending company, was co-founded in June 2013 by Russell McLoughlin and Ethan Senturia. Dealstruck serves as a marketplace for accredited and institutional investors to directly invest in small businesses through loans. Dealstruck underwrites the loans, shares profits with loan investors, and provides affordable capital access to small business owners. Dealstruck offers three types of loans: business term loans, funding \$50,000 to \$250,000; revenue secured term loans, funding up to \$250,000 but requiring pledged cash from fledgling companies as proof of ability to make monthly payments; and asset-based lines of credit, with a funding cap based on annual revenue. Pre-qualifications for Dealstruck term loans include a FICO score of 600+, at least one year in business, and at least \$20,000 in monthly revenue. Dealstruck charges a 3 to 4 percent origination fee depending on the type of loan chosen. Loan interest rates range from 15.68 to 20.63 percent and have a duration of up to three years.

The next section features equity crowdfunding platforms.

AngelList

AngelList, founded in 2010 by Naval Ravikant and Babak Nivi, is a U.S. website for start-ups, angel investors, and job seekers looking to work at startups. AngelList offers invest-ment syndicates, which allow investors to co-invest alongside accredited investors in exchange for carried interest. This setup makes it simpler for startups to get access to more capital with fewer meetings and to focus on dialogue with only one investor—the lead. AngelList has been dubbed by *Wired* magazine a "social network for entrepreneurs and investors." AngelList generates revenue by taking 5 percent per deal of carried inter-est from syndicate backers. On the job recruitment model, there are possible plans to roll out a premium package for larger companies. In 2014, $104 million was raised by 243 startups, from 2,673 investors.

CircleUp

CircleUp was founded in 2011 by ex-private-equity professionals Ryan Caldbeck and Rory Eakin with $1.5 million in backing from investors such as Clayton Christensen, David Topper, and Maveron (a venture capital firm founded by Howard Schultz). Cir-cleUp is an equity-based crowdfunding portal focusing on angel investments in con-sumer products companies. According to reports from PricewaterhouseCoopers, the categories that CircleUp is targeting (food and beverage, apparel, drugs, household, and specialty retail) at $91 billion are a substantially larger M&A market than Internet and software, which together form an M&A market a bit over $55 million. As of Septem-ber 2014, CircleUp had raised $40 million for forty different companies, an average of $1 million per company.

FundersClub

FundersClub was founded in July 2012 by Alexander Mittal and Boris Silver. It is built on a unique online marketplace that allows accredited investors to become equity hold-ers in FundersClub-managed venture funds. FundersClub's startup opportunities are prescreened by the FundersClub Investment Committee and a FundersClub Panel. Less than 2 percent of companies considered are selected to launch on the platform. To en-courage diversification, investments through FundersClub are typically much smaller than typical angel investments, $3,000 versus $25,000 to $100,000. FundersClub does not take an outright fee on either side but accrues carried interest on its investments. It does, nevertheless, set aside 10 percent of each pledge to a startup to handle legal and accounting costs. FundersClub is also a syndicate on AngelList.

To date, FundersClub has invested over $28 million in 111 companies.

WeFunder

WeFunder is a crowdfunding service that connects startups to investors online. Cur-rently, only accredited investors are able to fund startups on the platform, but WeFunder intends to use provisions in the 2012 JOBS Act that will allow unaccredited investors to provide equity for new firms. WeFunder was founded in 2011 by serial entrepreneurs Nick Tommarello, Mike Norman, and Greg Belote and launched out of Y Combinator. It is predicated on the idea that anyone, regardless of wealth, should be able to invest in a company. With one of the lowest minimums in the industry, WeFunder investments start at $1,000, and it intends to further reduce the barrier to investor entry to $100. WeFunder has raised over $6 million for more than fifty companies on its platform.

ACCELERATORS AND BUSINESS TRAINING PROGRAMS
Focused on Women

MergeLane (http://www.mergelane.com)
Based in Boulder, Colorado, MergeLane promotes "exceptional women leaders and the companies they run" through a combination of training, mentoring, and contacts with potential investors.

Springboard Enterprises (http://www.springboardenterprises.com)
Springboard is a national organization that provides coaching, mentoring, and contacts with Angel and VC investors (see Chapter 6).

Astia (http://www.astia.org)
Astia is an international organization that provides coaching, mentoring, and contacts with Angel and VC investors.

General

Global Accelerator Network (www.gan.co)
Global Accelerator Network (GAN) is an organization based on the seed-stage, mentorship-driven accelerator model and includes fifty of the most respected accelerators from six continents around the world. Its goal is to support the top accelerators that grow top companies. The efforts of GAN's members, mentors, investors, founders, and strategic partners have resulted in some impressive early numbers, with founders in GAN accelerators averaging over half a million dollars in funding. In total, GAN firms raised nearly $1 billion as of April 2015, and the accelerated companies have generated employment for thousands of people.

Seed Accelerator Rankings Project (www.seedrankings.com)
"The goal of the seed accelerator rankings project is to start a larger conversation about the accelerator phenomenon, its effects and its prospects for the future," according to a presentation by Professor Yael Hochberg, a faculty member at the MIT Sloan School of Management.

The top ten accelerators in 2014 were

1. Angelpad (http://angelpad.org)
2. Mucker Lab (http://www.muckercapital.com/muckerlab/about)
3. Techstars (http://www.techstars.com)
4. University of Chicago New Venture Challenge
   (https://research.chicagobooth.edu/nvc)
5. Alchemist (http://www.alchemistaccelerator.com)
6. StartX (http://startx.stanford.edu/accelerator)
7. Amplify.LA (http://amplify.la)
8. 500 Startups (http://www.500.co/accelerator)
9. Capital Innovators (http://capitalinnovators.com)
10. Dreamit (http://dreamit.com)

Other Business Training Programs

FastTrac (www.fasttrac.org)
FastTrac programs serve existing and aspiring entrepreneurs in non-academic environments. In addition, college students can earn course credit for completing courses using FastTrac materials. FastTrac has served more than three hundred thousand entrepreneurs since 1993.

Ice House Entrepreneurship Program (http://whoownstheicehouse.com)
The Ice House Entrepreneurship Program is designed to educate and engage participants in the fundamental aspects of an entrepreneurial mind-set and the unlimited opportunities it can provide. Built for rigor and relevance, this highly interactive program enables participants to learn directly from the first-hand experience of successful, "unlikely" entrepreneurs. The overall objective is to empower learners by exposing them to entrepreneurial thinking while immersing them in real-world entrepreneurial experiences.

Service Corps of Retired Executives (SCORE) (www.score.org)
SCORE provides free business counseling and mentoring through a nationwide network of over eleven thousand volunteers. In addition, SCORE provides inexpensive or free business workshops locally as well as online webinars. Last but not least, SCORE has a library of valuable tools, tips, and templates (including business plan templates) at http://www.score.org/resources/recommended.

Startups Illustrated (http://www.startupsillustrated.com)
Startups Illustrated was founded by Tom Chikoore, the founder of the Techstars Accelerator's Risingstars Program. Startups Illustrated partners with local economic development organizations, corporations, government entities, and accelerators to deliver

entrepreneurship training programs and boot camps that help underserved entrepreneurs build and grow successful firms in the innovation economy.

ENTREPRENEURSHIP GROUPS/ ENTREPRENEURSHIP ECOSYSTEM
Women Focused

Women Presidents' Organization (www.womenpresidentsorg.com)

The Women Presidents' Organization (WPO) is a nonprofit membership organization for women presidents of multimillion-dollar companies. Members of the WPO take part in professionally facilitated peer advisory groups in order to bring the "genius out of the group" and accelerate the growth of their businesses (see Chapter 10).

Ellevate (formerly 87 Broads) (www.ellevatenetwork.com)

Ellevate is a global professional women's network based on the premise that women are still an undertapped resource in the business world and in society at large—and that it's time to change that. Ellevate's founders and members believe that networking and lifelong learning are keys to business success. Further, they believe that by providing these capabilities, by working with companies and investors to help them see the opportunity, and by truly investing in women, Ellevate can be an active and positive part of that change.

National Association of Women Business Owners (www.nawbo.org)

The National Association of Women Business Owners (NAWBO) works to advance women entrepreneurs in the economic, social, and political spheres of power worldwide by

1. Strengthening the wealth-creating capacity of its members and promoting economic development within the entrepreneurial community
2. Creating innovative and effective change in the business culture
3. Building strategic alliances, coalitions, and affiliations
4. Transforming public policy and influencing opinion makers

National Women's Business Council (www.nwbc.gov)

The National Women's Business Council (NWBC), established in 1988, is a nonpartisan federal advisory council created to serve as an independent source of advice and counsel to the president, Congress, and the U.S. Small Business Administration on economic issues of importance to women business owners. The council is the government's only independent voice for women entrepreneurs. Members are prominent women business owners and leaders of women's business organizations. The NWBC is composed of fifteen members who are appointed to three-year terms.

Women's Business Enterprise National Council (www.wbenc.org)

The Women's Business Enterprise National Council (WBENC), founded in 1997, is the largest third-party certifier of businesses owned, controlled, and operated by women in the United States. WBENC, a national 501(c)(3) nonprofit, partners with fourteen Regional Partner Organizations to provide certification to women-owned businesses throughout the country. WBENC is also one of the nation's leading advocates of women-owned businesses as suppliers to America's corporations.

National Center for Women & Information Technology (www.ncwit.org)

The National Center for Women & Information Technology is a nonprofit community of more than six hundred prominent corporations, academic institutions, government agencies, and nonprofits working to increase women's participation in technology and computing. NCWIT helps organizations recruit, retain, and advance women from K–12 and higher education through industry and entrepreneurial careers.

Women's Business Centers (https://www.sba.gov)

Women's Business Centers (WBCs) are a national network of roughly a hundred educational centers located throughout the United States. The centers are designed to assist women in starting and growing small businesses and provide entrepreneurs with comprehensive training and counseling on a variety of topics in several languages. The U.S. Small Business Administration oversees the WBC network.

WEConnect International (http://weconnectinternational.org)

WEConnect's mission is to "help women-owned businesses succeed in global value chains." WEConnect identifies, educates, registers, and certifies women's business enterprises based outside of the United States and then connects them with multinational corporate buyers.

General

1 Million Cups (http://www.1millioncups.com)

1 Million Cups (1MC) is a simple way to engage entrepreneurs in communities around the world. Each week, the 1MC program offers two local entrepreneurs an opportunity to present their startups to a diverse audience of mentors, advisors, and entrepreneurs. Presenters prepare a six-minute educational presentation and engage in twenty minutes of feedback and questioning after they present. Entrepreneurs gain insight into possible ways they can improve their businesses, gather real-time feedback, and connect with a community that cares about their progress.

Startup Grind (www.startupgrind.com)

Startup Grind is a global startup community designed to educate, inspire, and connect entrepreneurs: one hundred cities, forty-two countries, seventy-five thousand entrepreneurs. Members have opportunities to interact through monthly events and an annual conference.

UpGlobal (www.up.co)

UpGlobal's mission is to improve the global human condition by amplifying the efforts of startup community leaders and their ability to create and sustain flourishing entrepreneurial communities around the world. It offers startup weekends globally, including women's editions that are focused specifically on women. UpGlobal also has a startup Next program that is a pre-accelerator type of program.

RESOURCES FOR FINANCIAL DOCUMENTS AND TEMPLATES

There are many freely available open-sourced model seed-financing documents on the web. As an example, the Techstars Accelerator website (http://www.techstars.com/docs) provides a variety of documents, including a term sheet that describes the basic characteristics of the investment. The term sheet lays out the proposed capitalization, in other words, the number and type of shares for each shareholder and their relative ownership percentages, post-financing. It also provides a description of the liquidation preference, mechanics of conversion, how the board of directors will be determined, protective provisions, and other rights and agreements.

Here are two other excellent financial document resources:

Foundry Group (http://www.askthevc.com/wp/resources) has some links to financial documents that can be great resources for startups, including term sheets, stock purchase agreements, investor rights agreements, bylaws, common M&A and sale documents, and more.

Series Seed (http://www.seriesseed.com) is another great website, with documents that can be helpful for young firms raising seed rounds of funding, including term sheet, stock investment agreement, certificate of incorporation, and more.

OTHER RESOURCES
Women Focused

Women Impacting Public Policy (www.wipp.org)

Women Impacting Public Policy, Inc. (WIPP) is a national nonpartisan public policy organization that advocates for and on behalf of women and minorities in business in the legislative processes of our nation, thereby creating economic opportunities and building bridges and alliances with other small business organizations.

Catalytic Women (http://catalyticwomen.wpengine.com)

Catalytic Women provides education, tools, and training to donors, investors, and advisors who want to align their money with their values. Their focus is on social impact investing, gender lens opportunities, and strategic giving.

Lean In (http://leanin.org/education)

The book *Lean In* is focused on encouraging women to pursue their ambitions and changing the conversation from what we can't do to what we can do. Consistent with that focus, LeanIn.Org is an online community committed to offering women the ongoing inspiration and support to help them achieve their goals.

General

Kauffman Foundation (www.kauffman.org)

Established in the mid-1960s by the late entrepreneur and philanthropist Ewing Marion Kauffman, the Kauffman Foundation is based in Kansas City, Missouri, and is among the largest private foundations in the United States, with an asset base of approximately $2 billion. Focused on education and entrepreneurship, the Kauffman Foundation's vision is to foster a society of economically independent individuals who are engaged citizens in their communities.

Aspen Network of Development Entrepreneurs (www.aspeninstitute.org)

The Aspen Network of Development Entrepreneurs (ANDE) is a global network of organizations dedicated to propelling entrepreneurship in emerging markets. ANDE members provide critical financial, educational, and business support services to small and growing businesses (SGBs) with the conviction that SGBs will create jobs, stimulate long-term economic growth, and produce environmental and social benefits. ANDE is part of the Aspen Institute, an educational and policy studies organization.

Endeavor (www.endeavor.org)

Endeavor's mission is to lead the global movement to catalyze long-term economic growth by selecting, mentoring, and accelerating the best high-impact entrepreneurs around the world. Endeavor helps entrepreneurs overcome barriers to growth by providing the key ingredients to success: mentorship, networks, strategic advice, talent, skills, access to smart capital, and inspiration.

Small Business Innovation Research Program (www.sbir.gov)

The Small Business Innovation Research (SBIR) program is a highly competitive program that encourages domestic small businesses to engage in federal research or research and development (R&D) that has the potential for commercialization. Through a competitive awards-based program, SBIR enables small businesses to explore their technological potential and provides the incentive to profit from its commercialization.

When qualified small businesses are included in the nation's R&D arena, high-tech innovation is stimulated and the United States gains entrepreneurial spirit as it meets its specific research and development needs (see Chapter 7).

Google for Entrepreneurs (www.googleforentrepreneurs.org)
Google for Entrepreneurs partners with startup communities and builds campuses where entrepreneurs can learn, connect, and create companies that will change the world. Since 2011, Google for Entrepreneurs has launched campuses and formed partnerships that support entrepreneurs across 125 countries.

NOTES

CHAPTER 1

1. In 2013, of the top one hundred women on the Forbes list of most influential women, twenty-four were corporate CEOs that controlled $893 billion in annual revenues and sixteen founded their own companies, including two of the three new billionaires on the list, Tory Burch, founder of the Tory Burch line of clothing, and Spanx's Sara Blakely. Five women in the field of technology also made the top twenty-five, including familiar names such as Facebook's Sheryl Sandberg (no. 6), Pepsi's Indira Rometty (no. 12) and HP's Meg Whitman (no. 15).

2. These "breadwinner moms" are made up of two very different groups: 5.1 million (37 percent) are married mothers who have a higher income than their husbands, and 8.6 million (63 percent) are single mothers.

CHAPTER 3

1. Everloop founder Hilary DeCesare's description of her firm's strategy for surviving and raising financial capital during the Great Recession (Coleman and Robb, 2012), pp. 168–169.

CHAPTER 4

1. In a priced round, the founders of a startup will agree on a current valuation of the company and allocate equity based on that valuation. For example, a company valued at $500,000 pre-money valuation would mean that an investor investing $500,000 would get 50 percent of the equity and own 50 percent of the value of the company ($1 million after investment). A convertible note allows the valuation to occur at a later point in time.

CHAPTER 6

1. Keiretsu Forum (www.keiretsuforum.com) is a global investment community of accredited private equity angel investors, venture capitalists, and corporate or institutional investors. It is a worldwide network of capital, resources, and deal flow with thirty-six chapters on three continents.

2. Astia has since focused less on programming for women entrepreneurs and more on pitch events that bring female entrepreneurs in front of potential investors and advisors. They have also launched an Angel group, Astia Angels, as well as a fund.

3. As we were submitting the final draft of this book, we found out that FundWell closed its doors. While we don't have details on the reasons behind the closing, we decided to keep the case study in this chapter as is.

CHAPTER 9

1. Springboard Enterprises' Dolphin Tank programs are "helpful feedback-driven" pitch sessions designed to provide entrepreneurs with actionable insights from knowledgeable people. The Dolphin Tank isn't about Sharks or Dragons or a competition for the best idea, it's about channeling the expertise of the people in the room to provide connections and advice to help entrepreneurs take the next step.

INTERVIEWS

Doreen Block, founder and CEO of Poshly, conducted by phone on February 26, 2014.

Emily Bruno, founder of Denizens Brewing Company, conducted by phone on April 25, 2014.

Maria Cirino, co-founder of .406 ventures, conducted by phone on February 24, 2014.

Trish Costello, founder and CEO of Portfolia, conducted by phone on March 7, 2014.

Manon Cox, president and CEO of Protein Sciences, Meriden, Connecticut, February 1, 2014.

Peggy Cross, founder of Ecotensils, conducted by phone on March 5, 2014.

Nancy Hayes, co-founder of MoolaHoop, conducted by phone on March 9, 2015.

Diane Hessan, CEO and founder of Communispace, conducted by phone on April 8, 2014.

Elizabeth Kraus, founder and CMO of MergeLane, conducted by phone on April 13, 2105.

Jo Anne Miller, managing director of Golden Seeds Angel Network, conducted by phone on May 23, 2014.

Kate Mitchell, co-founder and partner of Scale Venture Partners, conducted by phone on April 18, 2014.

Diane Mulcahy, senior fellow, Kauffman Foundation, conducted by phone on July 8, 2014.

Chinwe Onyeagoro, co-founder and CEO of FundWell, conducted by phone on February 26, 2014.

Mary Page Platerink, CEO and founder of First Aid Shot Therapy, conducted by phone on April 22, 2014.

Katie Rae, chairman of Techstars Boston, conducted by phone on August 11, 2014.

June Ressler, president and CEO of Cenergy International LLC, conducted by phone on October 2, 2014, and in person on March 3, 2015 during her visit to the University of Hartford, West Hartford, Connecticut.

Rachel Braun Scherl, co-founder and CEO of Semprae Laboratories, Inc., conducted by phone on July 9, 2014.

Sue Washer, president and CEO of Applied Genetics Technology Company (AGTC), conducted by phone on March 18, 2015.

Alexandra Wilkis Wilson, co-founder of the Gilt Groupe, on October 30, 2013 during her visit to the University of Hartford, West Hartford, Connecticut.

Dr. Natalie Wisniewski, co-founder and chief technical officer of Profusa, Inc., conducted by phone on April 22, 2014.

REFERENCES

Acs, Zoltan J., William Parsons, and Spencer Tracy. 2008. *High-Impact Firms: Gazelles Revisited.* Washington, DC: U.S. Small Business Administration, Office of Advocacy. Retrieved at http://www.sba.gov/advocacy on 1/9/14.

Adams, Ariel. 2014. The Future of Pebble Smartwatches: Interview with CEO Eric Migicovsky. Posted on January 30, 2014. Retrieved at http://www.forbes.com on February 26, 2014.

Aldrich, Howard E. 1989. Networking Among Women Entrepreneurs. In *Women-Owned Businesses*, ed. O. Hagan, C. Rivchun, and D. Sexton, 103–132. New York: Praeger.

Aldrich, Howard E., Pat Ray Reese, and Paola Dubini. 1989. Women on the Verge of a Breakthrough: Networking Among Entrepreneurs in the United States and Italy. *Entrepreneurship and Regional Development* 1 (4):339–356.

Allen, Kathleen, and Mark Lieberman. 2010. University of Southern California. In *The Development of University-Based Entrepreneurship Ecosystems*, ed. Michael L. Fetters, Mark P. Rice, and John Sibley Butler, 76–98. Northampton, MA: Edward Elgar.

Amatucci, F. M., and D. C. Crawley. 2011. Financial Self-Efficacy Among Women Entrepreneurs. *International Journal of Gender and Entrepreneurship* 3 (1):23–37.

Amatucci, Frances, and Jeffrey Sohl. 2004. Women Entrepreneurs Securing Business Angel Financing: Tales from the Field. *Venture Capital* 6 (2/3):181–196.

Amezcua, Alejandro S., and Alexander McKelvie. 2011. Incubation for All? Business Incubation and Gender Differences in New Firm Performance. *Frontiers of Entrepreneurship Research* 31 (8):Article 3. Available at http://digitalknowledge.babson.edu/fer/vol31/Iss8/3.

Amit, R., and P. Schoemaker. 1993. Strategic Assets and Organizational Rent. *Strategic Management Journal* 14 (1):33–46.

Anderson, Becky. 2012, November 15. $800 Million Biotech Business Started in a Garage. Retrieved at http://www.cnn.com/2012/11/15/business/kiran-mazumdar-shaw on February 1, 2013.

Ang, James S. 1992. On the Theory of Finance for Privately Held Firms. *The Journal of Small Business Finance* 1 (3):185–203.

Ang, James S., James Wuh Lin, and Floyd Tyler. 1995. Evidence On the Lack of Separation Between Business and Personal Risks Among Small Businesses. *The Journal of Entrepreneurial Finance* 4 (2):197–210.

Audretsch, David B. 2002. The Dynamic Role of Small Firms: Evidence from the U.S. *Small Business Economics* 18:13–40.

———. 2007. Entrepreneurship Capital and Economic Growth. *Oxford Review of Economic Policy* 23 (1):63–78.

Babcock, L., M. Gelfand, D. Small, and H. Stayn. 2006. Gender Differences in the Propensity to Initiate Negotiations. In *Social Psychology and Economics*, ed. D.D. Cremer, M. Zeelenberg, and J. K. Murnighan, 239–259. Mahway, NJ: Lawrence Erlbaum.

Babcock, L., and S. Laschever. 2003. *Women Don't Ask: Negotiation and the Gender Divide.* Princeton, NJ: Princeton University Press.

Bajtelsmit, V. L., and J. L. VanDerhei. 1997. Risk Aversion and Pension Investment Choices. In *Positioning Pensions for the Twenty-First Century*, ed. M. S. Gordon, O. S. Mitchell, and M. M. Twinney, 45–66. Philadelphia: University of Pennsylvania Press.

Bajtelsmit, V. L., A. Bernasek, and N. A. Jianakoplos. 1999. Gender Differences in Defined Contribution Pension Decisions. *Financial Services Review* 8:1–10.

Baker, T. 2007. Resources in Play: Bricolage in the Toy Store(y). *Journal of Business Venturing* 22:694–711.

Baker, T., and R. E. Nelson. 2005. Creating Something from Nothing: Resource Construction Through Entrepreneurial Bricolage. *Administrative Science Quarterly* 50 (3):329–366.

Barnett, Chance. 2013. Donation-Based Crowdfunding Sites: Kickstarter vs. Indiegogo. Retrieved at http://www.forbes.com on February 2, 2014.

Basu, Anuradha, and Simon C. Parker. 2001. Family Finance and New Business Start-Ups. *Oxford Bulletin of Economics and Statistics* 63:333–358.

Baum, Joel A. C., and Brian S. Silverman. 2004. Picking Winners or Building Them? Alliance, Intellectual, and Human Capital as Selection Criteria in Venture Financing and Performance of Biotechnology Startups. *Journal of Business Venturing* 19 (3):411–436.

Becker-Blease, John R., and Jeffrey E. Sohl. 2007. Do Women-Owned Businesses Have Equal Access to Angel Capital? *Journal of Business Venturing* 22 (4):503–521.

———. 2011, July. The Effect of Gender Diversity on Angel Group Investment. *Entrepreneurship Theory & Practice*, 709–733.

Beckman, C. M., M. D. Burton, and C. O'Reilly. 2007. Early Teams: The Impact of Team Demography on VC Financing and Going Public. *Journal of Business Venturing* 22 (2):147–173.

Berger, Allen N., and Gregory F. Udell. 1998. The Economics of Small Business Finance: The Roles of Private Equity and Debt Markets in the Financial Growth Cycle. *Journal of Banking & Finance* 22:613–673.

Bigelow, L., L. Lundmark, J. M. Parks, and R. Wuebker. 2014. Skirting the Issues: Experimental Evidence of Gender Bias in IPO Prospectus Evaluations. *Journal of Management* 40(6):1732–1759.

Blank, Steven. 2005. *The Four Steps to the Epiphany: Successful Strategies for Products That Win.* Cafepress.com.

———. 2013, May. Why the Lean Start-Up Changes Everything. *Harvard Business Review*, 3–9.

Bobbitt-Zeher, Donna. 2007. The Gender Income Gap and the Role of Education. *Sociology of Education* 80 (1):1–22.

Bosse, Douglas A., and Porcher L. Taylor III. 2012. The Second Glass Ceiling Impedes Women Entrepreneurs. *Journal of Applied Management and Entrepreneurship* 17 (1):52–68.

The Boston Beer Company, Inc. 2000. Brighton, MA: Harvard Business School Publishing. Retrieved at http://www.hbsp.harvard.edu on March 7, 2016.

Bowles, H. R., L. Babcock, and L. Lai. 2007. Social Incentives for Gender Differences in the Propensity to Initiate Negotiations: Sometimes It Does Hurt to Ask. *Organizational Behavior and Human Decision Processes* 103:84–103.

Bradford, Nicole. 2012, June 15. Cenergy International Services on Constant Hunt for Renegade Types. http://www.bizjournals.com. Retrieved on February 18, 2015.

Bruderl, J., and P. Preisendorfer. 1998. Network Support and the Success of Newly Founded Businesses. *Small Business Economics* 10 (3): 213–225.

Brush, C. G. 1992. Research on Women Business Owners: Past Trends, a New Perspective, and Future Directions. *Entrepreneurship Theory and Practice* 14 (4):5–31.

Brush, Candida. 2012, May. *Note on Internal Entrepreneurship Education Ecosystems.* Wellesley, MA: Babson College.

Brush, Candida G., Anne de Bruin, and Friederike Welter. 2009. A Gender-Aware Framework for Women's Entrepreneurship. *International Journal of Gender and Entrepreneurship* 1 (1):8–24.

Brush, Candida G., Linda F. Edelman, and Tatiana S. Manolova. 2008. The Effects of Initial Location, Aspirations, and Resources on Likelihood of First Sale in Nascent Firms. *Journal of Small Business Management* 46 (2):159–182.

Brush, Candida, Nancy Carter, Elizabeth Gatewood, Patricia Greene, and Myra Hart. 2001. *The Diana Project: Women Business Owners and Equity Capital: The Myths Dispelled.* Kansas City, MO: Kauffman Foundation.

———. 2004. *Gatekeepers of Venture Growth: A Diana Project Report on the Role and Participation of Women in the Venture Capital Industry.* Kansas City, MO: Kauffman Foundation.

———. 2006. The Use of Bootstrapping by Women Entrepreneurs in Positioning for Growth. *Venture Capital* 8 (1): 15–31.

Brush, Candida G., Nancy M. Carter, Patricia G. Greene, Myra M. Hart, and Elizabeth Gatewood. 2002. The Role of Social Capital and Gender in Linking Financial Suppliers and Entrepreneurial Firms: A Framework for Future Research. *Venture Capital* 4 (4):305–323.

Brush, Candida G., Patricia G. Greene, Lakshmi Balachandra, and Amy E. Davis. 2014, September. *Women Entrepreneurs 2014: Bridging the Gender Gap in Venture Capital.* Wellesley MA: Arthur M. Blank Center for Entrepreneurship, Babson College. Available at http://www.babson.edu/Academics/centers/blank-center/global-research/diana/Documents/diana-project-executive-summary-2014.pdf.

Brush, Candida G., Patricia G. Greene, and Myra M. Hart. 2001. From Initial Idea to Unique Advantage: The Entrepreneurial Challenge of Constructing a Resource Base. *Academy of Management Executive* 15 (1):64–78.

Building Bridges: 2014 Annual Report (2014). Washington DC: National Women's Business Council. Retrieved at http://www.nwbc.gov on April 7, 2015.

Burke, Elaine. 2014, July 4. Female Founders Forum: Top Advice from Founders and Investors. Siliconrepublic. Available at http://newsle.com/article/0/165021363.

Burns, Matt. 2013. Pebble Nabs $15M in Funding, Outs PebbleKit SDK and Pebble Sports API to Spur Smartwatch App Development. Posted May 16, 2013. Retrieved at http://techcrunch.com on February 26, 2014.

Butler, John Sibley. 2010. The University of Texas at Austin. In *The Development of University-Based Entrepreneurship Ecosystems*, ed. Michael L. Fetters, Mark P. Rice, and John Sibley Butler, 99–121. Northampton, MA: Edward Elgar.

Campbell, Kevin, and Antonio Minguez-Vera. 2008. Gender Diversity in the Boardroom and Firm Performance. *Journal of Business Ethics* 83:435–451.

Canizares, Sandra Ma Sanchez, and Fernando J. Fuentes Garcia. 2010. Gender Differences in Entrepreneurial Attitudes. *Equality, Diversity and Inclusion: An International Journal* 29 (8):766–786.

Carter, Nancy M., Heather Foust-Cummings, Liz Mulligan-Ferry, and Rachel Soares. 2013. High Potentials in the Pipeline: On Their Way to the Boardroom. Retrieved at http://www.catalyst.org on October 31, 2013.

Carter, Nancy M., William B. Gartner, Kelly G. Shaver, and Elizabeth J. Gatewood. 2003. The Career Reasons of Nascent Entrepreneurs. *Journal of Business Venturing* 18:13–39.

Carter, Sara, Eleanor Shaw, Wing Lam, and Fiona Wilson. 2007, May. Gender, Entrepreneurship, and Bank Lending: The Criteria and Processes Used by Bank Loan Officers in Assessing Applications. *Entrepreneurship Theory and Practice*, 427–444.

Cassar, Gavin. 2004. The Financing of Business Start-Ups. *Journal of Business Venturing* 19:261–283.

Certo, S. Travis, Jeffrey G. Covin, Catherine M. Daily, and Dan R. Dalton. 2001. Wealth and the Effects of Founder Management Among IPO-Stage New Ventures. *Strategic Management Journal* 22 (6–7):641–658.

Chen, C. C., P. C. Greene, and A. Crick. 1998. Does Entrepreneurial Self-Efficacy Distinguish Entrepreneurs from Managers? *Journal of Business Venturing*, 13:295–316.

Chowdhury, Sanjib. 2005. Demographic Diversity for Building an Effective Entrepreneurial Team: Is It Important? *Journal of Business Venturing* 20 (6):727–746.

Cliff, Jennifer E. 1998. Does One Size Fit All? Exploring the Relationship Between Attitudes Toward Growth, Gender and Business Size. *Journal of Business Venturing* 13:523–542.

Cohen, Susan, and Yael V. Hochberg. 2014. Accelerating Startups: The Seed Accelerator Phenomenon. Available at http://ssrn.com/abstract=2418000.

Cole, Rebel A. 2008. Who Needs Credit and Who Gets Credit? Evidence from the Surveys of Small Business Finances. Retrieved at http://mpra.ub.uni-muenchen.de/24691/ on May 14, 2014.

Cole, Rebel A., and Hamid Mehran. 2009. Gender and the Availability of Credit to Privately Held Firms: Evidence from the Surveys of Small Business Finances. Federal Reserve Bank of New York Staff Report no. 383.

Coleman, S. 2000. Access to Capital and Terms of Credit: A Comparison of Men- and Women-Owned Small Businesses. *Journal of Small Business Management* 38 (3):37–52.

———. 2003. Women and Risk: An Analysis of Attitudes and Investment Behavior. *Academy of Accounting and Financial Studies Journal* 7 (2): 99–115.

Coleman, Susan, and Dafna Kariv. 2016. *Creating the Social Venture.* New York: Routledge.

Coleman, Susan, and Alicia M. Robb. 2009. A Comparison of New Firm Financing by Gender: Evidence from the Kauffman Firm Survey Data. *Small Business Economics* 33:397–411.

Coleman, Susan, and Alicia M. Robb. 2012. *A Rising Tide: Financing Strategies for Women-Owned Firms.* Stanford, CA: Stanford University Press.

———. 2014. Financing High-Growth Women-Owned Enterprises: Evidence from the United States. Paper presented at the International Council of Small Business World Conference in Dublin, Ireland, June 12, 2014.

———. forthcoming. Financing High-Growth Women-Owned Enterprises: Evidence from the United States. In *Women's Entrepreneurship in Global and Local Contexts,* ed. Maria Diaz-Garcia, Candida G. Brush, Elizabeth G. Gatewood, and Frederike Welter. Cheltenham, UK, and Northampton, MA: Edward Elgar.

Constantinidis, C., A. Cornet, and S. Asandei. 2006. Financing of Women-Owned Ventures: The Impact of Gender and Other Owner- and Firm-Related Variables. *Venture Capital* 8 (2):133–157.

Cooper, Arnold C., F. Javier Gimeno-Gascon, and Carolyn Y. Woo. 1994. Initial Human and Financial Capital as Predictors of New Venture Performance. *Journal of Business Venturing* 9:371–395.

Davidsson, Per, and Magnus Henrekson. 2002. Determinants of the Prevalence of Start-Ups and High-Growth Firms. *Small Business Economics* 19:81–104.

De Clercq, Dirk, Vance H. Fried, Oskari Lehtonen, and Harry J. Sapienza. 2006. An Entrepreneur's Guide to the Venture Capital Galaxy. *Academy of Management Perspectives* 20 (3):90–112.

Debra Sterling's Mission to Inspire the Next Generation of Female Engineers. 2013. Retrieved at http://katiecouric.com on December 6, 2013.

Dempwolf, C. Scott, Jennifer Auer, and Michelle D'Ippolito. 2014, October. *Innovation Accelerators: Defining Characteristics Among Startup Assistance Organizations.* Washington, DC: U.S. Small Business Administration, Office of Advocacy. Retrieved at http://www.sba.gov/advocacy on January 22, 2015.

Desai, Juhi. 2014, January 27. Tory Burch Expands Nonprofit Aimed at Helping Women Entrepreneurs. Retrieved at http://blogs.wsj.com/accelerators/2014/01/27/tory-burch-expands-nonprofit-aimed-at-helping-women-entrepreneurs/ on March 9, 2016.

DeTienne, Dawn R. 2010. Entrepreneurial Exit as a Critical Component of the Entrepreneurial Process: Theoretical Development. *Journal of Business Venturing* 25 (2):203–2015.

Ding, Waverly W., Fiona Murray, and Toby E. Stuart. 2013. From Bench to Board: Gender Differences in University Scientists' Participation in Corporate Scientific Advisory Boards. *Academy of Management Journal* 56 (5):1443–1464.

Doing Business 2015: United States. 2014. Washington DC: The World Bank. Retrieved at http://www.doingbusiness.org on August 5, 2015.

Drnovsek, M., J. Wincent, and M. S. Cardon. 2010. Entrepreneurial Self-Efficacy and Business Start-Up: Developing a Multi-Dimensional Definition. *International Journal of Entrepreneurial Behavior and Research* 16 (4):329–348.

Ebben, Jay, and Alec Johnson. 2006. Bootstrapping in Small Firms: An Empirical Analysis of Change Over Time. *Journal of Business Venturing* 21:851–865.

The Education of Oprah Winfrey: How She Saved Her South African School. 2012, October 8. *Forbes Magazine.* Retrieved at http://www.forbes.com.

Eisenhardt, Kathleen M. 2013. Top Management Teams and the Performance of Entrepreneurial Firms. *Small Business Economics* 40:805–816.

Eisenmann, Thomas, Eric Ries, and Sarah Dillard. 2013. Hypothesis-Driven Entrepreneurship: The Lean Startup. Boston: Harvard Business School Publishing, 9-812-095.

Ellevate. 2011, April 11. Double Standards in Funding Sexual Satisfaction. Forbes.com. Available at http://www.forbes.com/sites/85broads/2011/04/11/double-standards-in-funding-sexual-satisfaction.

Ellsworth Lecture: The Future of Shopping Is Now. 2013. Presentation by Alexandra Wilkis Wilson, co-founder of the Gilt Groupe, on October 3 at the University of Hartford, West Hartford, CT.

Encyclopedia of World Biography, 2nd Ed. 2014. Farmington Hills, MI: Gale Research.

Eyden, Terri. 2013. SEC to Propose Crowdfunding Rules Under JOBS Act. Retrieved at http://www.accountingweb.com on March 11, 2014.

Farr, Christine. 2014. Indiegogo Founder Danae Ringelmann: "We Will Never Lose Sight of Our Vision to Democratize Finance." Retrieved at http://venturebeat.com/2014/02/21/indiegogo-founder-danae-ringelmann-we-will-never-lose-sight-of-our-vision-to-democratize-finance on August 6, 2015.

Fetters, Michael L., Patricia G. Greene, and Mark P. Rice. 2010. Babson College. In *The Development of University-Based Entrepreneurship Ecosystems*, ed. Michael L. Fetters, Mark P. Rice, and John Sibley Butler, 15–44. Northampton, MA: Edward Elgar.

Forbes.com. 2013, December 4. Why Equity Crowdfunding Is Good News for Women. Available at http://www.forbes.com/sites/women2/2013/12/04/why-equity-crowdfunding-is-good-news-for-women.

———. 2014, March 8. Women-Led Businesses: The Underserved Opportunity—SXSW 2014. Available at http://www.forbes.com/sites/chicceo/2014/03/08/women -led-businesses-the-underserved-opportunity-sxsw-2014.

———. 2014, March 26.Crowdfunding Site Targets the Gigantic Untapped Consumer Market. Available at http://www.forbes.com/sites/geristengel/2014/03/26/equity -crowdfunding-site-targets-the-gigantic-untapped-consumer-market.

Freel, Mark, Sara Carter, Stephen Tagg, and Colin Mason. 2012. The Latent Demand for

Bank Debt: Characterizing "Discouraged Borrowers." *Small Business Economics* 38 (4):399–418.

Fried, Vance H., and Robert D. Hisrich. 1994. Toward A Model of Venture Capital Investment Decision Making. *Financial Management* 23 (3):28–37.

———. 1995. The Venture Capitalist: A Relationship Investor. *California Management Review* 37 (2):101–113.

Friedman, Ann. 2015, March 29. The Real Lesson of the Ellen Pao Verdict. *New York* magazine. Available at http://nymag.com/thecut/2015/03/real-lesson-of-the-ellen-pao-verdict.html.

Ganotakis, Panagiotis. 2012. Founders' Human Capital and the Performance of UK New Technology-Based Firms. *Small Business Economics* 39:495–515.

Garber, Stella. 2013. Why Aren't More Women Entrepreneurs in Tech Accelerators? Retrieved at http://www.forbes.com on January 22, 2015.

Gatewood, Elizabeth J., Candida G. Brush, Nancy M. Carter, Patricia G. Greene, and Myra M. Hart. 2009. Diana: A Symbol of Women Entrepreneurs' Hunt for Knowledge, Money, and the Rewards of Entrepreneurship. *Small Business Economics* 32:129–144.

Goldin, Claudia. 2014. A Grand Gender Convergence: Its Last Chapter. *American Economic Review* 104 (4):1091–1119.

Gompers, Paul, and Josh Lerner. 2001. The Venture Capital Revolution. *The Journal of Economic Perspectives* 15 (2):145–168.

Gompers, Paul A., Vladimir Mukharlyamov, Emily Weisburst, and Yuhai Xuan. 2014, May 12. Gender Effects in Venture Capital. Available at SSRN: http://ssrn.com/abstract=2445497 or http://dx.doi.org/10.2139/ssrn.2445497.

Greenberg, Jason, and Ethan R. Mollick. 2014, July 3. Leaning In or Leaning On? Gender, Homophily, and Activism in Crowdfunding. Available at SSRN: http://ssrn.com/abstract=2462254.

Greene, Patricia G., Candida G. Brush, Myra M. Hart, and Patrick Saparito. 2001. Patterns of Venture Capital Funding: Is Gender a Factor? *Venture Capital* 3 (1):63–83.

Hackett, Sean M., and David M. Dilts. 2004. A Systematic Review of Business Incubation Research. *Journal of Technology Transfer* 29 (1):55–82.

Haltiwanger, John, Henry Hyatt, Erika McEntarfer, and Liliana Soufa. 2012. *Business Dynamics Statistics Briefing: Job Creation, Worker Churning, and Wages and Young Businesses*. Kansas City, MO: Kauffman Foundation.

Haltiwanger, John, Ron Jarmin, and Javier Miranda. 2010. Who Creates Jobs? Small vs. Large vs. Young. NBER Working Paper no. 16300.

———. 2013. Who Creates Jobs? Small Versus Large Versus Young. *The Review of Economics and Statistics* 95 (2):347–361.

Harrison, R., C. Mason, and P. Girling. 2004. Financial Bootstrapping and Venture Development in the Software Industry. *Entrepreneurship & Regional Development* 16 (3):307–333.

Harrison, Richard T., and Colin M. Mason. 2007. Does Gender Matter? Women Business Angels and the Supply of Entrepreneurial Finance. *Entrepreneurship Theory and Practice* 31 (3):445–472.

Haynes, George W., and Deborah C. Haynes. 1999. The Debt Structure of Small Businesses Owned by Women in 1987 and 1993. *Journal of Small Business Management* 37 (2):1–19.

Here's How the Pebble Smartwatch Became the Most Funded Project in Kickstarter History. 2014, November 11. Retrieved at http://www.huffingtonpost.com/michaelprice/heres-how-the-pebble-smar_b_5798406.html on March 8, 2016.

Hinz, R. P., D. D. McCarthy, and J. A. Turner. 1997. Are Women Conservative Investors? Gender Differences in Participant-Directed Pension Investments. In *Positioning Pensions for the Twenty-First Century*, ed. M. S. Gordon, O. S. Mitchell, and M. M. Twinney, 99–106). Philadelphia: University of Pennsylvania Press.

Hisrich, R. D., and C. Brush. 1984. The Woman Entrepreneur: Management Skills and Business Problems. *Journal of Small Business Management*, 22(1):30–37.

How He Invented the Smart Watch. 2013. Retrieved at http://www.technologyreview.com/lists/innovators-under-35/2013 on February 26, 2014.

Hsu, David H. 2007. Experienced Entrepreneurial Founders, Organizational Capital, and Venture Capital Funding. *Research Policy* 36:722–741.

Hudson, Kenneth. 2006. The New Labor Market Segmentation: Labor Market Dualism in the New Economy. *Social Science Research* 36:286–312.

Inverso, Emily. 2014, May 28. The World's Most Powerful Female Entrepreneurs of 2014. Retrieved from http://www.forbes.com/sites/emilyinverso/2014/05/28/the-worlds-most-powerful-female-entrepreneurs-of-2014/#3ae3389a4521 on April 15, 2016.

Isenberg, Daniel J. 2010, June. How to Start an Entrepreneurial Revolution. *Harvard Business Review*, 1–11. Retrieved at http://hbr.org on January 20, 2015.

Ivory, Danielle. 2013. Women Lose More Ground in U.S. Small Business Contracts Race. Retrieved at http://www.bloomberg.com on February 6, 2014.

Jianakoplos, N. A., and A. Bernasek. 1998. Are Women More Risk Averse? *Economic Inquiry* 36 (4):620–631.

Johnson, Mark W., Clayton M. Christensen, and Henning Kagermann. 2008, December. Reinventing Your Business Model. *Harvard Business Review*. Retrieved at http://www.hbr.org.

Jones, Oswald, and Dilani Jayawarna. 2010. Resourcing New Businesses: Social Networks, Bootstrapping, and Firm Performance. *Venture Capital* 12 (2):127–152.

Kakarika, Maria. 2013. Staffing an Entrepreneurial Team: Diversity Breeds Success. *Journal of Business Strategy* 34 (4):31–38.

Kariv, Dafna, and Susan Coleman. 2015. Toward a Theory of Financial Bricolage. *Journal of Small Business and Enterprise Development* 22 (2):196–224.

Kay, Katty, and Claire Shipman. 2014a. The Confidence Gap. Retrieved at http://www.theatlantic.com/magazine/archive/2014/05/the-confidence-gap/359815 on March 7, 2017.

———. 2014b. *The Confidence Code: The Science and Art of Self-Assurance—What Women Should Know.* New York: HarperCollins.

Kelley, Donna J., Candida G. Brush, Patricia G. Greene, and Yana Litovsky. 2012. *Global Entrepreneurship Monitor 2012 Women's Report.* Retrieved at http://www.gemconsortium.org on November 12, 2013.

Kenny, Martin, and Donald Patton. 2015. Gender, Ethnicity and Entrepreneurship in Initial Public Offerings: Illustrations from an Open Database. *Research Policy* 44 (9):1773–1784.

Kepler, E., and S. Shane. 2007, September. *Are Male and Female Entrepreneurs Really That Different?* Washington, DC: U.S. Small Business Adminstration, Office of Advocacy. Available at http://www.sba.gov/advo.

Kirkwood, J. 2009. Is a Lack of Self-Confidence Hindering Women Entrepreneurs? *International Journal of Gender and Entrepreneurship* 1 (2):118–133.

Kirsner, Scott. 2012, December 3. CyPhy Works, Startup from iRobot Co-Founder Helen Greiner, Unveils Two Hover-drones. Retrieved at http://www.boston.com/business/technology/innoeco/2012/12/cyphy_works_startup_from_irobo.html on March 9, 2016.

Koellinger, P., M. Minniti, and C. Schade. 2008. Seeing the World with Different Eyes: Gender Differences in Perceptions and the Propensity to Start a Business. Tinbergen Institute discussion paper, TI 2008-035/3. Available at http://www.tinbergen.nl.

Korn, Brian. 2013. The Trouble with Crowdfunding. Retrieved at http://www.forbes.com on March 11, 2014.

Kroll, Mark, Bruce A. Walters, and Son A. Le. 2007. The Impact of Board Composition and Top Management Team Ownership Structure on Post-IPO Performance in Young Entrepreneurial Firms. *The Academy of Management Journal* 50 (5):1198–1216.

Lam, Wing. 2010. Funding Gap, What Funding Gap? Financial Bootstrapping. *International Journal of Entrepreneurial Behavior & Research* 16 (4):268–295.

Landivar, Liana Christen. 2013. *Disparities in STEM Employment by Sex, Race, and Hispanic Origin.* Washington, DC: U.S. Department of Commerce. Retrieved at http://www.census.gov on October 30, 2013.

Laneri, Raquel. 2010. Gilt Groupe Founders: The Most Powerful People in Fashion? Retrieved at http://www.forbes.com on November 5, 13.

Leader-Chivee, Lauren. 2013, October 23. America Loses When VC Money Ignores Women. Inc.com blog. Retrieved from http://www.inc.com/lauren-leader-chiv%C3%83%C2%A9e/america-loses-when-vc-money-ignores-women.html on March 7, 2016.

Lerner, Josh. 1999. The Government as Venture Capitalist: The Long-Run Impact of the SBIR Program. *Journal of Business* 72 (3):285–318.

Levi-Strauss, C. 1967. *The Savage Mind.* Chicago: The University of Chicago Press.

Liao, Kianwen, Harold Welsch, and Chad Moutray. 2004. Start-Up Resources and Entrepreneurial Discontinuance: The Case of Nascent Entrepreneurs. *Journal of Small Business Strategy* 19 (2):1–15.

Lindenmayer, Michael. 2012. Inspiring Girls to Become Engineers: Meet Goldie Blox. Retrieved from http://www.forbes.com on December 6, 2013.

Lowrey, Ying. 2011, September. *Developments in Women-Owned Businesses.* Washington,

DC: U.S. Small Business Administration, Office of Advocacy. Retrieved at http://
www.sba.gov/advo on October 27, 2013.

Maani, Sholeh A., and Amy A. Cruickshank. 2010. What Is the Effect of Housework on
the Market Wage, and Can It Explain the Gender Wage Gap? *Journal of Economic
Surveys* 24 (3):402–427.

Malone, Michael S. 2014. An Innovation Slowdown at the Tech Giants. *Wall Street Journal,* July 2, 2014, A13.

Manning, Alan, and Joanna Swaffield. 2008. The Gender Gap in Early-Career Wage
Growth. *Economic Journal* 118 (530):983–1024.

Marlow, Susan, and Maura McAdam. 2012. Analyzing the Influence of Gender Upon
High-Technology Venturing Within the Context of Business Incubation. *Entrepreneurship Theory and Practice* 36 (4):655–676.

———. 2013, August. Incubation or Induction? Gendered Identity Work in the Context
of Technology Business Incubation. *Entrepreneurship Theory and Practice*, 1–26.

Marom, Dan, Alicia Robb, and Orly Sade. 2014, May 29. Gender Dynamics in Crowdfunding (Kickstarter): Evidence on Entrepreneurs, Investors, Deals and Taste-Based
Discrimination. Available at SSRN: http://ssrn.com/abstract=2442954.

Maschke, Konstantin, and Dodo zu Knyphausen-Aufseb. 2012. How the Entrepreneurial
Top Management Team Setup Influences Firm Performance and the Ability to Raise
Capital: A Literature Review. *BuR-Business Research* 5 (1):83–123.

Mason, Colin, and Richard Harrison. 1999. Venture Capital: Rationale, Aims, and Scope.
Venture Capital 1 (1):1–46.

Massolution. 2015. *2015CF—Crowdfunding Industry Report.* Available at http://reports
.crowdsourcing.org/index.php?route=product/product&product_id=54#oid=
1001_23_banner_38.

McAdam, Maura, and Susan Marlow. 2010. Female Entrepreneurship in the Context
of High Technology Business Incubation: Strategic Approaches to Managing Challenges and Celebrating Success. *Innovating Women: Contributions to Technological
Advancement,* 55–75.

McClatchy, Martin C. 2007, November 27. *Barack Obama Enlists Oprah Winfrey to Woo
Voters.* Washington DC: Tribune Business News.

McGinn, Daniel. 2012, October 20. What VCs Really Care About. *Inc.* magazine. Available at http://www.inc.com/magazine/201211/daniel-mcginn/what-vcs-really-care-
about.html.

McManus, Lillian F. 2012. The Anatomy of a Helping Hand: Women-Owned Small Business and Federal Contract Procurement. *William & Mary Journal of Women and the
Law* 18 (3):625–650.

Meek, W. R., and D. M. Sullivan. 2015. Kickstarting New Businesses: Exploring the Dynamics of Gender and Crowdfunding. Presented at the 2015 Diana International
Research Conference, Wellesley, Massachusetts, June 9–10, 2015.

Mesch, Debra L. 2010, October. *Women Give.* The Center for Philanthropy at Indiana University, Indianapolis. Available at https://philanthropy.iupui.edu/files/.../
women_give_2010_report.pdf.

———. 2012, August. *Women Give*. The Center for Philanthropy at Indiana University, Indianapolis. Available at https://scholarworks.iupui.edu/handle/1805/6339.

Minnitti, Maria. 2010. Female Entrepreneurship and Economic Activity. *European Journal of Development Research* 23 (3):294–312.

Missing Pieces: Women and Minorities on Fortune 500 Boards (2013). Retrieved at http://www.catalyst.org/knowledge/missing-pieces-women-and-minorities-fortune-500-boards-2012-alliance-board-diversity on October 31, 2013.

Mitchell, Lesa. 2011, September. *Overcoming the Gender Gap: Women Entrepreneurs as Economic Drivers*. Kansas City, MO: Kauffman Foundation. Retrieved at http://www.kauffman.org on October 27, 2013.

Mollick, Ethan. 2013. The Dynamics of Crowdfunding: An Exploratory Study. *Journal of Business Venturing* 29: 1–16.

Mollick, Ethan R., and Venkat Kuppuswamy. 2014. After the Campaign: Outcomes of Crowdfunding. UNC Kenan-Flagler Research Paper no. 2376997.

Morris, Michael H., Nola N. Miyasaki, Craig E. Watters, and Susan Coombes. 2006. The Dilemma of Growth: Understanding Venture Size Choices of Women Entrepreneurs. *Journal of Small Business Management* 44 (2):221–244.

Morris, Michael, Minet Schindehutte, and Jeffrey Allen (2005). The Entrepreneur's Business Model: Toward a Unified Perspective. *Journal of Business Research* 58, 726–735.

Murray, Sara. 2013, October 23. Crowdfunding Site Launches for the Female Entrepreneur. *Wall Street Journal Moneybeat*. Available at http://blogs.wsj.com/moneybeat/2013/10/23/crowdfunding-site-launches-for-the-female-entrepreneur.

Nanda, Ramana, and Liz Kind. 2013. *AngelList*. Boston: Harvard Business School Publishing.

National Center for Education Statistics. 2013. Fast Facts. Retrieved at http://www.nces.ed.gov on December 4, 2013.

National Science Foundation. 2011, June. S&E Degrees: 1966–2008. Retrieved at http://www.nsf.gov/statistics/nsf11316/content.cfm?pub_id=4062&id=2 on December 4, 2013.

National Venture Capital Association. 2014, December 8. NVCA Forms Diversity Task Force to Foster Greater Inclusion Across the Innovation Ecosystem. Retrieved from http://nvca.org/pressreleases/nvca-forms-diversity-task-force-foster-greater-inclusion-across-innovation-ecosystem on April 18, 2016.

National Venture Capital Association Yearbook 2010. 2010, March. New York: Thomson Reuters. Retrieved at growthandjustice.typepad.com/files/nvca_2010_yearbook.pdf on March 7, 2016.

National Venture Capital Association Yearbook 2015. 2015, March. New York: Thomson Reuters.

Nelson, Teresa, and Laurie L. Levesque. 2007. The Status of Women in Corporate Governance in High-Growth, High-Potential Firms. *Entrepreneurship Theory and Practice*, 209–232.

Nelson, Teresa, Sylvia Maxfield, and Deborah Kolb. 2009. Women Entrepreneurs and Venture Capital: Managing the Shadow Negotiation. *International Journal of Gender and Entrepreneurship* 1 (1):57–76.

New Communispace CEO Will Accelerate Innovation and Global Reach. Retrieved at http://www.prnewswire.com on April 9, 2014.

1997 Survey of Business Owners. Washington DC: U.S. Census Bureau.

OECD. 2012. Closing the Gender Gap: Act Now. OECD Publishing. Retrieved at http://dx.doi.org/10.1787/9789264179370-en on December 1, 2013.

Orser, B., and S. Hogarth-Scott. 2002. Opting for Growth: Gender Dimensions of Choosing Enterprise Development. *Canadian Journal of Administrative Sciences* 19 (3):284–300.

Orser, B., A. Riding, and K. Manley. 2006. Women Entrepreneurs and Financial Capital. *Entrepreneurship Theory and Practice* 30:643–665.

Orser, Barbara. 2009. *Procurement Strategies to Support Women-Owned Enterprises.* Ottawa: WEConnect Canada.

Osterwalder, Alexander, and Yves Pigneur. 2010. *Business Model Generation.* Hoboken, NJ: John Wiley & Sons.

Padnos, Cindy. 2010. High Performance Entrepreneurs: Women in High Tech. White paper. Available at http://www.illuminate.com.

Parker, Simon C., and Yacine Belghitar. 2006. What Happens to Nascent Entrepreneurs? An Econometric Analysis of the PSED. *Small Business Economics* 27:81–101.

Patel, Pankaj C., James O. Fiet, and Jeff Sohl. 2011. Mitigating the Limited Scalability of Bootstrapping Through Stratetgic Alliances to Enhance New Venture Growth. *International Small Business Journal* 29 (5):421–447.

Persaud, Christine. 2014, November 27. Women-Led Companies Confident & Thriving, But Need Access to Capital. Retrieved at http://whatsyourtech.ca/2014/11/27 on April 7, 2015.

Petty, J. William, William D. Bygrave, and Joel M. Shulman. 1994. Harvesting the Entrepreneurial Venture: A Time for Creating Value. *Journal of Applied Corporate Finance* 7 (1):48–58.

Piacentini, Mario. 2013. Women Entrepreneurs in the OECD: Key Evidence and Policy Challenges. OECD Social Employment and Migration Working Papers, no. 147, OECD Publishing. Retrieved at http://dx.doi.org/10.1787/5k43bvtkmb8v-edn on January 7, 2014.

Pieri, Jules. 2013, February 11. Visit a VC: and Party Like It's 1969. Daily Grommet. Available at http://jules.thegrommet.com/2013/02/11/visit-a-vc-and-party-like-its-1969.

———. 2014, May 22. To Crack the Glass Ceiling, Start with Venture Capital. Daily Grommet. Available at http://blogs.hbr.org/2014/05/to-crack-the-glass-ceiling-start-with-venture-capital.

Post, Corinne, and Kris Byron. 2015. Women on Boards and Firm Financial Performance: A Meta-Analysis. *Academy of Management Journal* 58 (5):1546–1571.

Primack, Dan. 2014, February 6. Venture Capital's Stunning Lack of Female Decision-Makers. Fortune.com blog. Available at http://fortune.com/2014/02/06/venture-capitals-stunning-lack-of-female-decision-makers.

Procurement. 2014. Retrieved at http://wipp.org on February 6, 2014.

Ranga, M., and H. Etzkowitz. 2010. Athena in the World of Techne: The Gender Dimension of Technology, Innovation, and Entrepreneurship. *Journal of Technology Management and Innovation* 5(1):1–12.

Reader, Ruth. 2015, March 30. The Ellen Pao Trial Verdict Is a Loss for the Tech Industry and a Loss for Women. VentureBeat. Available at http://venturebeat.com/2015/03/30/the-ellen-pao-trial-verdict-is-a-loss-for-the-tech-industry-and-a-loss-for-women.

Reinventing CT: An Economic Development Progress Report. 2013. Retrieved at http://www.ct.gov on March 11, 2014.

Reynolds, Paul D., Nancy M. Carter, William B. Gartner, and Patricia G. Greene. 2004. The Prevalence of Nascent Entrepreneurs in the United States: Evidence from the Panel Study of Entrepreneurial Dynamics. *Small Business Economics* 23 (4):263–284.

Ries, Eric. 2011. *The Lean Startup.* New York: Crown Press.

Robb, Alicia. 2013. *Access to Capital Among Young Firms, Minority-Owned Firms, Women-Owned Firms, and High-Tech Firms.* Washington, DC: U.S. Small Business Administration. Retrieved at http://www.sba.gov on November 4, 2013.

Robinett, Judy. 2014. *How to Be a Power Connector: The 5+50+100 Rule for Turning Your Business Network into Profits.* New York: McGraw-Hill Education.

Rodriguez-Dominguez, Luis, Isabel-Maria Garcia-Sanchez, and Isabel Gellego-Alvarez. 2012. Explanatory Factors of the Relationship Between Gender Diversity and Corporate Performance. *European Journal of Law and Economics* 33:603–620.

Ross, Stephen A., Randolf W. Westerfield, and Bradford D. Jordan. 2014. *Essentials of Corporate Finance,* 8th ed. New York: McGraw-Hill Irwin, p. 564.

Rumbaugh, Andrea. 2010, July 25. Woman Helps Make Researchers' Products a Reality. *The Gainesville Sun.* Retrieved at http://www.gainsville.com on March 23, 2015.

Santinelli, Angelo, and Candida Brush. 2013. *Designing and Delivering the Perfect Pitch.* Wellesley, MA: Babson College.

Sapienza, Harry J., Sophie Manigart, and Wim Vermeir. 1996. Venture Capitalist Governance and Value Added in Four Countries. *Journal of Business Venturing* 11 (6):439–469.

Sarasvathy, S. D. 2001. Causation and Effectuation: Toward a Theoretical Shift from Economic Inevitability to Entrepreneurial Contingency. *Academic Management Review* 26 (2):243–288.

———. 2004. Making It Happen: Beyond Theories of the Firm to Theories of Firm Design. *Entrepreneurship Theory and Practice* 28 (6):519–531.

Schjoedt, Leon, and Sascha Kraus. 2009. Entrepreneurial Teams: Definition and Performance Factors. *Management Research News* 32 (6):513–524.

Schooley, D. K., and D. D. Worden. 1996. Risk Aversion Measures: Comparing Attitudes and Asset Allocation. *Financial Services Review* 5 (2):87–99.

Schumpeter, Joseph. 1934. *The Theory of Economic Development.* Cambridge, MA: Harvard University Press.

Scott, Robert H. III. 2009. *The Use of Credit Card Debt by New Firms.* Kansas City, MO.: Kauffman Foundation.

Securities and Exchange Commission. 2015, October 30. Crowdfunding. Available at https://www.sec.gov/rules/final/2015/33-9974.pdf.

Sellers, Patricia. 2014, February 5. Fortune.com blog. Available at @pattiesellers.

Sirmon, D. G., and M. A. Hitt. 2003, Summer. Managing Resources: Linking Unique Resources, Management, and Wealth Creation in Family Firms. *Entrepreneurship Theory and Practice*, 339–358.

Slade, Hollie. 2014, March 26. Forbes.com blog. Available at http://www.forbes.com/sites/hollieslade/2014/03/26/we-need-more-women-in-venture-capital-say-female-midas-listers/#757b4af5557e.

Snider, Keith F., Max V. Kidalov, and Rene. G. Rendon. 2013, Fall. Diversity Governance by Convenience? Federal Contracting for Minority-Owned Small Businesses. *Public Affairs Quarterly*, 394–432.

Sohl, Jeffrey E. 2005. *The Angel Investor Market in 2004: The Angel Market Sustains a Modest Recovery*. Durham, NH: University of New Hampshire, Center for Venture Research.

———. 2014. *The Angel Investor Market in 2013: A Return to Seed Investing*. Durham, NH: University of New Hampshire, Center for Venture Research.

———. 2015. *The Angel Investor Market in 2014: A Market Correction in Deal Size*. Durham, NH: University of New Hampshire, Center for Venture Research.

Sohl, Jeffrey E., and Laura Hill. 2007. Women Business Angels: Insights from Angel Groups. *Venture Capital* 9 (3):207–222.

Spanx Mogul Sara Blakely Becomes First Female Billionaire to Join Gates-Buffett Giving Pledge. 2013. Retrieved at http://www.forbes.com on October 22, 2013.

Srinivasan, Sujata. 2013. Protein Sciences' Eggless Vaccine Seen as Game Changer. Retrieved at http://www.hartfordbusiness.com on January 21, 2014.

Stimulating Small Business Growth: Progress Report on Goldman Sachs 10,000 Small Businesses. 2014. Wellesley, MA: Babson College. Retrieved at http://www.goldmansachs.com on March 10, 2015.

Stuhlmacher, A. R., and A. E. Walters. 1999. Gender Differences in Negotiation Outcome: A Meta-Analysis. *Personnel Psychology* 52:654–677.

Sunden, A. E., and B. J. Surette. 1998. Gender Differences in the Allocation of Assets in Retirement Savings Plans. *The American Economic Review* 88 (2):207–211.

Swartz, Ethne, Frances Amatucci, and Susan Coleman. 2016. Still a Man's World? Second Generation Gender Bias in External Equity Term Sheet Negotiations. Paper presented at the 2016 Annual Conference of the United States Association of Small Business and Entrepreneurship (USASBE), San Diego, January 12, 2016.

Tansley, A. G. 1935. The Use and Abuse of Vegetational Concepts and Terms. *Ecology* 16 284–307.

Terjesen, Siri, Jan Lepoutre, Rachida Justo, and Neils Bosma. 2012. *Global Entrepreneurship Monitor 2009 Report on Social Entrepreneurship*. Wellesley, MA: Babson College.

Tinkler, Justine, Manwai Ku, Kjersten Bunker Whittington, and Andrea Rees Davies. 2014. Gender and Venture Capital Decision-Making: The Effects of Technical Background and Social Capital on Entrepreneurial Evaluations. Working Paper, Michelle R. Claymen Center for Gender Research at Stanford University.

Tomorrow's Philanthropist. 2009. Barclays Wealth Management. Retrieved at http://www.barclayswealth.com on July 14, 2014.

Tracy, Spencer L. Jr. 2011. *Accelerating Job Creation in America: The Promise of High-Impact Companies.* Washington, DC: U.S. Small Business Administration, Office of Advocacy. Retrieved at http://www.sba.gov/advocacy on November 13, 2013.

Treichel, Monica Zimmerman, and Jonathan A. Scott. 2006. Women-Owned Businesses and Access to Bank Credit: Evidence from Three Surveys Since 1987. *Venture Capital* 8 (1):51–67.

2002 Survey of Business Owners. Washington, DC: U.S. Census Bureau.

2007 Survey of Business Owners. Washington, DC: U.S. Census Bureau.

2012 Catalyst Census. Retrieved at http://www.catalyst.org on October 31, 2013.

2012 Survey of Business Owners. Washington, DC: U.S. Census Bureau.

The 2013 State of Women-Owned Businesses Report. 2013. Retrieved at https://www.open forum.com/womensbusinessreport on 1/7/14.

2015 Survey of Business Owners. Washington, DC: U.S. Census Bureau.

Tyebjee, Tyzoon T., and Albert V. Bruno. 1984. A Model of Venture Capitalist Investment Activity. *Management Science* 30 (9):1051–1066.

UNH Center for Venture Research. Various years. Analysis Reports. Durham, NH: University of New Hampshire. Available at https://paulcollege.unh.edu/research/center-venture-research/cvr-analysis-reports.

U.S Bureau of Labor Statistics. 2013. *Labor Force Statistics from the Current Population Survey.* Available at http://www.bls.gov/cps/earnings.htm#demographics.

U.S. Bureau of Labor Statistics. 2015a. *Labor Force Statistics from the Current Population Survey.* Available at http://www.bls.gov/cps/tables.htm#empstat_m.

U.S. Bureau of Labor Statistics. 2015b. *Employment and Unemployment Among Youth Summary.* Available at http://www.bls.gov/news.release/youth.nro.htm.

U.S. Internal Revenue Service, Statistics of Income Division. 2008, July. SOI Data Tables. Retrieved at https://www.irs.gov/uac/SOI-Tax-Stats-All-Top-Wealthholders-by-Size-of-Net-Worth.

———. 2012, January. SOI Tax Stats—Personal Wealth Statistics. Available at http://www.irs.gov/uac/SOI-Tax-Stats-Personal-Wealth-Statistics.

Van Osnabrugge, Mark. 2000. A Comparison of Business Angel and Venture Capitalist Investment Procedures: An Agency Theory-based Analysis. *Venture Capital* 2 (2):91–109.

Vos, Ed, Andrew Jia-Yuh Yeh, Sara Carter, and Stephen Tagg. 2007. The Happy Story of Small Business Financing. *Journal of Banking and Finance* 31 (9):2648–2672.

Vyakarnam, S., R. Jacobs, and J. Handelberg. 1999. Exploring the Formation of Entrepreneurial Teams: The Key to Rapid Growth Business. *Journal of Small Business and Enterprise Development* 6 (2):153–165.

Wadhwa, V., and F. Chideya. 2014. *Innovating Women: The Changing Face of Technology.* New York: Diversion Books.

Wang, Quinfang. 2013. The Industrial Concentration of Ethnic Minority- and Women-Owned Businesses in the United States. *Journal of Small Business & Entrepreneurship* 26 (3):299–321.

Wang, Wendy, Kim Parker, and Paul Taylor. 2013. *Breadwinner Moms.* Washington DC: Pew Research Center. Available at http://www.pewsocialtrends.org/2013/05/29/bread winner-moms.

Watson, J., and R. Newby. 2005. Biological Sex, Stereotypical Sex-Roles, and SME Owner Characteristics. *International Journal of Entrepreneurial Behavior and Research* 11 (2):129–143.

Watson, John. 2006. External Funding and Firm Growth: Comparing Female- and Male-Controlled SMEs. *Venture Capital* 8 (1):33–49.

Watson, John, Rick Newby, and Anna Mahuka. 2009. Gender and the SME "Finance Gap." *International Journal of Gender and Entrepreneurship* 1 (1):42–56.

Wennekers, Sander, and Roy Thurik. 1999. Linking Entrepreneurship and Economic Growth. *Small Business Economics* 13:27–55.

Wernerfelt, B. 1984. A Resource-Based View of the Firm. *Strategic Management Journal* 5:171–180.

White, Laurel. 2014. A Cold One for Every One: Craft Beer Sales Surged in 2013. Retrieved at http://www.npr.og on April 28, 2014.

Willis, A. J. 1997. Forum. *Functional Ecology* 11:268–271.

Wilson, Fiona, J. Kickul, and D. Marlino. (2007). Gender, Entrepreneurial Self-Efficacy, and Entrepreneurial Career Intentions: Implications for Entrepreneurship Education. *Entrepreneurship Theory and Practice* 31 (3):387–406.

Winborg, Joakim, and Hans Landstrom. 2000. Financial Bootstrapping in Small Businesses: Examining Small Business Managers' Resource Acquisition Behaviors. *Journal of Business Venturing* 16:235–254.

Wired.com. 2014, May 20. The Inside Story of Oculus Rift and How Virtual Reality Became Reality. Available at http://www.wired.com/2014/05/oculus-rift-4.

Wolfe, Alexandra. 2013. Sara Blakely. *Wall Street Journal,* October 12–13, C11.

Women CEOs of the Fortune 1000. Retrieved at http://www.catalyst.org on October 31, 2013.

Women in the Labor Force: A Databook. 2013, February. Washington, DC: U.S. Bureau of Labor Statistics, Report no. 1040. Retrieved at http://www.bls.gov on December 5, 2013.

Zhang, Junfu. 2011. The Advantage of Experienced Start-Up Founders in Venture Capital Acquisition: Evidence from Serial Entrepreneurs. *Small Business Economics* 36 (2):187–208.

Zhao, H., S. E. Seibert, and G. E. Hills. 2005. The Mediating Role of Self-Efficacy in the Development of Entrepreneurial Intentions. *Journal of Applied Psychology* 90 (6):1265–1272.

INDEX

Aardvark, 73

Abbott Labs, 212

accelerators, 139, 140, 254–56; Global Accelerator Network (GAN), 106–7, 254; MergeLane, 101, 107, 108, 177, 224, 254; and pitches to investors, 117–18; vs. incubators, 104–8, 117. *See also* Astia; Springboard Enterprises

Accel Partners, 229, 240

Acs, Zoltan, J.: on high-impact firms, 21–22

Adams, Ariel, 146

Adams, Dan, 126

AdvanceMe, 251

advisory boards, 113, 117, 164

Alachua, 212

Alchemist, 255

Aldrich, Howard E., 20

Allen, Jeffrey, 71

Allen, Kathleen, 136

alternative scenarios, 66, 77

Amatucci, F. M., 42, 48, 174, 175

Amazon.com, 154

Amezcua, Alejandro S., 105, 106

Amit, R., 34

Amplify, 255

Anderson, Becky, 8, 9, 10

Anderson, Derek, 135

Ang, James S., 60, 180

Angel Capital Association (ACA), 221, 245–46

angel investors, 12, 31, 54, 61, 97–118, 144, 243–46, 247, 250, 253, 261n1; defined, 98, 220–21; and early stage firms, 94, 99, 158, 221; gender differences regarding financ-

ing from, 21, 26, 33, 97, 100, 101–2, 114–15, 151, 223–24, 236, 237; growth-oriented entrepreneurs as, 221; homophily among, 40–41, 101, 116, 224, 237; investor groups, 65, 99, 101–3, 221, 223–24, 227, 238, 245–46; networks of, 53, 68, 73, 81, 97, 99–100, 115, 116, 151, 155, 158–59, 221, 227, 244, 245–46; relations with entrepreneurs, 27–28, 29, 97, 101–4, 105, 106–10, 111–18, 129, 155, 159, 163, 164, 165, 167–68, 174, 205, 236, 253, 254; and survival stage firms, 97–104, 113–16, 158–59; tax credits for, 129; vs. venture capitalists, 98, 99–100, 115, 116–17, 158–59, 160, 162, 228; women as, 41, 100–102, 108–10, 116, 155, 220, 221, 223–28, 236, 238, 240, 243–45

AngelList, 113–15, 149, 155, 159, 253

Angelpad, 255

Angel Resource Institute (ARI), 246; Women First Enterprise, 245

AOL, 50

Apple, 16, 170, 204

application program interface (API), 66

Applied Genetic Technologies Corporation (AGTC), 212–14

Ariel (minesweeper), 188–89

ARI's WFE, 245

Asandei, S., 47, 186

Aspect Ventures, 229, 246

Aspen Network of Development Entrepreneurs (ANDE), 259

asset structure, 58, 60

Astia, 11, 43, 77, 108, 116, 176, 177, 236, 241; as accelerator, 104, 107, 154; Astia Angels, 65, 66, 101, 227–28, 243–44, 262n2

asymmetric/incomplete information, 58, 60, 99, 160, 169, 192
Athena Foundation's PowerLink Program, 134
Atlantic, The, 48
Audretsch, David B., 3, 121
Auer, Jennifer, 105
Austin, Texas, 133
Australia: women entrepreneurs in, 47

Babcock, Linda, 174
Babson College, 45, 131, 132; Babson Entrepreneurship Ecosystem Project (BEEP), 132
Bajtelsmit, V. L., 46
Baker, T., 82
Baker Hughes, 189
Balachandra, Lakshmi, 229
balance of work and family, 16, 41, 44, 93, 236
bank loans, 12, 83, 84, 96, 99, 111, 147, 148, 181, 182; as difficult to secure, 46, 87–89, 93, 94, 95, 146, 180; gender differences regarding, 25–26, 158, 180, 186–88; and profitability, 94, 180; secured by personal assets, 41, 87, 180
Bank of America, 216
Barclays Wealth Management, 216
Barnett, Chance, 143, 144
Basu, Anuradha, 82–83
Baum, Joel A. C., 91
Bazan, Brenda, 152–53
beauty products industry, 64–66, 74
Becker-Blease, John R., 40–41, 100, 101, 102
Beckman, C. M., 91
Begley, Larry, 172
Belghitar, Yacine, 57
Belgium: women entrepreneurs in, 47
Belote, Greg, 254
Berger, Allen N., 41–42
Bernasek, A., 46
Bia Sport, 155
Bigelow, Lyda, 190–91
BioFlorida, 214
Biogen, 8–9, 10, 14
Biomedical Advanced Research and Development Authority (BARDA), 127

Blakely, Sara, 13, 176, 214, 261n1; and Empowerment Plan, 9; as founder of Spanx, 1–3; and Giving Pledge, 1, 9; motivation of, 14; as role model, 10
Blank, Steven: *The Four Steps to the Epiphany,* 68–69; *How to Build a Startup,* 71
Block, Doreen, 64–66, 67, 74, 76, 77
Blue Sky laws, 198
boards of directors, 6, 39, 91–92, 161, 175, 203, 209
Bobbitt-Zeher, Donna, 80
bootstrapping, 79, 206, 208; and early stage firms, 42, 65, 84–86, 87, 93–94, 95, 99, 155; vs. Lean Startup Model, 69, 76; and networks, 86; and rapid-growth stage firms, 83, 93, 157
Bosma, Neils, 215
Bosse, Douglas A., 164, 165
Boston, 133
Boston Beer, 87
Boulder, Colorado, 133
Bowles, H. R., 174
Bradford, Nicole, 143, 181, 183
bricolage, 81–82
bridge financing, 158
Brodbeck, Christina A., 247
Bruderl, J., 86
Bruno, Albert V., 162–64
Bruno, Emily, 87–90, 93, 94–95, 96
Brush, C., 48
Brush, Candida G., 12, 19, 34, 45, 48, 57, 63, 85, 86, 118, 131, 164, 229; and Diana Project, 30, 32, 40, 49, 165–66, 176, 237
Bryzek, Mike, 50
Buffett, Warren: Giving Pledge, 1
Bulgari, 50, 54
Burch, Tory, 216, 218, 261n1
Burke, Elaine, 81
Burns, Matt, 145
Burton, M. D., 91
Business Model Canvas, 71, 72
business models, 66, 68–73, 75, 76, 78, 84, 170, 175
business plans, 89, 175, 218, 234, 255; benefits of, 67–68, 73; vs. Lean Startup Model, 68–71, 73, 76, 78
Butler, John Sibley, 136

Byron, Kris, 92

Caldbeck, Ryan, 253
California: Marin County, 130; Silicon
    Valley, 64, 112, 130, 133, 229; Small Busi-
    ness Development Center, 130; Venture
    Greenhouse, 130
Campbell, Kevin, 92
Canaan Partners, 246
Canada, 47, 124, 144
Can Capital, 251–52
CanFel Therapeutics, 205, 207–8
Canizares, Sandra Ma Sanchez, 47
Capital, 255
Cardon, M. S., 48
Carter, Nancy, 6, 12, 57, 63, 85, 86, 164; and
    Diana Project, 30, 32, 40, 49, 165, 176, 237
Carter, Sara, 48, 186
cash flow, 84, 85
Cassar, Gavin, 58, 60
Catalyst, 6, 39
Catalytic Women, 259
Cenergy International, 180, 181–85, 210, 211
Center for Talent Innovation, 230
certification: of minority-owned firms, 125,
    140; of women-owned firms, 125, 138, 140,
    211, 257
certified development companies (CDCs),
    120
Certo, S. Trevis, 194, 197
Charles River Ventures, 145
Chase, Robin, 176
Chen, C., 47
Chen, Jane, 215–16
Chideya, F.: Innovating Women, 154
Chikoore, Tom, 255
Chowdhury, Sanjib, 91
Christensen, Clayton, 71, 253
Circle Up, 149, 154, 253
Cirino, Maria, 172–74, 246
Cisco, 204
Clapham, Arthur Roy, 131
Cliff, Jennifer E., 44, 47, 63, 165
Clinton, Hillary, 43
Coca-Cola, 26
Cohen, Susan, 106
Cole, Rebel A., 186

Communispace, 167–69, 170, 171, 177, 179,
    190
Community Sourced Capital (CSC), 148–49
confidence, 16, 21, 48–49, 54, 55, 109
Connecticut: Connecticut Innovations
    (CI), 129; CTNext, 128–29; Department
    of Economic and Community Develop-
    ment, 129; Jobs Bill of 2011, 128–29; Tech-
    nology Council, 209
Constantinidis, C., 47, 186
construction industry, 58
consultants, 28, 29
consumer products industry, 26, 29, 109, 166
Coombes, Susan, 44, 63
Cooper, Arnold C., 60
Cornet, A., 47, 186
Costello, Trish, 152
Covin, Jeffrey G., 194, 197
Cowboy Ventures, 246
Cox, Manon, 123, 126–28, 209, 211
craft brewing industry, 87–90, 93
Craigslist, 113
Crawley, D. C., 48
credit cards, 86–87, 94, 95–96, 180
Crick, A., 48
critical success factors, 75
Cross, Peggy, 102–4, 116
crowdfunding, 13, 95, 141–57, 208; as debt-
    based/lending-based, 141, 143–49, 151,
    155, 156, 198, 239, 249–52; as donation-
    based, 143, 149, 151, 156, 239; and early
    stage firms, 144–45, 147, 153, 155–57;
    as equity-based, 141, 143, 149, 150–52,
    154, 155, 156, 157, 198, 239, 253–54; Fixed
    Funding option, 143; Flexible Fund-
    ing option, 143–44; gender differences
    regarding, 142, 144, 146, 151; growth of,
    141, 149; and growth-oriented firms,
    147, 150, 151, 154, 155, 156, 157, 239; as
    hybrid-based, 141, 149; and the Pebble
    Smartwatch, 145; pre-purchase model,
    143, 151, 155, 248–49; as reward-based,
    143, 149, 151, 152–54, 155, 198, 248–49; as
    royalty-based, 141, 149; SEC regulation
    of, 150–51, 198–99
Cruickshank, Amy A., 45
CyPhy Works, 198, 204–5

Daily, Catherine M., 194, 197

Daily Grommet, 232, 237

Dalton, Dan R., 194, 197

Daric, 148, 249

Davidsson, Per, 56

Davies, Andrea Rees, 233

Davis, Amy E., 229

Dawson, Cooper, 250

Dealstruck, 147, 252

de Bruin, Anne, 45

debt capital, 34, 67, 79, 83; credit cards, 86–87, 94, 95–96, 180; gender differences regarding, 12, 61, 80, 185, 186–88; Kiva, 146–47, 148, 238–39; microlending, 146–47. *See also* bank loans; crowdfunding; family and friends

DeCesare, Hilary, 261n1

De Clerq, Dirk, 159, 160, 161, 163, 169–70

Defense Advanced Research Projects Agency (DARPA), 137

Dempwolf, C. Scott, 105

Denizens Brewing Company, 87–90, 93, 94–95, 96

Desai, Juhi, 216

Desai, Samir, 252

Deshpande, Rohan, 250

DeTienne, Dawn R., 191, 196–97

developed vs. developing economies, 19, 43

DFJ, 229

Diana Project, 30–31, 32, 40, 49, 165–66, 176, 237

Dillard, Sarah, 69, 70

Dilts, David M., 104

Ding, Waverly W., 5

D'Ippolito, Michelle, 105

Direct Selling News, 210

diversity, experiential, 91–92

Doerr, John, 233

Dominion Ventures, 167, 168

Donohue, Liam, 172

dot-com bust, 159, 195

Dow Jones VentureSource, 229, 230

Dreamit, 255

Drnovsek, M., 48

drones, 198, 204–5

Dropbox, 73

drug industry, 123, 126–28, 205–8

Dubini, Paola, 20

Eakin, Rory, 253

early stage firms, 13, 57, 58, 73, 79–97, 108, 172, 206, 216, 218–19; and angel investments, 94, 99, 158–59, 221; and bank loans, 88–89, 180; and bootstrapping, 42, 65, 84–86, 87, 93–94, 95, 99, 155; and credit cards, 86–87, 94, 95–96; and crowdfunding, 144–45, 147, 153, 155–57; and entrepreneur's personal funds, 42, 45, 79–82, 84, 86, 89, 92, 94, 95, 99, 155, 180, 206; and family and friends, 79, 82–84, 87, 93, 95, 103, 155; and resources of family and friends, 79, 82–84, 87, 93, 95, 99, 102

earnings: gender differences regarding, 7–8, 20, 38, 39–40, 45, 53, 54, 79, 80, 81, 92–93, 155, 261n2; of women, 7–8, 20, 38, 39–40, 45, 53, 54, 79, 80, 81, 92–93, 155, 214, 217, 221, 261n2

eBay, 50, 170, 208

Ebben, Jay, 84–85, 86

e-commerce, 51

economic conditions, 168, 193, 206; dot-com bust, 159, 195; financial crisis, 97, 183, 186, 188, 223, 228; Great Recession, 137, 159, 180, 183, 186, 188, 212, 228, 261n1; industry expansion, 74; job creation, 3–4, 17, 23, 46, 60, 119, 134, 170, 176, 217

Ecotensils, 102–4, 116

Edelman, Linda F., 57

education: gender differences regarding, 35, 62; of growth-oriented women entrepreneurs, 5–6, 15, 18, 49, 54, 64, 126, 127, 136, 139, 153, 188, 212; of women, 5–6, 15, 18, 35–36, 40, 49, 53, 54, 62, 64, 74, 109, 126, 127, 136, 139, 153, 173, 188, 212, 221, 230, 232, 243, 257

effectuation, 81

Eisenhardt, Kathleen M., 80

Eisenmann, Thomas, 69, 70

Eli Lilly, 212

Elizabeth Street Capital, 216

Ellevate, 256

Embrace, 215–16

Emergent BioSolutions, 126, 127

Emerging Women, 77, 177
Employee Stock Ownership Plan (ESOP), 190
employer firms, 17, 18, 20, 41, 58, 59–61
Empowerment Plan, 9
Endeavor, 259
"Enterprising Women of the Year", 210
entrepreneurial ecosystems, 131–36, 256–58; defined, 131; Isenberg on, 131–33, 140; role of universities in, 136, 139, 140
entrepreneurial self-efficacy (ESE), 47–49, 128, 175
entrepreneurship groups, 43, 256–58
equity capital: from crowdfunding, 141, 143, 149, 150–52, 154, 155, 156, 157, 198, 239, 253–54; gender differences regarding, 12, 26, 30, 40–41, 53, 60–62, 80, 164–65, 237, 238; private equity, 12, 73, 158, 174; and Springboard Enterprises, 31, 49, 53. *See also* angel investors; initial public offerings (IPOs); venture capitalists
Ernst & Young's Entrepreneur of the Year, 210–11
Esty, Elizabeth, 209
Etzkowitz, H., 35
Eventbrite, 81
Everloop, 261n1
exit funnel outcomes, 170–71, 176
exit strategies, 117, 197, 200
exports, 119, 121, 125, 217
external sources of capital, 67–68, 79, 84, 85, 206; vs. bootstrapping, 92, 94; gender differences regarding, 42, 54, 61, 100, 158, 238; and growth-oriented firms, 12, 30, 40, 42, 51, 54, 56, 58, 60, 61, 62, 73, 80–81, 100, 115, 157, 169; vs. internal sources, 12, 21, 41, 42, 59, 60, 61, 84, 92, 92–93, 97, 116, 138, 155, 180; and profitability, 75. *See also* angel investors; bank loans; initial public offerings (IPOs); investors; Springboard Enterprises; venture capitalists
Eyden, Terri, 151

Facebook, 16, 113, 145, 204, 261n1
family and friends (F&F), 25, 26, 116, 185; and early stage firms, 79, 82–84, 87, 93, 95, 103, 155

Farr, Christine, 144
Farrington, Deborah, 246
FastTrac, 255
fear of failure, 21, 47, 48, 49
Federal Acquisition Streamlining Act, 124
Fetters, Michael L., 136
Fiet, James O., 94
financial documents resources, 258
financial growth cycle: Development Stage, 41, 42; Maturity Stage, 42; Rapid-Growth Stage, 42, 54; Startup Stage, 41, 42; Survival Stage, 41–42, 115, 116
Firestone, Marsha, 185
First Aid Shot Therapy, 26–29, 32, 56, 61
5 C's of Credit, 180
500 Startups, 107, 255
flash sales, 51–52, 75
flexibility, 52, 236
Flublok vaccine, 126–27
focus groups, 167
Fonstad, Jennifer, 229, 246
Forbes 400, 7, 261n1
Forbes.com, 142, 235
Forbes Midas List, 229, 237
Forerunner Ventures, 246
Fortune magazine: Fortune 500 firms, 6, 39, 164, 169, 231; "Top Ten Innovators Under 40", 195; "World's Most Powerful Women" list, 210
Founder Dating (website), 95
founding teams. *See* teams, entrepreneurial
Foundry Group, 258
.406 Ventures, 172–74, 246
Freel, Mark, 48
Fried, Vance H., 159, 160, 161, 163, 169–70, 171
Friedman, Ann, 233
Frohwein, Rob, 251
Fundation, 148, 250
Fundera, 147–48, 250–51
FundersClub, 253
Funding Circle, 147, 148, 252
FundWell, 110–13, 116, 204, 262n3

Gadowsky, Debbie: as founder of Cookies Direct, 2
Ganotakis, Panagiotis, 80
Garber, Stella, 106

Garcia, Fernando J. Fuentes, 47
Garcia-Sanchez, Isabel-Maria, 47, 92
Garrison Investment Group, 148
Gartner, William B., 57
Gates, Bill, 8; Giving Pledge, 1
Gatewood, Elizabeth, 12, 30, 40, 57, 85
Gelfand, M., 174
Gellego-Alvarez, Isabel, 92
GEM. *See* Global Entrepreneurship Monitor
gender differences: regarding angel financing, 21, 26, 33, 97, 100, 101–2, 114–15, 151, 223–24, 236, 237; regarding bank loans, 25–26, 158, 180, 186–88; regarding CEO positions, 231; regarding confidence, 21, 48–49, 109, 110, 173–74, 175; regarding critical feedback, 172–73; regarding crowdfunding, 142, 144, 146, 151; regarding debt capital, 12, 61, 80, 185, 186–88; regarding earnings, 7–8, 20, 38, 39–40, 45, 53, 54, 79, 80, 81, 92–93, 155, 261n2; regarding education, 35, 62; regarding elected office, 43; regarding employees, 20, 62, 63, 63–64; regarding employer firms, 20; regarding entrepreneurial activity, 19, 20, 21, 31, 39; regarding equity capital, 12, 26, 30, 40–41, 53, 60–62, 80, 164–65, 237, 238; regarding external sources of capital, 42, 54, 61, 100, 158, 238; regarding financial success, 57; regarding firm launches, 15, 32, 57, 60–62, 81; regarding firm ownership, 4–5, 10, 23; regarding firm revenues, 62, 63; regarding firm size, 17–18, 20, 21, 24, 31, 34, 46, 61–62, 100, 199; regarding government support, 119, 120, 122, 123–24, 140; regarding growth expectations, 24, 25, 30, 57; regarding growth-oriented entrepreneurship, 4–5, 8, 10, 15, 24, 26, 30, 31–32, 44, 46, 47, 57, 60–64, 80, 83, 92–93, 105, 133, 164–65, 185, 199; regarding harvesting value, 179, 190–91, 199–200; regarding high-impact firms, 23, 32–33; regarding human capital, 6, 20, 35, 39, 52–53, 62; regarding incubators and accelerators, 105, 106–7; regarding innovation, 19, 57; regarding insider financing, 83; regarding internal equity, 61; regarding international expansion, 19; regarding IPOs, 190–91; regarding managerial experience, 6, 20, 39; regarding motivation, 44–45, 63, 165; regarding negotiation, 174–75; regarding networks, 40, 53, 100, 158, 165; regarding paid and unpaid work, 44–45; regarding personal sources of financing, 25–26, 40, 45, 80, 81, 185, 238; regarding philanthropy, 214, 216, 217, 219; regarding preference for self-employment, 21; regarding risk, 46–48, 49, 89, 165, 187, 188; regarding self-efficacy, 47–49, 128, 175; regarding social capital, 20, 40; regarding social entrepreneurship, 215; regarding startup capital, 60–62, 80; regarding venture capital financing, 21, 26, 33, 40, 97, 114–15, 151, 164–66, 185, 226, 230–31, 232, 236, 237, 239–40, 244; regarding wealth accumulation, 5, 39, 40, 45, 53, 54, 79, 80, 81, 92–93, 95, 155, 185, 221–23
gender stereotypes and myths, 20, 30, 35, 43, 49, 54, 165, 185
Genentech, 205, 206
gene therapies, 212–14
GGV Capital, 229
Gilt Groupe, 50–52, 54, 56, 60, 61, 62, 75, 177
Gimeno-Gascon, F. Javier, 60
Girling, P., 84, 85, 86
Gist-Brocades, 126
Giving Pledge, 9
glass ceiling, 6
Global Accelerator Network (GAN), 106–7, 254
Global Entrepreneurship Monitor (GEM), 48; *2010 Women's Report*, 19–20
Global InvestHer, 247
Goldcrest Investments, 250
Golden Seeds, 43, 65, 66, 101, 164, 236, 241; Knowledge Institute, 11; and Jo Anne Miller, 108–10, 115, 116, 117, 118; and Stephanie Newby, 226, 244
GoldieBlox, 36–37, 54
Goldin, Claudia, 80
Goldman Sachs 10,000 Small Businessesgov, 45–46

Gompers, Paul, 160, 161, 230–31
Google, 16, 170
Google for Entrepreneurs, 260
Gordon, Doug, 250
Gorlin, Marc, 251
go-to market strategy, 103
Gouw, Theresia, 229, 246
government contracts, 43, 75, 123–25, 138, 139–40, 188, 189
government programs, 110, 144; federal programs 120–25, 126, 127, 137, 138; gender differences regarding, 119, 120, 122, 123–24, 140; government grants, 25, 75, 121–23, 137, 138, 139–40, 212; and growth-oriented firms, 119, 120, 123; state and local programs, 128–31, 138, 139; and survival stage firms, 119, 120, 127, 138–39
Grameen Bank, 146
Graziano, Sam, 250
Great Recession, 137, 159, 180, 183, 186, 188, 212, 228, 261n1
Green, Kristen, 246
Greenberg, Jason, 142, 156
Greene, Patricia, 19, 20, 34, 48, 57, 86, 136, 164, 176, 229
Greiner, Helen, 188–89, 204–5, 209–10, 211, 217; and harvesting value, 195–98, 200, 201, 202, 204
Grockit, 73
growth expectations, 47, 49, 50, 51–52, 54, 55, 57; vs. actual growth, 24, 25
growth-oriented firms: and bootstrapping, 83, 93, 157; and crowdfunding, 147, 150, 151, 154, 155, 156, 157, 239; and entrepreneurial teams, 62, 67, 80–81, 87–88, 136–37; and external sources of capital, 12, 30, 40, 42, 51, 54, 56, 58, 60, 61, 62, 73, 80–81, 100, 115, 157, 169; financial growth cycle of, 41–42; first sales of, 57; and government programs, 119, 120, 123; and harvesting value, 179, 190, 193, 195–98; and insider financing, 83; job creation by, 3–4, 119; life cycle of, 12–13, 16; vs. lifestyle firms, 2, 41, 42, 50, 56, 93; rapid-growth stage, 42, 54, 83, 93, 150, 157, 162, 228. See also early stage firms; nascent firms; survival stage firms

growth-oriented women entrepreneurs: challenges faced by, 11–12, 15, 26, 32, 33, 55, 92–93, 96, 115, 158, 174, 187–88, 237, 238; education of, 5–6, 15, 18, 49, 54, 64, 126, 127, 136, 139, 153, 188, 212; exit strategies, 117, 197, 200; impact beyond own companies, 9–10, 14, 16; as investors, 11, 12, 13, 15–16, 203, 204; as mentors, 10–11, 77, 214, 218–19, 241; motivation of, 2–3, 6–10, 12, 14, 16, 26, 29, 49–50, 54–55, 57–58, 64, 87, 89; number of, 25, 32, 191; as philanthropists, 191, 203, 204, 214–15, 216, 217–18, 219, 220; previous work experience, 5–6, 15, 18, 49, 53, 54, 64, 102, 126, 127–28, 188, 212, 234; recognition as leaders, 8–9, 14, 16, 203, 208–11, 217, 220; as role models, 10–11, 14, 158, 217, 220, 241; as serial entrepreneurs, 197–98, 200, 202, 203, 204–8, 216–17, 218, 220; as social entrepreneurs, 215–16, 219. See also growth-oriented firms; teams, entrepreneurial; women; women-owned firms

Hackett, Sean M., 104
Haltiwanger, John, 3, 4
Handelberg, J., 91
Harris, Carla A., 91
Harrison, Richard T., 12, 84, 85, 86, 159, 163; on women angel investors, 41, 100, 101, 223
Hart, Myra, 12, 34, 165
Hartz, Julia, 81
Harvard Business Review, 71, 131–32
Harvard University, 50, 54
harvesting value, 13, 16, 99, 100, 165, 190–98, 199–201, 228; entrepreneurs after, 191, 192, 196–97, 200, 201, 202, 203, 209, 211, 213–14, 216, 218–19, 236; gender differences regarding, 179, 190–91, 199–200; and Helen Greiner, 195–98, 200, 201, 202, 204; and growth-oriented firms, 179, 190, 193, 195–98; and Diane Hessan, 169, 177, 179, 190, 200; and investment banks, 179, 194–96, 201; as management buyout (MBO), 190; as merger, 31, 170, 185, 191, 216; as sale of the firm, 106, 159, 179, 190,

191, 193, 199, 200, 205, 206–7, 214, 216, 218, 221, 228, 236, 237. *See also* initial public offerings (IPOs)

Hasbro, 189

Hayes, Nancy, 152–53

Haynes, Deborah C., 12

Haynes, George W., 12

health care industry, 16, 21, 26–27, 29, 31, 160, 161, 166

Hecht, Jared, 250

Henrekson, Magnus, 56

Hessan, Diane: and harvesting value, 169, 177, 179, 190, 200; on venture capitalists, 167–69, 171, 175, 177, 178, 179, 190

Hewlett-Packard, 261n1

high growth potential (HGP), 16, 84, 186, 187

high-impact firms, 21–23, 32–33

Hill, Laura, 221, 223, 224

Hills, G. E., 48

Hinz, R. P., 46

Hisrich, R. D., 48, 163, 171

Hitt, M. A., 34

Hochberg, Yael, 106, 254

Hogarth-Scott, S., 47

Hollender, Meika and Jeffrey, 154

home-based firms, 2, 41, 62, 63

Home Depot, 170

home equity loans, 41, 180

homophily, 40–41, 101, 116, 142, 155–56, 224, 237

Hsu, David H., 205

Hudson, Kenneth, 5

human capital, 52–54, 55, 63, 73, 74, 81, 91, 121, 128, 157, 177, 217; defined, 34, 52–53, 221; gender differences regarding, 6, 20, 35, 39, 52–53, 62; investors as source of, 160, 176; previous work experience as, 5–6, 34, 49, 52, 62, 109. *See also* education

Hunt, Helen LaKelly, 214–15

Hunt, Swanee, 214–15

Hurricane Katrina, 180

Hwang, Rebeca, 247

Hyatt, Henry, 3

Ice House Entrepreneurship Program, 255

Illuminate Ventures, 240, 246

Impact Angel Group, 224–25

Inc. magazine, 164; *Inc.* 5000 list, 25–26, 32, 33, 183

incubators, 136, 140, 145, 212; vs. accelerators, 104–8, 117

India, 8–9, 10

Indiana University Center on Philanthropy, 214

Indiegogo, 143–44, 156, 208, 248

initial public offerings (IPOs), 13, 176, 177, 179, 185, 190–98, 218, 221, 228, 229; advantages, 191–92, 201; disadvantages, 192–93; entrepreneurs after, 191, 192, 196–97, 200, 201, 202, 203, 209, 211, 213–14, 216, 218–19; frequency of, 106, 170–71, 200; investment banks during, 179, 194–96, 201; and JOBS Act, 199, 231; pricing of stock, 194–95, 196; road show regarding, 194–95, 196, 213; role of entrepreneurs during, 194–96, 201–2, 209, 212–13; S-1 for SEC, 194, 195–96; timing of, 193

Innovus Pharmaceuticals, 236

insider investors. *See* family and friends

institutional investors, 28, 29

InStyle, 65

Intel Corp., 170

intellectual property, 62, 63

internal sources of capital, 79, 163; credit cards, 86–87, 94, 95–96, 180; defined, 41; vs. external sources, 12, 21, 41, 42, 59, 60, 61, 84, 92, 92–93, 97, 116, 138, 155, 180; home equity loans, 41, 180; personal savings, 25–26, 41, 80, 83, 92–93, 185. *See also* bank loans

international trade, 119, 121, 125, 217

Internet, 51, 113, 141, 146–48, 154. *See also* websites

Inverso, Emily, 216

investment banks, 179, 194–96, 201

Investor Circle, 224, 225

investors: accredited investors, 114, 149, 198, 199, 221, 239, 246, 252, 253–54, 261n1; and asymmetric/incomplete information, 58, 60, 99, 160, 169, 192; as mentors, 103, 227, 238, 243, 244; non-accredited investors, 150, 198, 199, 239, 254; patience of, 82, 93, 98, 115, 127, 159, 193; pitches to, 29, 66, 103,

106, 109, 110, 117–18, 137, 140, 178, 218, 232, 235, 237, 262n2; relations with entrepreneurs, 27–29, 33, 39, 40–41, 49, 53, 54, 62, 65–66, 67–68, 73, 76, 77, 90, 93, 94, 97, 98, 101–4, 105, 106–10, 111–18, 129, 137, 139, 140, 141, 145, 151–52, 155, 157, 159, 161–62, 163, 164–78, 192, 193, 194, 197, 198–99, 200, 201, 205, 206–8, 212, 223–24, 234–35, 236, 237, 240, 253, 254, 262n2; as source of human capital, 160, 176; as source of social capital, 33, 101, 157, 160, 176; women as, 11, 12, 13, 15–16, 28, 46, 100–102, 108–10, 116, 142, 149, 151–52, 155–56, 157, 164, 176, 203, 204, 218, 220, 221, 223–29, 235, 236–41, 243–45, 246–47. *See also* angel investors; family and friends; venture capitalists

iRobot, 31, 188–89; IPO of, 108, 195–98, 200, 201, 204

Isabella Capital Fund, 245

Isenberg, Daniel J.: on entrepreneurial ecosystems, 131–33, 140

Ivory, Danielle, 124

Jackley, Jessica, 146–47

Jackson, Deborah, 154

Jacobs, Mitch, 251

Jacobs, R., 91

Jaensch, Mary Wallace, 234

Jarmin, Ron, 3

Jayawarna, Dilani, 86

JetBlue, 170

Jianakoplos, N. A., 46

Jimmy Choo, 51

job creation, 3–4, 17, 23, 46, 60, 119, 134, 170, 176, 217

Jobs, Steve, 8

JOBS Act, 143, 149, 150–51, 157, 239, 254; and IPOs, 199, 231; and SEC, 198–99

Johnson, Alec, 84–85, 86

Johnson, Mark W., 71

Johnson, Whitney, 246

Jones, Oswald, 86

Jordan, Bradford D., 180

J.P. Morgan, 195

Jumpstart Our Business Startups (JOBS) Act. *See* JOBS Act

Justo, Rachida, 215

Kabbage, 147, 251

Kagermann, Henning, 71

Kakarika, Maria, 92

Kariv, Dafna, 82, 215

Karrot, 251

Kauffman Fellows, 247

Kauffman Firm Survey (KFS), 13, 15, 24–25, 35, 59–64, 83–84, 86, 186–87

Kauffman Foundation, 4–5, 15, 259; BDS Statistic Briefing, 4; 1 Million Cups program, 77, 134, 139, 257

Kay, Katty: *The Confidence Code*, 48–49

Keiretsu Forum, 103, 261n1

Kelley, Donna J., 19, 20

Kenny, Martin, 190

Kepler, E., 47

key contacts, 49, 54, 55, 121, 131, 145, 160, 176, 177

Kickstarter, 37, 142, 143, 144, 145–47, 249

Kickul, J., 48

Kidalov, Max V., 123

Kind, Liz, 113

Kirkwood, J., 48

Kirsner, Scott, 205

Kiva, 146–47, 148, 238–39

Kleiner Perkins Caufield & Byers (KPCB), 229, 230, 233

Knyphausen-Aufseb, Dodo zu, 80

Koellinger, P., 48

Kolb, Deborah, 174

Koplovitz, Kay, 246

Kopp, Wendy, 215

Korn, Brian, 150

Kraus, Elizabeth, 224–26, 237

Kraus, Sascha, 91, 92

Kroll, Mark, 192, 197

Ku, Manwai, 233

Kuppuswamy, Venkat, 144

Lai, L., 174

Lamont, Ann, 229

Landivar, Liana Christen, 5

Landstrom, Hans, 86

Laneri, Raquel, 51

Laschever, S., 174

Le, Son A., 192, 197

Lean In, 259

Lean Startup Model, 68–71, 73, 76, 78, 84
Leader-Chivee, Lauren, 230
Lee, Jenny, 229, 230
Lehtonen, Oskar, 159, 160, 161, 163, 169–70
Lending Club, 148, 249–50
Lepoutre, Jan, 215
Lerner, Josh, 121, 160, 161
Levesque, Laurie L., 6
Levi-Strauss, Claude, 82
Liao, Kianwen, 58
Lieberman, Mark, 136
lifestyle firms, 2, 41, 42, 50, 56
Lin, James Wuh, 180
Lindenmayer, Michael, 37
LinkedIn, 113
Litovsky, Yana, 19, 20
L'Oreal's NEXT Generation Award, 65
Louis Vuitton, 50, 54
Lowrey, Ying, 3
Lundmark, L., 191
Lynn, Rebecca, 229

Maani, Sholeh A., 45
MacroGenics, 206–7
Mahuka, Anna, 186
Maier, Jennifer, 211
Malloy, Dannel, 209
Malone, Michael S., 204
management buyout (MBO), 190
Manigart, Sophie, 169, 171
Manley, K., 48, 186
Manning, Alan, 80
Manolova, Tatiana S., 57
manufacturing industry, 58
Marc Jacobs, 51
market share, 74
Marlino, D., 48
Marlow, Susan, 35, 106
Marom, Dan, 142, 156
Maschke, Konstantin, 80
Mason, Colin, 12, 48, 84, 85, 86, 159, 163; on
    women angel investors, 41, 100, 101, 223
Massolution, 141, 149
Mather, Jennie, 205–8, 217
Matrix Partners, 52
Maveron, 253
Maxfield, Sylvia, 174

Maybank, Alexis, 50, 62
Mazumdar-Shaw, Kiran, 13; as founder of
    Biogen, 8–9, 10, 14; motivation, 14; as role
    model, 10
McAdam, Maura, 35, 106
McCarthy, D. D., 46
McClatchy, Martin C., 10
McEntarfer, Erika, 3
McGinn, Daniel, 164
McKelvie, Alexander, 105, 106
McLoughlin, Russell, 252
McManus, Lillian F., 124
Meckings, James, 252
medical/health/life science industries, 160,
    161, 176, 212–14
Medtronic, Inc., 170
Meek, W. R., 142
Meeker, Mary, 229
Mehraein, Shadi, 247
Mehran, Hamid, 186
mentors, 16, 108, 134, 139, 164, 216, 240, 255;
    advantages of, 66, 77, 90, 130; growth-
    oriented women entrepreneurs as, 10–11,
    77, 214, 218–19, 241; investors as, 103, 227,
    238, 243, 244
MergeLane, 101, 107, 108, 177, 224, 254
mergers, 31, 170, 185, 191, 216
Merian Ventures, 247
Mesch, Debra L., 214
mezzanine financing, 158
microlending, 146–47
Microsoft, 170
Migicovsky, Eric, 145–47
Milk Street Ventures, 109
Miller, Jo Anne, 108–10, 115, 116, 117, 118
Mills, Kathy, 210
Minguez-Vera, Antonio, 92
minimum viable products (MVPs), 69–71
Minniti, Maria, 4, 48
Minority Business Development Agency
    (MBDA), 125
minority-owned firms, 125, 140
Minute Clinic, 108
Miranda, Javier, 3
Missing Pieces, 6
MIT Artificial Intelligence Laboratory, 188
Mitchell, Kate, 231–32, 237

Mitchell, Lesa, 5, 15
Mittal, Alexander, 253
Miyasaki, Nola N., 44, 63
Mollick, Ethan, 142, 144, 156
Monroe, Cindy, 210, 211
MoolaHoop, 152–53, 154, 239, 248
moonlighting, 81
Moos, Kathryn, 154
Moran, Andres, 250
Morgan Stanley, 195
Morris, Michael H., 44, 63, 71
motivation: financial rewards as, 6–8, 14, 16,
    29, 50, 57, 87; gender differences regard-
    ing, 44–45, 63, 165; giving back as, 11, 218;
    of growth-oriented women entrepre-
    neurs, 2–3, 6–10, 12, 14, 16, 26, 29, 44–45,
    49–50, 54–55, 57–58, 64, 87, 89; recogni-
    tion as leader, 8–9, 50; risk as, 89–90; of
    women investors, 110, 155–56, 157, 220,
    224–26
Moutray, Chad, 58
Mucker Lab, 255
Mullinger, Andrew, 252
Murray, Fiona, 5
Murray, Sara, 154
myUsearch.com, 224

Nanda, Ramana, 113
nascent firms, 13, 19, 56–78, 99, 102, 163,
    218–19; and asymmetric information, 58,
    60, 99; defined, 56; failure rate, 58–59,
    87, 113, 228; founded by teams, 52, 62, 67,
    77, 80–81, 87–88, 91–92, 93, 94, 109, 117,
    136–37, 152, 166, 172–73, 177, 188, 201, 208,
    212, 239, 250, 251, 252, 253, 254; gender
    differences regarding, 15, 32, 57, 60–62, 81;
    growth rates of, 59–60; and Lean Startup
    Model, 68–71, 73, 75, 78, 84; survival of,
    56–59, 68, 87, 92, 93, 97, 113
Nasdaq, 191, 196, 213
National Aeronautics and Space Adminis-
    tration (NASA), 123, 188
National Association of Women Business
    Owners (NAWBO), 131, 210, 256
National Center for Education Statistics, 35
National Center for Women & Information
    Technology, 257

National Institutes of Health (NIH), 137;
    SBIR grants, 122, 123
National Science Foundation, 35, 36, 123
National Venture Capital Association
    (NVCA), 228–29, 231–32, 247
National Women's Business Council
    (NWBC), 87, 90–91, 256
Nelson, R. E., 82
Nelson, Teresa, 6, 174
networks, social, 16, 20, 49, 54, 55, 66, 80,
    95, 107, 131, 132, 152, 162, 176, 177, 184, 204,
    216, 217, 248; of angel investors, 53, 68,
    73, 81, 97, 99–100, 115, 116, 151, 155, 158–59,
    221, 227, 244, 245–46; and bootstrapping,
    86; and crowdfunding, 141, 151–52; entre-
    preneurship groups, 43; and founding
    teams, 62, 95; gender differences regard-
    ing, 40, 53, 100, 158, 165; and 1 Million
    Cups, 77, 134, 139, 257; and Startup Grind,
    77, 135, 139, 257–58; of venture capital-
    ists, 151, 165–66; as women-focused, 43,
    256–57
Newby, R., 47, 186
Newby, Stephanie, 226, 244
NewLogic Business Loans, 251
New York Stock Exchange, 191
Next Wave Ventures, 238, 243; Angel Train-
    ing Program, 243; Next Wave Fund, 238;
    Rising Tide Fund, 238, 243
Nguyen, Phong, 50
Nielsen, Spencer, 135
Nivi, Babak, 113–14, 253
Norman, Mike, 254

Obama, Barack, 10, 209, 217
Oculus Rift, 144–45, 155
OECD, 39, 44–45; women entrepreneurs in,
    20–21
Office of Economic Development, 139
Office of Naval Research, 188
O-H Community Partners, 110, 111
oil and gas industry, 180, 181–85, 189
Omnicom Group, 169, 190
OnDeck, 147, 251
1 Million Cups, 77, 134, 139, 257
Onyeagoro, Chinwe, 110–13, 115, 116, 117,
    204, 217

O'Reilly, C., 91
Organization for Economic Cooperation and Development. *See* OECD
Orser, B., 47, 48, 124, 186
Osterwalder, Alexander, 70
Ouya, 146

PackBot, 189
Padnos, Cindy, 223, 240, 246
Panel Study of Entrepreneurial Dynamics (PSED), 56–58
Pao, Ellen, 233
Parker, Kim, 8
Parker, Simon C., 57, 82–83
Parks, J. M., 191
Parsons, Williams, 21
Patel, Pankaj C., 94
Patton, Donald, 190
Pebble Smartwatch, 145–46
Pepsi, 261n1
Persaud, Christine, 185
persistence, 29, 33, 90, 96
personal savings, 25–26, 41, 80, 83, 92–93, 185. *See also* wealth accumulation
Petralia, Kathryn, 251
Petty, J. William, 190, 191, 193, 194
Pew Research Center, 8
philanthropy: gender differences regarding, 214, 216, 217, 219; of growth-oriented women entrepreneurs, 191, 203, 204, 214–15, 216, 217–18, 219, 220
Piacentini, Mario, 20–21, 22
Pieri, Jules, 232–33, 237
Pigneur, Yves, 71
Pipeline Angels, 11, 129–30, 227, 236, 241, 244–45
Platerink, Mary Page, 26–29, 31, 32, 33, 56
Plum Alley, 153–54, 239, 248
political capital, 34, 42–43, 53, 55, 73, 211, 217
Portfolia, 149, 151–52, 154, 157, 239, 248
Poshly, 64–66, 67, 74, 75, 76
Post, Corinne, 92
Preisendorfer, P., 86
Presidential Ambassador for Global Entrepreneurship (PAGE), 209–10, 217
priced rounds, 65, 261n1
PriceWaterhouseCoopers, 210–11, 253

Primack, Dan, 231
profitability, 58, 69, 71–73, 75–76, 77, 94, 130, 180, 193
Profusa, Inc., 136–38, 139, 140
proof of concept, 114, 137, 138
Prosper, 148, 249
Protein Sciences, 123, 126–28, 138, 209
Prunier, Christy, 154

QVC, 1

Ramachandran, Vasant, 250
Ranga, M., 35
Raven Biotechnologies, 205–8
Ravikant, Naval, 113–14, 253
Reader, Ruth, 233
Reese, Pat Ray, 20
Regulation A+, 198–99
Rendon, Rene G., 123
Resource-Based View (RBV), 34, 52, 81–82
Ressler, June, 180, 181–85, 210, 211, 217
retail sector, 2, 5, 16, 21, 50–52, 75, 160, 164
revenue models, 67, 71–73, 75, 77, 82, 92
Reynolds, Paul D., 57
Rice, Condaleeza, 43
Rice, Mark P., 136
Riding, A., 48, 186
Ries, Eric, 70; *The Lean Startup*, 69
Ringelmann, Danae, 144
Rising Tide, A, 2, 8, 10, 49–50, 83, 94, 159, 176, 232
Rising Tide Europe Fund, 238
Rising Tide Fund, 238, 243
Rising Tide Program, 77
risk, 16, 54, 58, 73, 87, 92, 93, 97, 105, 163, 225, 226, 228; acceptance of, 30, 32, 49, 52, 110, 117, 180, 184; aversion to, 21, 46–47, 49, 89, 165, 180, 187, 188; gender differences regarding, 46–48, 49, 89, 165, 187, 188; as motivation, 89–90
Rivet Ventures, 247
Robinett, Judy: *How to Be a Power Connector*, 164; on venture capital, 164
Rodriguez-Dominguez, Luis, 92
role models, 10–11, 14, 158, 217, 220, 241
Rometty, Indira, 261n1
Roomba, 189

Ross, Stephen A., 180
Rumbaugh, Andrea, 212
Ryan, Greg, 250
Ryan, Kevin, 50–51, 52

Sade, Orly, 142, 156
Sam Adams ales, 87
Sandberg, Sheryl, 261n1; *Lean In*, 229
Santinelli, Angelo, 118
Santy, Deb, 121, 123
Saparito, Patrick, 165
Sapienza, Harry J., 159, 160, 161, 163, 169–70, 171
Sarasvathy, S. D., 81
Sarbanes-Oxley Act, 193
SBA. *See* Small Business Administration
SBIR grants, 25, 121–23, 259–60
Scale Venture Partners, 231–32, 246
Schade, C., 48
Scherl, Rachel Braun, 233–34, 237
Schindehutte, Minet, 71
Schjoedt, Leon, 91, 92
Schoemaker, P., 34
Schooley, D. K., 46
Schultz, Howard, 253
Schumpeter, Joseph: on creative destruction, 3
Scott, Jonathan A., 186
Scott, Robert H., III, 86
Securities and Exchange Commission (SEC), 192, 213; crowdfunding regulations, 150–51, 198–99; and JOBS Act, 198–99; S-1 registration document, 194, 195–96
Seed Accelerator Rankings Project, 254
Seibert, S. E., 48
Seidenberg, Beth, 230
self-efficacy, 47–49, 54, 55, 128, 175
Sellers, Patricia, 229
Semprae Laboratories, Inc., 234–36, 237
Senturia, Ethan, 252
Seraph Capital Forum, 245
serial entrepreneurs, 50, 80–81, 110, 111, 126, 177, 254; growth-oriented women entrepreneurs as, 197–98, 200, 202, 203, 204–8, 216–17, 218, 220; investor preference for, 39, 68

Series A funding, 52, 66, 112, 145
Series B funding, 145
Series Seed, 258
Service Corps of Retired Executives (SCORE), 255
service sector, 2, 5, 16, 21, 58, 62, 63, 160, 164
Shane, S., 47
Shaver, Kelly G., 57
Shebooks, 152
Shipman, Claire: *The Confidence Code*, 48–49
Siedenberg, Beth, 229
Silicon Valley, 64, 112, 130, 133, 229
Silver, Boris, 253
Silverman, Brian S., 91
Sinosun Technology, 229
Sirmon, D. G., 34
Slade, Hollie, 230
SLO Seed Ventures, 109
Small, D., 174
Small Business Administration (SBA), 91, 139, 257; certification program, 125; definition of small business, 3, 120; 8(a) Business Development Program, 125; 504 loan program, 120–21; and government contracts, 124–25; on high-impact firms, 21; loans from, 111, 120–21, 250; Patriot Express, 121; 7(a) loan program, 120–21; Women-Owned Small Business Federal Contract Program, 124
Small Business Innovation Research program (SBIR), 25, 121–23, 259–60
Small Business Reauthorization Act, 124
smartwatches, 145–46
Snider, Keith F., 123
social capital, 29, 51–52, 53–54, 55, 63, 73, 74, 80, 81, 88, 91, 109, 121, 128, 144, 157, 162, 177, 217; defined, 40; gender differences regarding, 20, 40; investors as source of, 33, 101, 157, 160, 176; key contacts, 34, 49, 54, 55, 121, 131, 145, 160, 176, 177. *See also* networks, social
Social Capital Markets (SOCAP), 148
social entrepreneurship, 215–16, 219, 245–46
social media, 89, 147, 153, 175
software industry, 31, 160, 161

Sohl, Jeffrey, 42, 94, 174, 221; on angel investors, 41, 99, 100, 101, 102, 223–24
Soufa, Liliana, 3
South Africa, Leadership Academy for Girls, 9
Spanx, 1–3, 9, 176, 210, 214, 261n1
Springboard Enterprises, 11, 31, 33, 41, 43, 53, 77, 101, 176, 177, 236, 241, 246; as accelerator, 107–8, 110, 254; Dolphin Tank programs, 164, 262n1; Springboard forums, 30, 49, 165
Springboard Fund, 246
Srinivasan, Sujata, 127
Staples, 170
Starbucks, 170
Startup Grind, 77, 135, 139, 257–58
Startups Illustrated, 255–56
Startup Weekends, 71, 77, 135, 258
StartX, 255
Starvation Valley Farms, 148–49
Starvest Partners, 246
Stayn, H., 174
STEM fields (science, technology, engineering, and math), 5, 35–37, 53
Sterling, Debbie, 36–37, 54–55
Stimulating Small Business Growth, 45, 46
Strategic Communications, 210
STTR grants, 25
Stuart, Toby E., 5
Stuhlmacher, A. R., 174
Sullivan, D. M., 142
Sullivan, Jeanne, 246
Sunden, A. E., 46, 47
Surette, B. J., 46, 47
Survey of Business Owners, 4, 17, 18, 41
Survey of Consumer Finances (1998), 46
survival stage firms, 13, 147; and angel investors, 97–104, 113–16, 158–59; and crowdfunding, 151, 155; defined, 97, 116, 120; in financial growth cycle, 41–42; and government programs, 119, 120, 127, 138–39
sustainability, 130, 142, 246
Swaffield, Joanna, 80
Swartz, Ethne, 175

Tagg, Stephen, 186
Take it OUT! Fitness, 224

Tansley, Arthur, 131
Tantisook, Jessika, 148–49
Taylor, Paul, 8
Taylor, Porcher L., III, 164, 165
Teach for All, 215
Teach for America, 215
teams, entrepreneurial, 87–88, 136–37, 152, 172–73, 188–89, 201, 250, 251, 252, 253, 254; advantages of, 52, 62, 67, 77, 80–81, 88, 91–92, 93, 95, 117, 166, 177, 208; experiential diversity of, 91–92; risks of, 92, 109; serial entrepreneurs on, 80–81
technology, 106, 163, 176, 229–30, 245, 261n1; biotechnology/bioscience firms, 31, 35, 58, 75, 123, 126–28, 136–38, 138, 159, 160, 161, 166, 205–8, 209, 211, 212–14; computer science, 35; high-tech firms, 16, 21, 23, 31, 62, 64–66, 74, 75–76, 89, 107, 109, 121, 129, 136–38, 144–45, 161, 164, 165, 166, 170, 188–89, 204, 205–8, 209–10, 211, 212–14, 231, 257; information technology, 161, 166, 257; Internet, 51, 113, 141, 146–48, 154; robotics, 31, 188–89, 209–10, 211; Silicon Valley, 64, 112, 130, 133, 229; virtual reality (VR), 144–45, 155
Technology Review, 195
Techstars, 107, 255, 258
Teen Vogue, 66
Terjesen, Siri, 215
term sheets, 175
37 Angels, 43, 101, 226–27, 236, 241, 244
Thirty-One Gifts, 210, 211
Thurik, Roy, 3
Tinkler, Justine, 233
Tommarello, Nick, 254
Tomorrow's Philanthropist, 216
Topper, David, 253
Tory Burch Foundation, 216
toy industry, 36–37
Tracy, Spencer, 21
Tracy, Spencer L., Jr., 23, 32
transportation, 58
Treichel, Monica Zimmerman, 186
Turner, J. A., 46
2012 Catalyst Census, 5
Tyebjee, Tyzoon T., 162–64
Tyler, Floyd, 180

Udell, Gregory F., 41–42

Uhrman, Julie, 146

"Ultimate Guide to Finding Women Investors", 246

United Kingdom, 144, 252; angel investors in, 100; Asian entrepreneurs in, 83

United States, 18, 144, 252; African Americans, 7; Bureau of Labor Statistics, 3, 7–8, 39; Census Bureau, 8, 18; Department of Commerce, 125; Department of Defense, 121, 123, 137, 188, 189; Department of Energy, 123; Department of Health and Human Services, 123; Department of Transportation, 123; economic conditions, 23; Environmental Protection Agency, 123; Food and Drug Administration, 126, 127; high-impact firms in, 23; Latinas, 7; NASA, 123, 188; self-employment in, 21; women entrepreneurs in, 19–20, 32–33; and World Bank "Doing Business" indicators, 133. *See also* Securities and Exchange Commission; Small Business Administration

University of Chicago New Venture Challenge, 255

University of Florida, 212, 214

University of New Hampshire Center for Venture Research, 98–99, 101, 223

unmanned aerial vehicles (UAVs), 198, 204–5

UpGlobal (UP), 77, 135, 258

Valentino, 51

value proposition, 69, 71, 72, 117–18

VanDerhei, J. L., 46

Van Osnabrugge, Mark, 169

VentureBeat, 144

venture capitalists (VCs), 12, 31, 41, 52, 61, 73, 81, 84, 105, 127, 144, 158–78, 248, 261n1; amount invested over time, 159–60, 161, 228; vs. angel investors, 98, 99–100, 115, 116–17, 158–59, 160, 162, 228; decision-making process, 162–64; evaluation of potential deals by, 163; gender differences regarding financing by, 21, 26, 33, 40, 97, 114–15, 151, 164–66, 185, 226, 230–31, 232, 236, 237, 239–40, 244; Diane Hessan on,

167–69, 171, 175, 177, 178, 179, 190; industry specialization of, 160, 161, 163, 164, 166, 169, 172, 175, 176, 177, 178; networks of, 151, 165–66; number of deals, 159–60, 161, 228; relations with entrepreneurs, 40, 53, 54, 62, 68, 94, 101, 106, 109–10, 112–13, 115, 141, 145, 157, 161–62, 163, 164–78, 192, 193, 194, 197, 200, 201, 205, 206–8, 212, 234–35, 236, 237, 240, 253, 254; as source of human capital, 157, 160, 176; as source of social capital, 157, 160, 176; and term sheets, 175; Tyebjee and Bruno on, 162–64; women as, 155, 165–67, 172–74, 176, 177, 220, 223, 228–34, 235, 236, 237, 239–40, 246–47

Venture Census survey (2011), 229

Venture Greenhouse, 130–31

Venture Hacks, 113

Venture Valkyrie, 247

Vermeir, Wim, 169, 171

Viacord, 31

Vinetta Project, 77

virtual reality (VR), 144–45, 155

Vitamin Water, 26

Vos, Ed, 186

Vrou, 154

Vyakarnam, S., 91

Wadhwa, V.: *Innovating Women*, 154

Walters, A. E., 174

Walters, Bruce A., 192, 197

Wang, Quinfang, 5

Wang, Wendy, 8

Washer, Sue, 211, 212–14

Watson, John, 47, 186

Watters, Craig E., 44, 63

WDS (Women's Distribution Services), 211

wealth accumulation: gender differences regarding, 5, 39, 40, 45, 53, 54, 79, 80, 81, 92–93, 95, 155, 221–23; of women, 5, 39, 40, 45, 53, 54, 79, 80, 81, 92–93, 95, 155, 185, 200, 201, 203, 204–5, 214–15, 217, 218, 219, 220, 221–23, 240–41

Wealthfront, 73

websites: AGTC, 212; Alchemist, 255; Amplify, 255; Angel Capital Association, 221; Angelpad, 255; Angel Resource Institute (ARI), 246; Aspect Ventures, 246;

Aspen Network of Development Entrepreneurs (ANDE), 259; Astia, 254; Biocon, 9; Canaan Partners, 246; CanFel Therapeutics, 207; Capital, 255; Catalyst, 39; Catalytic Women, 259; Cenergy, 181; Circle Up, 149; Communispace, 167; Community Sourced Capital, 148; Cowboy Ventures, 246; CyPhy Works, 204; Daric, 148; Dealstruck, 147; Denizens Brewing Co., 87; Dreamit, 255; Ellevate, 256; Embrace, 215; Emerging Women, 77; Endeavor, 259; Ernst & Young's Entrepreneur of the Year, 211; FastTrac, 255; First Aid Shot Therapy, 26; 500 Startups, 107, 255; Forbes, 7; Forerunner Ventures, 246; Founder Dating, 95; Foundry Group, 258; .406 Ventures, 246; Fundation, 148; Funding Circle, 147; FundWell, 110; Gilt, 50; Giving Pledge, 9; Global Accelerator Network, 254; Global InvestHer, 247; Golden Seeds, 11; GoldieBlox, 37; Goldman Sach, 45; Google for Entrepreneurs, 260; *How to Build a Startup*, 71; Ice House Entrepreneurship Program, 255; Illuminate Ventures, 246; Indiegogo, 143; Isabella Capital Fund, 245; Judy Robinett, 164; Kabbage, 147; Kauffman Fellows, 247; Kauffman Foundation, 259; Keiretsu Forum, 261n1; Kickstarter, 37; Kiva, 146; Lean In, 259; lean startup movement, 71; Lending Club, 148; MergeLane, 108; Merian Ventures, 247; MoolaHoop, 152; Mucker Lab, 255; National Association of Women Business Owners (NAWBO), 256; National Center for Women & Information Technology, 257; National Venture Capital Association (NVCA), 247; National Women's Business Council (NWBC), 256; Next Wave Ventures, 238; OnDeck, 147; 1 Million Cups, 134; Pebble Smartwatch, 145; Pipeline Fellowship, 129; Plum Alley, 248; Portfolia, 151; Poshly, 64; Prosper, 148; Protein Sciences, 209; Rivet Ventures, 247; Scale Venture Partners, 231; Seed Accelerator Rankings Project, 254; Seraph Capital Forum, 245; Series Seed, 258; Service Corps of Retired Executives (SCORE), 255; Small Business Innovation Research program (SBIR), 259; Springboard Enterprises, 254; Startup Grind, 135; Startups Illustrated, 255; StartX, 255; Starvest Partners, 246; Strategic Communications, 210; Teach for America, 215; Techstars, 255; 37 Angels, 226; Thirty-One Gifts, 210; Tory Burch Foundation, 216; "Ultimate Guide to Finding Women Investors", 246; University of Chicago New Venture Challenge, 255; UpGlobal, 258; Venture Valkyrie, 247; Vinetta Project, 77; Vrou, 154; WDS, 211; WEConnect International, 257; WeFunder, 149; Women Business Center of NOVA, 245; Women First Enterprise, 245; Women Impacting Public Policy, 258; Women Moving Millions, 214; Women Presidents' Organization, 185; Women's Business Centers(WBCs), 257; Women's Business Enterprise National Council, 257; Women's Technology Network, 245; Women's Venture Capital Fund, 246; Zestra Essential Arousal Oils, 234

WEConnect International, 257
WeFunder, 149, 253–54
Welsch, Harold, 58
Welter, Friederike, 45
Wennekers, Sander, 3
Wernerfelt, B., 34
Westerfield, Randolf W., 180
White, Laurel, 87
Whitman, Meg, 261n1
Whittington, Kjersten Bunker, 233
Whole Foods, 154, 170
Wildstein, Amy, 246
Willa, 154
Willis, A. J., 131
Wilson, Alexandra Wilkis, 50–52, 54–55, 56, 62
Wilson, Fiona, 48
Winborg, Joakim, 86
Wincent, J., 48
Winfrey, Oprah, 1, 9–10, 13, 189; Leadership Academy for Girls, 9; motivation, 6–7, 14;

as role model, 10, 14; wealth accumulation, 6–7, 214
Wired.com, 145
Wired magazine, 253
Wisniewski, Natalie, 136–38, 139, 140
Wolfe, Alexandra, 1
women: aspirations of, 8, 14, 19–20, 24, 25,
30, 32, 41, 49–50, 51, 57–58, 63, 64, 74, 87;
as CEOs, 6, 26, 39, 50, 109, 152, 154, 164,
166, 169, 180, 181–85, 191, 197, 203, 209,
212–13, 231, 232, 237, 261n1; earnings, 7–8,
20, 38, 39–40, 45, 53, 54, 79, 80, 91, 92–93,
155, 214, 217, 221, 261n2; education of,
5–6, 15, 18, 35–36, 40, 49, 53, 54, 62, 64,
74, 109, 126, 127, 136, 139, 153, 173, 188, 212,
221, 230, 232, 243, 257; as elected officials,
43; as family caregivers, 39, 44–45, 47, 53,
80, 93; as investors, 11, 12, 13, 15–16, 28,
46, 100–102, 108–10, 116, 142, 149, 151–52,
155–56, 157, 164, 176, 203, 204, 218, 220,
221, 223–29, 235, 236–41, 243–45, 246–47;
management experience, 6, 20, 39, 126;
as married, 81, 261n2; as mothers, 8, 20,
39, 44–45, 47, 53, 80, 93, 261n2; previous
work experience, 5–6, 15, 18, 20, 39, 40,
49, 52–53, 54, 62, 64, 74, 80, 81, 87, 89,
90, 102, 126, 127–28, 153, 158, 164, 165–66,
177, 188, 205, 212, 221, 234, 240; as social
entrepreneurs, 215–16; stereotypes and
myths about, 20, 30, 35, 43, 49, 54, 165,
185; wealth accumulation, 5, 39, 40, 45, 53,
54, 79, 80, 81, 92–93, 95, 155, 200, 201, 203,
204–5, 214–15, 217, 218, 219, 220, 221–23,
240–41. *See also* gender differences;
growth-oriented women entrepreneurs;
women-owned firms
Women Business Center of NOVA, 245
Women First Enterprise, 245
Women Growth Capital, 167, 168
Women Impacting Public Policy (WIPP),
211, 217, 258
Women in Technology International Hall of
Fame, 209

Women Moving Millions, 214–15
women-owned firms, 223, 224, 238–39; vs.
all firms, 17, 18; certification of, 125, 138,
140, 211, 257; as employer firms, 17, 18,
20, 41; and government programs, 119,
120, 121, 122, 123–24; growth rates, 17, 18;
as high-impact firms, 23; number of, 17,
120; number of employees, 17, 18, 24, 31,
62, 63–64; revenues of, 17, 18, 24, 31, 41, 62,
63; size of, 2, 17–18, 20, 21, 24–25, 31, 34, 41.
See also growth-oriented women entre-
preneurs; women
Women-Owned Small Business Federal
Contract Program, 124
Women Presidents' Organization (WPO),
184, 185, 210, 211, 256
Women's Business Centers (WBCs), 257
Women's Business Enterprise National
Council (WBENC), 257
Women's Business Ownership Act, 90
Women's Funding Network (WFN), 215
Women's Technology Network, 245
Women's Venture Capital Fund, 246
Woo, Carolyn Y., 60
Worden, D. D., 46
work-life balance, 16, 41, 44, 93, 236
World Bank "Doing Business" indicators,
133
World Economic Forum, 9
Wuebker, R., 191

Xenogen, 31

Yahoo, 64, 204
Y Combinator, 105, 107, 145, 254
Yeh, Andrew Jia-Yuh, 186
Yelp reviews, 147
Yunis, Mohammed, 146

Zestra Essential Arousal Oils, 234–36, 237
Zhang, Junfu, 205
Zhao, H., 48
Zipcar, 31, 108, 176